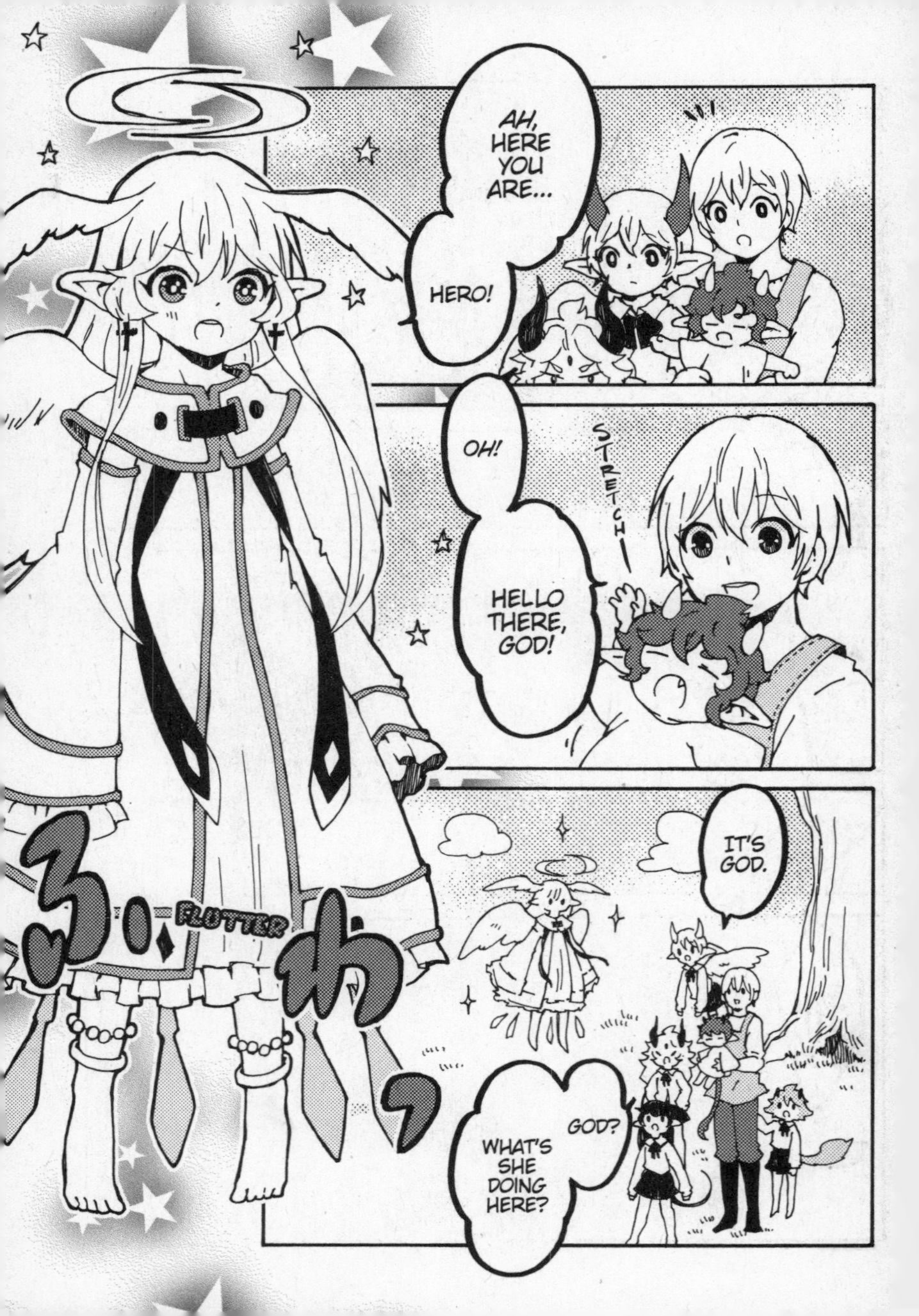
AH, HERE YOU ARE...
HERO!
STRETCH
OH!
HELLO THERE, GOD!
IT'S GOD.
GOD?
WHAT'S SHE DOING HERE?
FLUTTER

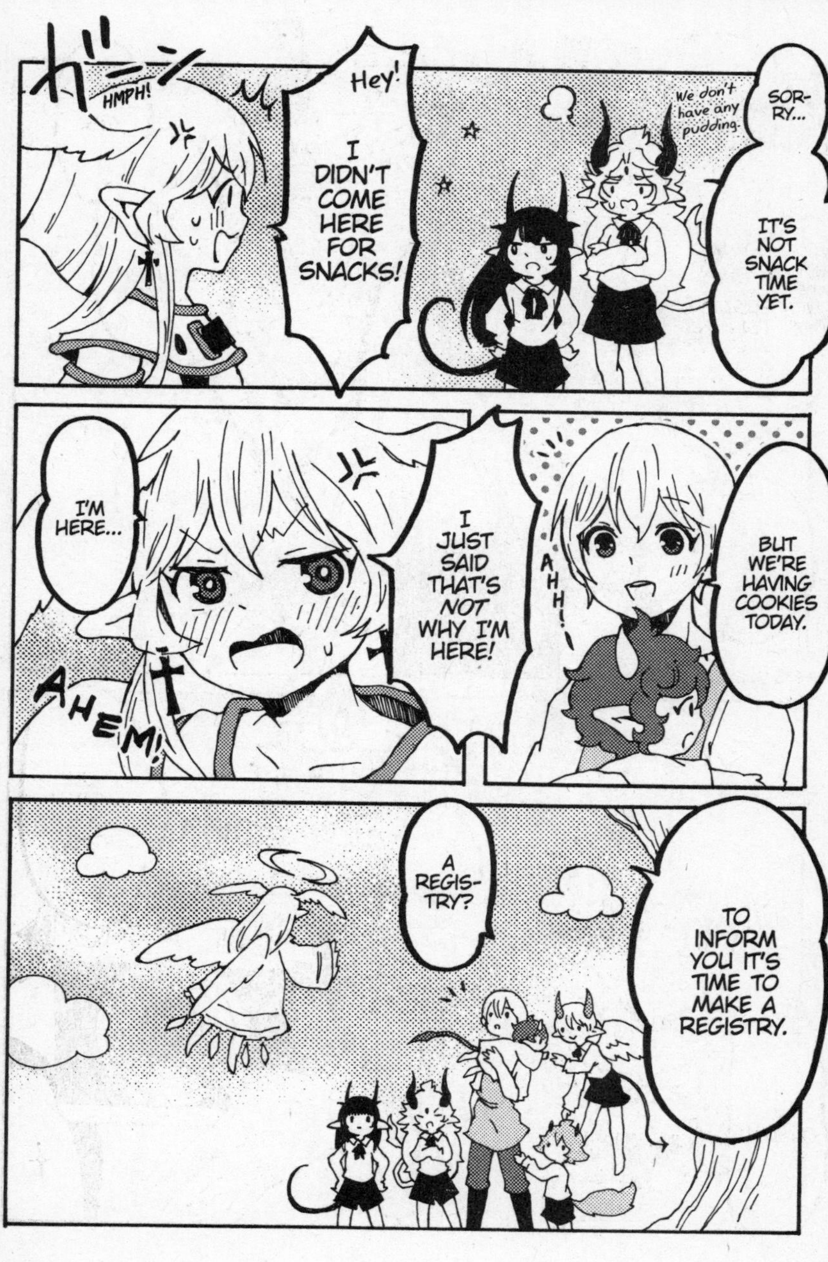
SORRY...
IT'S NOT SNACK TIME YET.
We don't have any pudding.
Hey!
I DIDN'T COME HERE FOR SNACKS!
HMPH!
ガーン
BUT WE'RE HAVING COOKIES TODAY.
AHH!
I JUST SAID THAT'S *NOT* WHY I'M HERE!
AHEM!
I'M HERE...
TO INFORM YOU IT'S TIME TO MAKE A REGISTRY.
A REGISTRY?

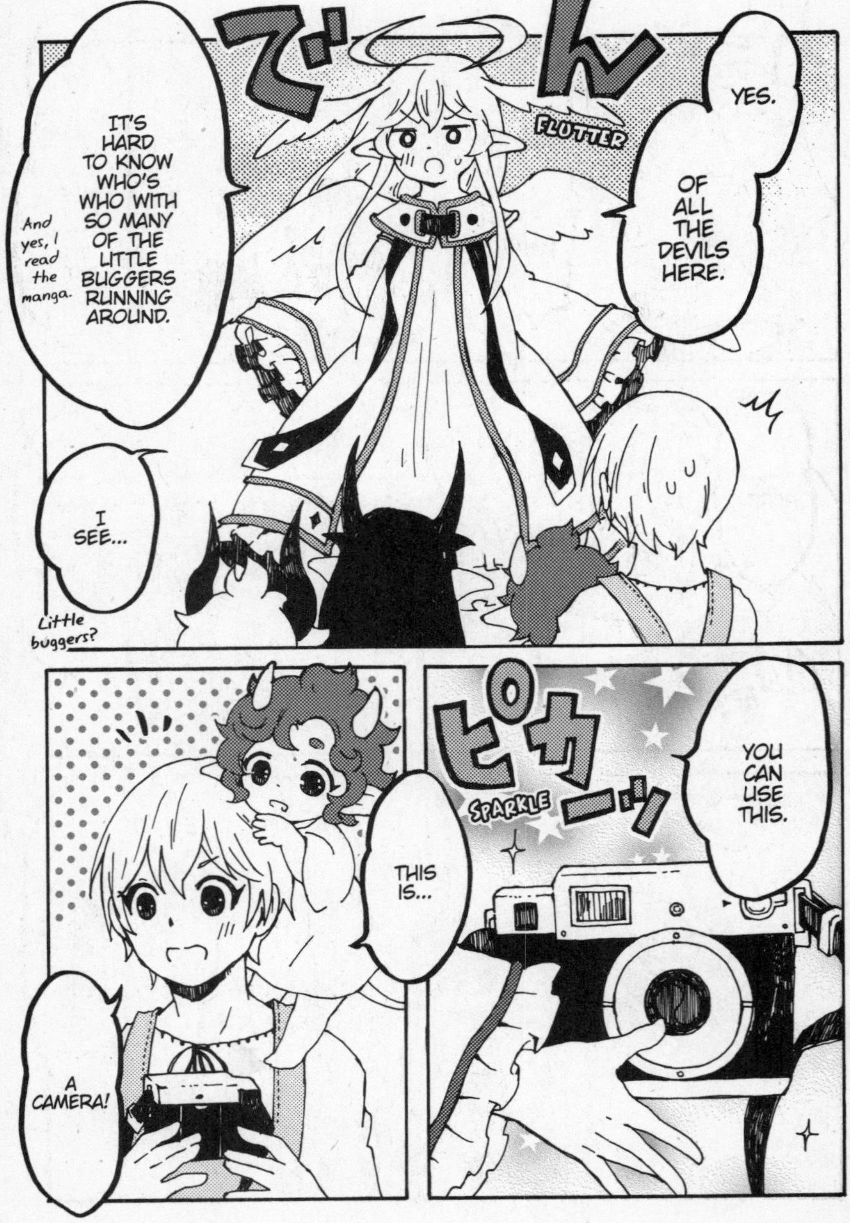
でーん
YES.
OF ALL THE DEVILS HERE.
FLUTTER
IT'S HARD TO KNOW WHO'S WHO WITH SO MANY OF THE LITTLE BUGGERS RUNNING AROUND.
And yes, I read the manga.
I SEE...
Little buggers?
ピカーッ
SPARKLE
YOU CAN USE THIS.
THIS IS...
A CAMERA!

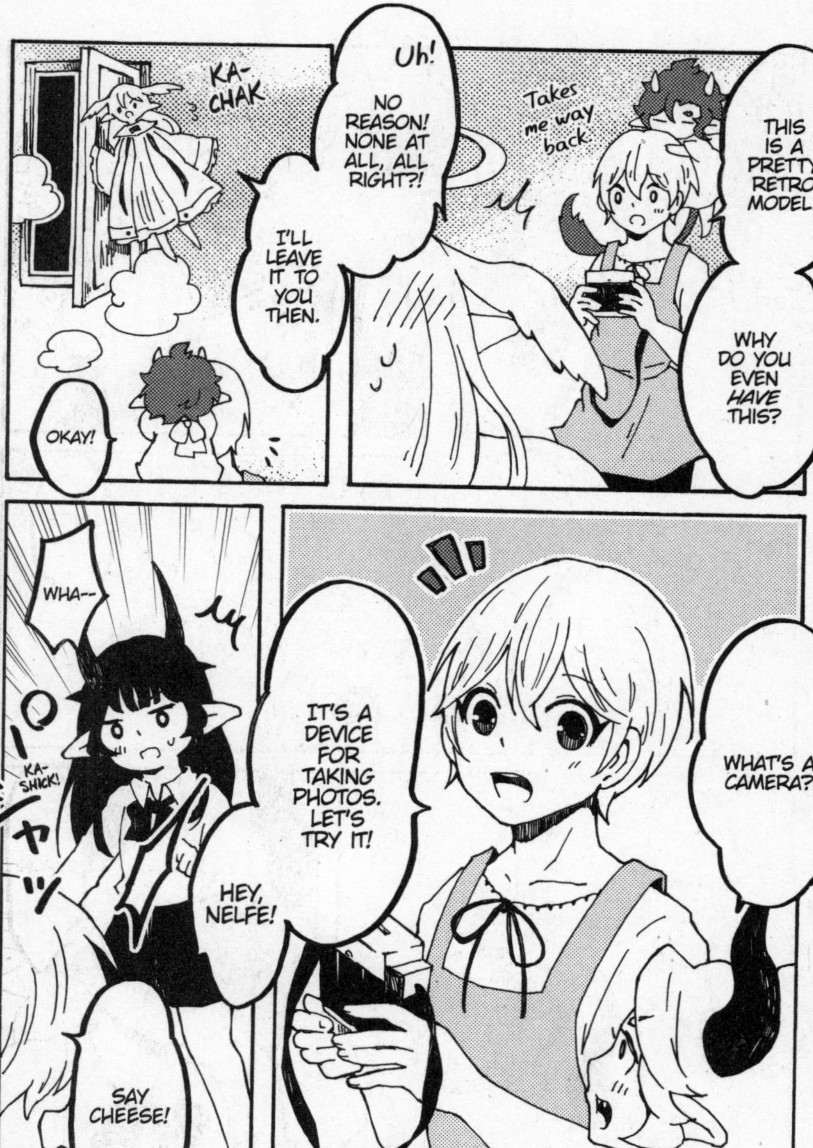
THIS IS A PRETTY RETRO MODEL.
Takes me way back
WHY DO YOU EVEN *HAVE* THIS?
Uh!
NO REASON! NONE AT ALL, ALL RIGHT?!
I'LL LEAVE IT TO YOU THEN.
KA-CHAK
OKAY!
WHAT'S A CAMERA?
IT'S A DEVICE FOR TAKING PHOTOS. LET'S TRY IT!
HEY, NELFE!
WHA--
KA-SHICK!
パシャッ
SAY CHEESE!

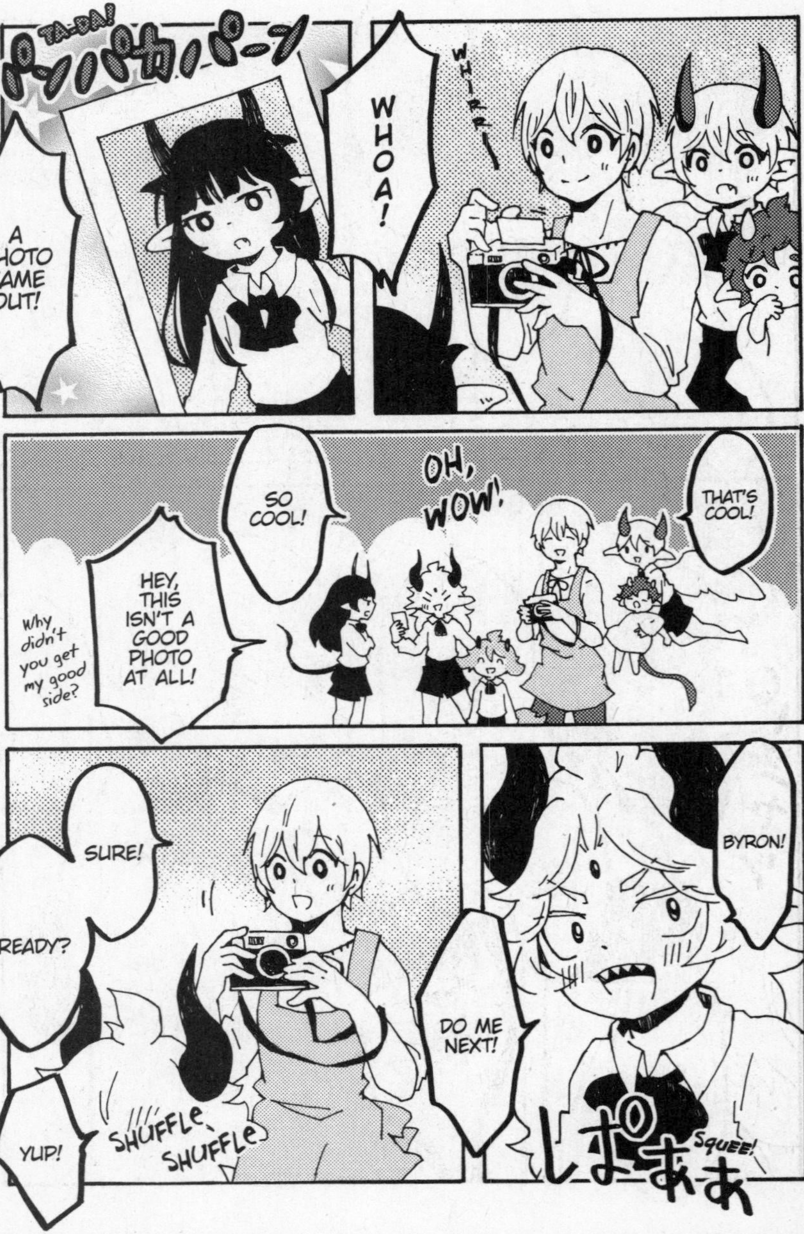
WHIRR—
WHOA!
TA-DA!
パンパカパーン
A PHOTO CAME OUT!
THAT'S COOL!
OH, WOW!
SO COOL!
HEY, THIS ISN'T A GOOD PHOTO AT ALL!
Why didn't you get my good side?
BYRON!
DO ME NEXT!
SQUEE!
しぱああ
SURE!
READY?
SHUFFLE SHUFFLE
YUP!

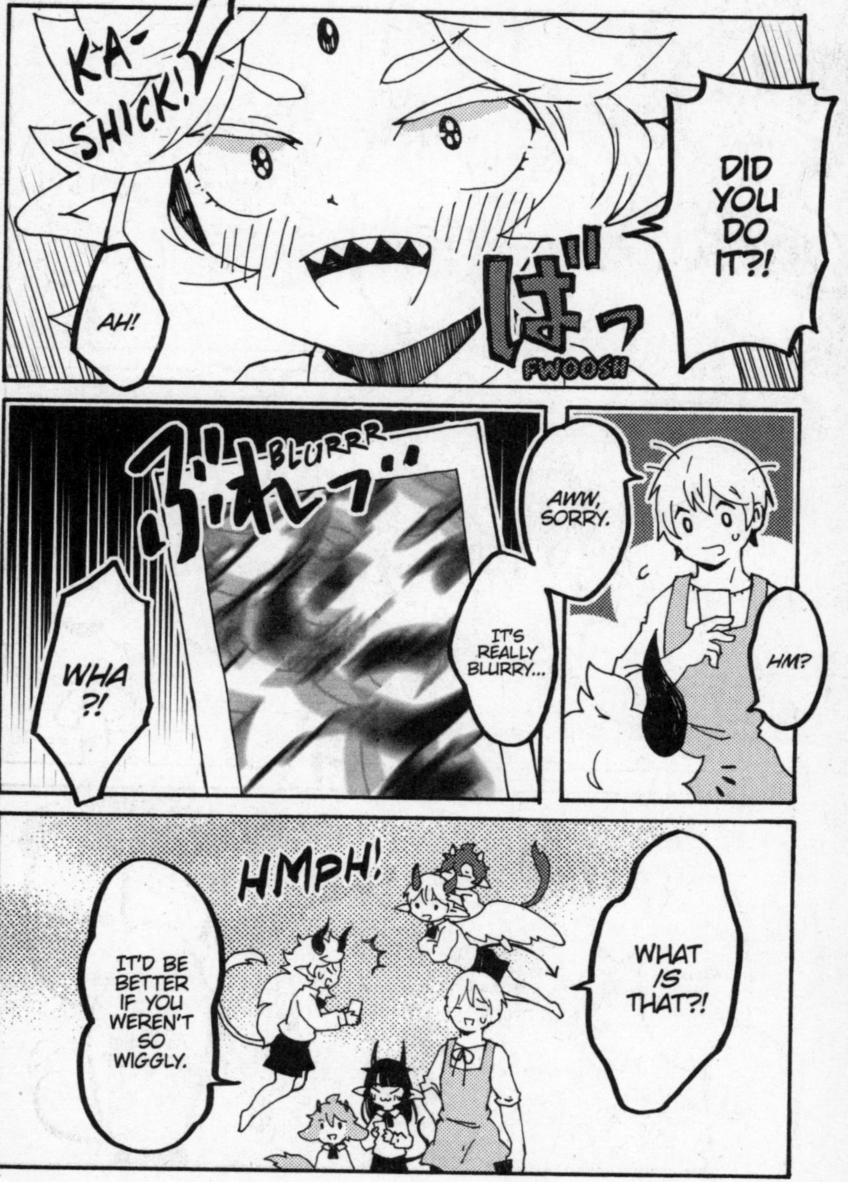
DID YOU DO IT?!
K-A-SHICK!
ばっ
FWOOSH
AH!
HM?
AWW, SORRY.
IT'S REALLY BLURRY...
ぶれっ
BLURRR
WHA?!
WHAT *IS* THAT?!
HMPH!
IT'D BE BETTER IF YOU WEREN'T SO WIGGLY.

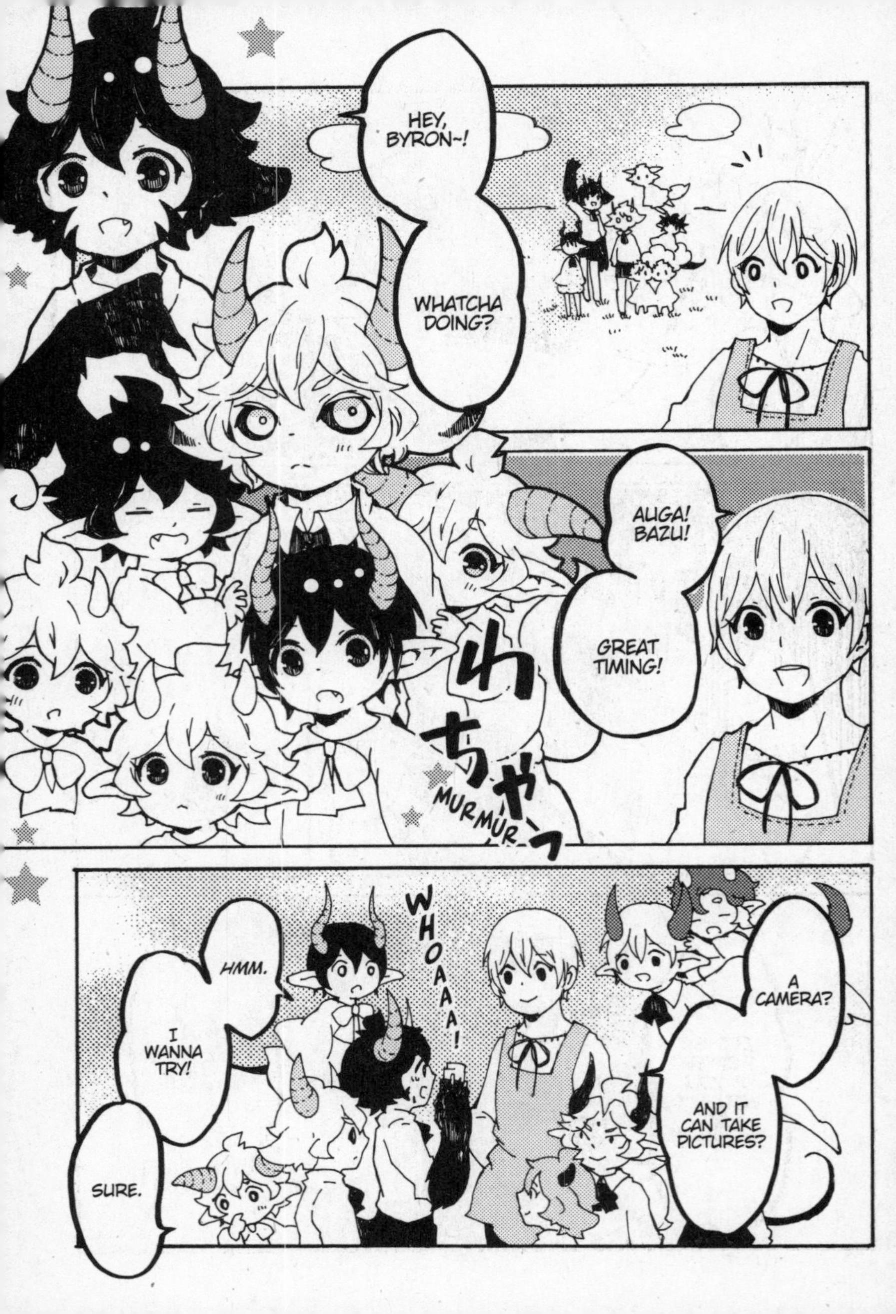
HEY, BYRON~! WHATCHA DOING?
AUGA! BAZU! GREAT TIMING!
わちゃ~っ
MURMUR
A CAMERA? AND IT CAN TAKE PICTURES?
WHOAAAA!
HMM. I WANNA TRY!
SURE.

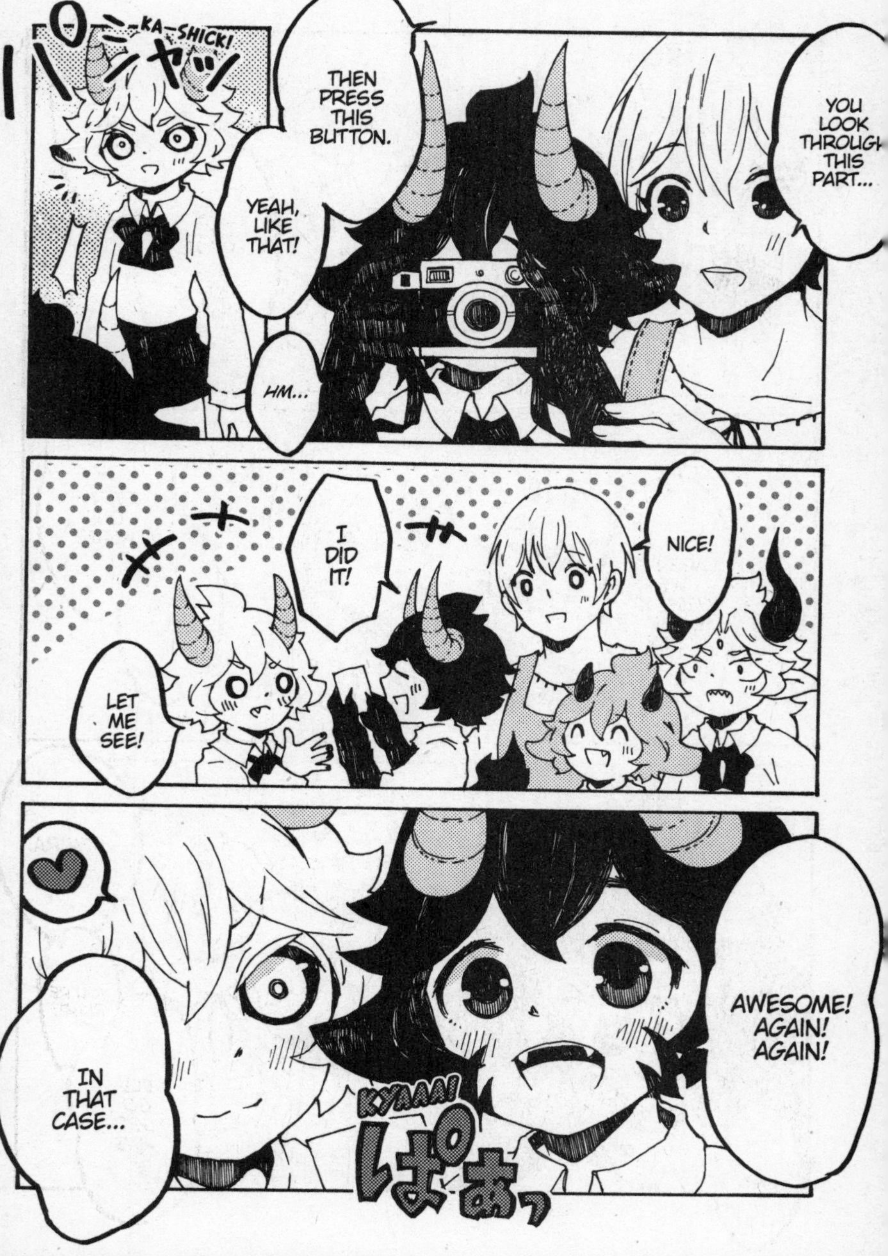
YOU LOOK THROUGH THIS PART...
THEN PRESS THIS BUTTON.
HM...
KA-SHICK!
YEAH, LIKE THAT!
NICE!
I DID IT!
LET ME SEE!
AWESOME! AGAIN! AGAIN!
KYAAA!
ぱあっ
IN THAT CASE...

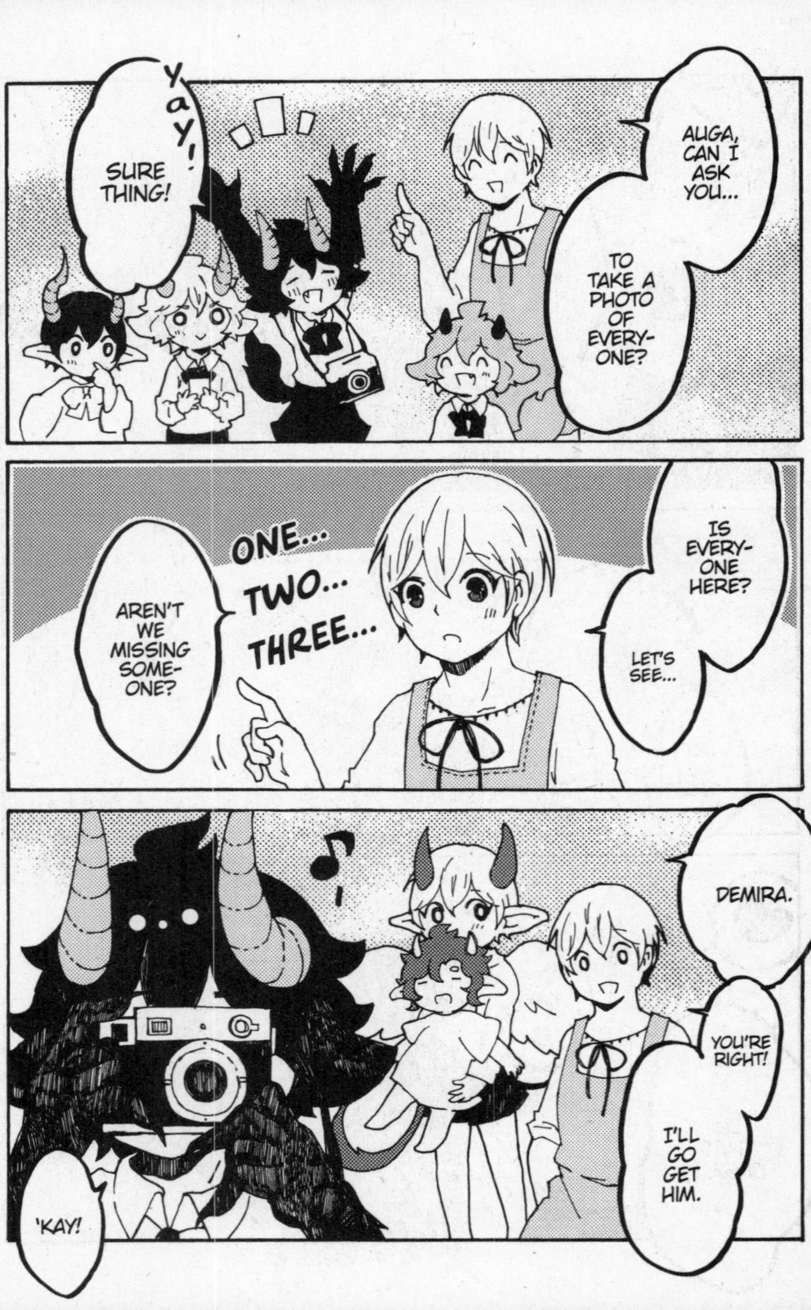
AUGA, CAN I ASK YOU...
TO TAKE A PHOTO OF EVERY-ONE?
YAY!
SURE THING!
IS EVERY-ONE HERE?
LET'S SEE...
ONE... TWO... THREE...
AREN'T WE MISSING SOME-ONE?
DEMIRA.
YOU'RE RIGHT!
I'LL GO GET HIM.
'KAY!

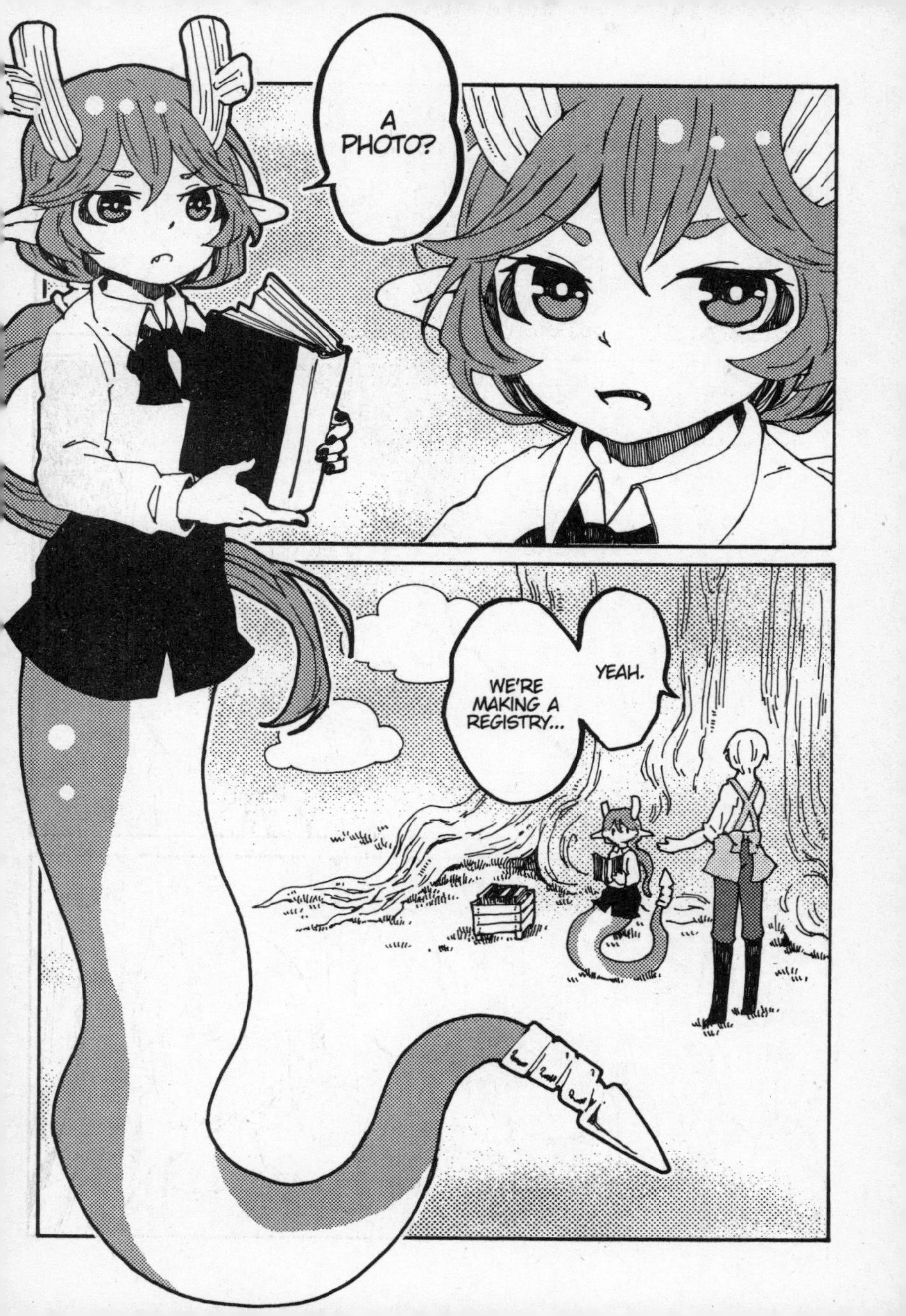
A PHOTO?
YEAH.
WE'RE MAKING A REGISTRY...

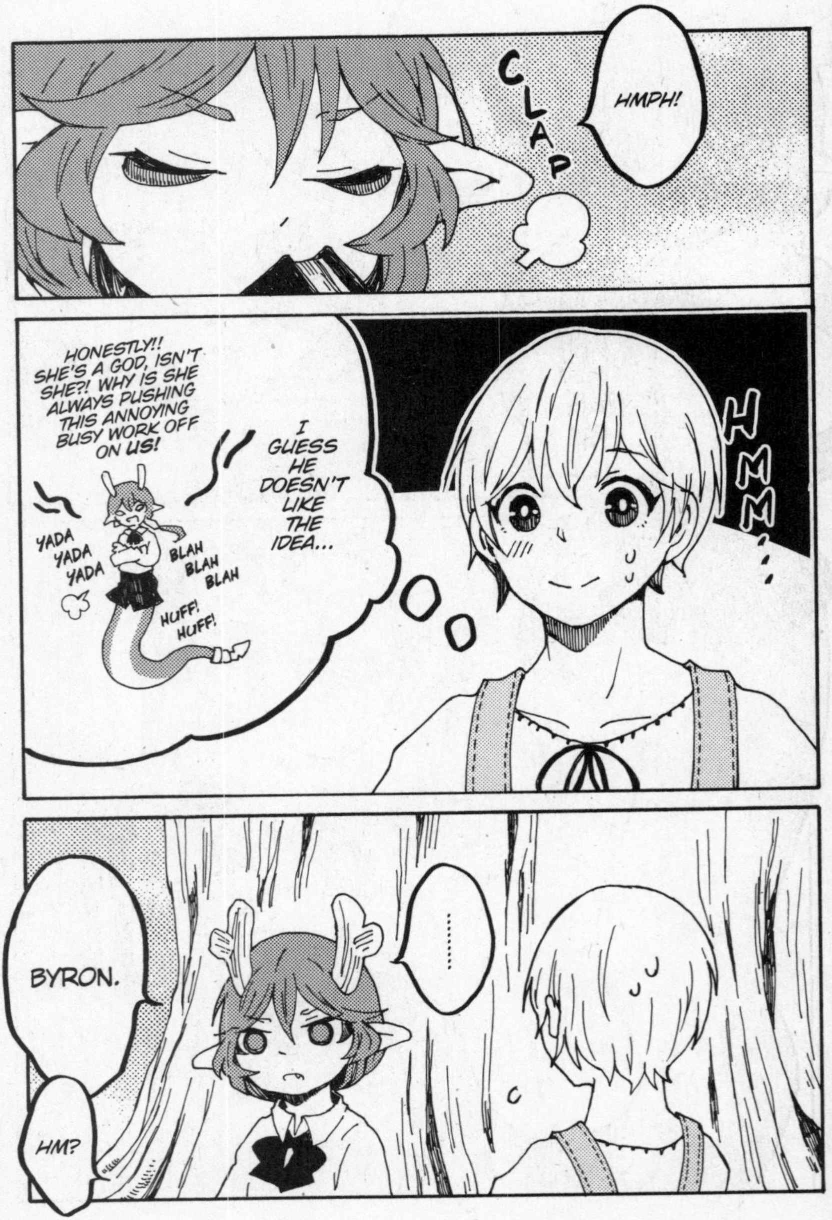
HMPH!
CLAP
HMMM...
I GUESS HE DOESN'T LIKE THE IDEA...
HONESTLY!! SHE'S A GOD, ISN'T SHE?! WHY IS SHE ALWAYS PUSHING THIS ANNOYING BUSY WORK OFF ON US!
BLAH BLAH BLAH
YADA YADA YADA
HUFF! HUFF!
......
BYRON.
HM?

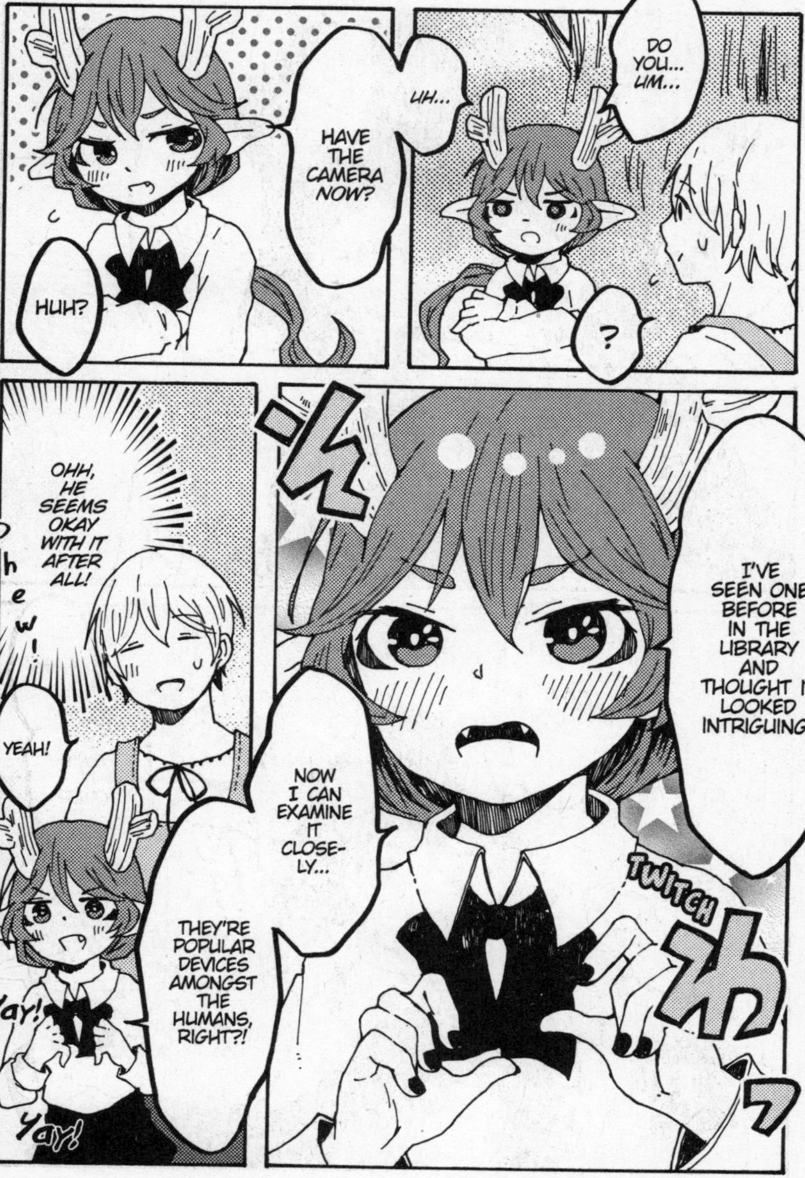
DO YOU... UM...
UH...
HAVE THE CAMERA NOW?
?
HUH?
ん
I'VE SEEN ONE BEFORE IN THE LIBRARY AND THOUGHT IT LOOKED INTRIGUING.
TWITCH
わっ
NOW I CAN EXAMINE IT CLOSE-LY...
THEY'RE POPULAR DEVICES AMONGST THE HUMANS, RIGHT?!
OHH, HE SEEMS OKAY WITH IT AFTER ALL!
Phew!
YEAH!
Yay!
Yay!

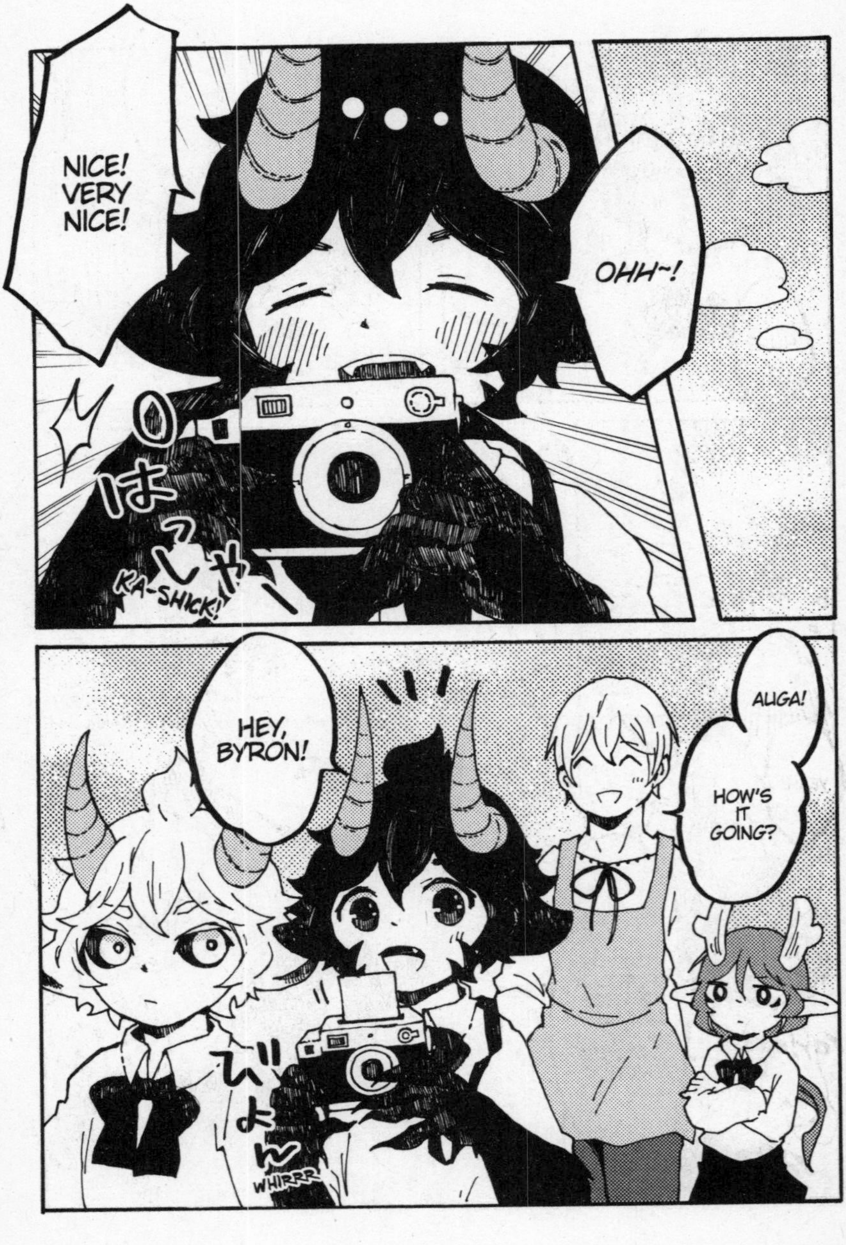
OHH~!
NICE! VERY NICE!
ぱしゃ
KA-SHICK!
AUGA!
HOW'S IT GOING?
HEY, BYRON!
びよん
WHIRRR

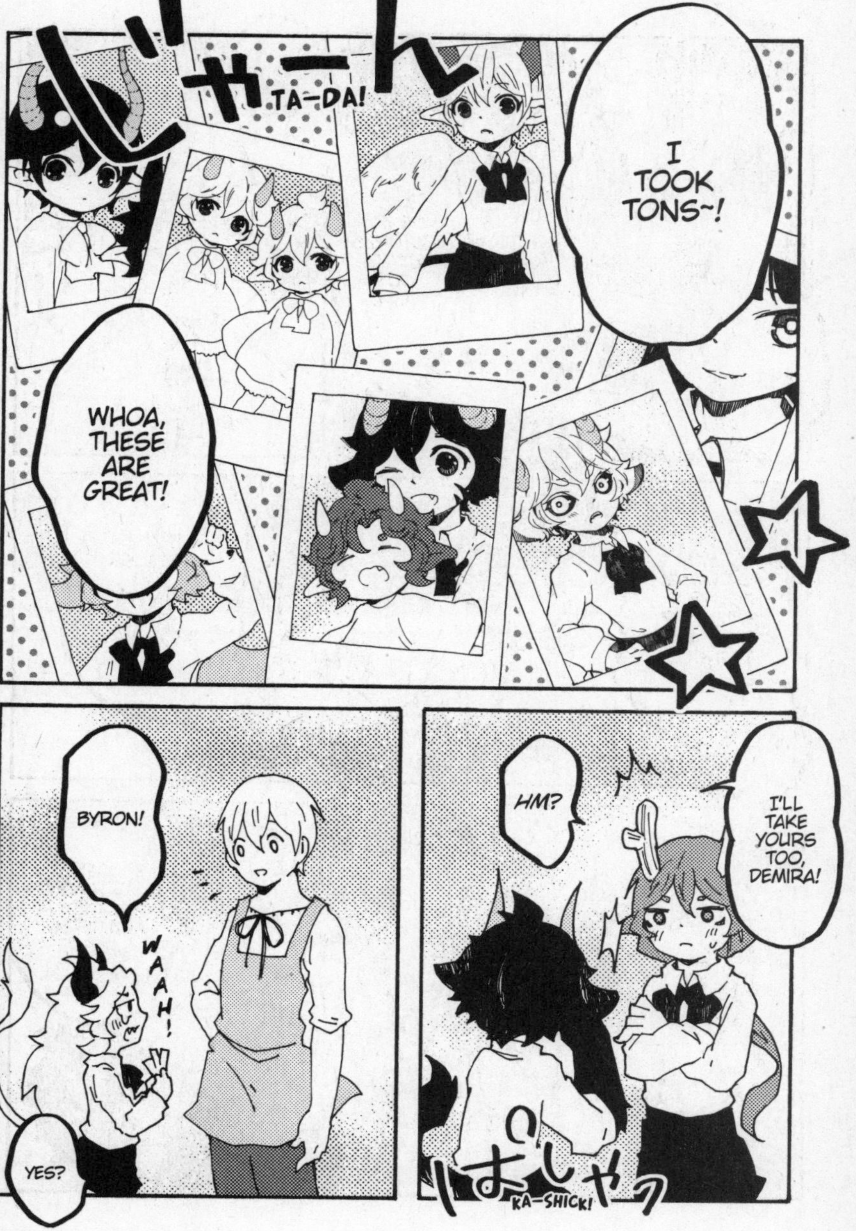

じゃーん
TA-DA!
I TOOK TONS~!
WHOA, THESE ARE GREAT!
I'LL TAKE YOURS TOO, DEMIRA!
HM?
ぱしゃっ
KA-SHICK!
BYRON!
WAAH!
YES?

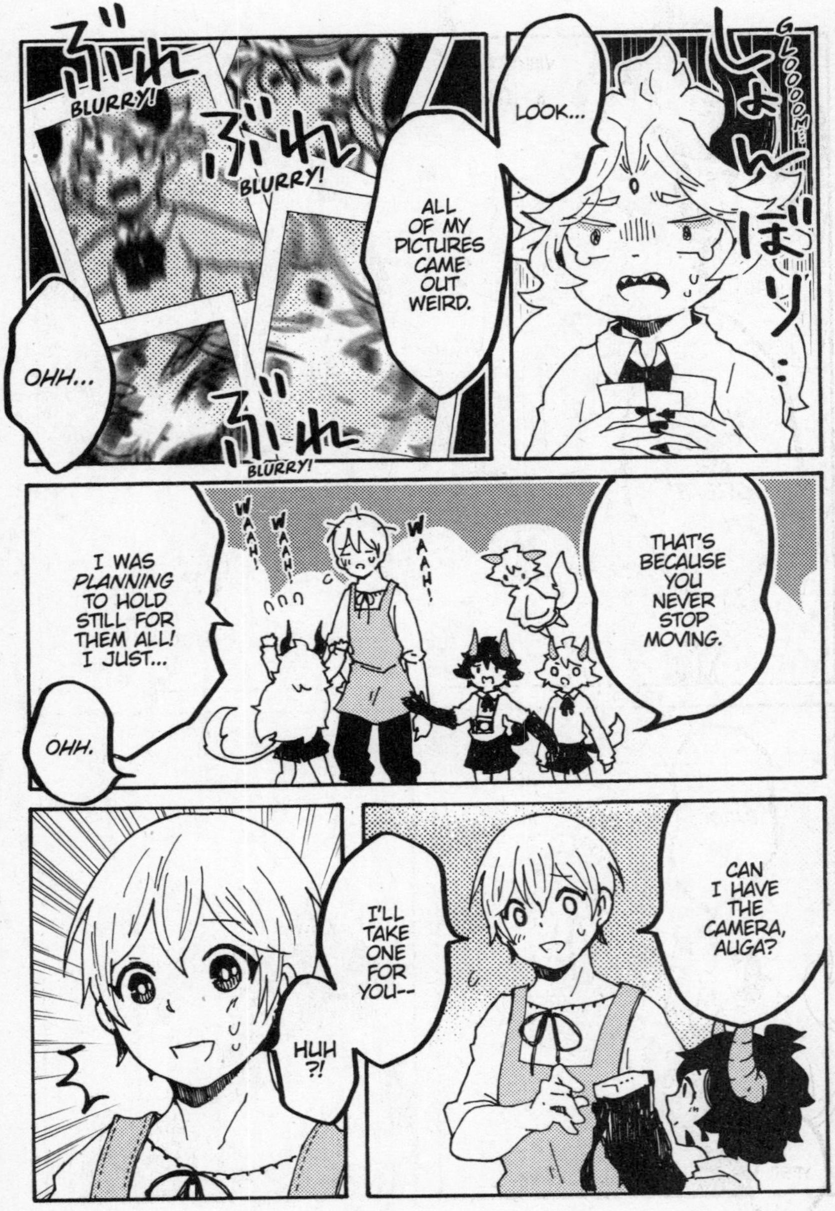
LOOK...
しょんぼり…
GLOOOOOM...
ALL OF MY PICTURES CAME OUT WEIRD.
ぶれ
BLURRY!
ぶれ
BLURRY!
ぶれ
BLURRY!
OHH...
THAT'S BECAUSE YOU NEVER STOP MOVING.
WAAH!
WAAH!
WAAH!
I WAS *PLANNING* TO HOLD STILL FOR THEM ALL! I JUST...
OHH.
CAN I HAVE THE CAMERA, AUGA?
I'LL TAKE ONE FOR YOU--
HUH?!

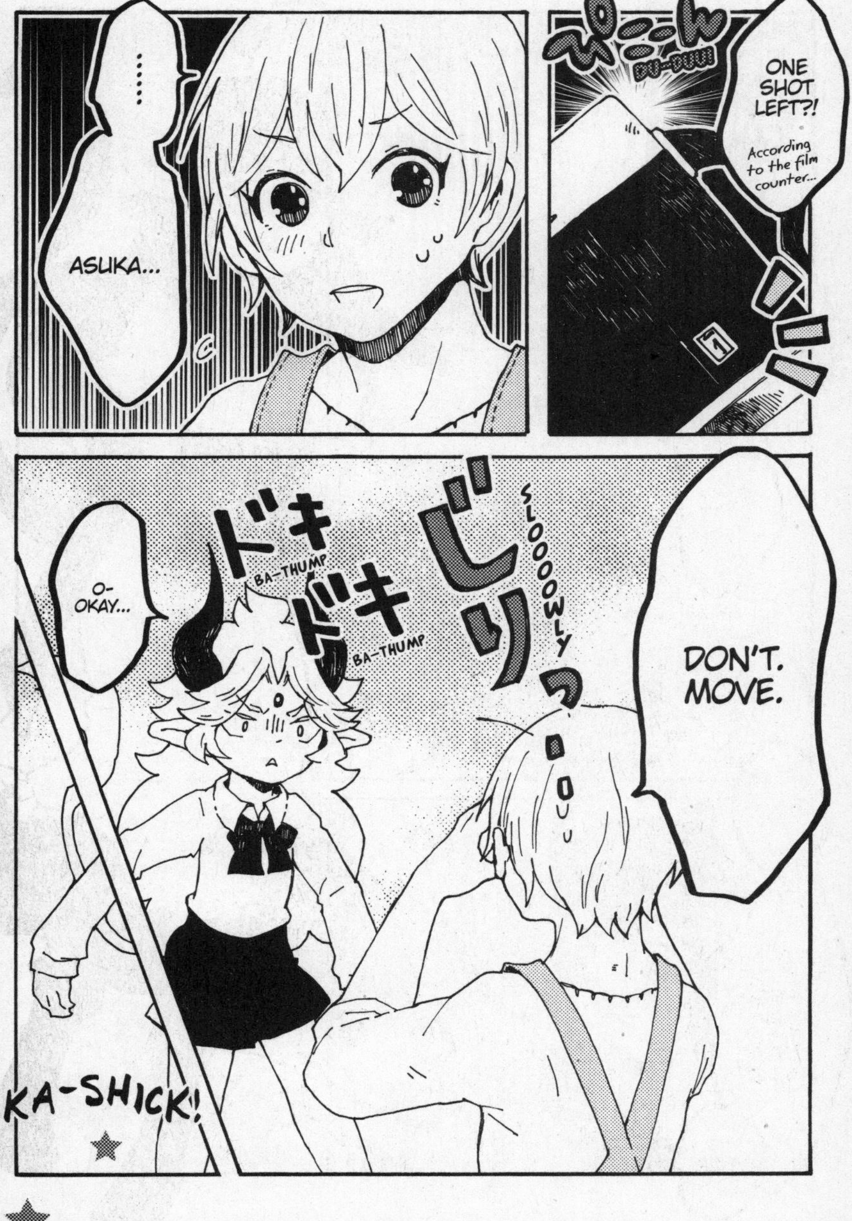
ONE SHOT LEFT?!
According to the film counter...
......
ASUKA...
DON'T. MOVE.
SLOOOOOWLY
BA-THUMP
BA-THUMP
O-OKAY...
KA-SHICK!

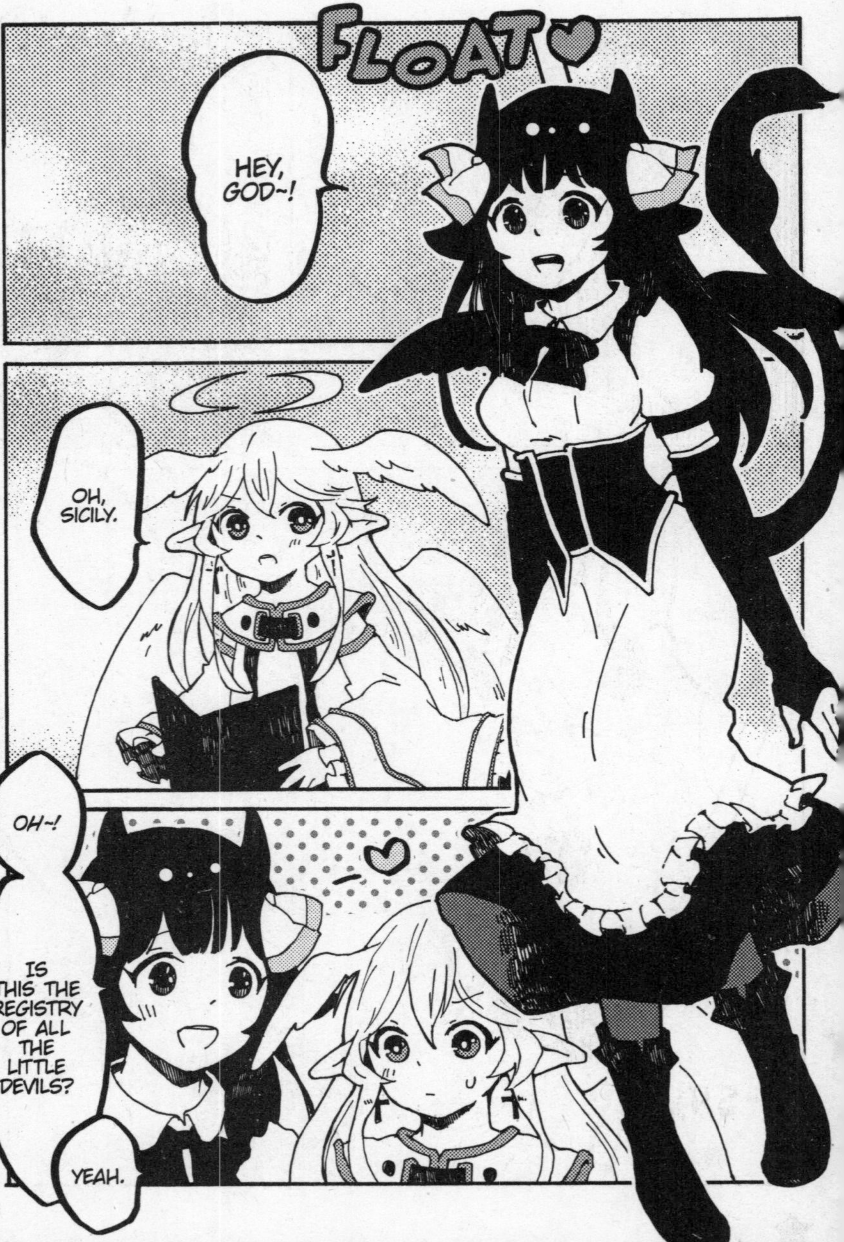
FLOAT♥
HEY, GOD~!
OH, SICILY.
OH~!
IS THIS THE REGISTRY OF ALL THE LITTLE DEVILS?
YEAH.

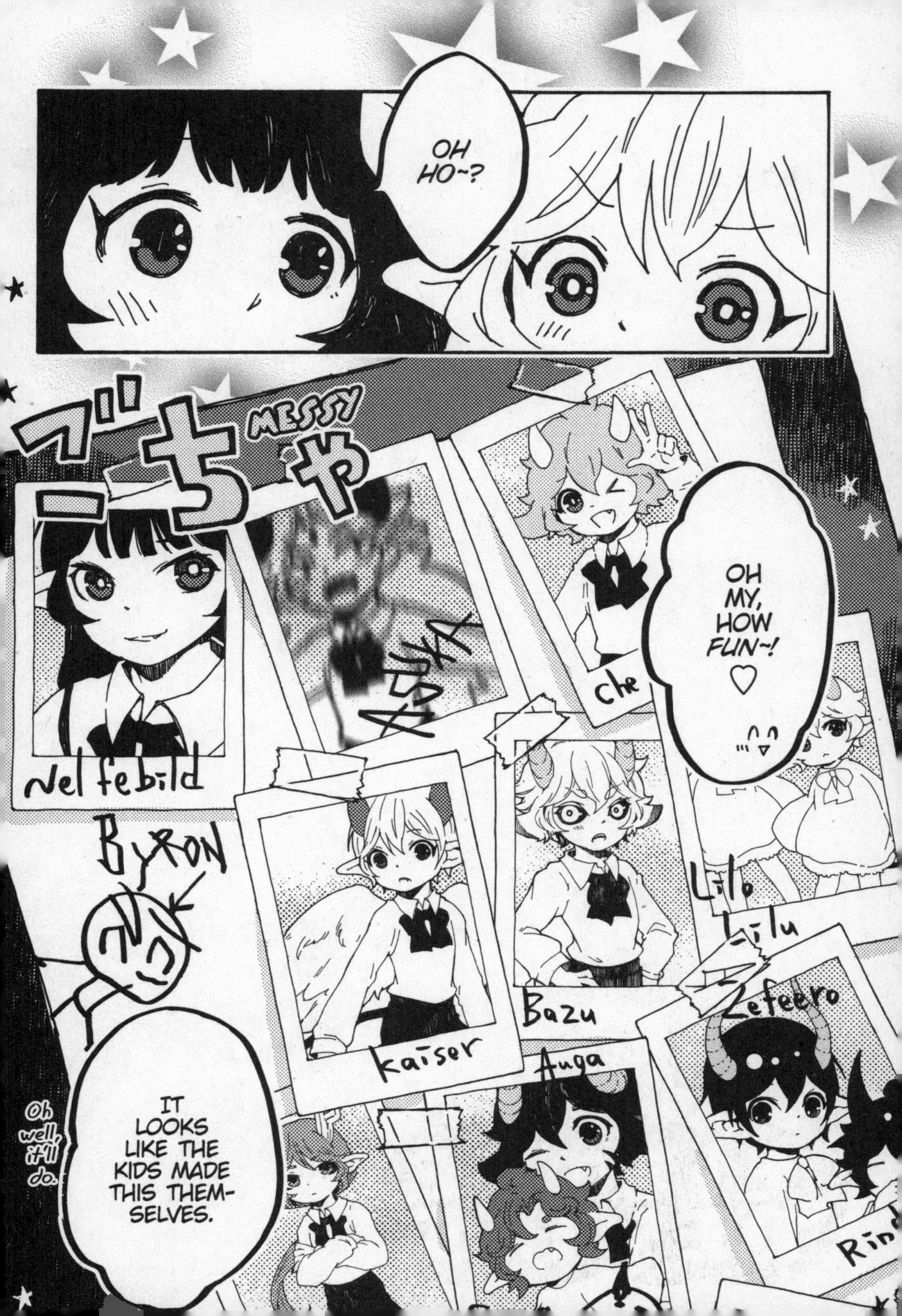
OH HO~?
OH MY, HOW FUN~! ♡
ごちゃ
MESSY
Che
Lilo
Lilu
Zefeero
Bazu
kaiser
Nel febild
BYRON
Auga
IT LOOKS LIKE THE KIDS MADE THIS THEMSELVES.
Oh well, it'll do.

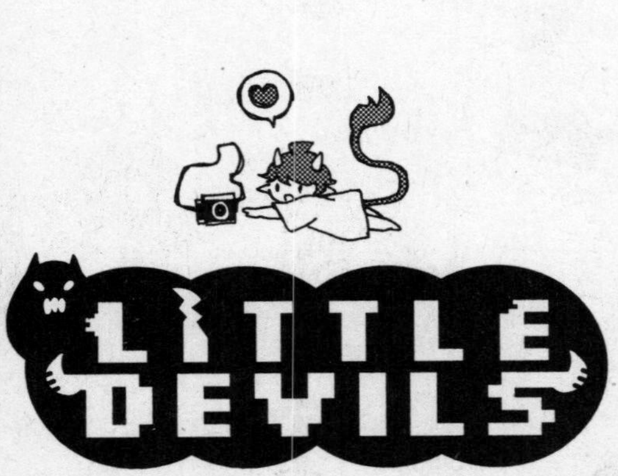

LITTLE
DEVILS

DEVIL OF THE HEART - GIEG ▼

Recently hatched, he is the youngest
devil by far.
Has a head of charming, fluffy red hair.
His horns have already come through.
Right now, his primary hobby is
teething.

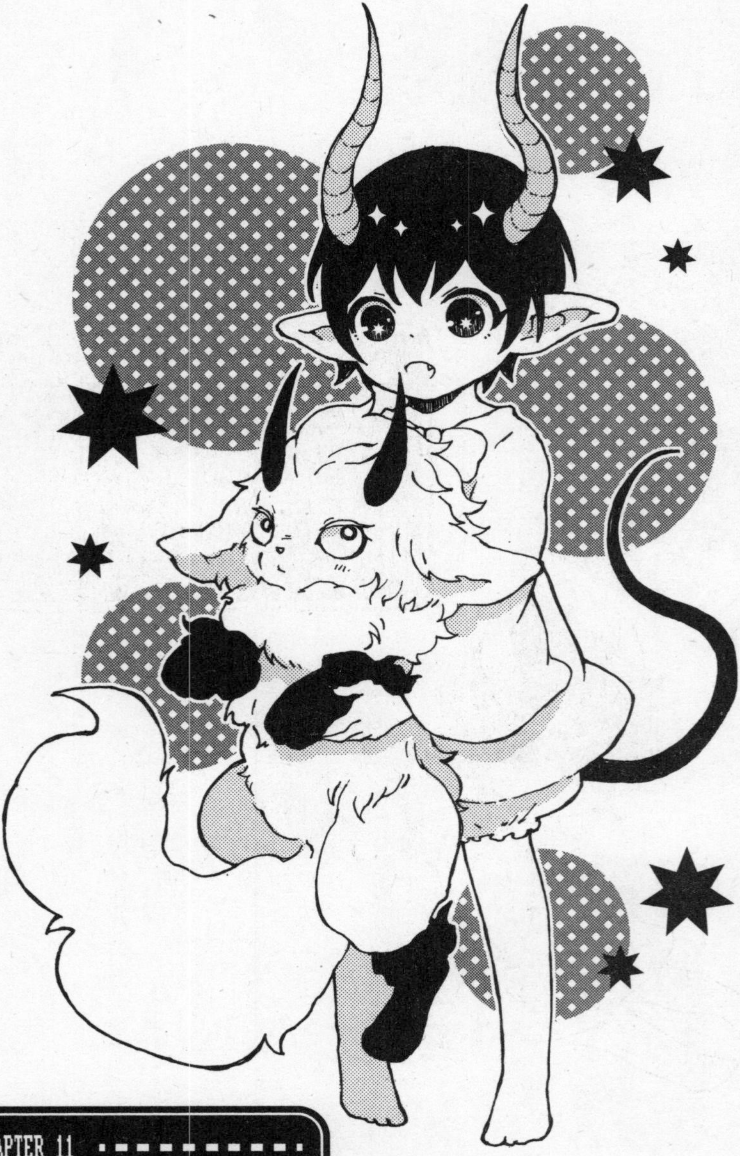

CHAPTER 11
YOUNG CATASTROPHIC MONSTER

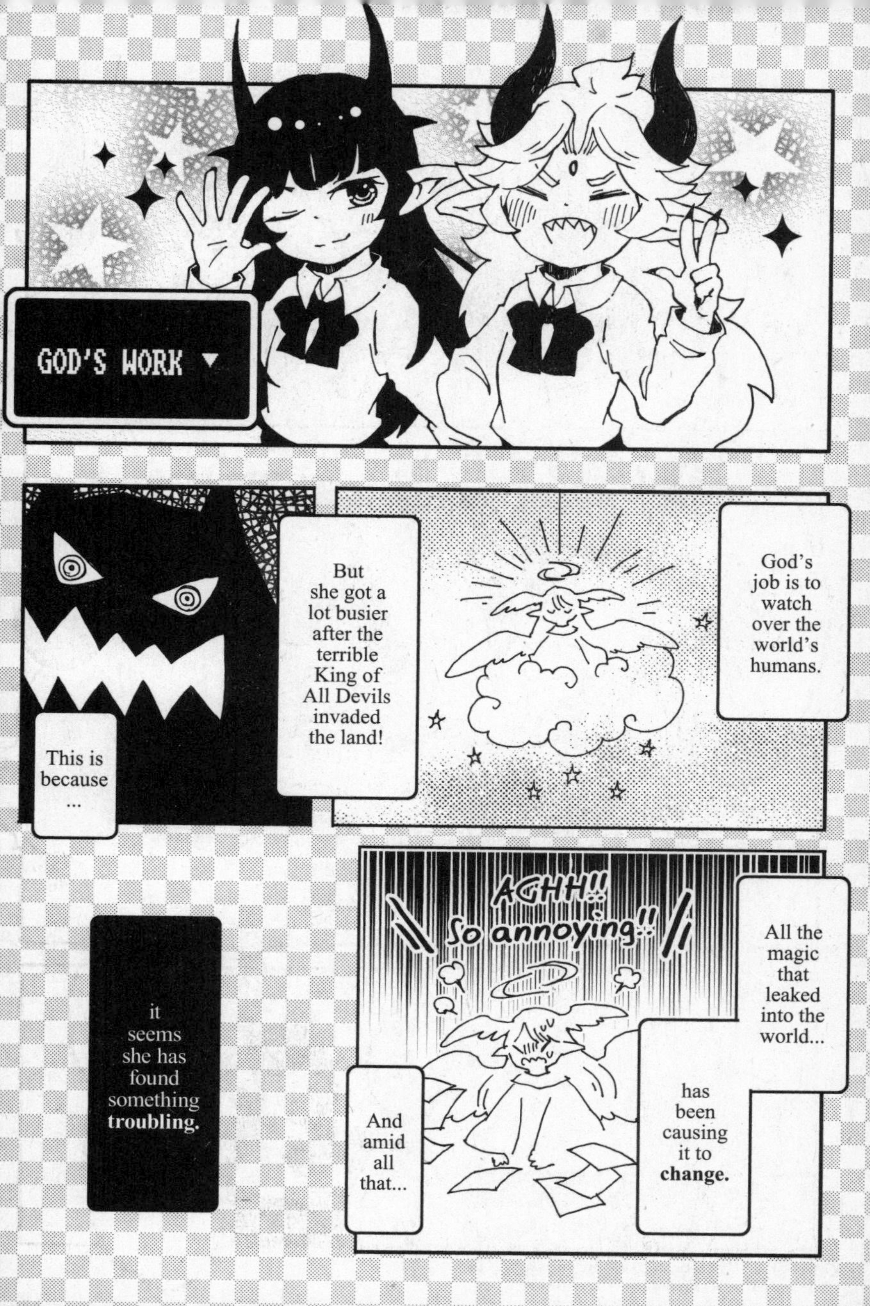
GOD'S WORK ▼
God's job is to watch over the world's humans.
But she got a lot busier after the terrible King of All Devils invaded the land!
This is because ...
All the magic that leaked into the world...
has been causing it to change.
AGHH!! So annoying!!
And amid all that...
it seems she has found something **troubling.**

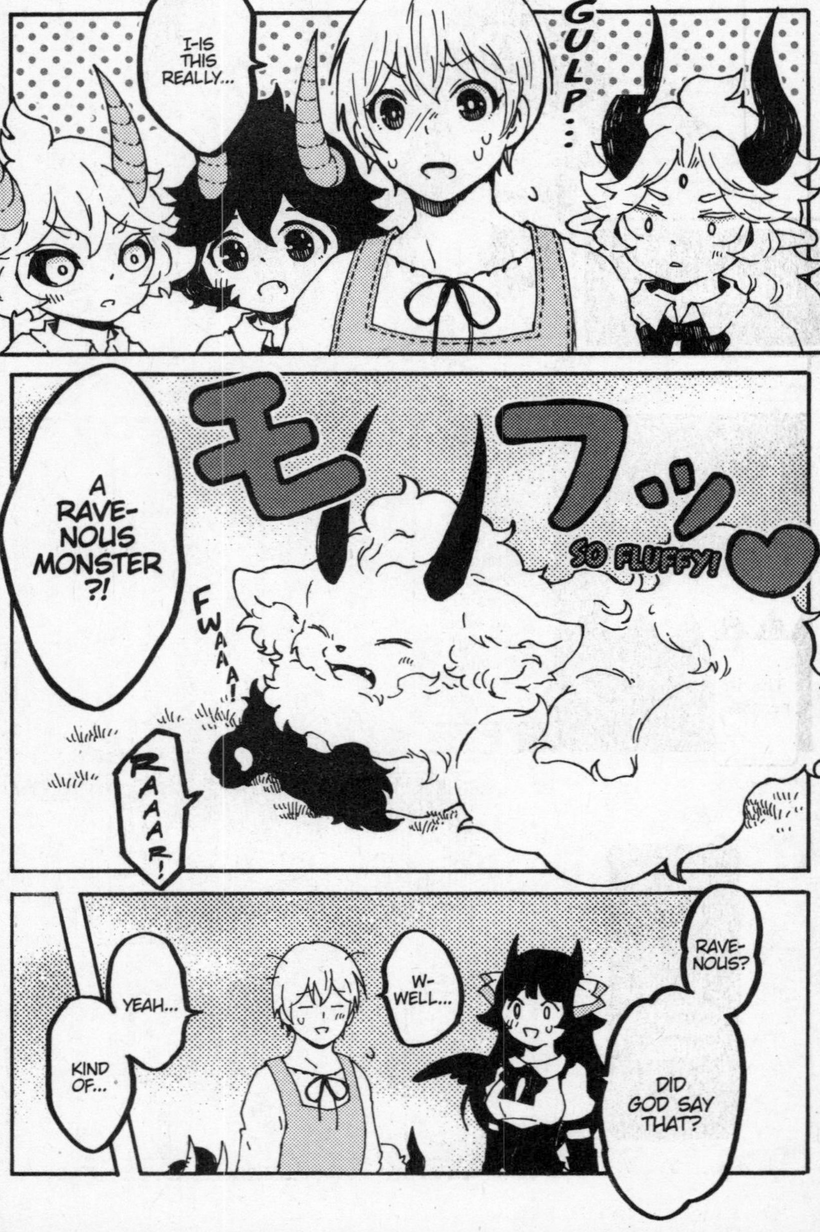
GULP...
I-IS THIS REALLY...
モフッ
SO FLUFFY!
A RAVE-NOUS MONSTER?!
FWAAAA!
RAAAR!
RAVE-NOUS?
DID GOD SAY THAT?
W-WELL...
YEAH...
KIND OF...

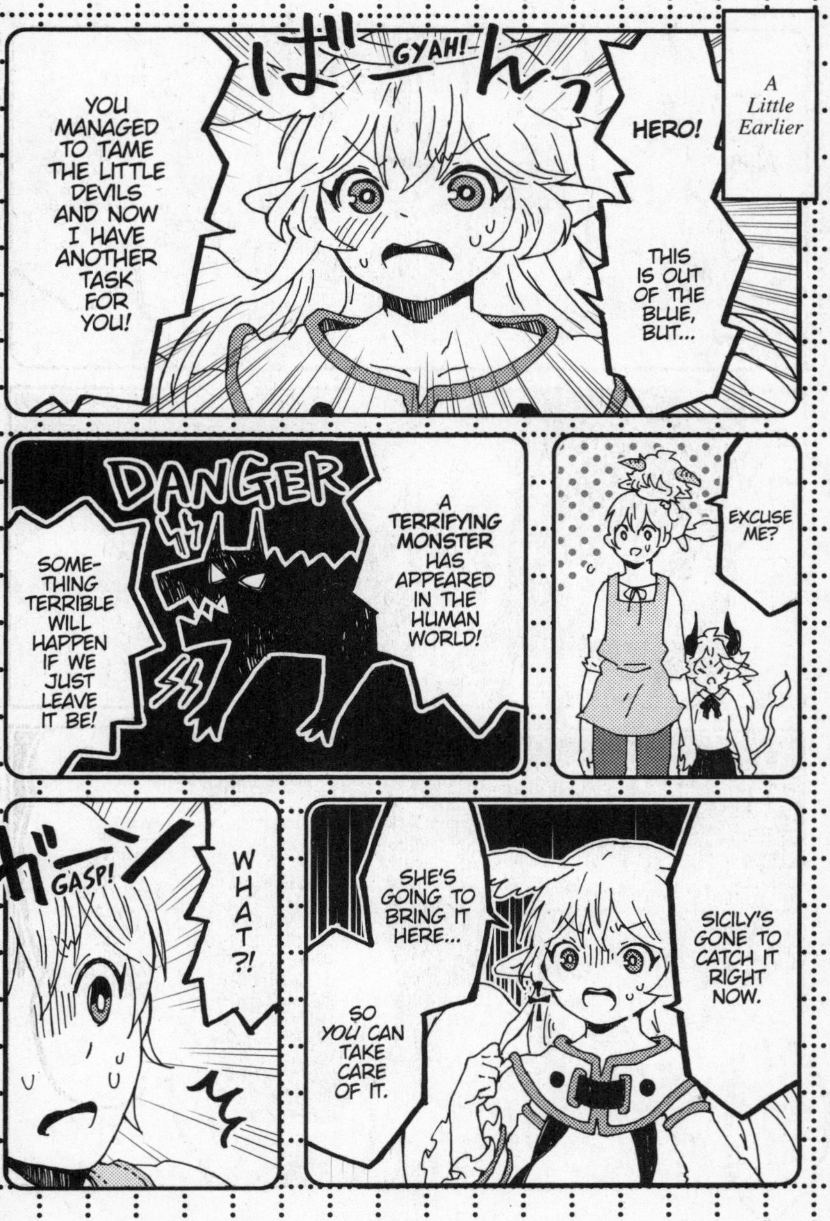
A Little Earlier
HERO!
THIS IS OUT OF THE BLUE, BUT...
GYAH!
YOU MANAGED TO TAME THE LITTLE DEVILS AND NOW I HAVE ANOTHER TASK FOR YOU!
EXCUSE ME?
A TERRIFYING MONSTER HAS APPEARED IN THE HUMAN WORLD!
DANGER
SOMETHING TERRIBLE WILL HAPPEN IF WE JUST LEAVE IT BE!
SICILY'S GONE TO CATCH IT RIGHT NOW.
SHE'S GOING TO BRING IT HERE...
SO YOU CAN TAKE CARE OF IT.
WHAT?!
GASP!

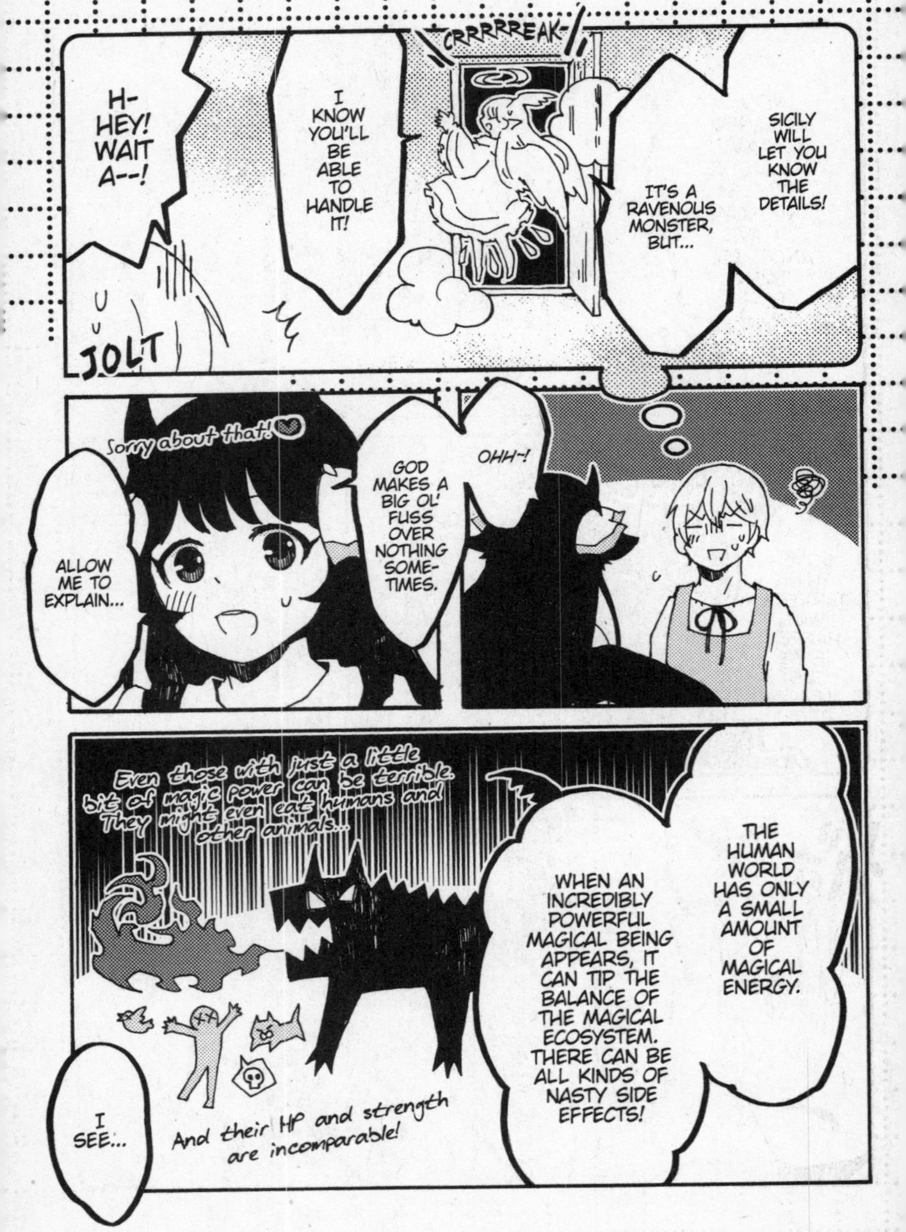
SICILY WILL LET YOU KNOW THE DETAILS!
IT'S A RAVENOUS MONSTER, BUT...
CRRRRREAK
I KNOW YOU'LL BE ABLE TO HANDLE IT!
H-HEY! WAIT A--!
JOLT
OHH~!
GOD MAKES A BIG OL' FUSS OVER NOTHING SOME-TIMES.
Sorry about that!
ALLOW ME TO EXPLAIN...
THE HUMAN WORLD HAS ONLY A SMALL AMOUNT OF MAGICAL ENERGY.
WHEN AN INCREDIBLY POWERFUL MAGICAL BEING APPEARS, IT CAN TIP THE BALANCE OF THE MAGICAL ECOSYSTEM. THERE CAN BE ALL KINDS OF NASTY SIDE EFFECTS!
Even those with just a little bit of magic power can be terrible. They might even eat humans and other animals...
And their HP and strength are incomparable!
I SEE...

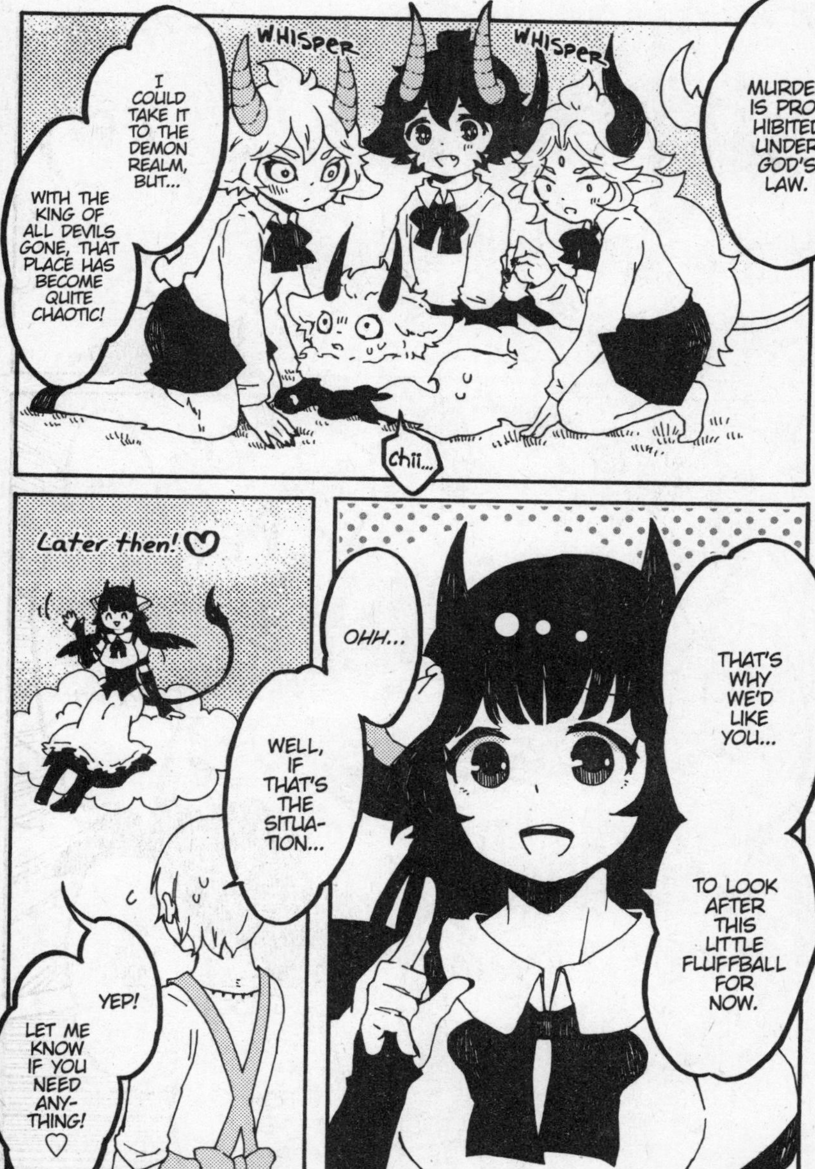
WHISPER
WHISPER
MURDER IS PROHIBITED UNDER GOD'S LAW.
I COULD TAKE IT TO THE DEMON REALM, BUT...
WITH THE KING OF ALL DEVILS GONE, THAT PLACE HAS BECOME QUITE CHAOTIC!
Chii...
THAT'S WHY WE'D LIKE YOU...
TO LOOK AFTER THIS LITTLE FLUFFBALL FOR NOW.
OHH...
WELL, IF THAT'S THE SITUATION...
Later then! ♡
YEP!
LET ME KNOW IF YOU NEED ANYTHING! ♡

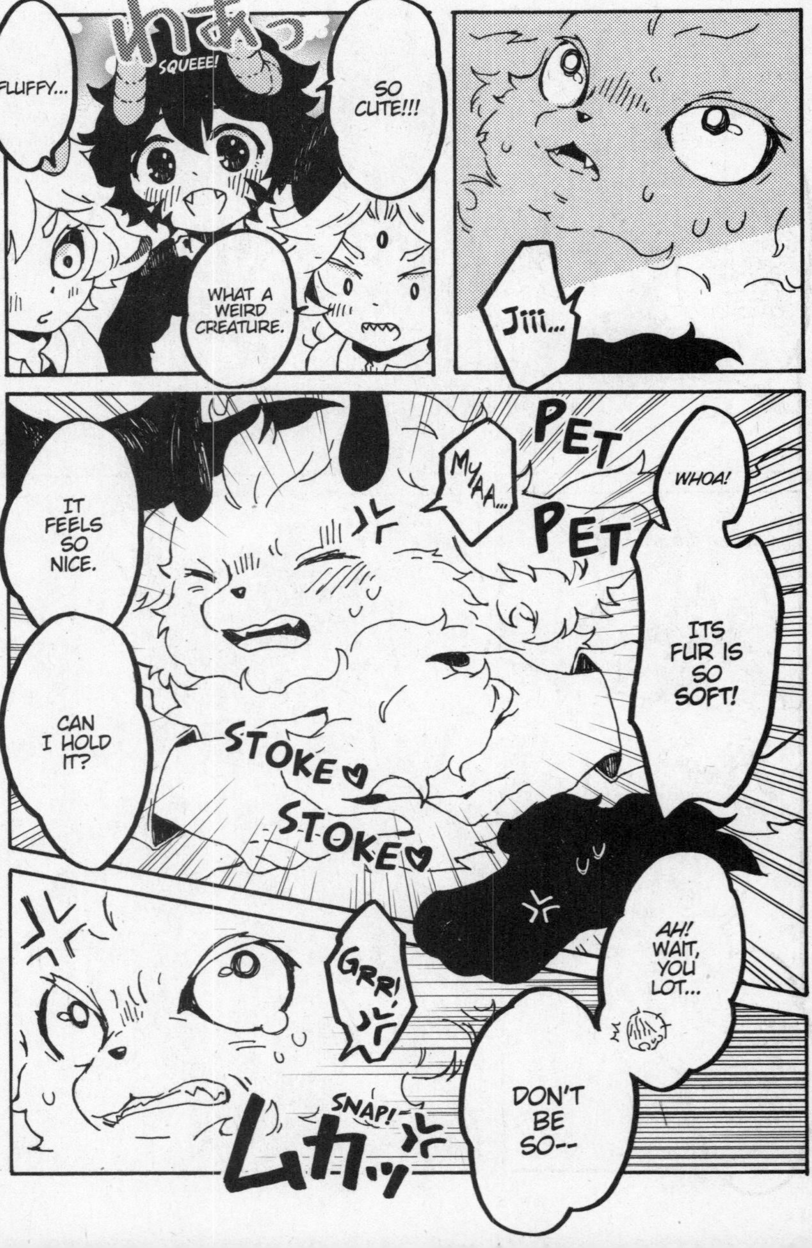
Jiii...
SO CUTE!!!
わぁっ
SQUEEE!
FLUFFY...
WHAT A WEIRD CREATURE.
WHOA!
PET
PET
MYAA...
IT FEELS SO NICE.
ITS FUR IS SO SOFT!
CAN I HOLD IT?
STOKE♡
STOKE♡
AH! WAIT, YOU LOT...
GRR!
DON'T BE SO--
ムカッ
SNAP!

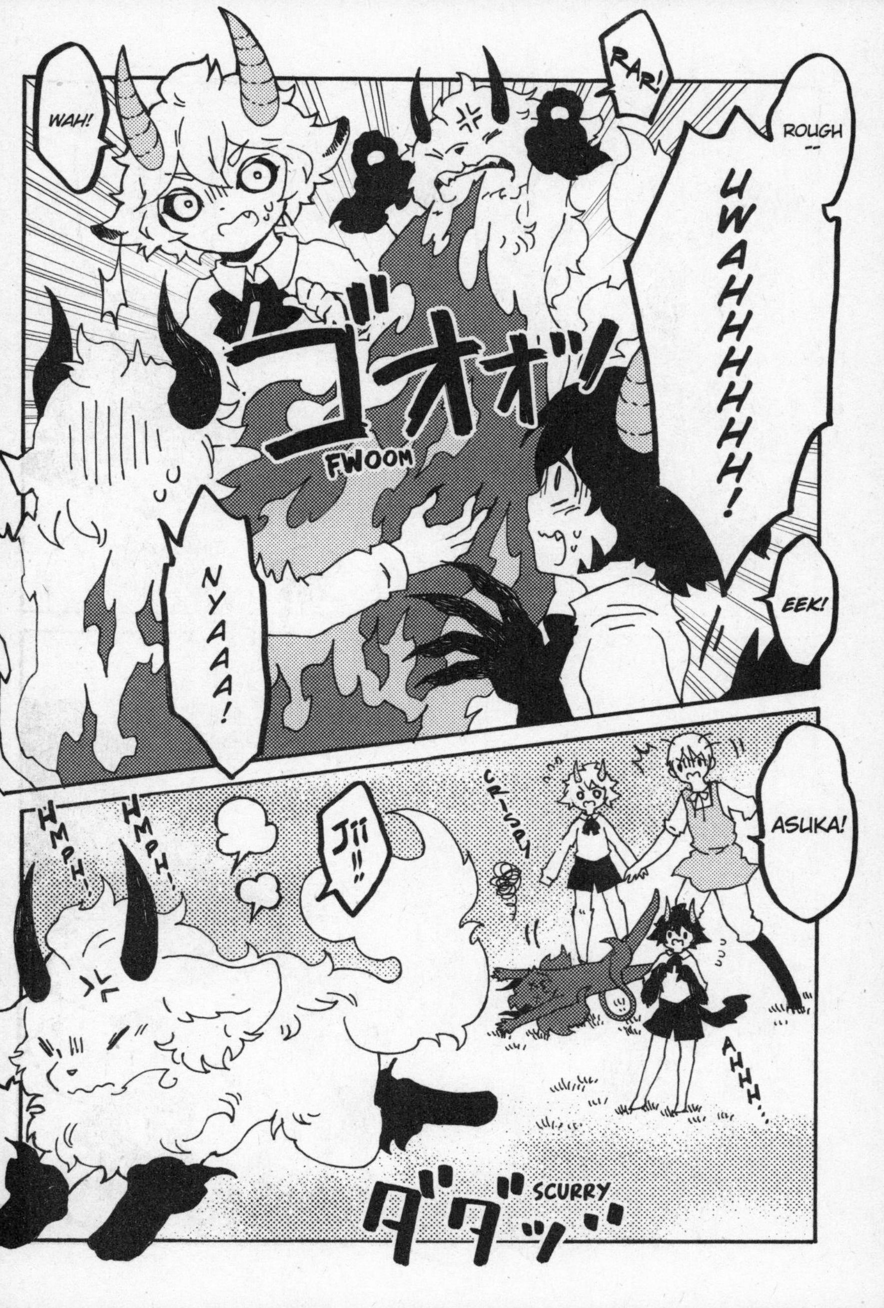
ROUGH --
UWAHHHHHHHH!
RAR!
EEK!
WAH!
ゴオオッ
FWOOM
NYAAAA!
ASUKA!
CRI-SPY
AHHH...
Jii!!
HMPH! HMPH!
ダダッ
SCURRY

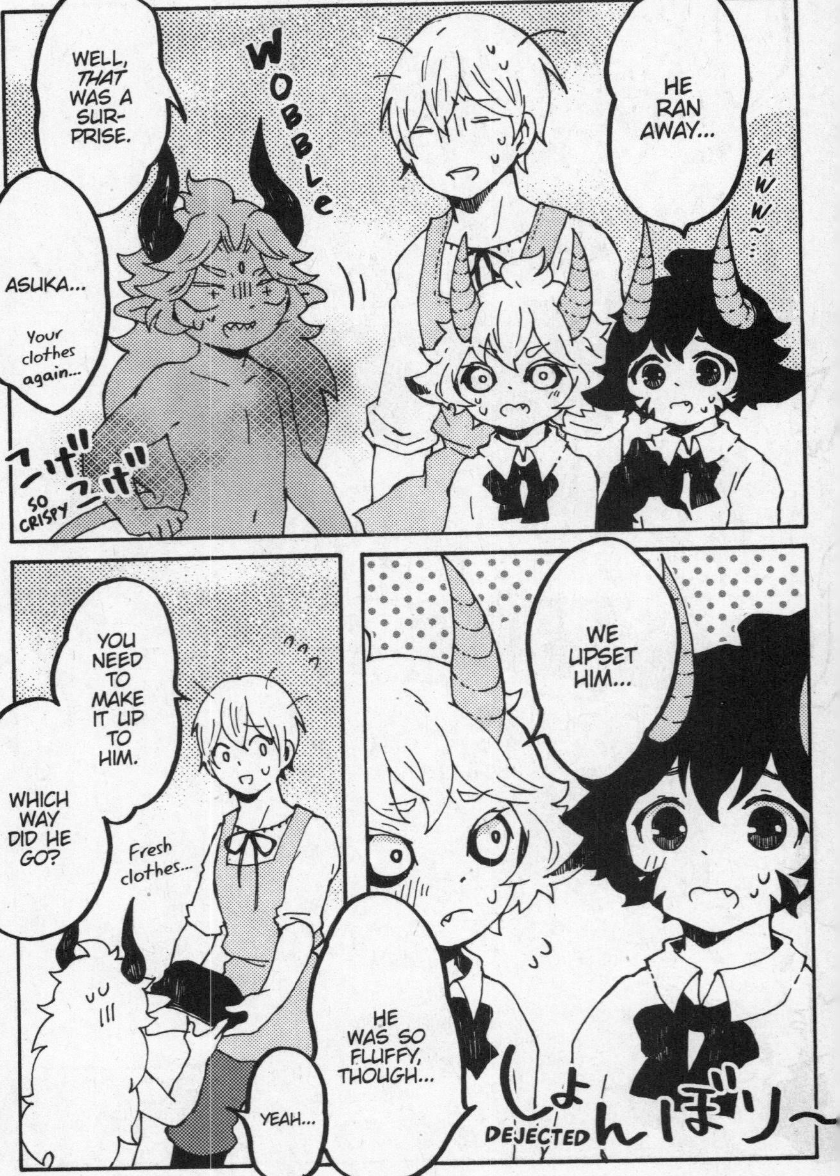
HE RAN AWAY...
AWW~...
WOBBLE
WELL, *THAT* WAS A SURPRISE.
ASUKA...
Your clothes again...
こげこげ
SO CRISPY
WE UPSET HIM...
HE WAS SO FLUFFY, THOUGH...
YEAH...
しょんぼり〜
DEJECTED
YOU NEED TO MAKE IT UP TO HIM.
WHICH WAY DID HE GO?
Fresh clothes...

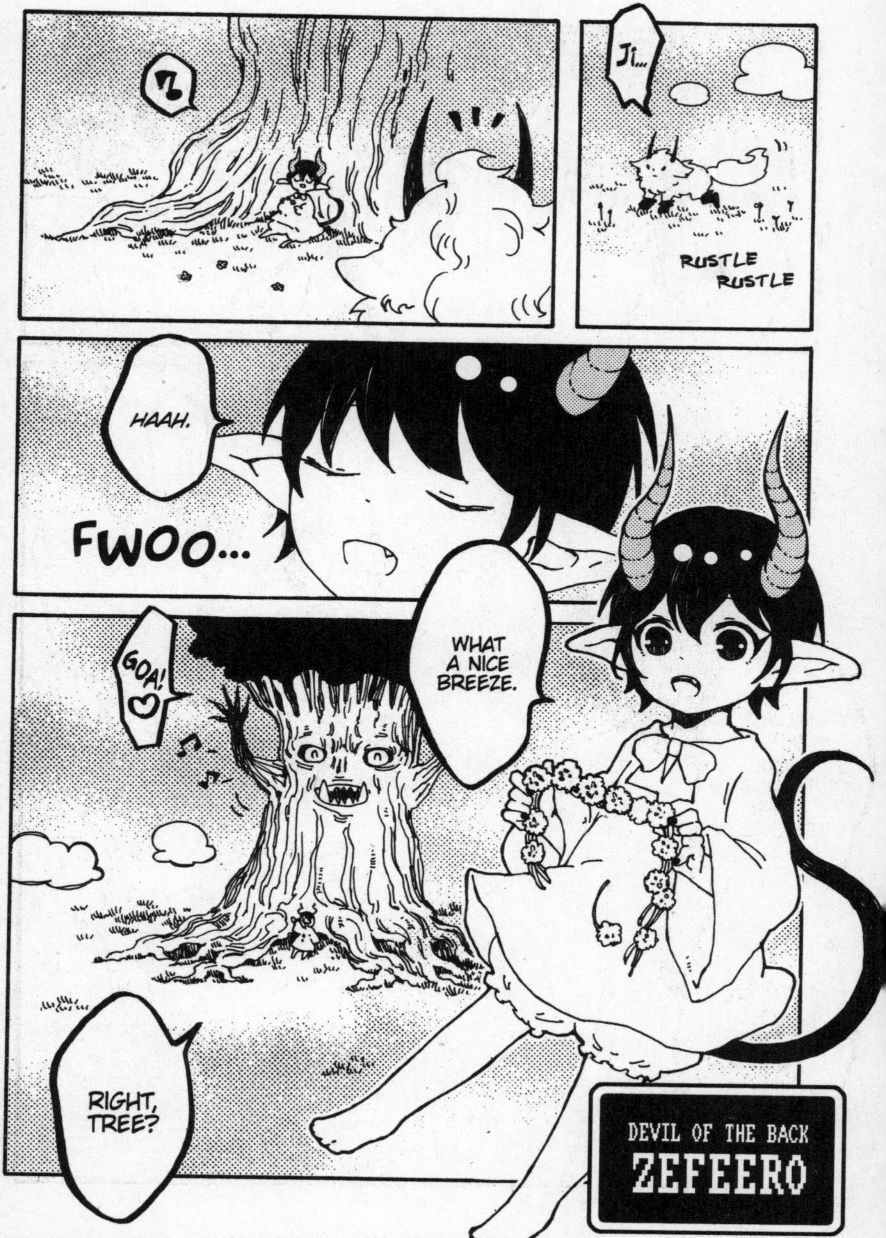
Ji...
RUSTLE RUSTLE
HAAH.
FWOO...
WHAT A NICE BREEZE.
GOA!
RIGHT, TREE?
DEVIL OF THE BACK
ZEFEERO

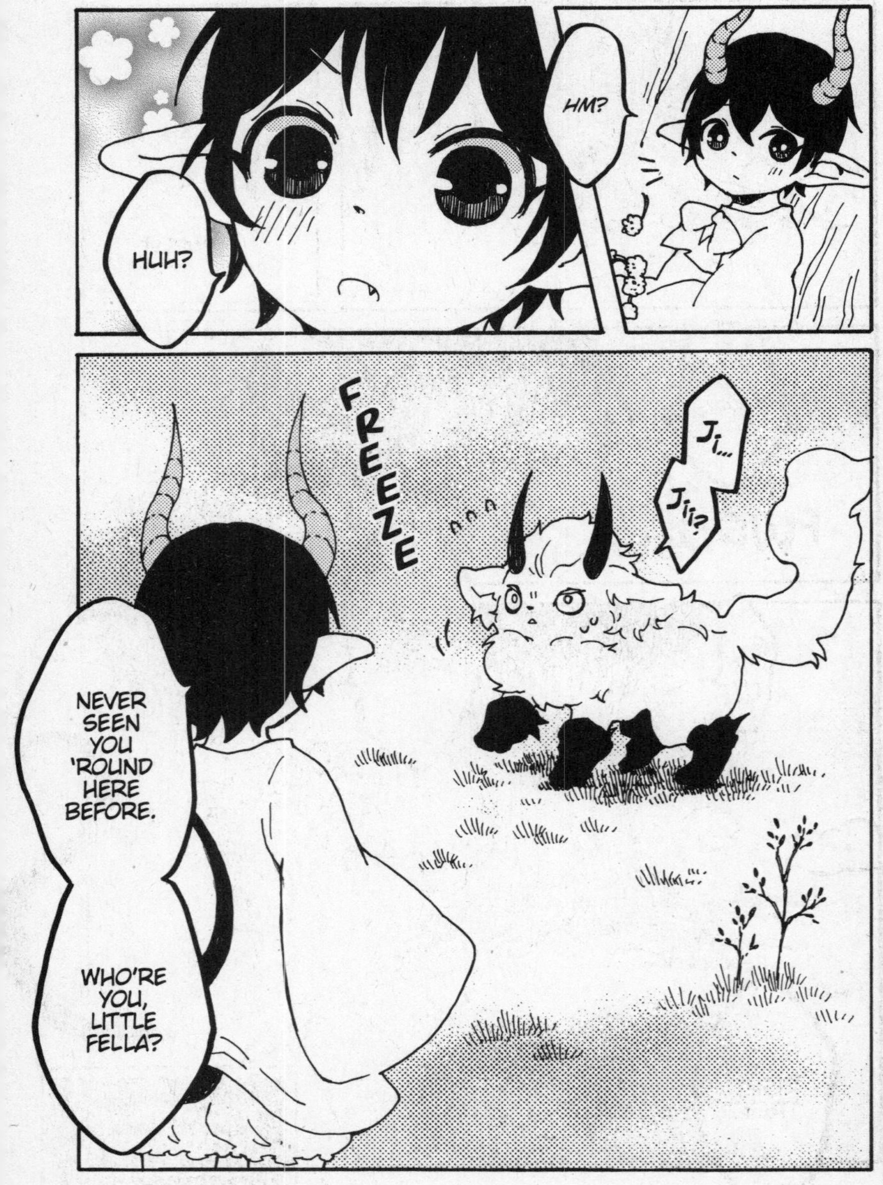
HM?
HUH?
JI...
JII?
FREEZE
NEVER SEEN YOU 'ROUND HERE BEFORE.
WHO'RE YOU, LITTLE FELLA?

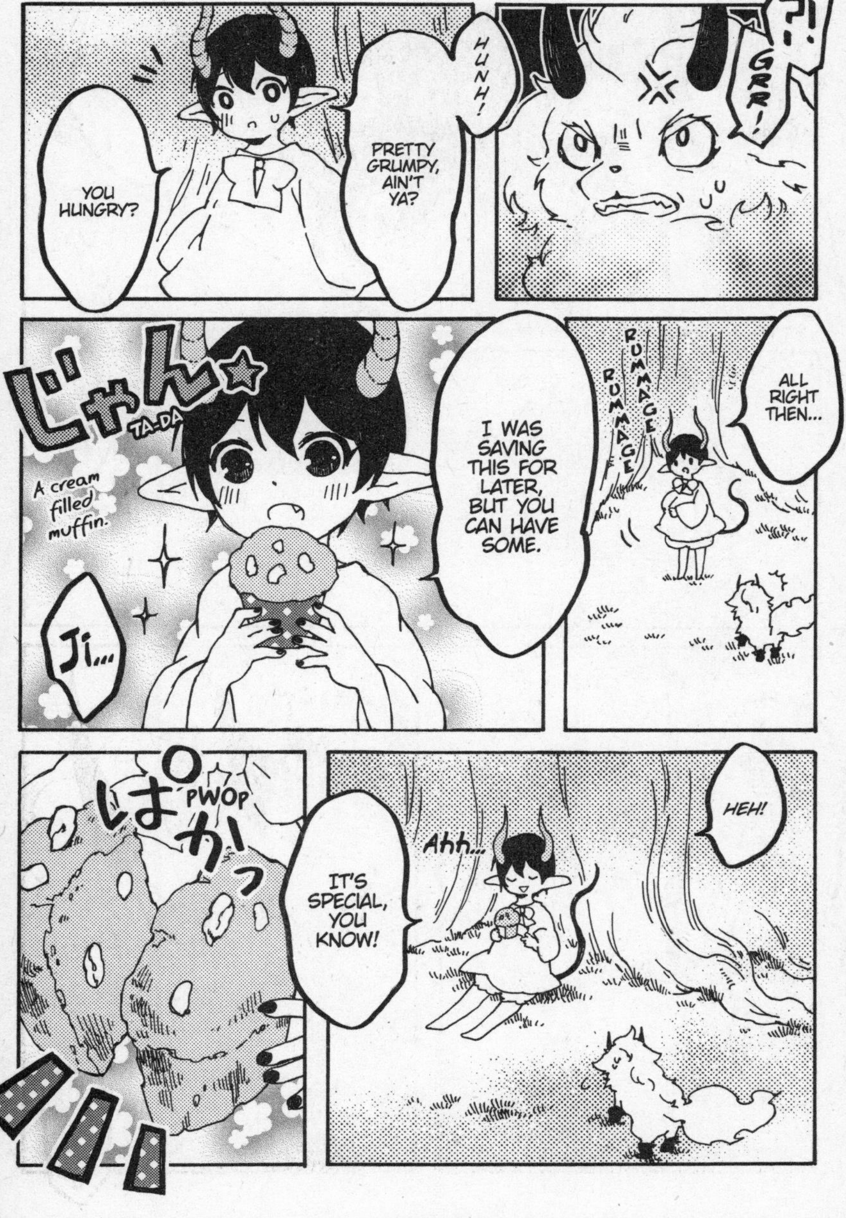
?!
GRR!
HUNH!
PRETTY GRUMPY, AIN'T YA?
YOU HUNGRY?
ALL RIGHT THEN...
RUMMAGE RUMMAGE
I WAS SAVING THIS FOR LATER, BUT YOU CAN HAVE SOME.
じゃん☆
TA-DA
A cream filled muffin.
Ji...
HEH!
Ahh...
IT'S SPECIAL, YOU KNOW!
ぱかっ
PWOP

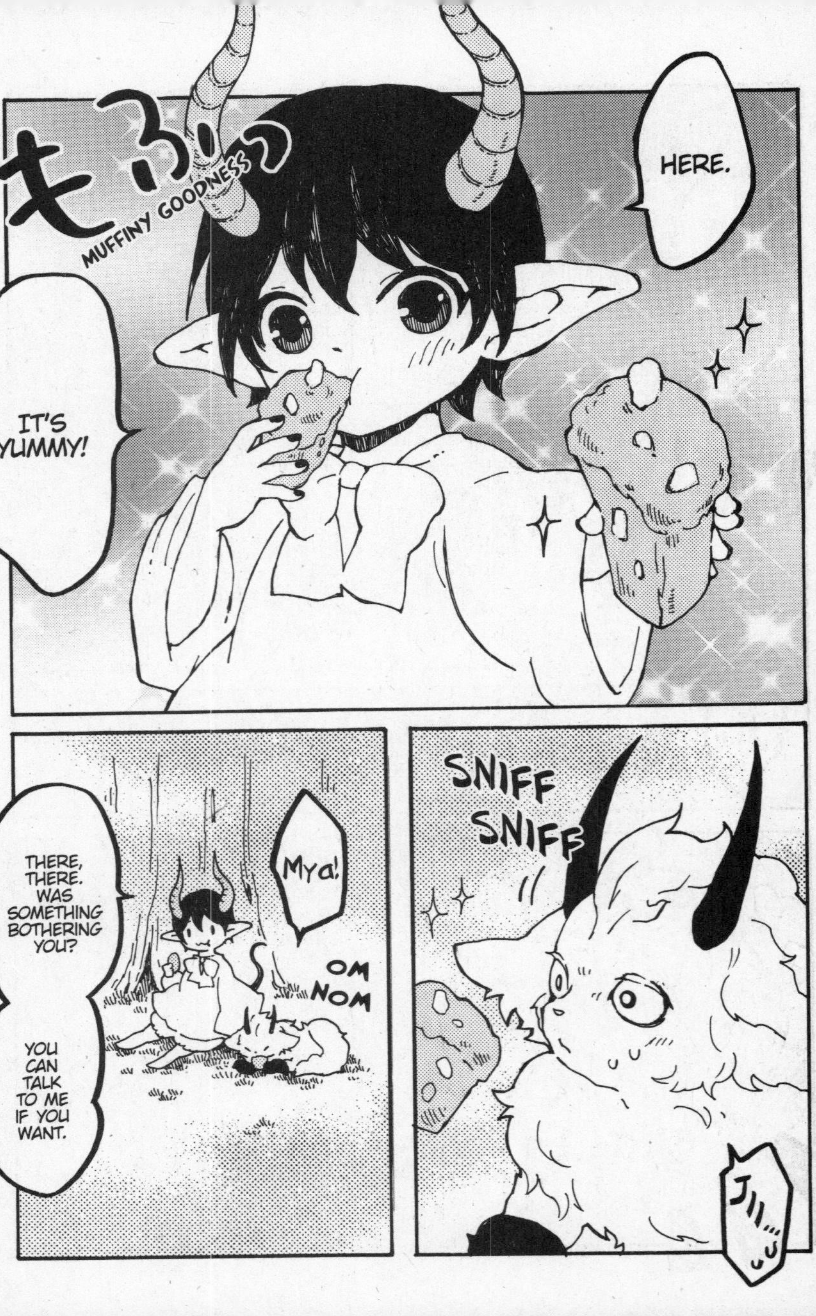
HERE.
もふっ
MUFFINY GOODNESS
IT'S YUMMY!
SNIFF SNIFF
JII...
Mya!
OM NOM
THERE, THERE. WAS SOMETHING BOTHERING YOU? YOU CAN TALK TO ME IF YOU WANT.

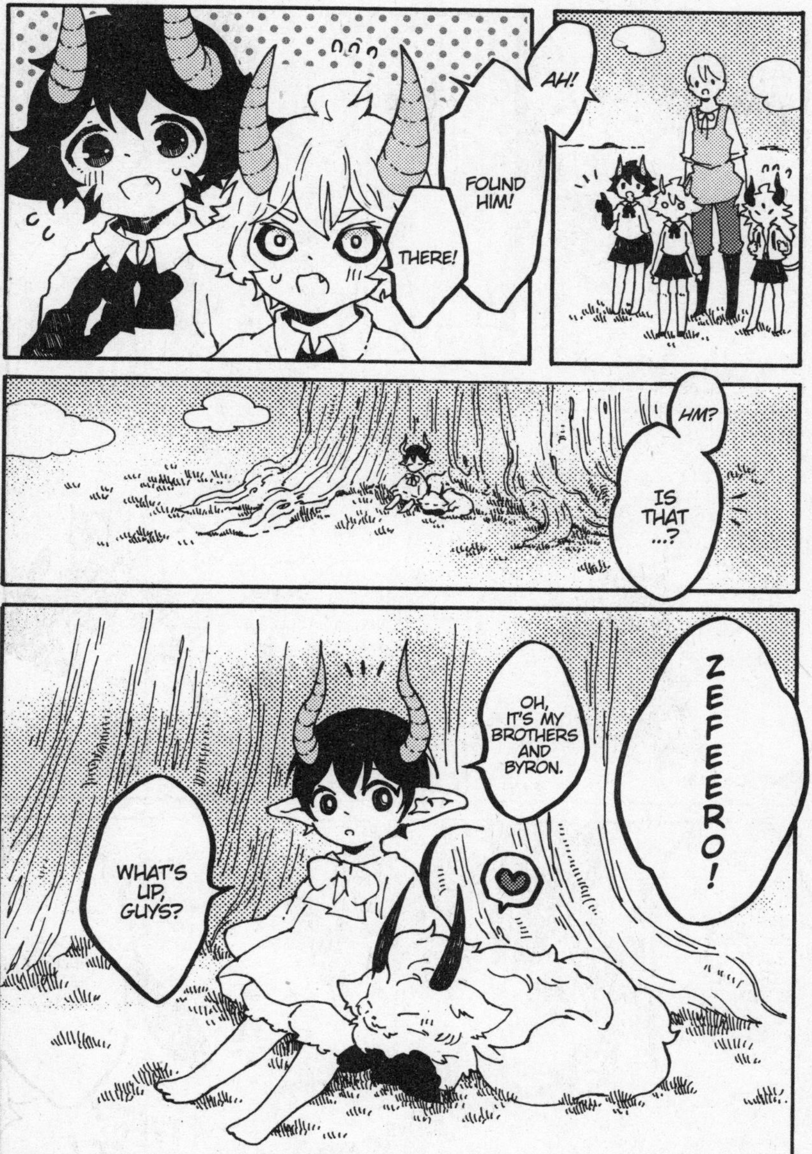
AH!
FOUND HIM!
THERE!
HM?
IS THAT ...?
ZEFEERO!
OH, IT'S MY BROTHERS AND BYRON.
WHAT'S UP, GUYS?

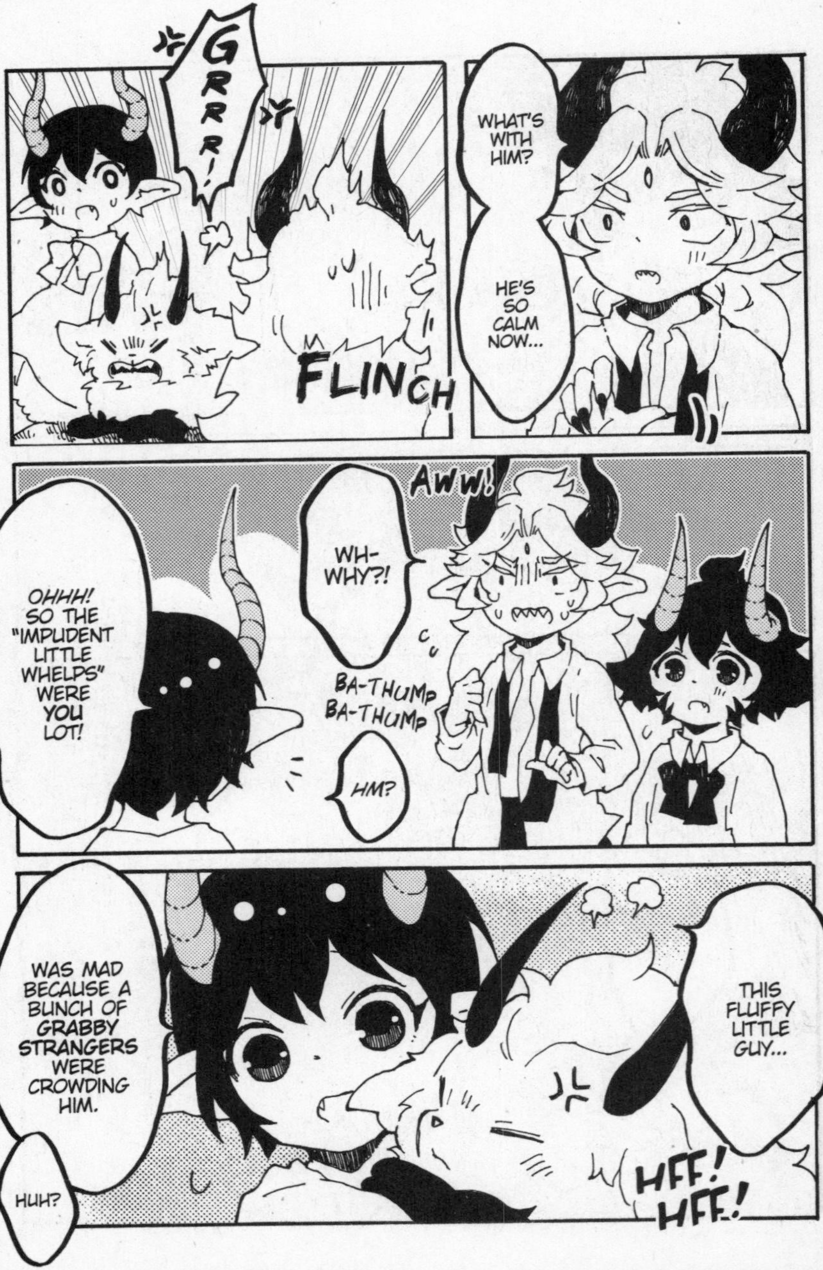
WHAT'S WITH HIM?
HE'S SO CALM NOW...
GRRR!
FLINCH
AWW!
WH- WHY?!
BA-THUMP BA-THUMP
HM?
OHHH! SO THE "IMPUDENT LITTLE WHELPS" WERE YOU LOT!
THIS FLUFFY LITTLE GUY...
HFF! HFF!
WAS MAD BECAUSE A BUNCH OF GRABBY STRANGERS WERE CROWDING HIM.
HUH?

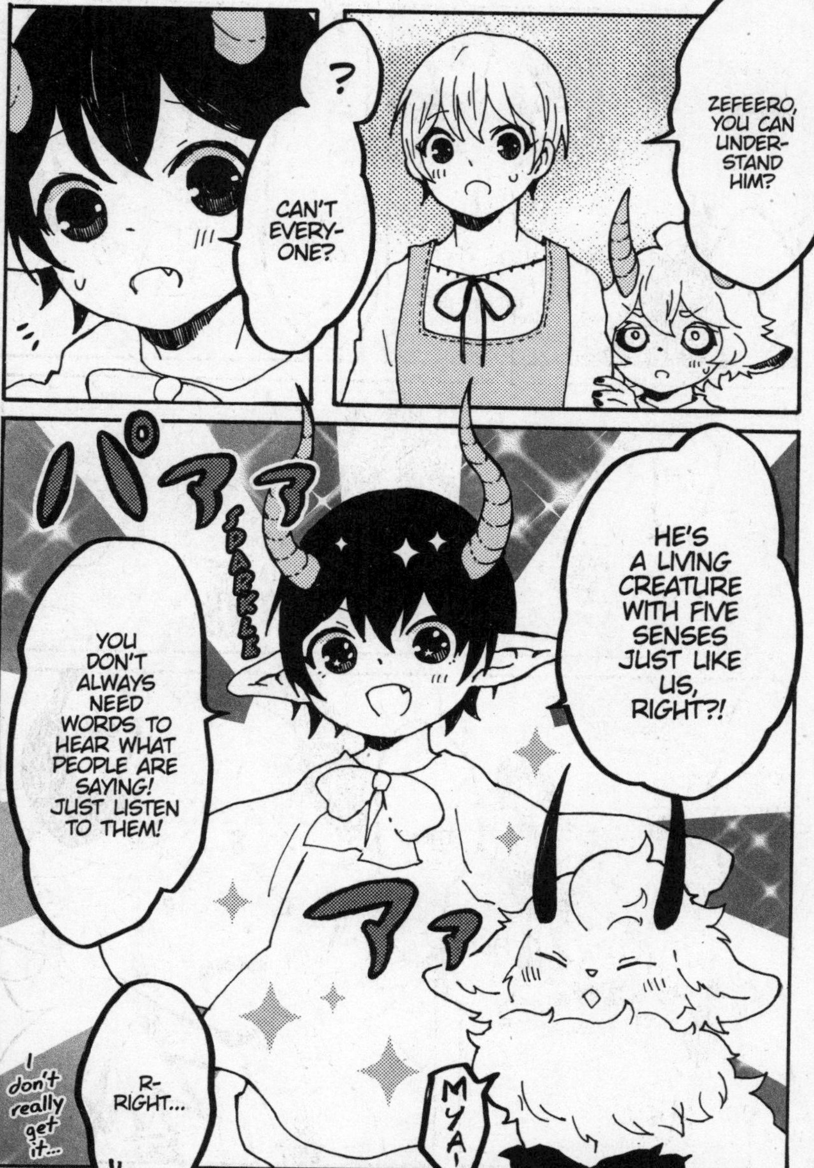
ZEFEERO, YOU CAN UNDER-STAND HIM?
?
CAN'T EVERY-ONE?
HE'S A LIVING CREATURE WITH FIVE SENSES JUST LIKE US, RIGHT?!
パアア
SPARKLE
YOU DON'T ALWAYS NEED WORDS TO HEAR WHAT PEOPLE ARE SAYING! JUST LISTEN TO THEM!
MYA!
R-RIGHT...
I don't really get it...
UU

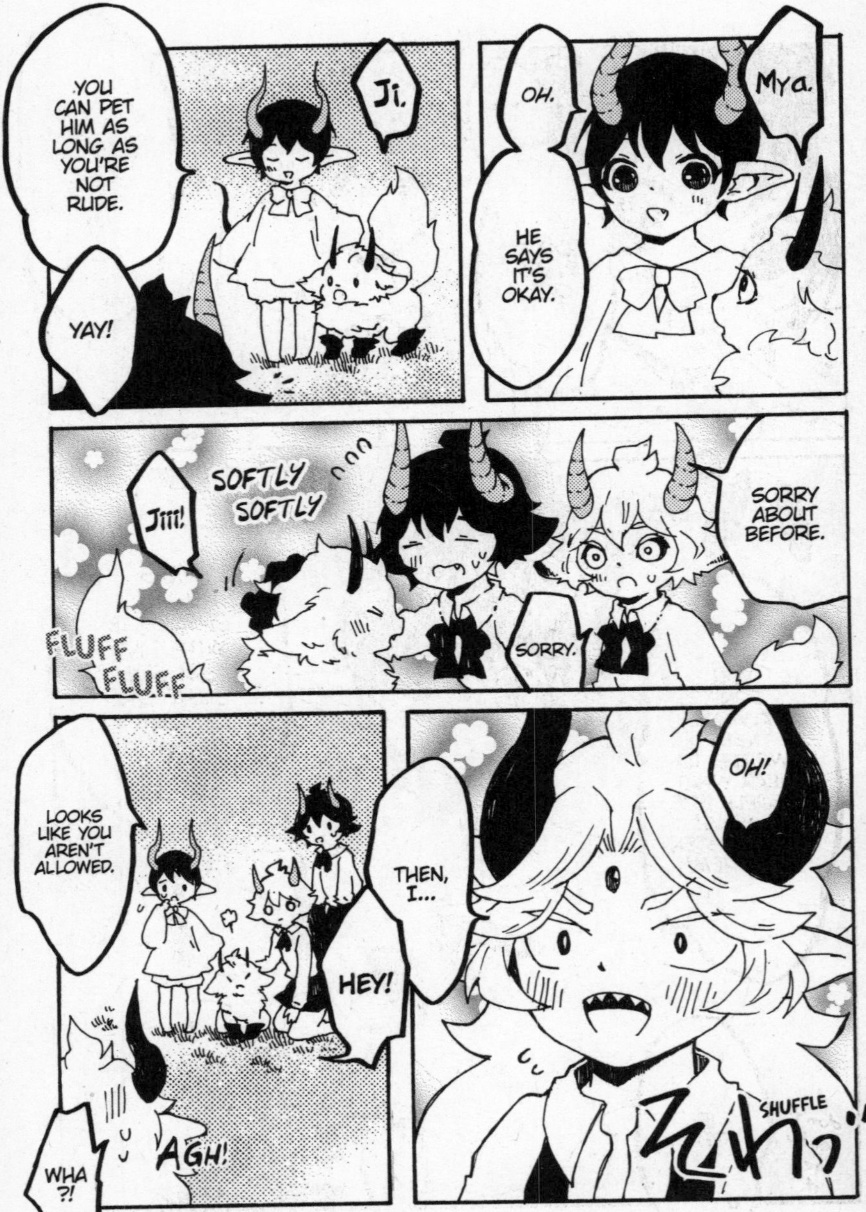
Mya.
OH.
HE SAYS IT'S OKAY.
Ji.
YOU CAN PET HIM AS LONG AS YOU'RE NOT RUDE.
YAY!
SORRY ABOUT BEFORE.
SORRY.
SOFTLY SOFTLY
Jiii!
FLUFF FLUFF
OH!
THEN, I...
HEY!
SHUFFLE
LOOKS LIKE YOU AREN'T ALLOWED.
AGH!
WHA?!

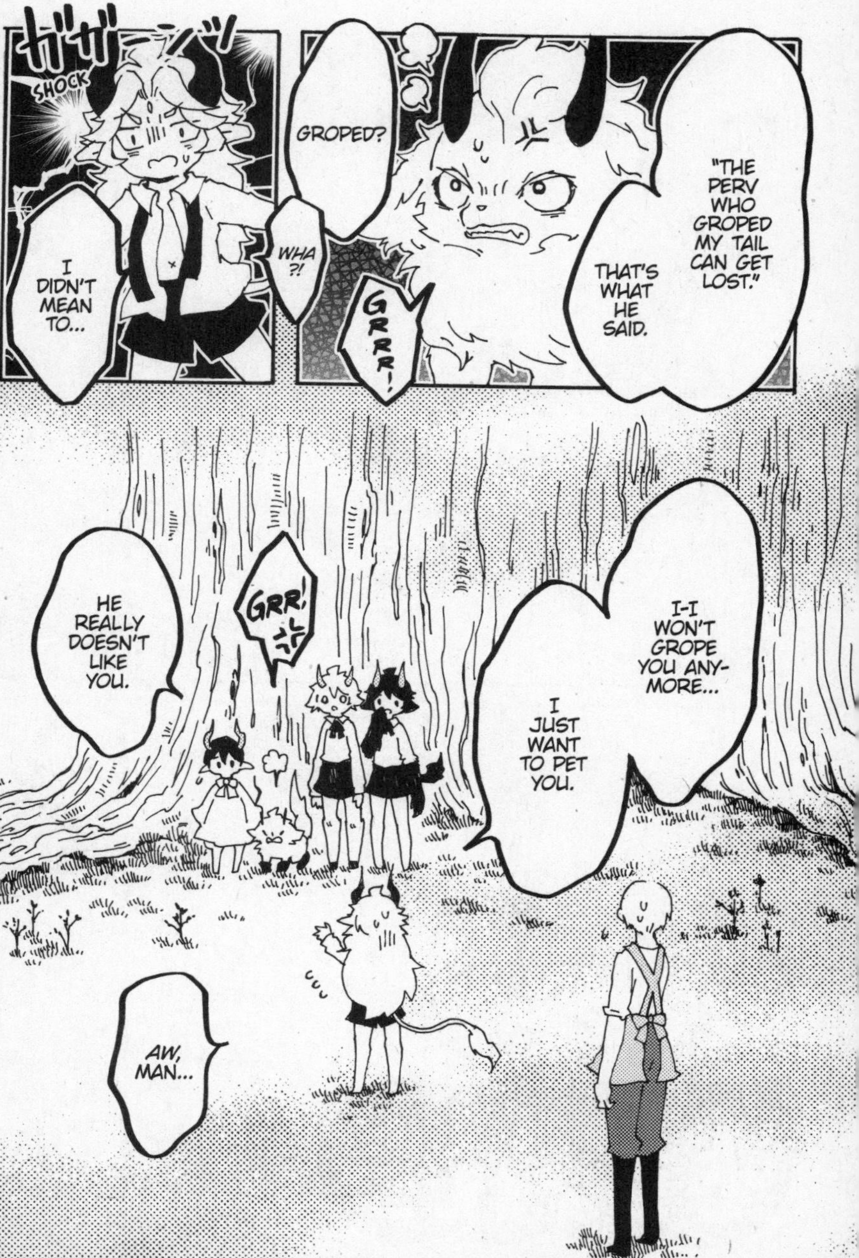
"THE PERV WHO GROPED MY TAIL CAN GET LOST."
THAT'S WHAT HE SAID.
GROPED?
GRRR!
WHA?!
SHOCK
I DIDN'T MEAN TO...
I-I WON'T GROPE YOU ANY-MORE...
I JUST WANT TO PET YOU.
GRR!
HE REALLY DOESN'T LIKE YOU.
AW, MAN...

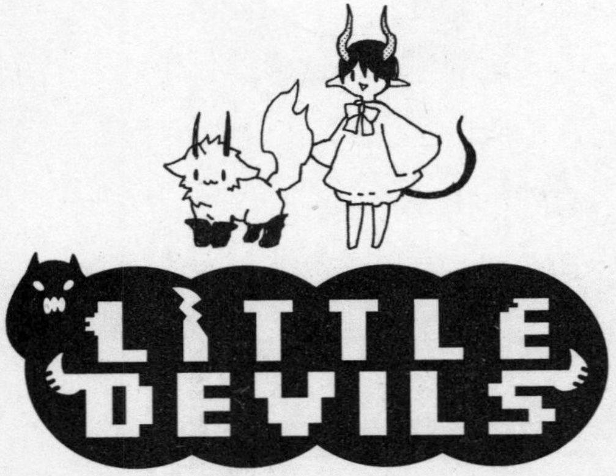

LITTLE DEVILS

LITTLE MONSTER - NIEZ ▼
- - - - - - - - - - - - - - - - -
God discovered him in the
human world.
A little creature with magical
powers.
Doesn't mind being pet, but ask
first!

DEVIL OF THE BACK - ZEFEERO ▼
- - - - - - - - - - - - - - - - -
The very friendly eighth Little Devil.
He talks like an old man and is wise
beyond his years.
He's kind to everyone, monsters and
men alike.

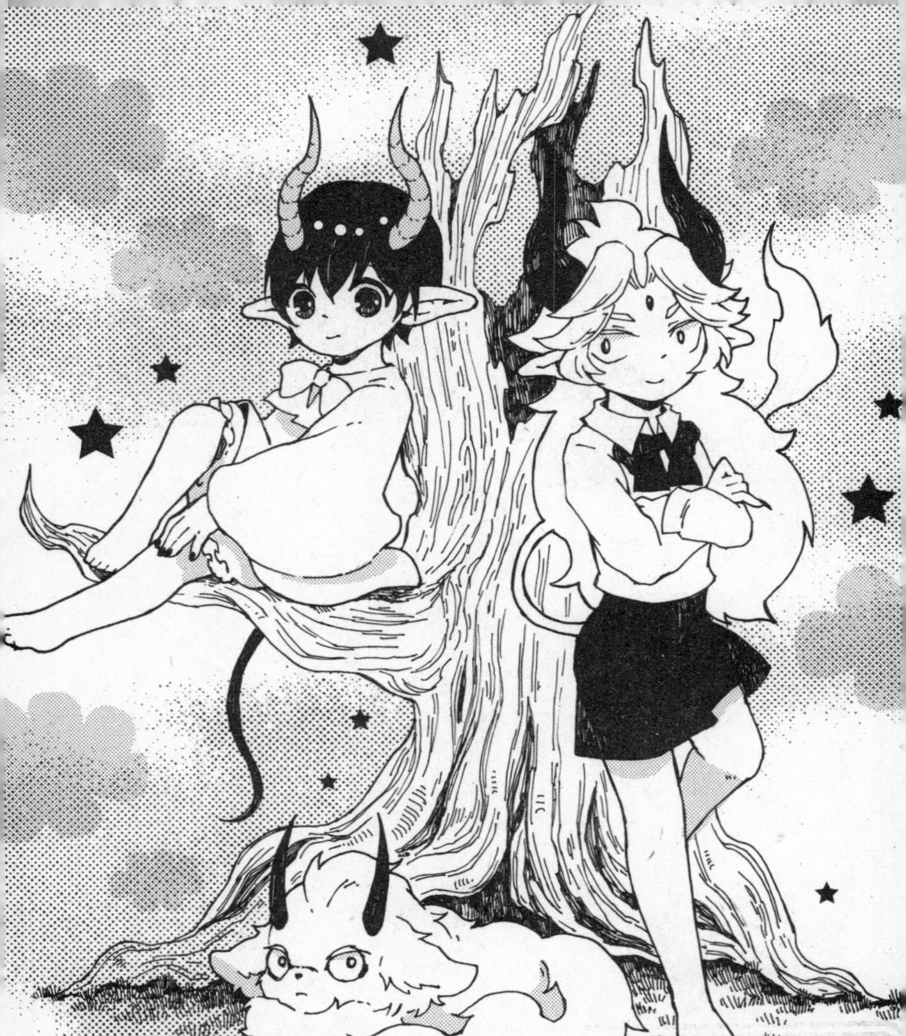

CHAPTER 12
A SOMEWHAT DARING RESCUE

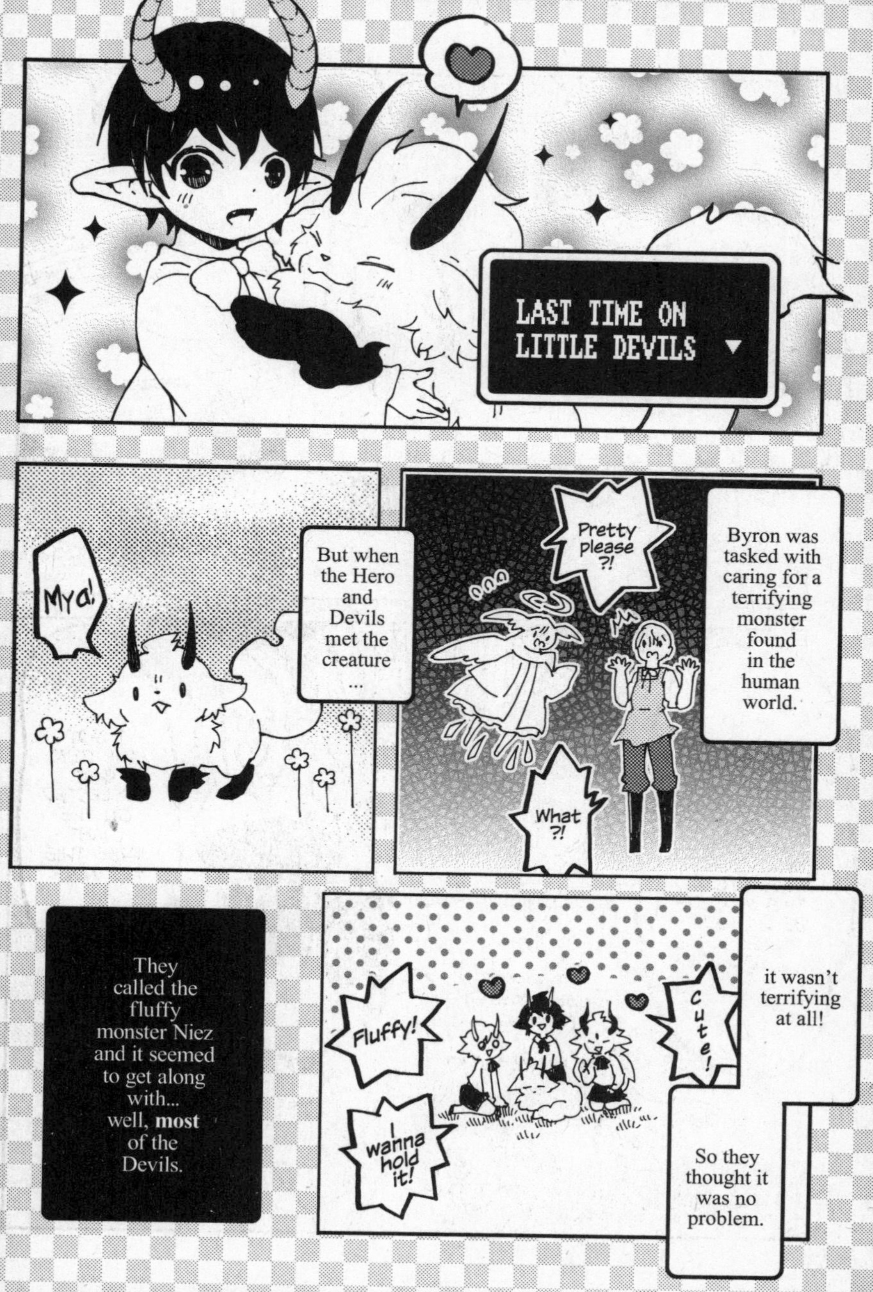
LAST TIME ON LITTLE DEVILS ▼
Byron was tasked with caring for a terrifying monster found in the human world.
Pretty please ?!
What ?!
But when the Hero and Devils met the creature ...
Mya!
it wasn't terrifying at all!
Cute!
Fluffy!
I wanna hold it!
So they thought it was no problem.
They called the fluffy monster Niez and it seemed to get along with... well, **most** of the Devils.

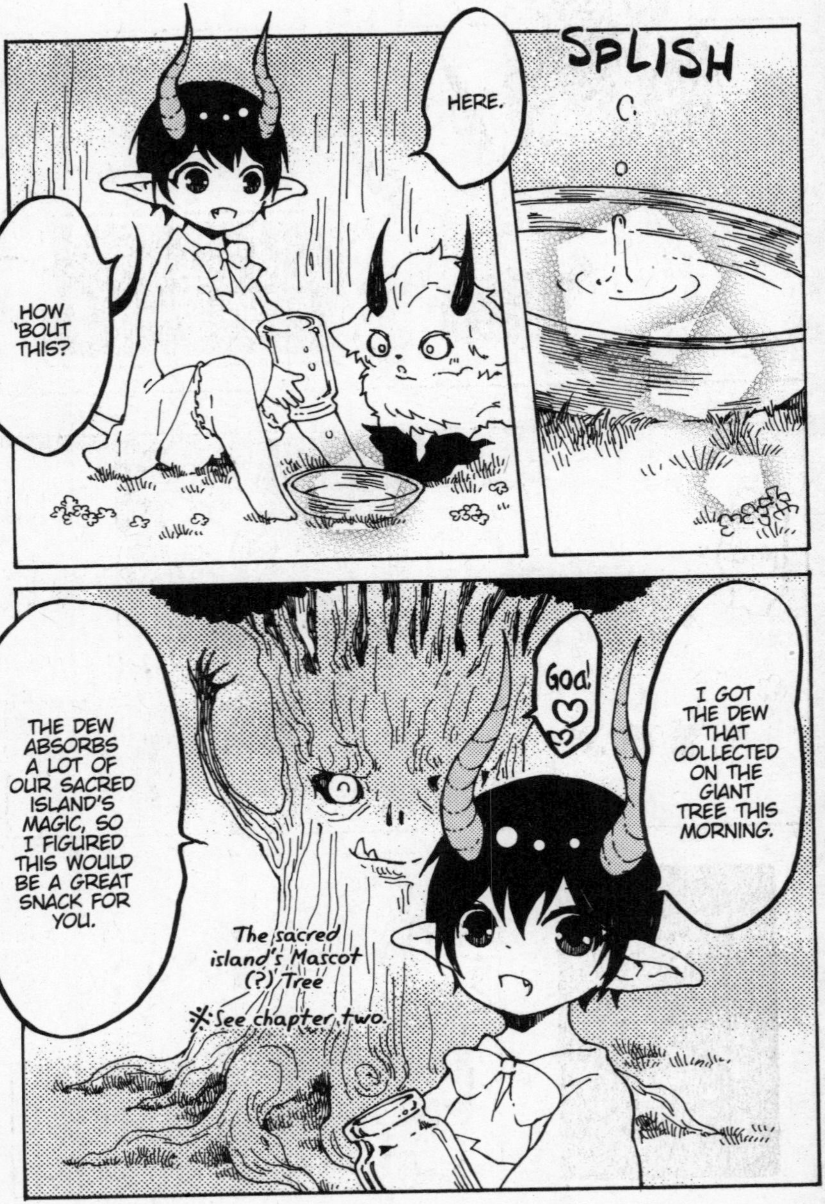
SPLISH
HERE.
HOW 'BOUT THIS?
I GOT THE DEW THAT COLLECTED ON THE GIANT TREE THIS MORNING.
Goa! ♡
THE DEW ABSORBS A LOT OF OUR SACRED ISLAND'S MAGIC, SO I FIGURED THIS WOULD BE A GREAT SNACK FOR YOU.
The sacred island's Mascot (?) Tree
※See chapter two.

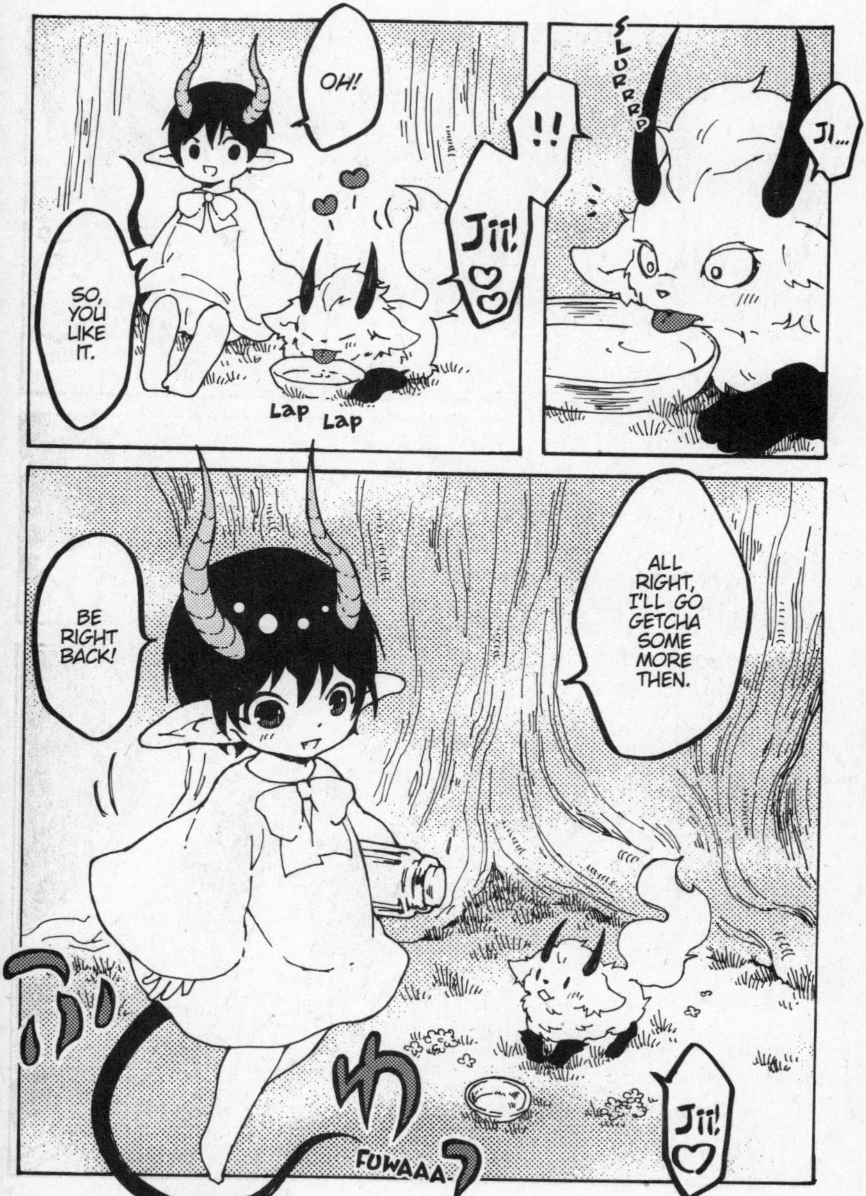
SLURRRP
JI...
!!
OH!
Jii!
SO, YOU LIKE IT.
Lap Lap
ALL RIGHT, I'LL GO GETCHA SOME MORE THEN.
BE RIGHT BACK!
Jii!
ふわ
FUWAAA

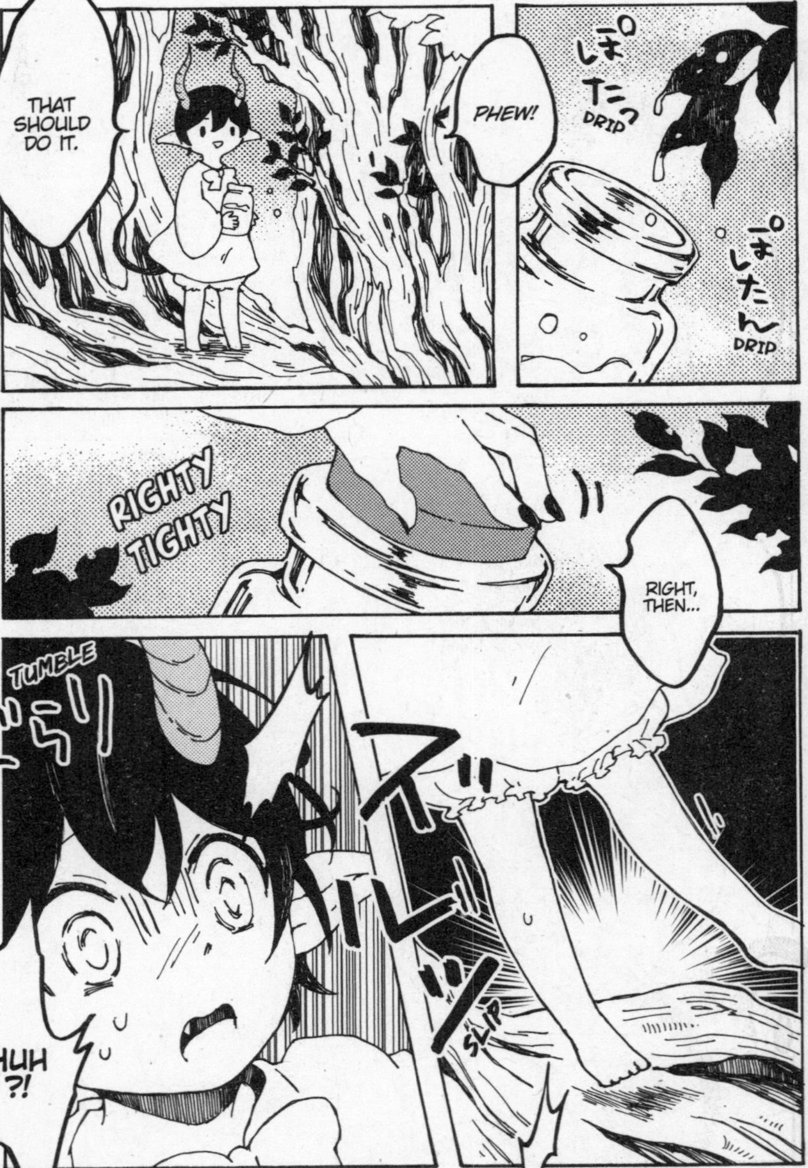
PHEW!
DRIP
DRIP
THAT SHOULD DO IT.
RIGHT, THEN...
RIGHTY TIGHTY
SLIP
TUMBLE
HUH ?!

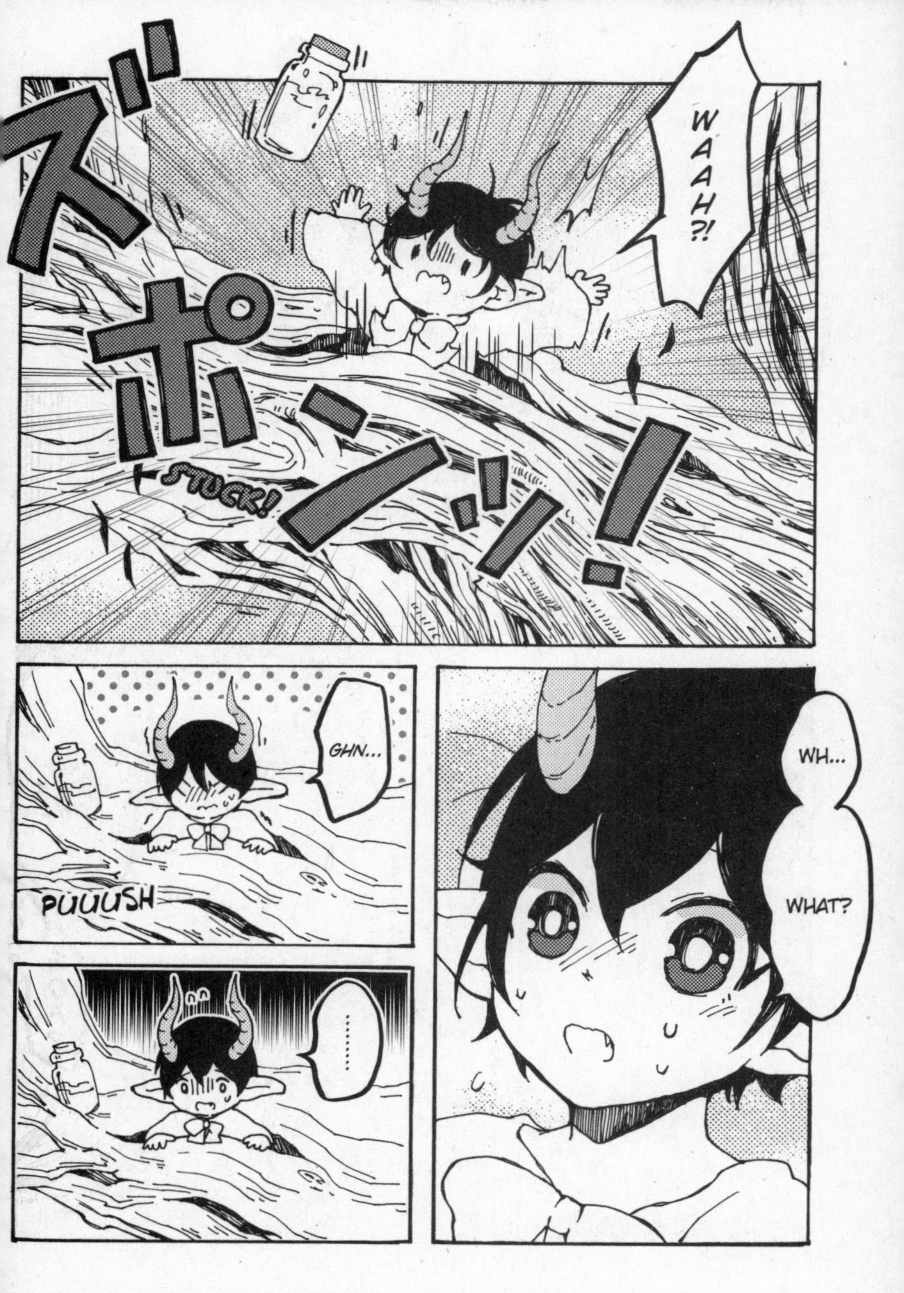
WAAAH?!
ズポーン!
STUCK!
WH...
WHAT?
GHN...
PUUUSH
......

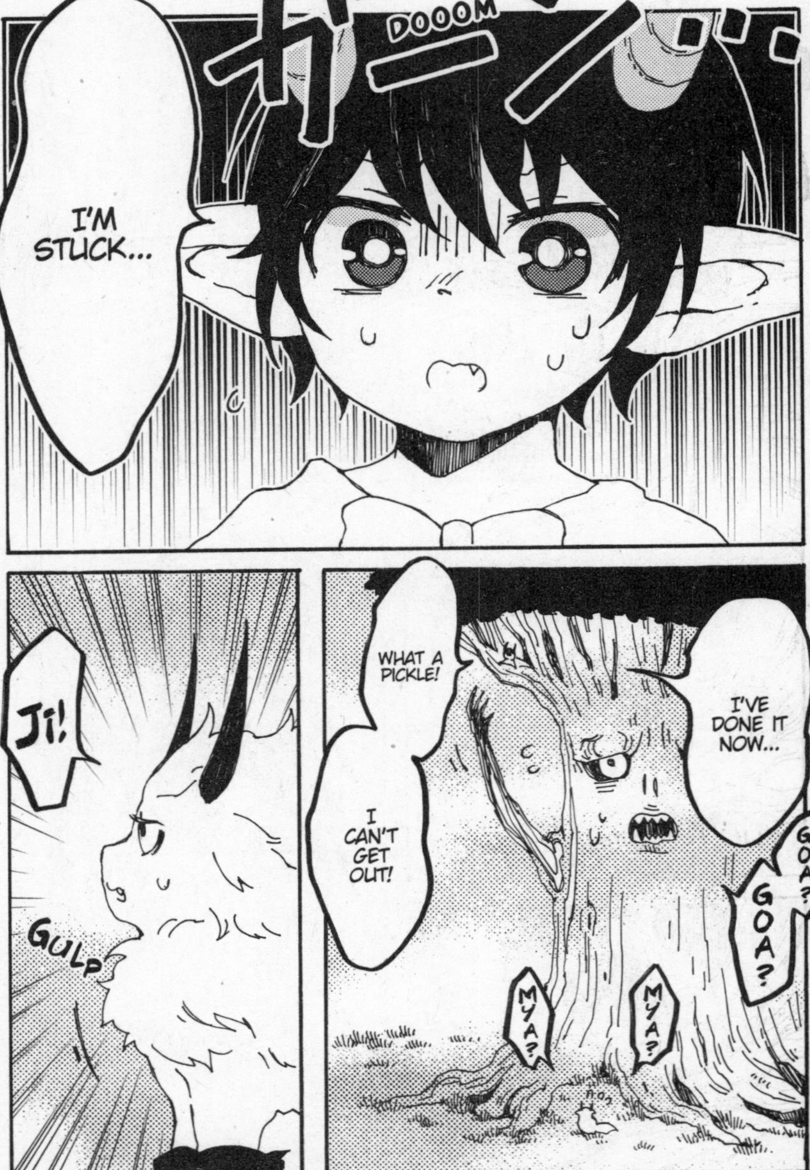
ガーン
DOOOM
I'M STUCK...
I'VE DONE IT NOW...
WHAT A PICKLE!
GOA?
GOA?
I CAN'T GET OUT!
MYA?
MYA?
Ji!
GULP

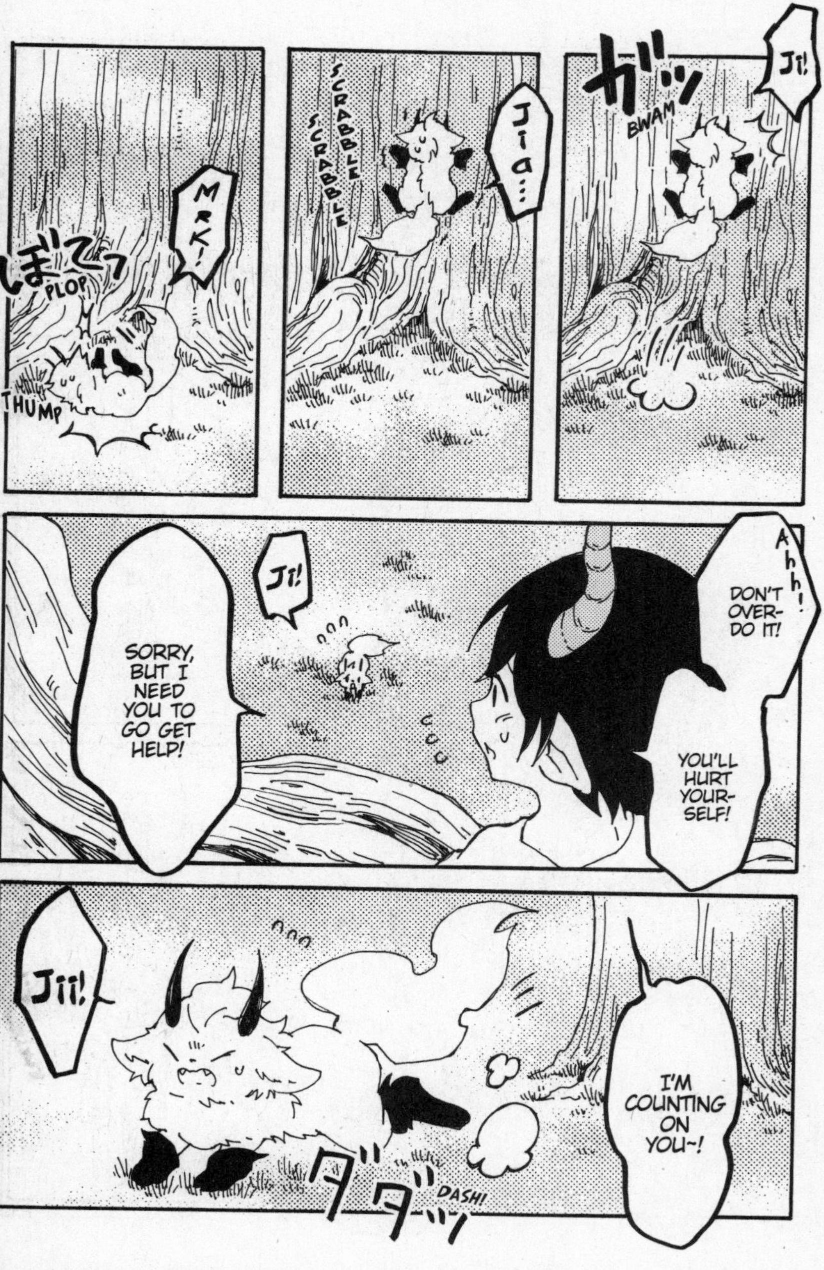
ガッ
BWAM
Ji!
SCRABBLE
SCRABBLE
Jia...
ぼてっ
PLOP
THUMP
Mrk!
Ahhh!
DON'T OVER-DO IT!
YOU'LL HURT YOURSELF!
Ji!
SORRY, BUT I NEED YOU TO GO GET HELP!
I'M COUNTING ON YOU~!
Jii!
ダダッ
DASH!

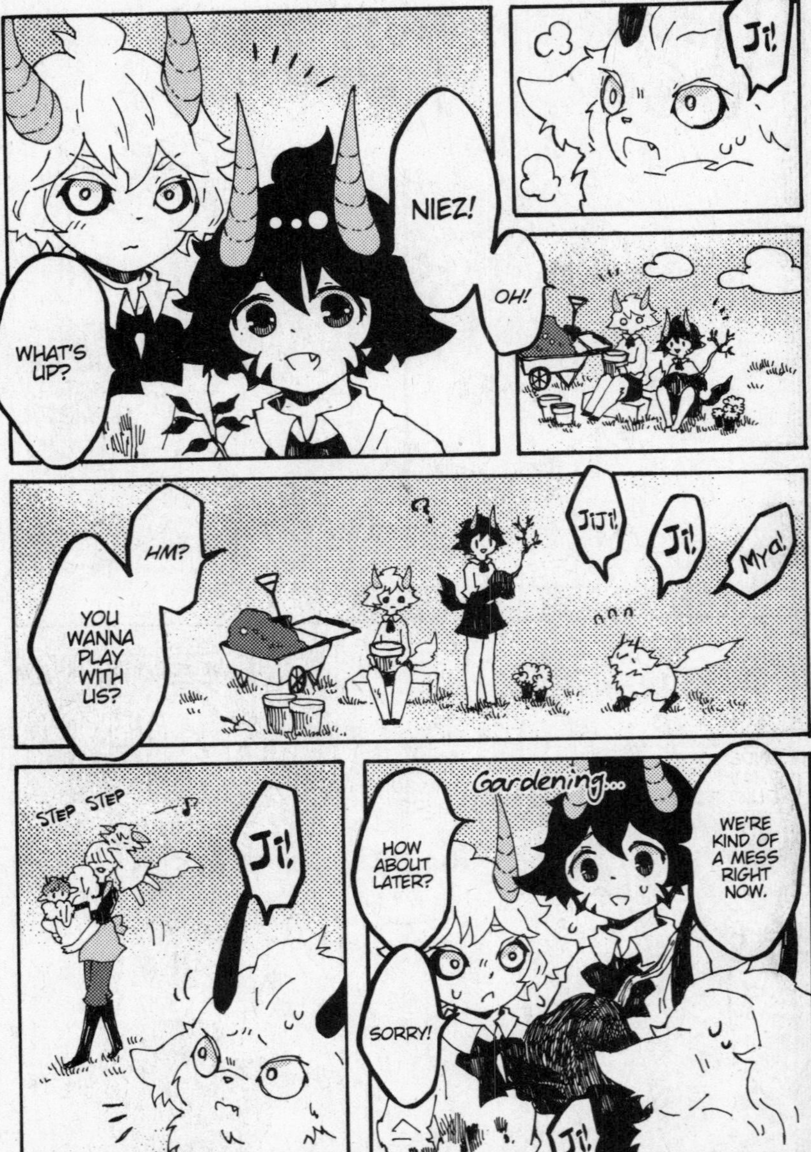
Ji!
NIEZ!
OH!
WHAT'S UP?
Mya!
Ji!
JiJi!
?
HM?
YOU WANNA PLAY WITH US?
WE'RE KIND OF A MESS RIGHT NOW.
Gardening...
HOW ABOUT LATER?
SORRY!
Ji!
Ji!
STEP STEP

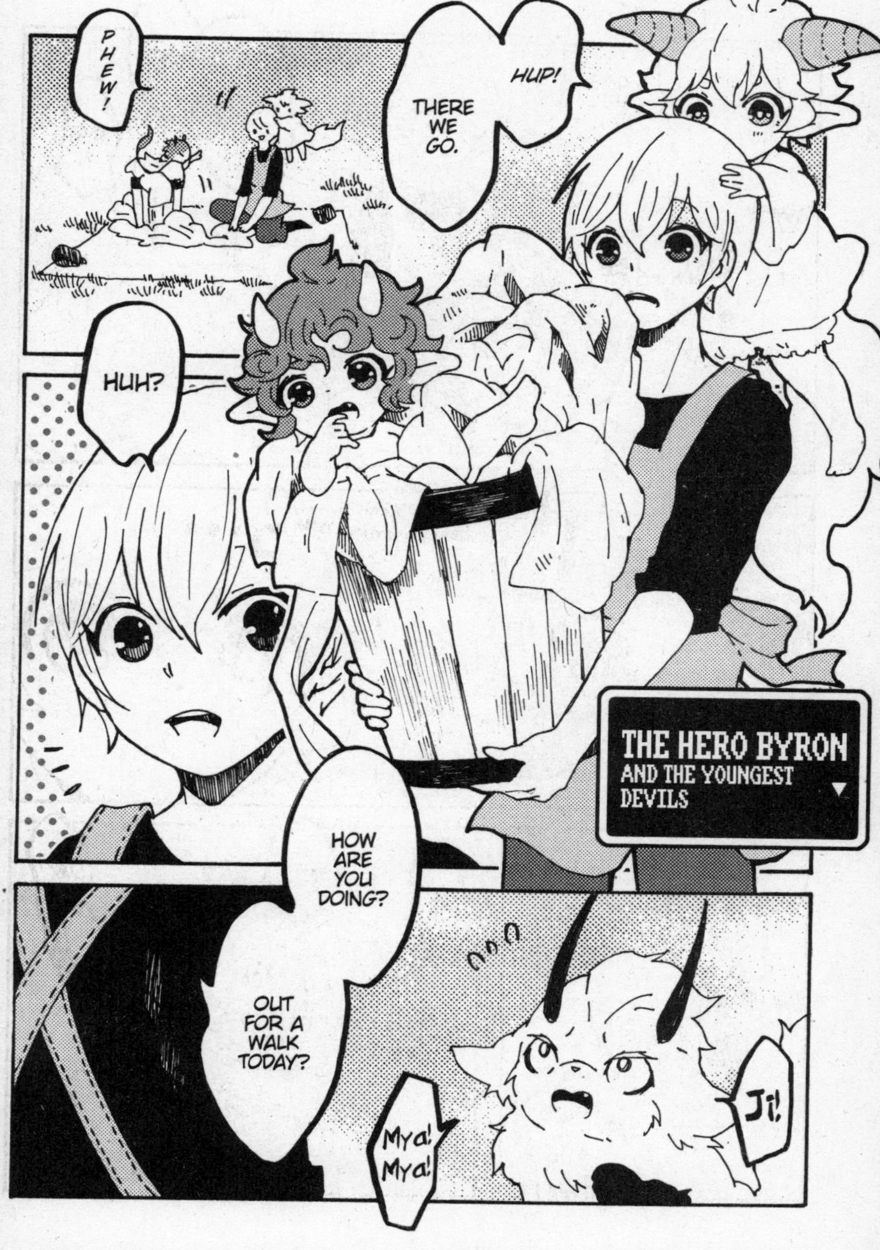
HUP!
THERE WE GO.
THE HERO BYRON
AND THE YOUNGEST DEVILS
PHEW!
HUH?
HOW ARE YOU DOING?
OUT FOR A WALK TODAY?
Ji!
Mya! Mya!

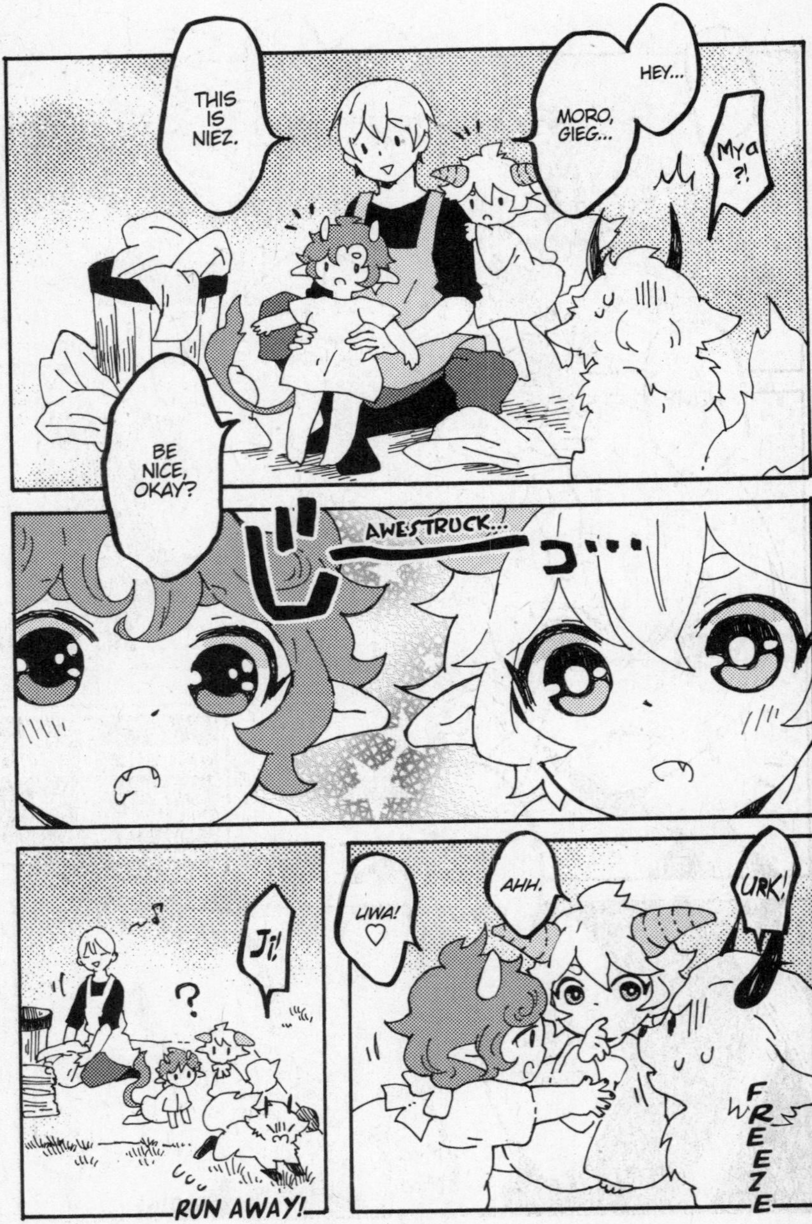
HEY...
MORO, GIEG...
Mya?!
THIS IS NIEZ.
BE NICE, OKAY?
AWESTRUCK...
URK!
AHH.
UWA! ♡
FREEZE
Ji!
?
RUN AWAY!

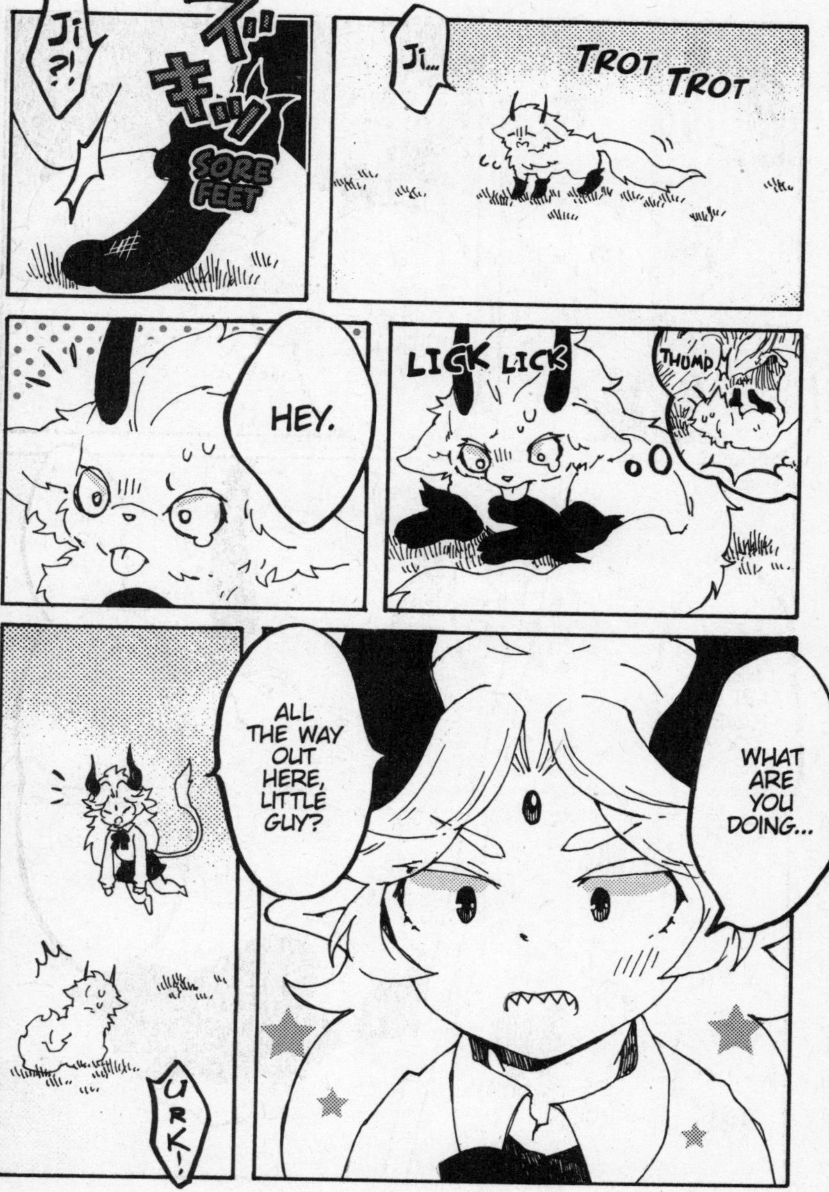
Ji...
TROT TROT
Ji ?!
イ゛キッ
SORE FEET
THUMP
LICK LICK
HEY.
WHAT ARE YOU DOING...
ALL THE WAY OUT HERE, LITTLE GUY?
URK!

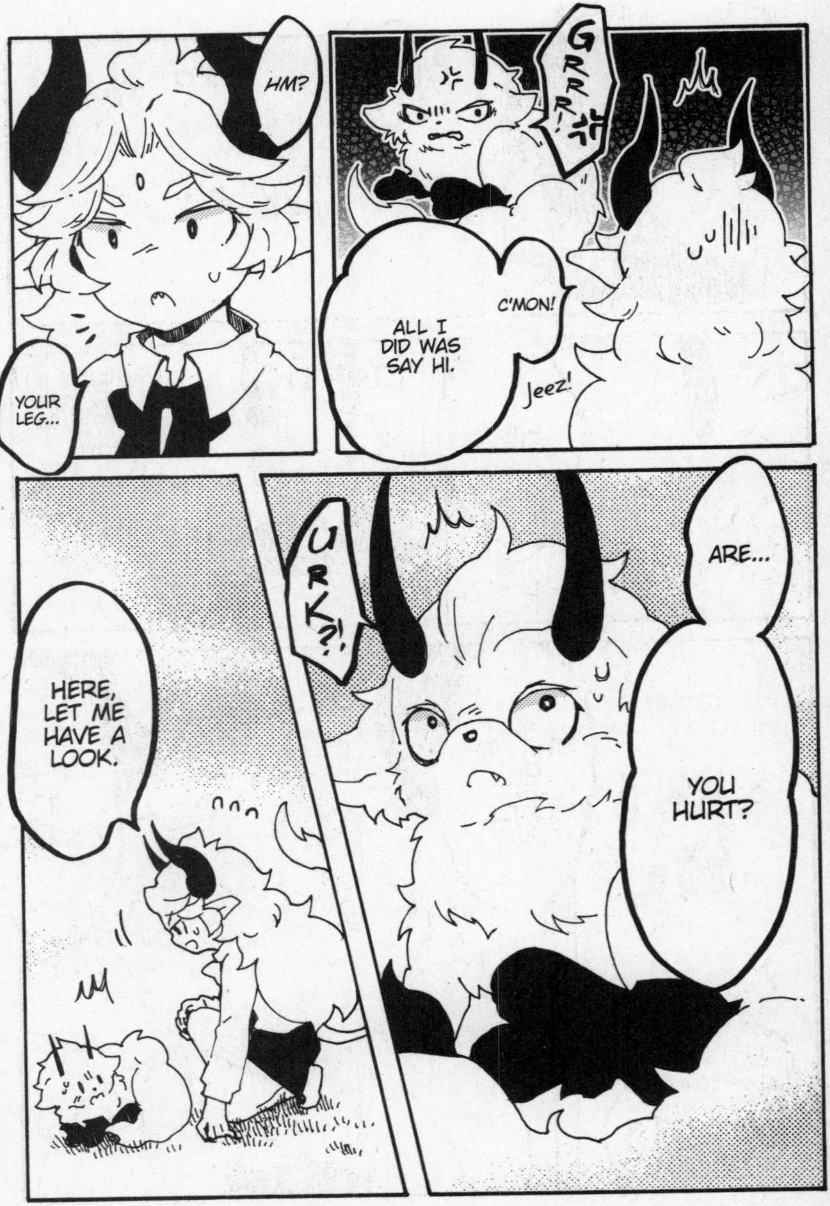
GRRR!
C'MON! ALL I DID WAS SAY HI.
Jeez!
HM?
YOUR LEG...
ARE... YOU HURT?
URK?!
HERE, LET ME HAVE A LOOK.

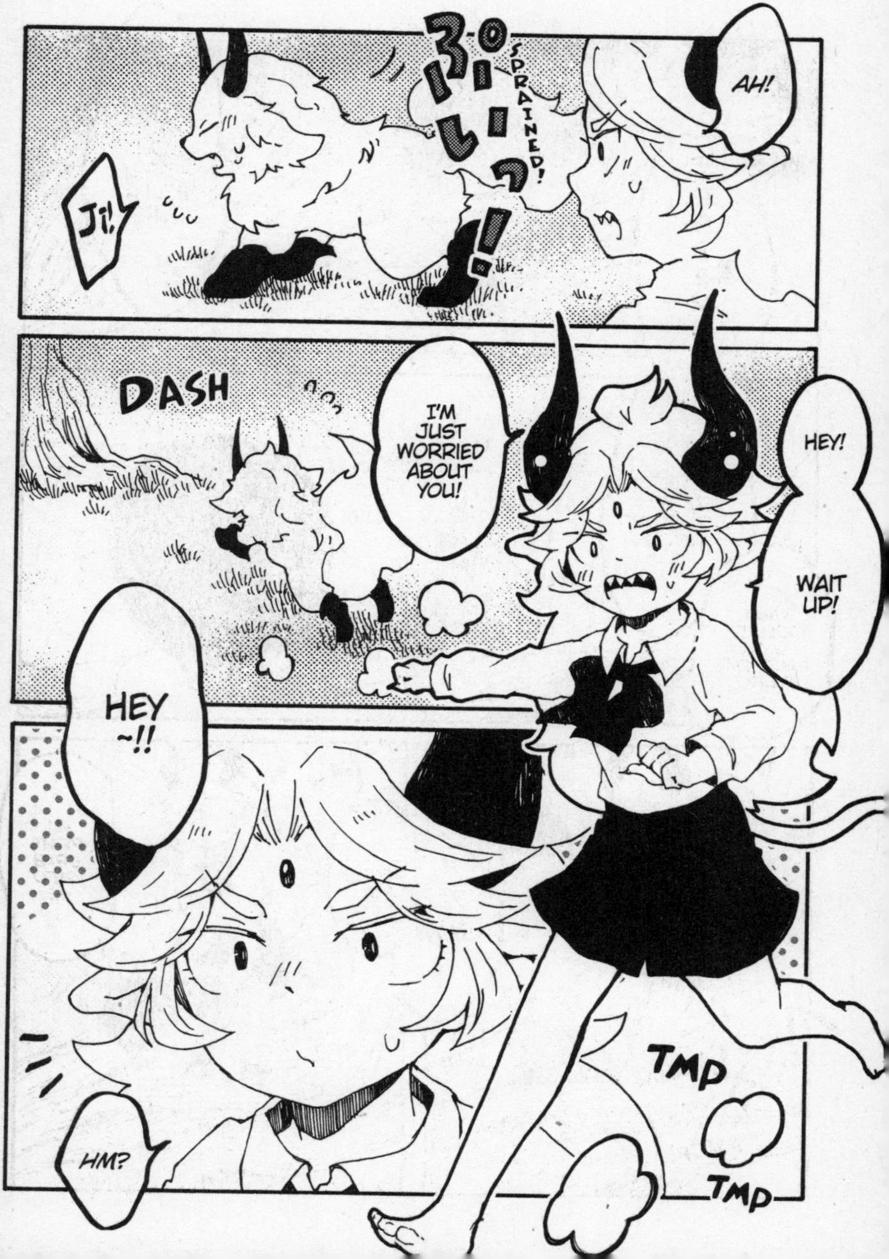

AH!
SPRAINED!
JI!
HEY!
WAIT UP!
I'M JUST WORRIED ABOUT YOU!
DASH
HEY ~!!
TMP
TMP
HM?

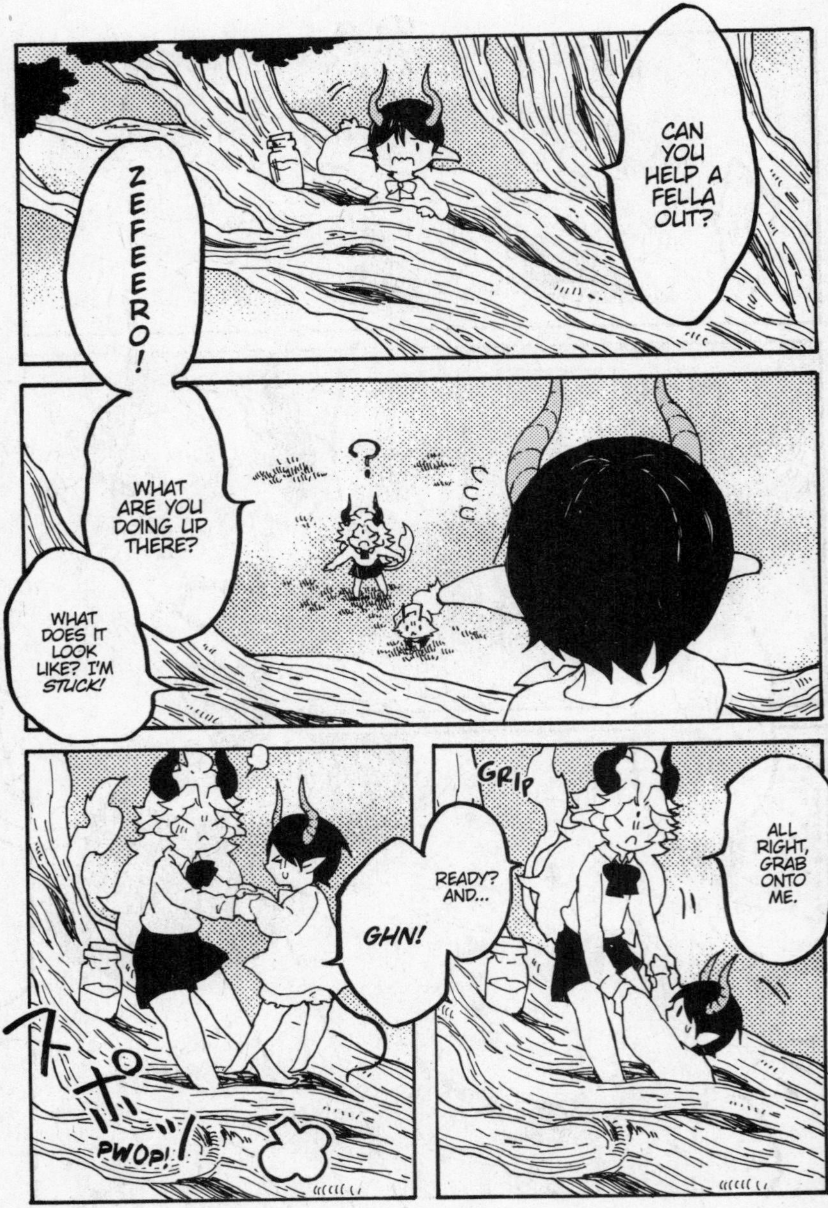
CAN YOU HELP A FELLA OUT?
ZEFEERO!
WHAT ARE YOU DOING UP THERE?
?
WHAT DOES IT LOOK LIKE? I'M STUCK!
GRIP
ALL RIGHT, GRAB ONTO ME.
READY? AND...
GHN!
スポッ!
PWOP!

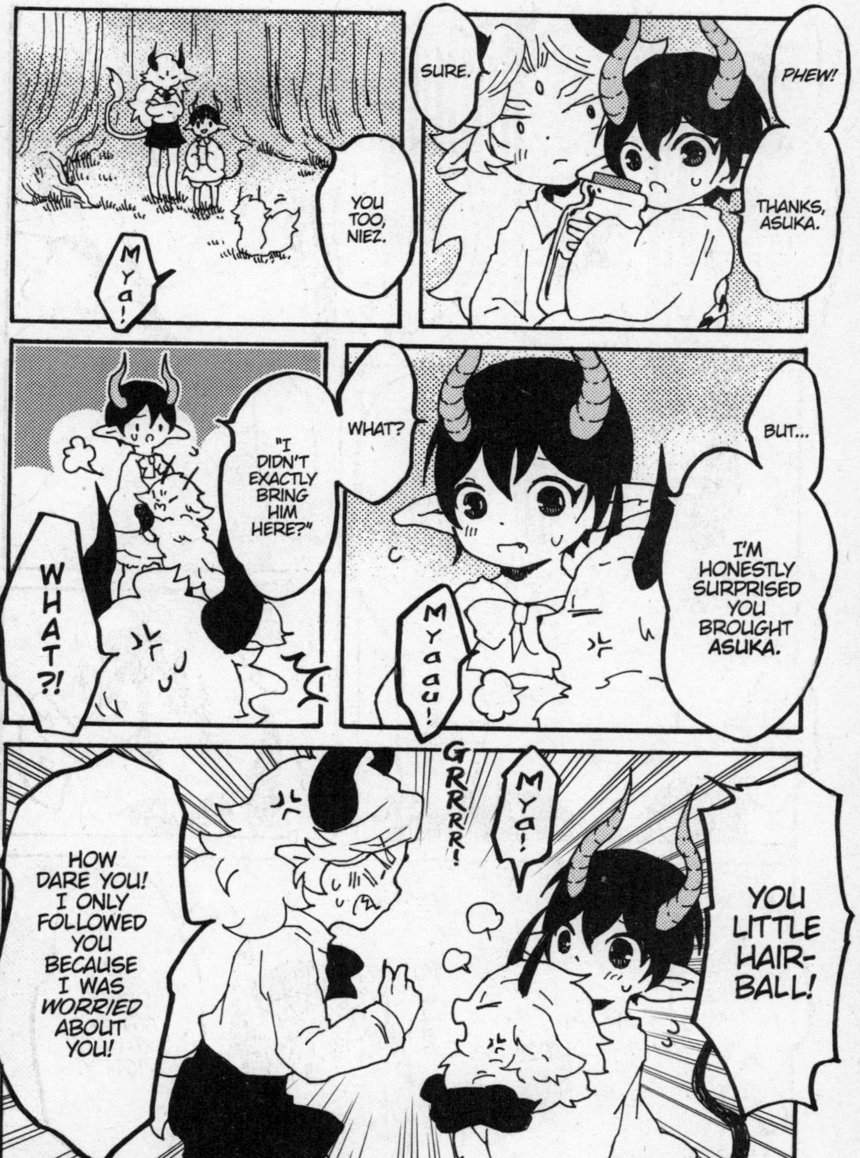
PHEW!
THANKS, ASUKA.
SURE.
YOU TOO, NIEZ.
Mya!
BUT...
I'M HONESTLY SURPRISED YOU BROUGHT ASUKA.
WHAT?
Myaau!
"I DIDN'T EXACTLY BRING HIM HERE?"
WHAT?!
YOU LITTLE HAIR-BALL!
Mya!
GRRRR!
HOW DARE YOU! I ONLY FOLLOWED YOU BECAUSE I WAS *WORRIED* ABOUT YOU!

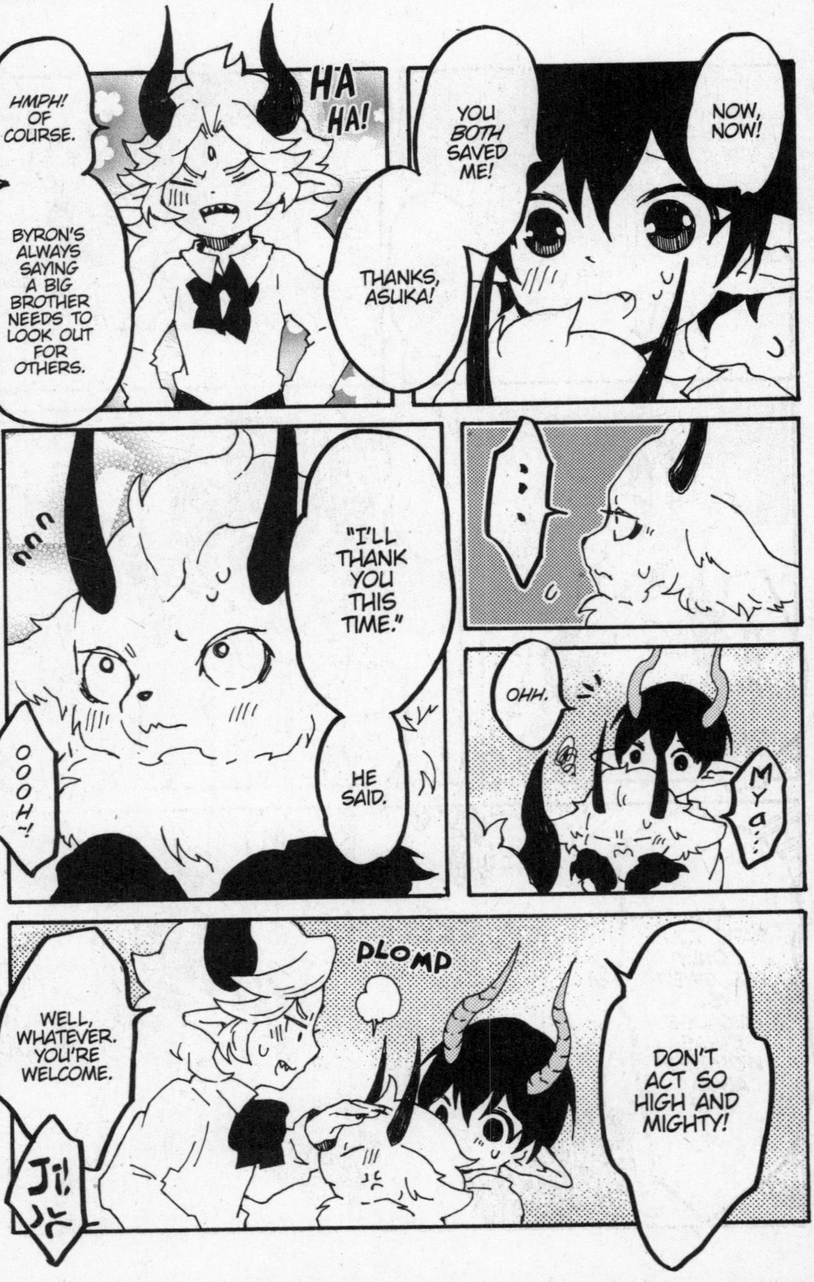
NOW, NOW!
YOU BOTH SAVED ME!
THANKS, ASUKA!
HA HA!
HMPH! OF COURSE.
BYRON'S ALWAYS SAYING A BIG BROTHER NEEDS TO LOOK OUT FOR OTHERS.
...
OHH.
MYa...
"I'LL THANK YOU THIS TIME."
HE SAID.
OOOOH~!
DON'T ACT SO HIGH AND MIGHTY!
PLOMP
WELL, WHATEVER. YOU'RE WELCOME.
Ji!

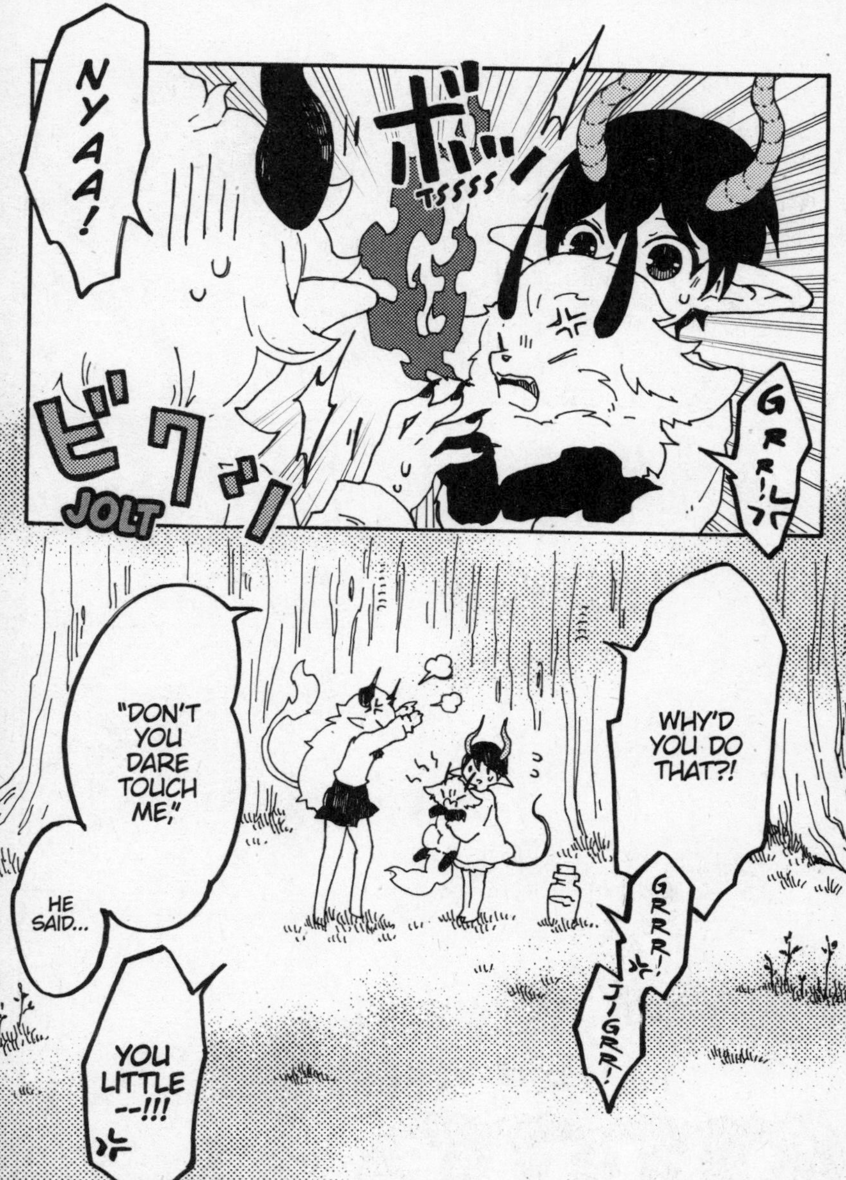

ボッ
TSSSS
GRR!
NYAA!
ビクッ
JOLT
WHY'D YOU DO THAT?!
GRRR!
JIGRR!
"DON'T YOU DARE TOUCH ME,"
HE SAID...
YOU LITTLE --!!!

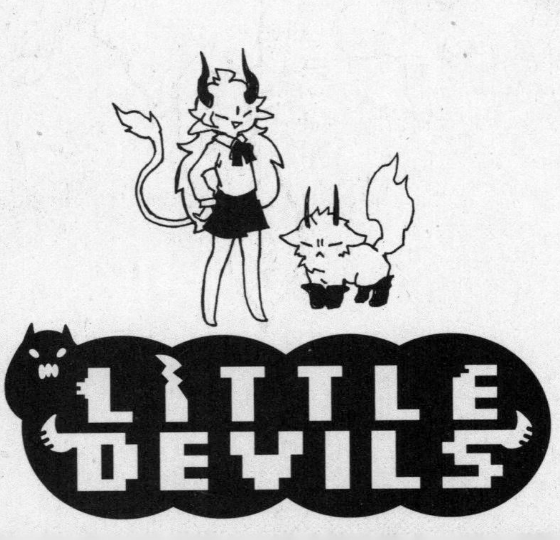

LITTLE DEVILS

THE LITTLE DEVILS' CLOTHES

God made them using human children's clothes for reference. ▼

A dress shirt with decorative bow. Because it's a button-up, it doesn't get caught on their horns. Most of them can't tie the bows on their own.

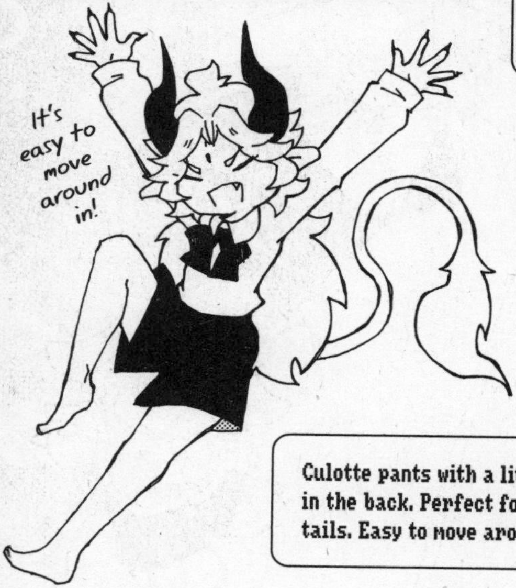
It's easy to move around in!

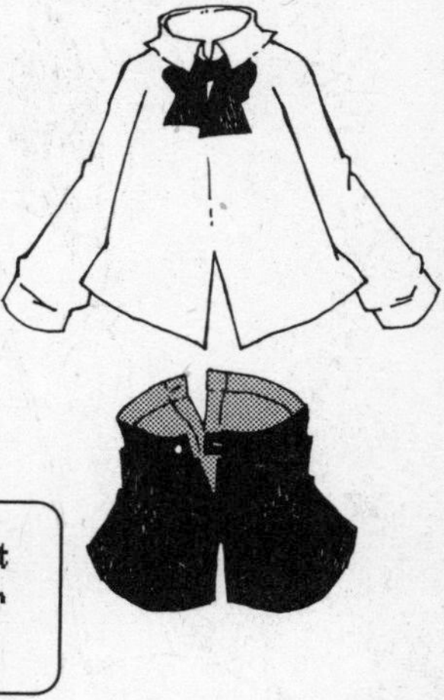

Culotte pants with a little slit in the back. Perfect for their tails. Easy to move around in.

The babies' clothes open at the back. No holes for the tail to go through.

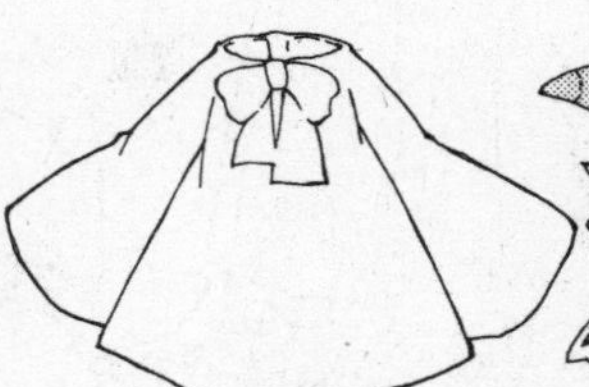

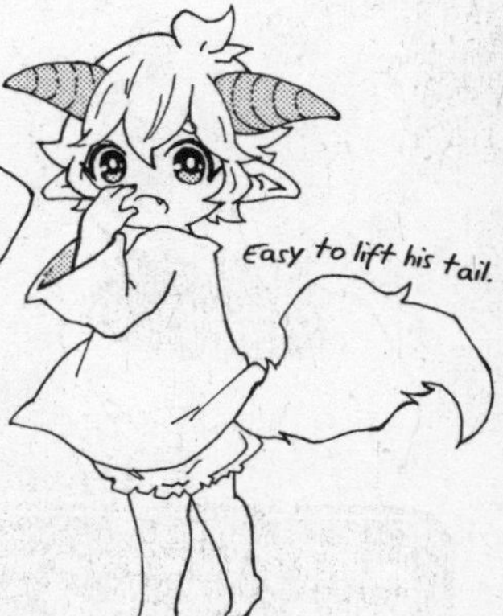
Easy to lift his tail.

Puffy pants with a hole for the tail. Made from soft fabric that's comfortable to wear.

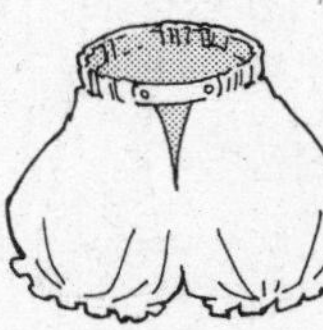

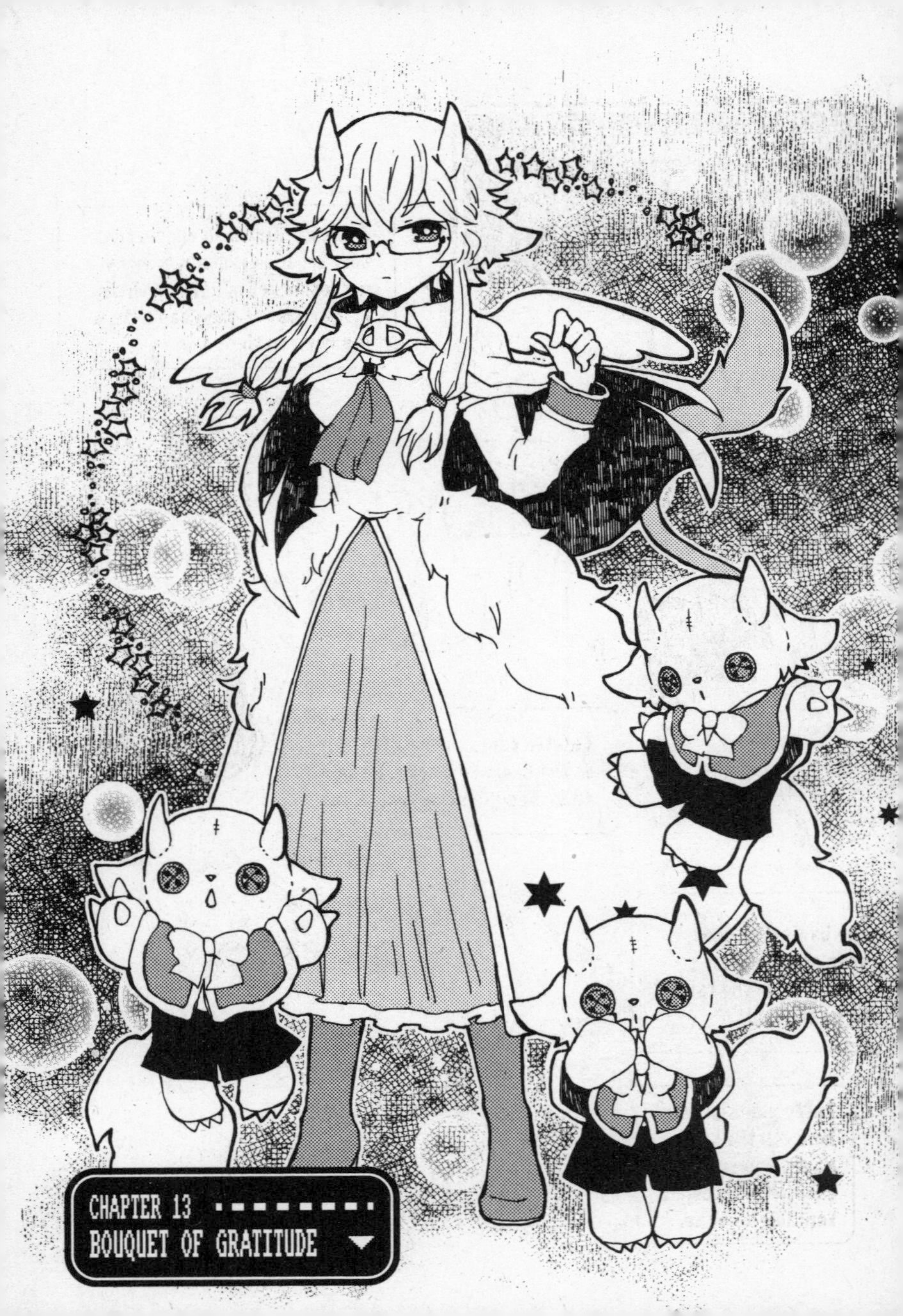
CHAPTER 13
BOUQUET OF GRATITUDE

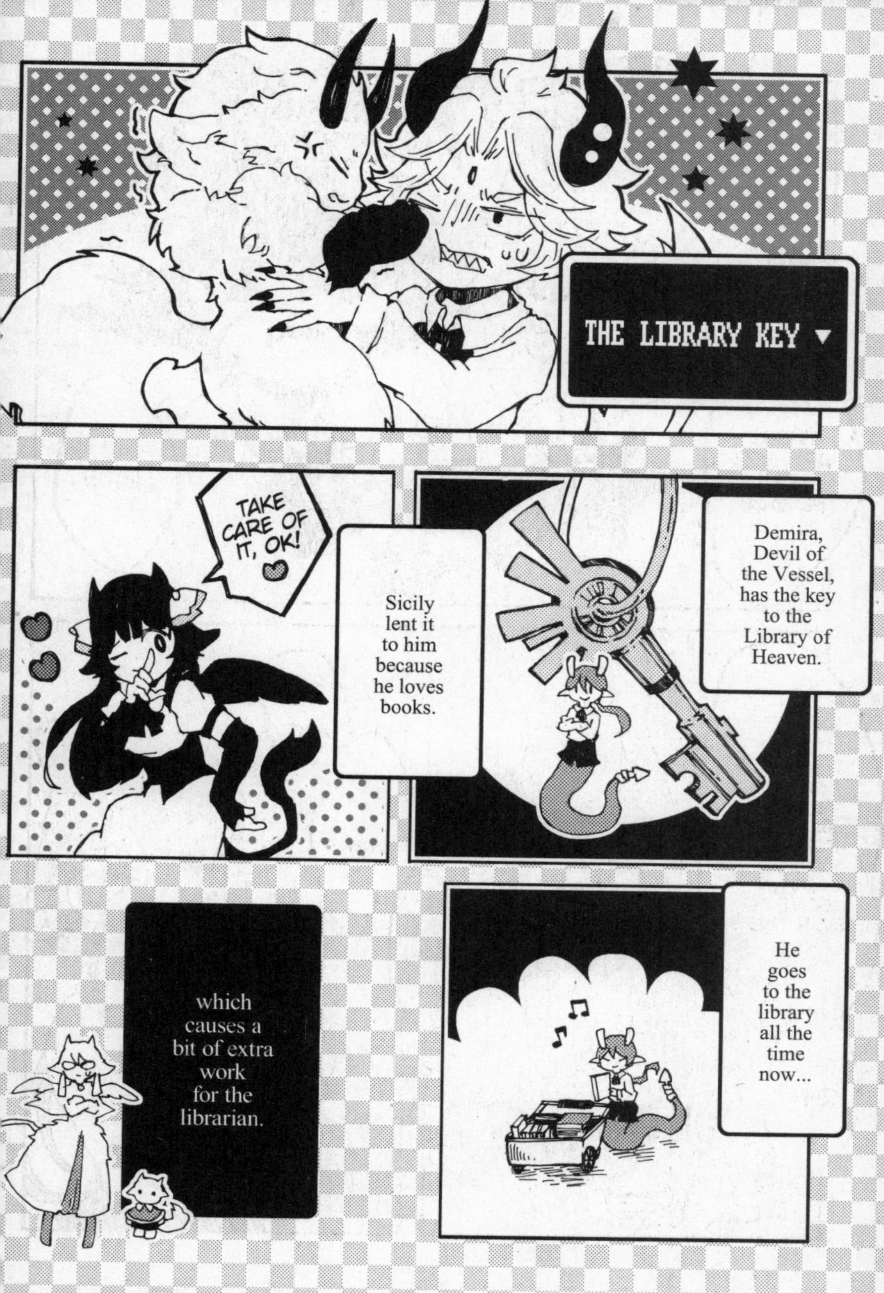
THE LIBRARY KEY ▼
Demira, Devil of the Vessel, has the key to the Library of Heaven.
Sicily lent it to him because he loves books.
TAKE CARE OF IT, OK!
He goes to the library all the time now...
which causes a bit of extra work for the librarian.

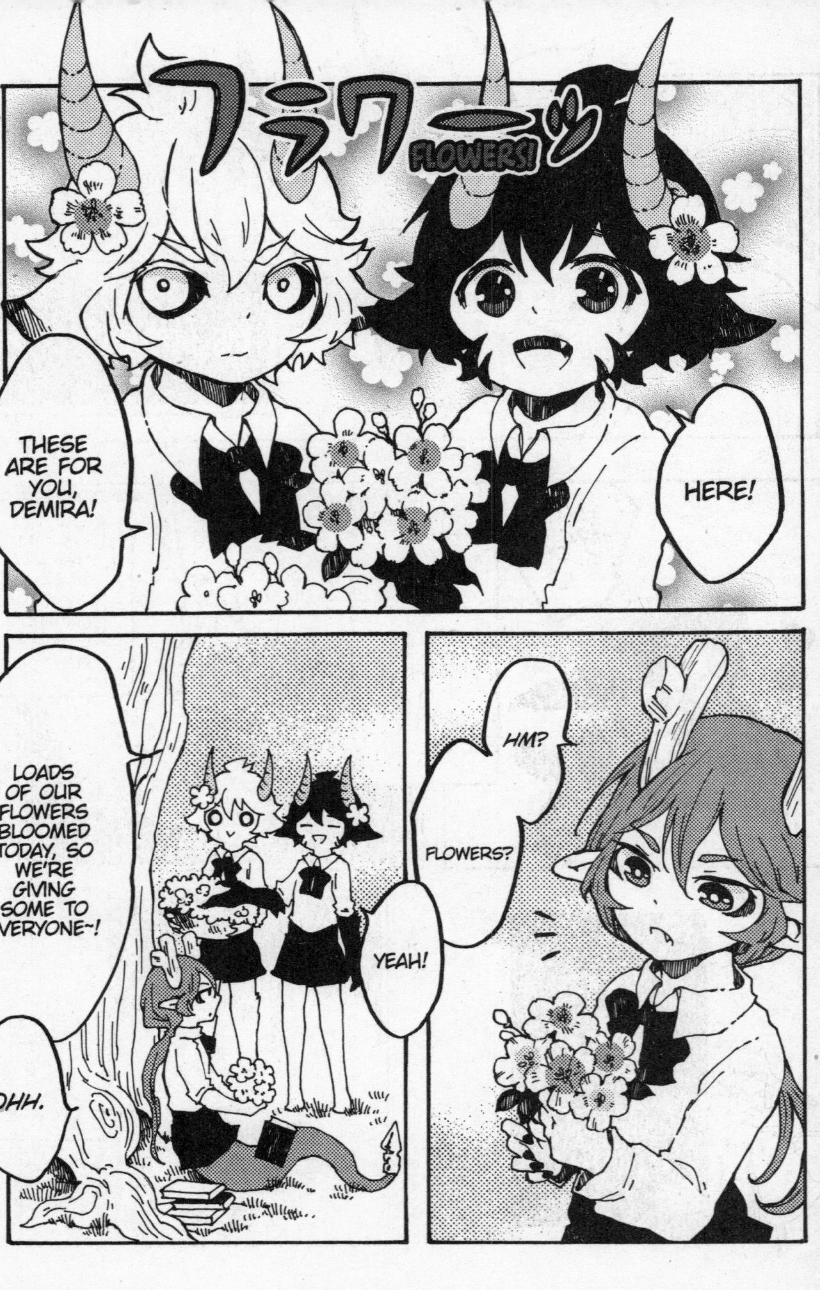
フラワーッ
FLOWERS!
HERE!
THESE ARE FOR YOU, DEMIRA!
HM?
FLOWERS?
LOADS OF OUR FLOWERS BLOOMED TODAY, SO WE'RE GIVING SOME TO EVERYONE~!
YEAH!
OHH.

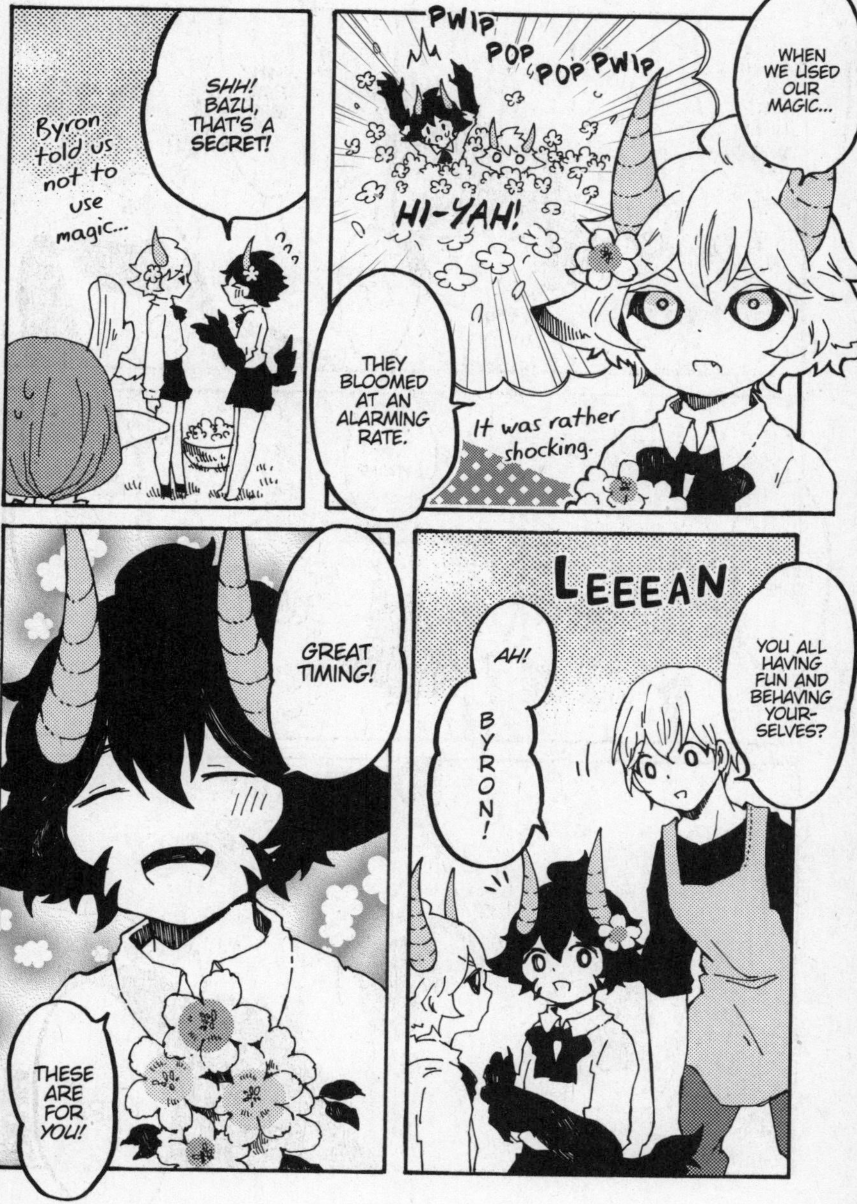
WHEN WE USED OUR MAGIC...
PWIP
POP
POP PWIP
HI-YAH!
THEY BLOOMED AT AN ALARMING RATE.
It was rather shocking.
SHH! BAZU, THAT'S A SECRET!
Byron told us not to use magic...
LEEEAN
YOU ALL HAVING FUN AND BEHAVING YOUR-SELVES?
AH! BYRON!
GREAT TIMING!
THESE ARE FOR YOU!

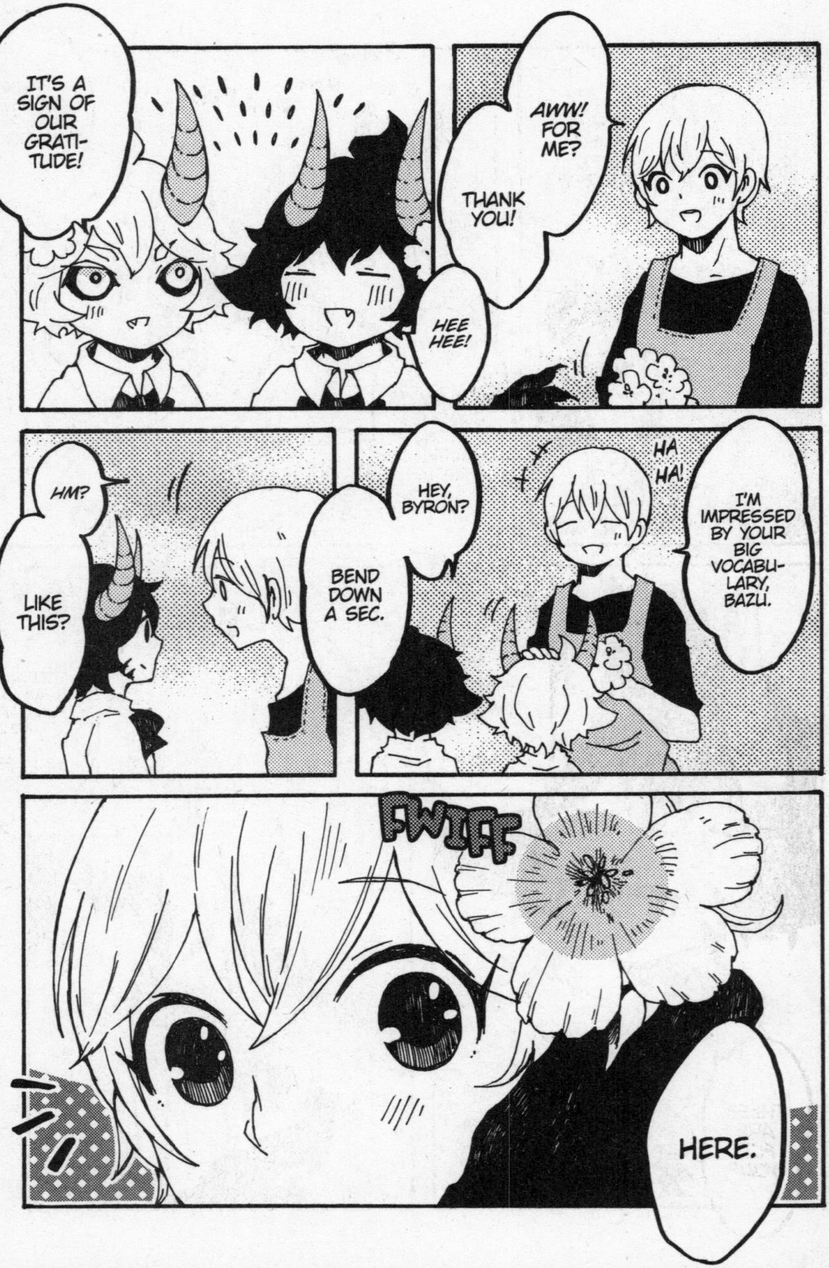
AWW! FOR ME?
THANK YOU!
IT'S A SIGN OF OUR GRATITUDE!
HEE HEE!
HA HA!
I'M IMPRESSED BY YOUR BIG VOCABULARY, BAZU.
HEY, BYRON?
BEND DOWN A SEC.
HM?
LIKE THIS?
FWIFF
HERE.

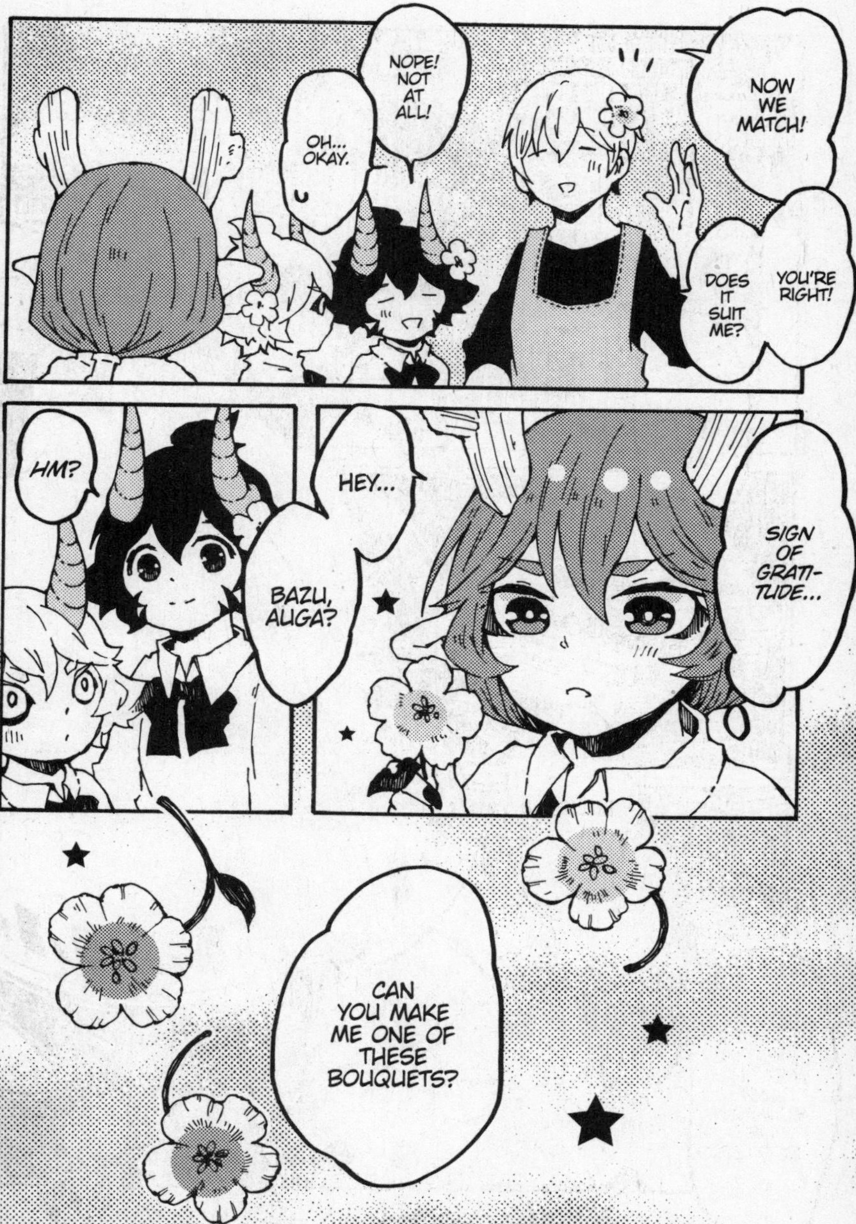
NOW WE MATCH!
YOU'RE RIGHT!
DOES IT SUIT ME?
NOPE! NOT AT ALL!
OH... OKAY.
SIGN OF GRATI-TUDE...
HEY...
BAZU, AUGA?
HM?
CAN YOU MAKE ME ONE OF THESE BOUQUETS?

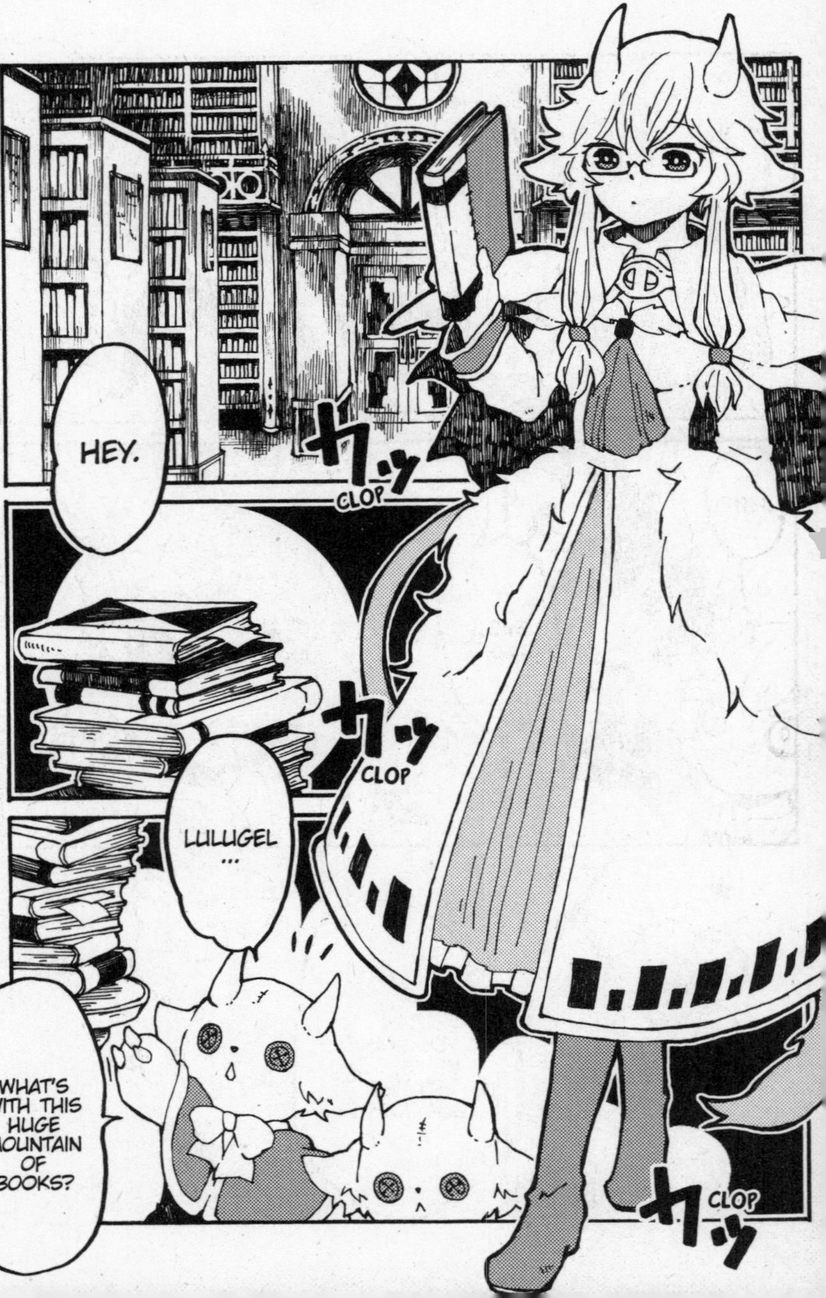
HEY.
カッ
CLOP
カッ
CLOP
LULUGEL ...
WHAT'S WITH THIS HUGE MOUNTAIN OF BOOKS?
カッ
CLOP

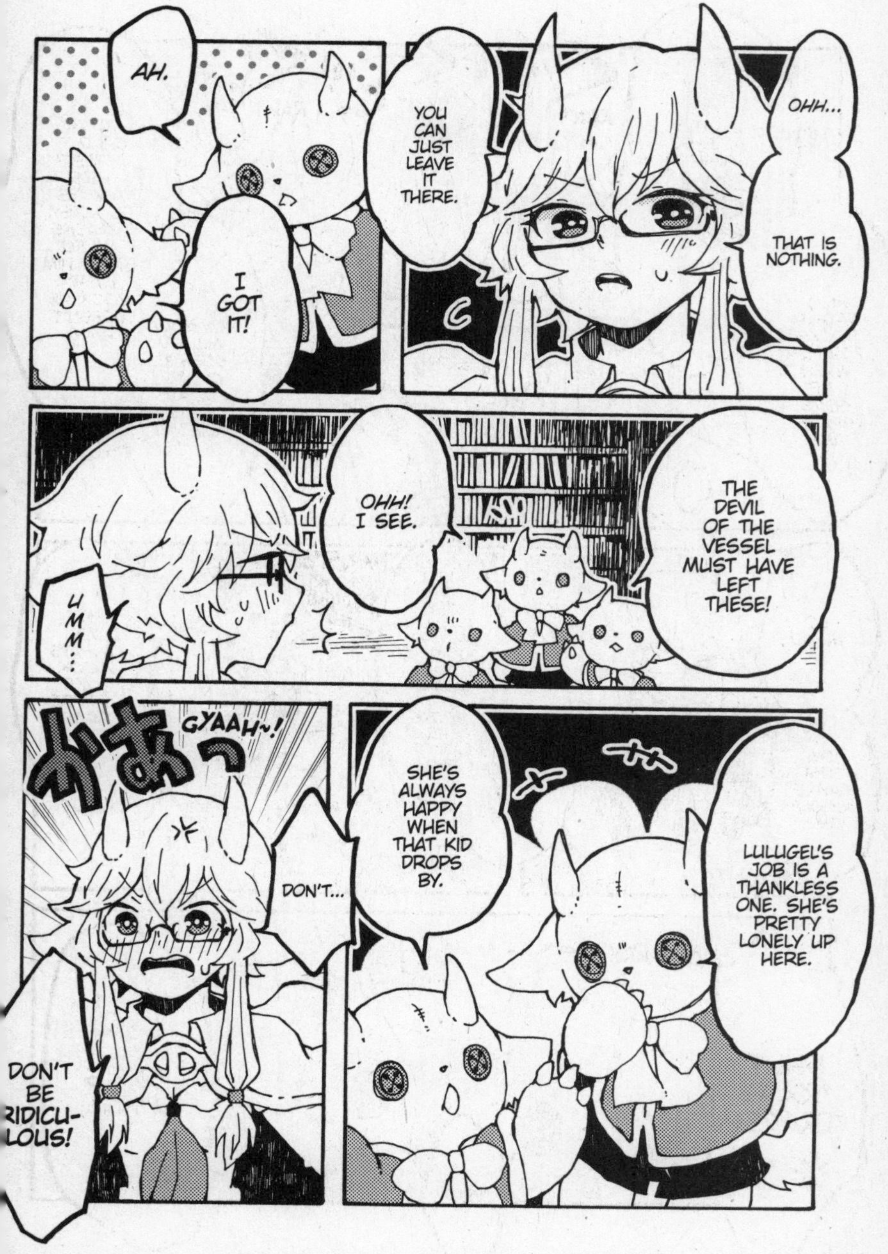
OHH...
THAT IS NOTHING.
YOU CAN JUST LEAVE IT THERE.
AH.
I GOT IT!
THE DEVIL OF THE VESSEL MUST HAVE LEFT THESE!
OHH! I SEE.
UMM...
LULUGEL'S JOB IS A THANKLESS ONE. SHE'S PRETTY LONELY UP HERE.
SHE'S ALWAYS HAPPY WHEN THAT KID DROPS BY.
GYAAH~!
DON'T...
DON'T BE RIDICULOUS!

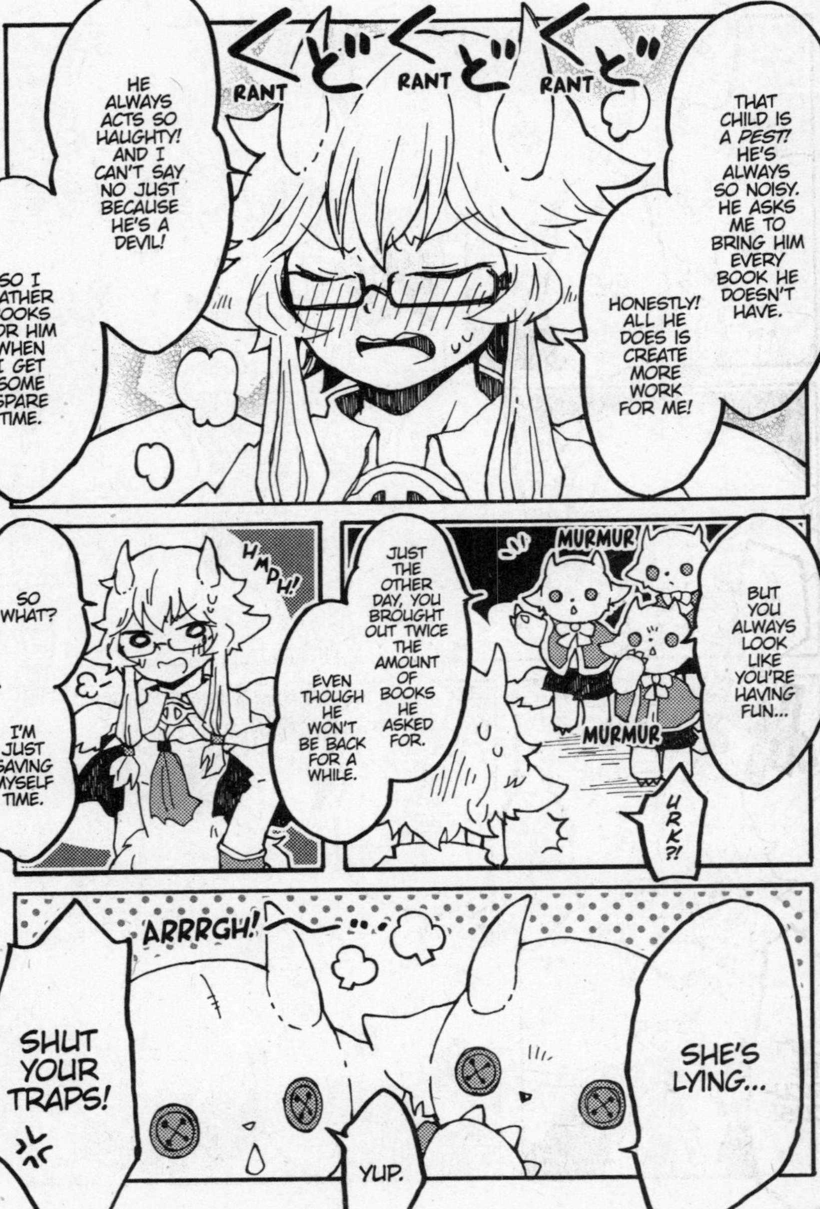
THAT CHILD IS A PEST! HE'S ALWAYS SO NOISY. HE ASKS ME TO BRING HIM EVERY BOOK HE DOESN'T HAVE.
HONESTLY! ALL HE DOES IS CREATE MORE WORK FOR ME!
くどくどくど
RANT RANT RANT
HE ALWAYS ACTS SO HAUGHTY! AND I CAN'T SAY NO JUST BECAUSE HE'S A DEVIL!
SO I GATHER BOOKS FOR HIM WHEN I GET SOME SPARE TIME.
BUT YOU ALWAYS LOOK LIKE YOU'RE HAVING FUN...
MURMUR
MURMUR
JUST THE OTHER DAY, YOU BROUGHT OUT TWICE THE AMOUNT OF BOOKS HE ASKED FOR.
EVEN THOUGH HE WON'T BE BACK FOR A WHILE.
URK?!
HMPH!
SO WHAT?
I'M JUST SAVING MYSELF TIME.
SHE'S LYING...
YUP.
ARRRGH!
SHUT YOUR TRAPS!

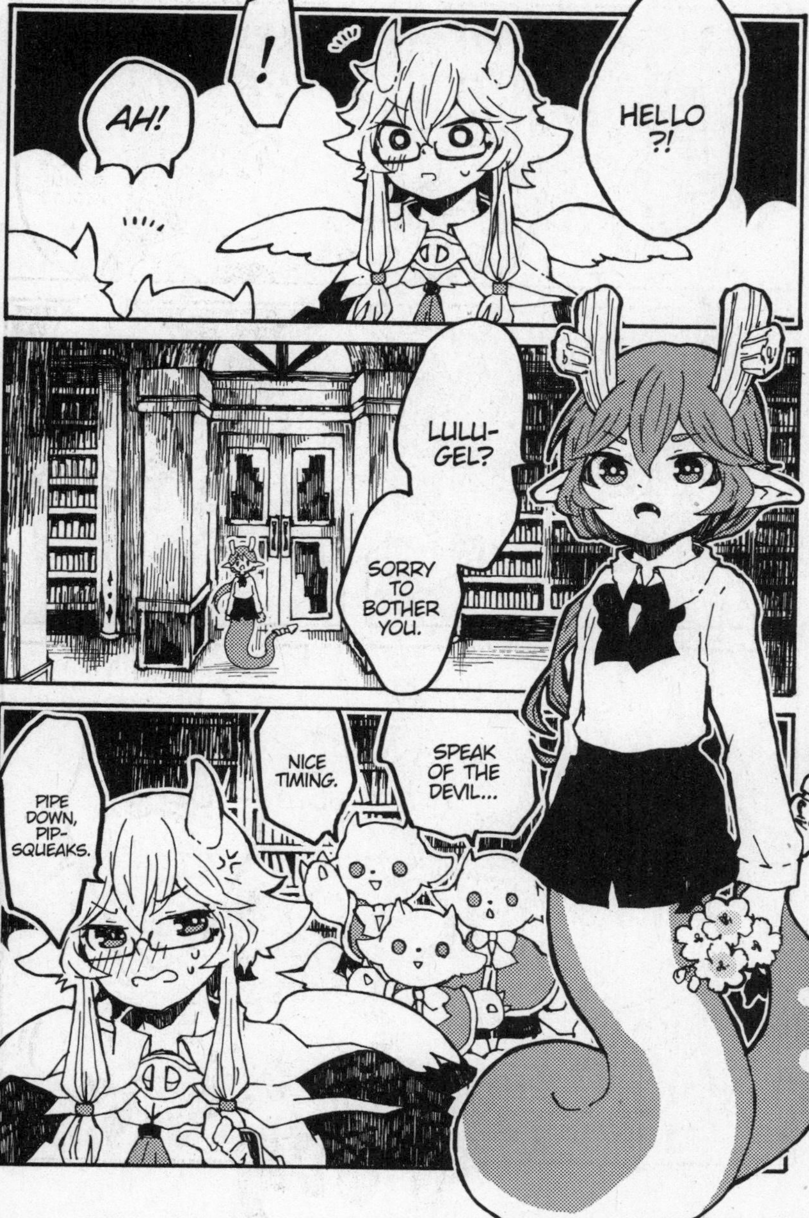
HELLO ?!
!
AH!
LULU-GEL?
SORRY TO BOTHER YOU.
SPEAK OF THE DEVIL...
NICE TIMING.
PIPE DOWN, PIP-SQUEAKS.

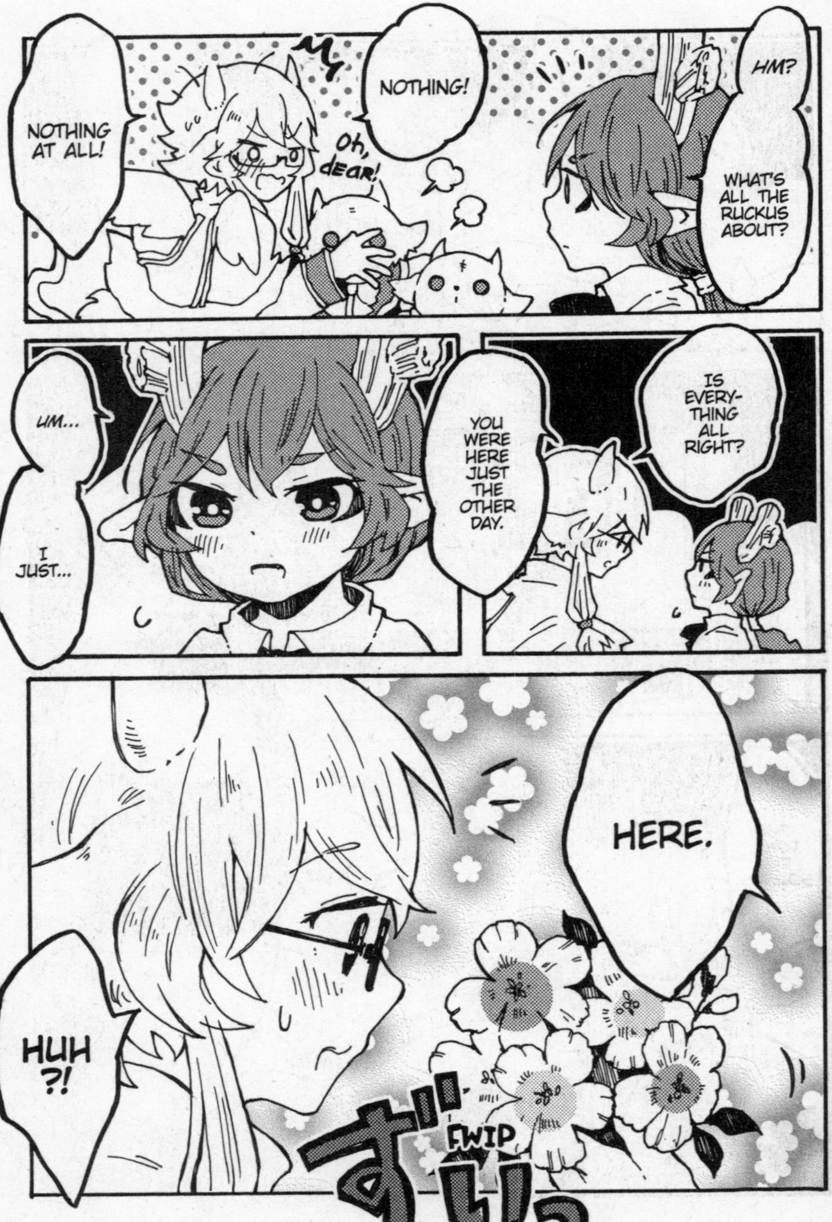
HM?
WHAT'S ALL THE RUCKUS ABOUT?
NOTHING!
Oh, dear!
NOTHING AT ALL!
IS EVERY-THING ALL RIGHT?
YOU WERE HERE JUST THE OTHER DAY.
UM...
I JUST...
HERE.
FWIP
すいっ
HUH?!

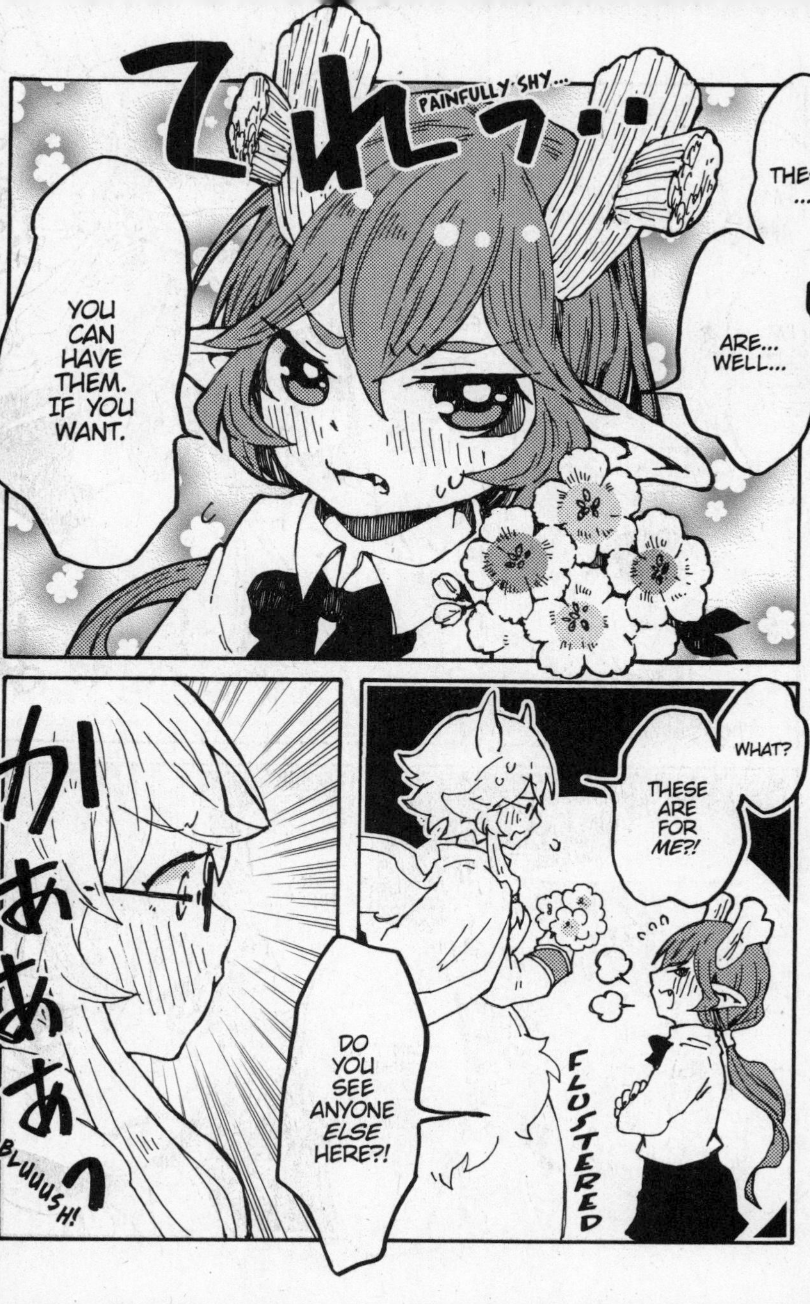
てれっ..
PAINFULLY SHY...
THESE ...
ARE... WELL...
YOU CAN HAVE THEM. IF YOU WANT.
WHAT? THESE ARE FOR *ME*?!
FLUSTERED
DO YOU SEE ANYONE *ELSE* HERE?!
かーあああっ
BLUUUSH!

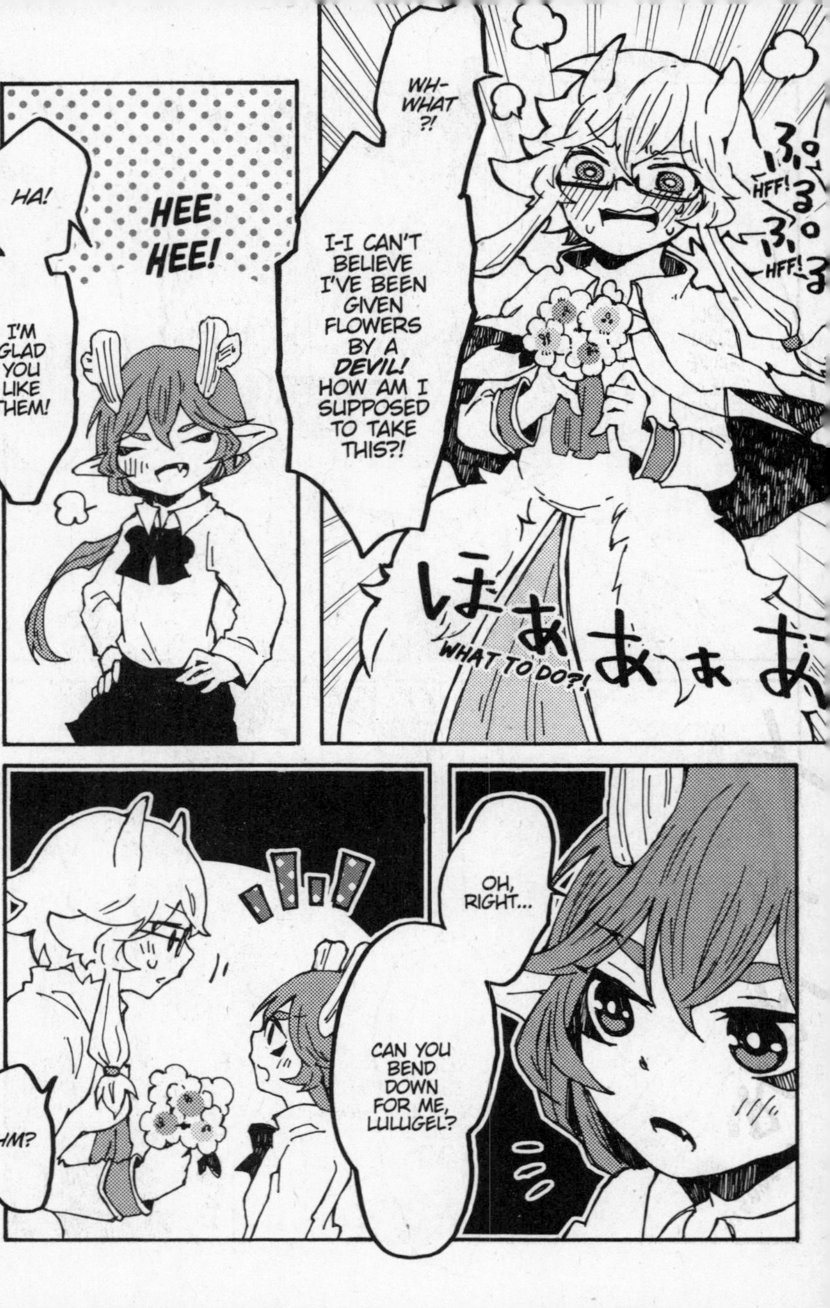
WH- WHAT ?!
I-I CAN'T BELIEVE I'VE BEEN GIVEN FLOWERS BY A DEVIL! HOW AM I SUPPOSED TO TAKE THIS?!
HFF!
HFF!
WHAT TO DO?!
HA!
HEE HEE!
I'M GLAD YOU LIKE THEM!
OH, RIGHT...
CAN YOU BEND DOWN FOR ME, LULLIGEL?
HM?

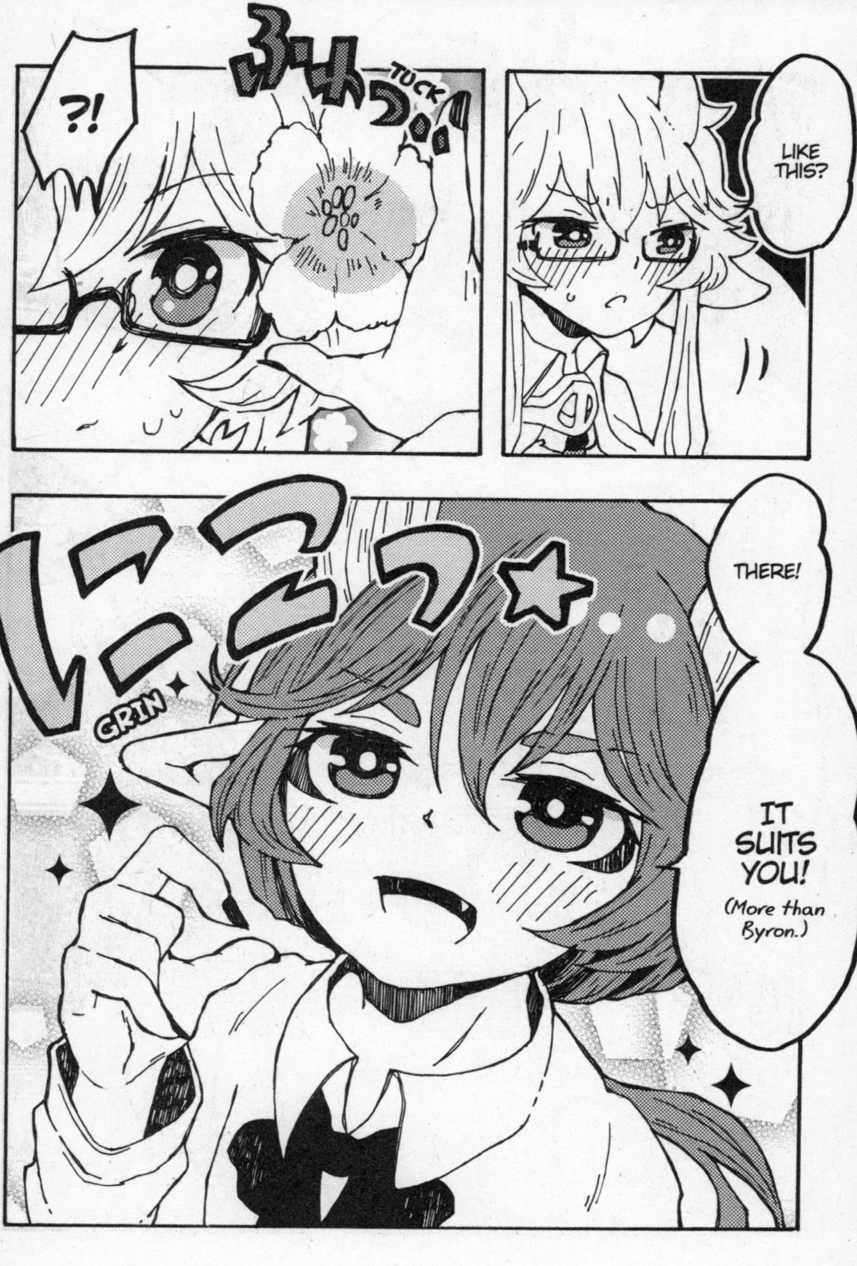
LIKE THIS?
ふわっ
TUCK
?!
THERE!
IT SUITS YOU!
(More than Byron.)
にこっ
GRIN

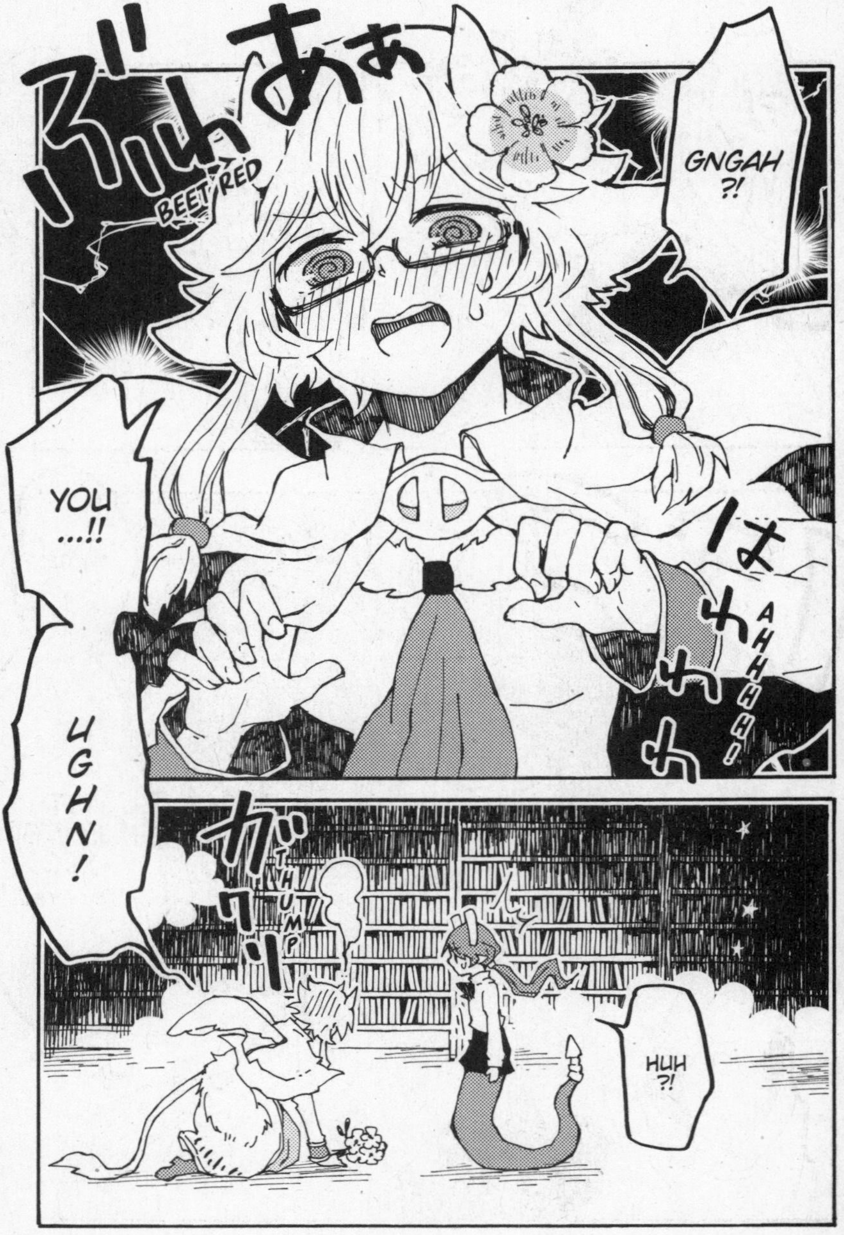
GNGAH ?!
BEET RED
AHHHHHH!
はわわわ
YOU ...!!
UGHN!
HUH ?!
THUMP

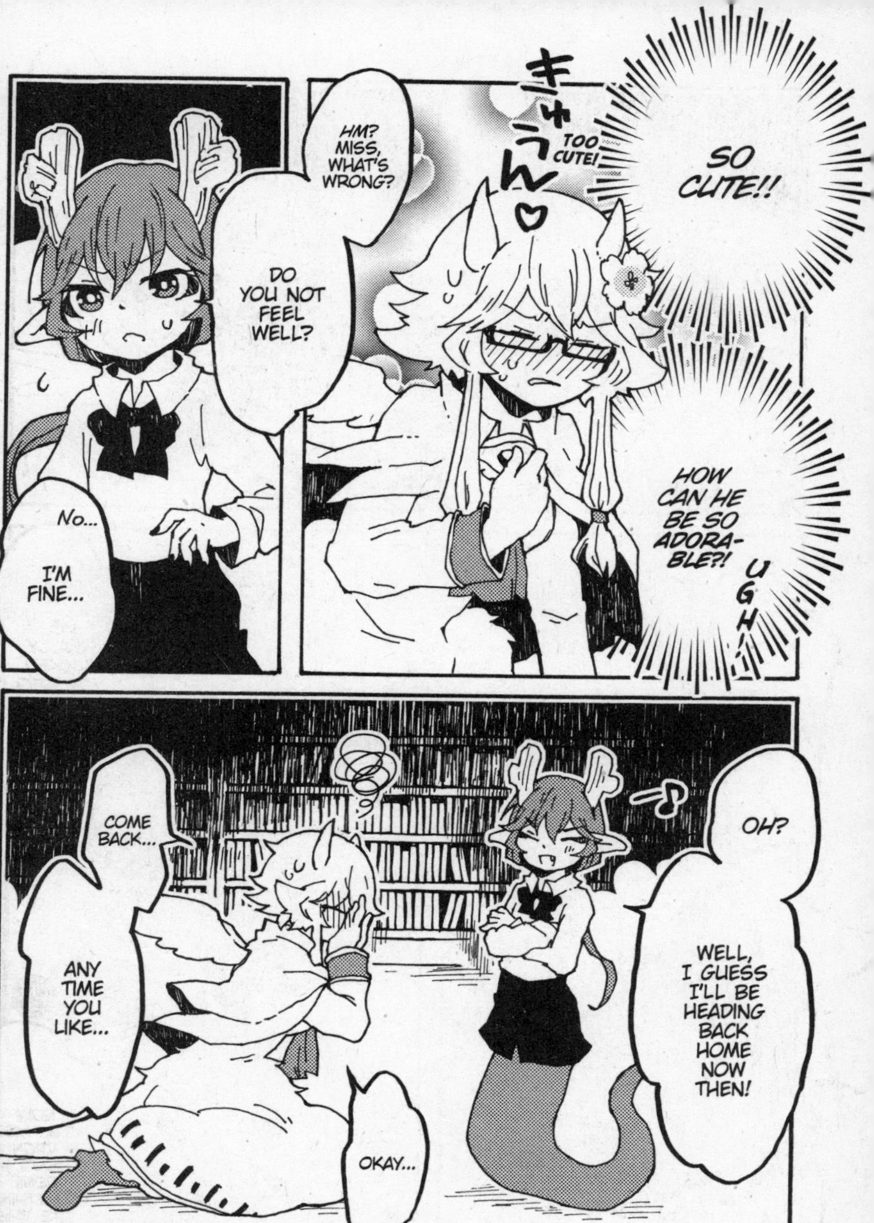
SO CUTE!!
きゅうん
TOO CUTE!
HM? MISS, WHAT'S WRONG?
DO YOU NOT FEEL WELL?
HOW CAN HE BE SO ADORA-BLE?!
UGH...
No...
I'M FINE...
OH?
WELL, I GUESS I'LL BE HEADING BACK HOME NOW THEN!
COME BACK...
ANY TIME YOU LIKE...
OKAY...

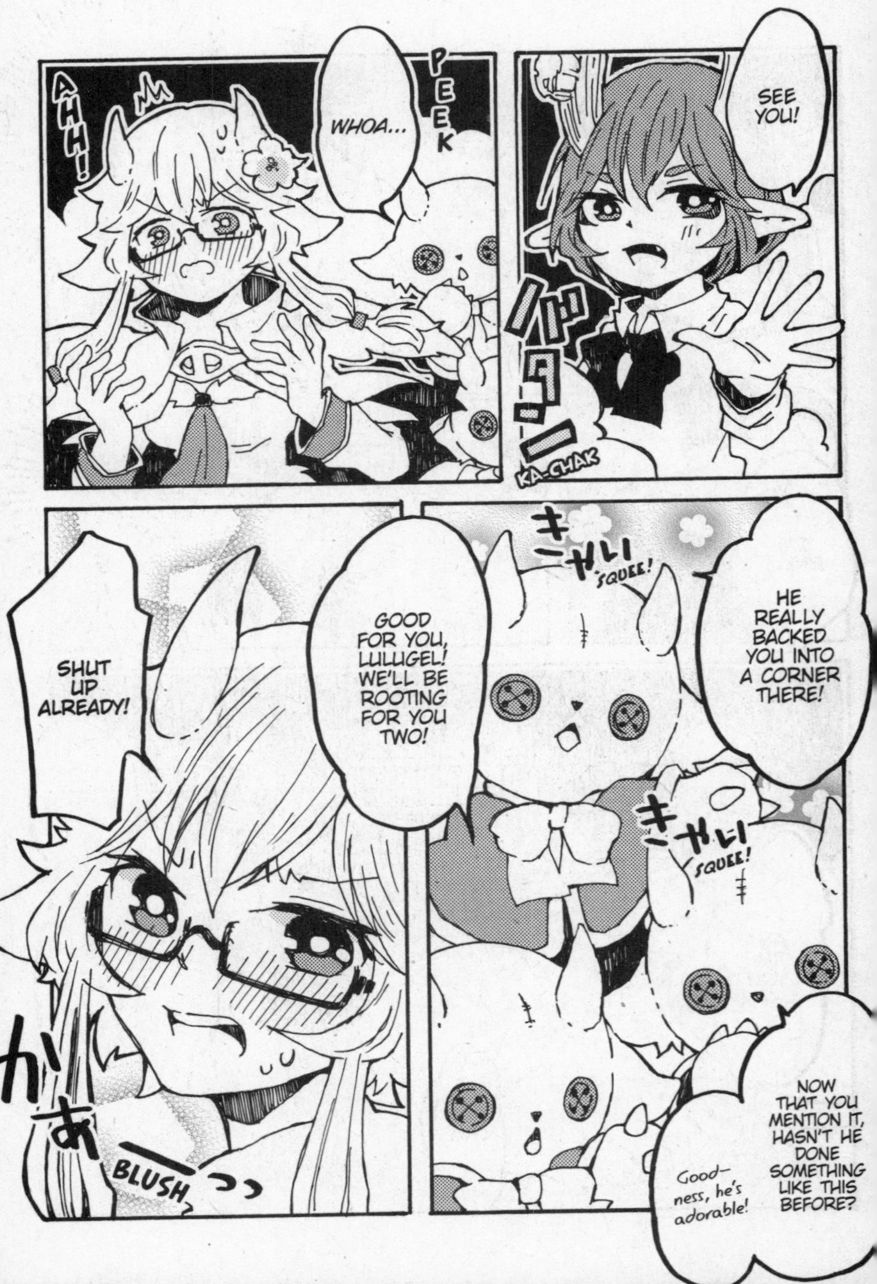
SEE YOU!
KA-CHAK
WHOA...
PEEK
AHHH!
HE REALLY BACKED YOU INTO A CORNER THERE!
SQUEE!
SQUEE!
NOW THAT YOU MENTION IT, HASN'T HE DONE SOMETHING LIKE THIS BEFORE?
Goodness, he's adorable!
GOOD FOR YOU, LULUGEL! WE'LL BE ROOTING FOR YOU TWO!
SHUT UP ALREADY!
BLUSH

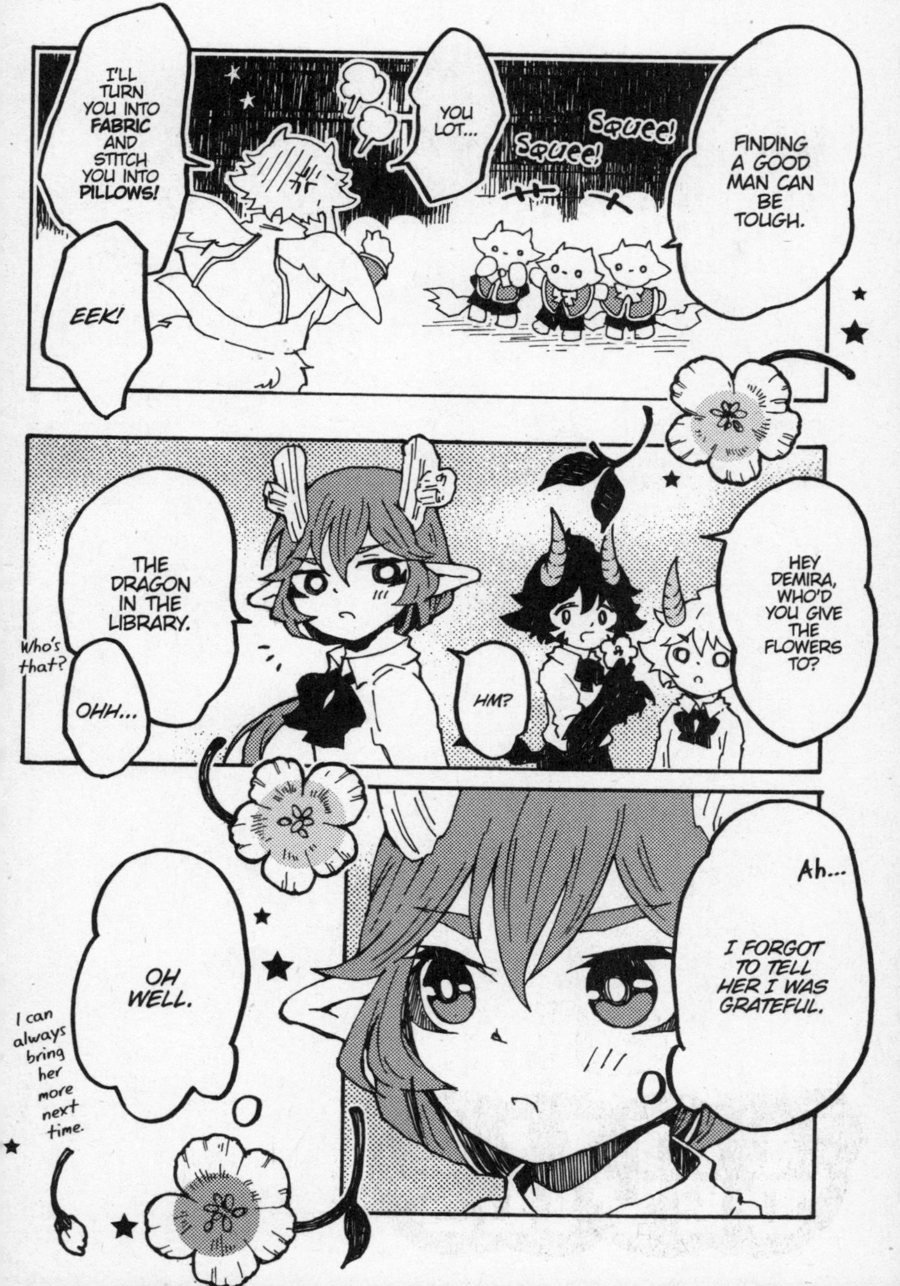
FINDING A GOOD MAN CAN BE TOUGH.
Squee!
Squee!
YOU LOT...
I'LL TURN YOU INTO FABRIC AND STITCH YOU INTO PILLOWS!
EEK!
HEY DEMIRA, WHO'D YOU GIVE THE FLOWERS TO?
HM?
THE DRAGON IN THE LIBRARY.
Who's that?
OHH...
Ah...
I FORGOT TO TELL HER I WAS GRATEFUL.
OH WELL.
I can always bring her more next time.

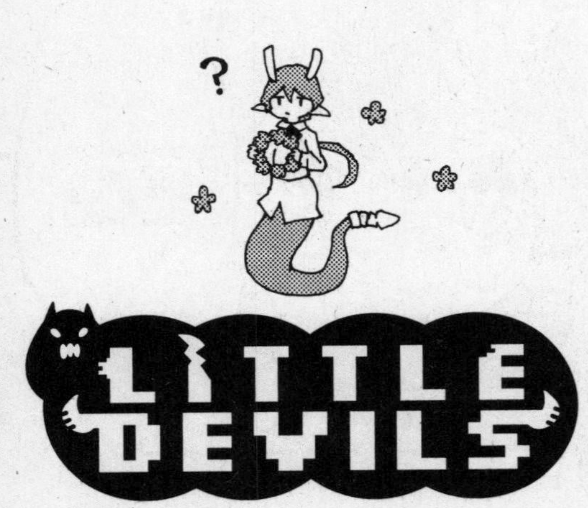

LITTLE DEVILS

THE LITTLE DEVILS' MAGIC: PART 1
SPELL OF SPECTACULAR GROWTH!

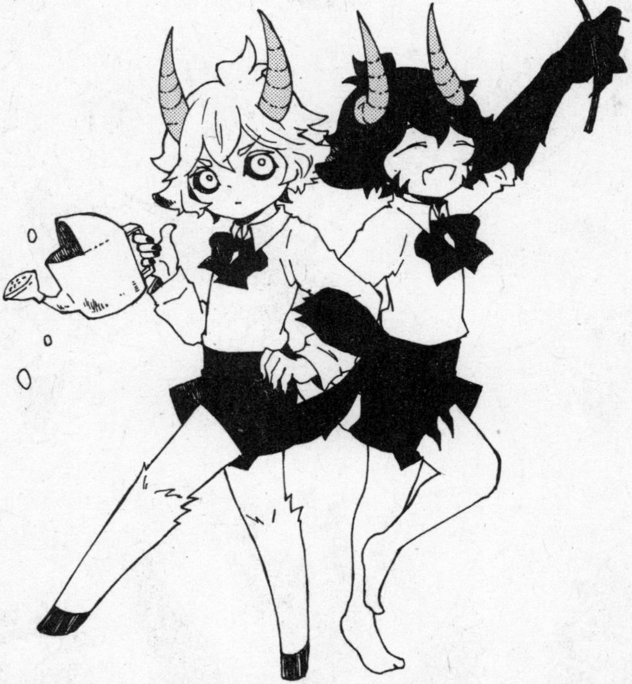

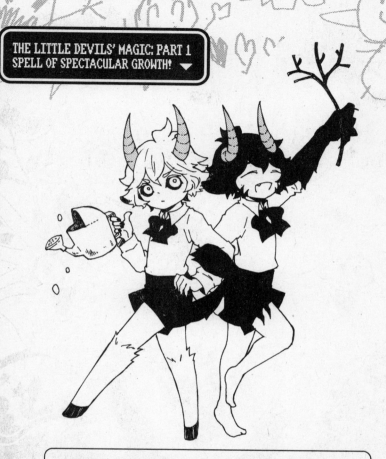

Bazu and Auga created this spell because they love gardening so much.
They can give plants energy to grow all at once.
But they have to be careful. When cast too powerfully, too many plants grow...or the plants turn into monsters!

The chant and dance they use for this spell is different every time.
They kinda make it up as they go along.

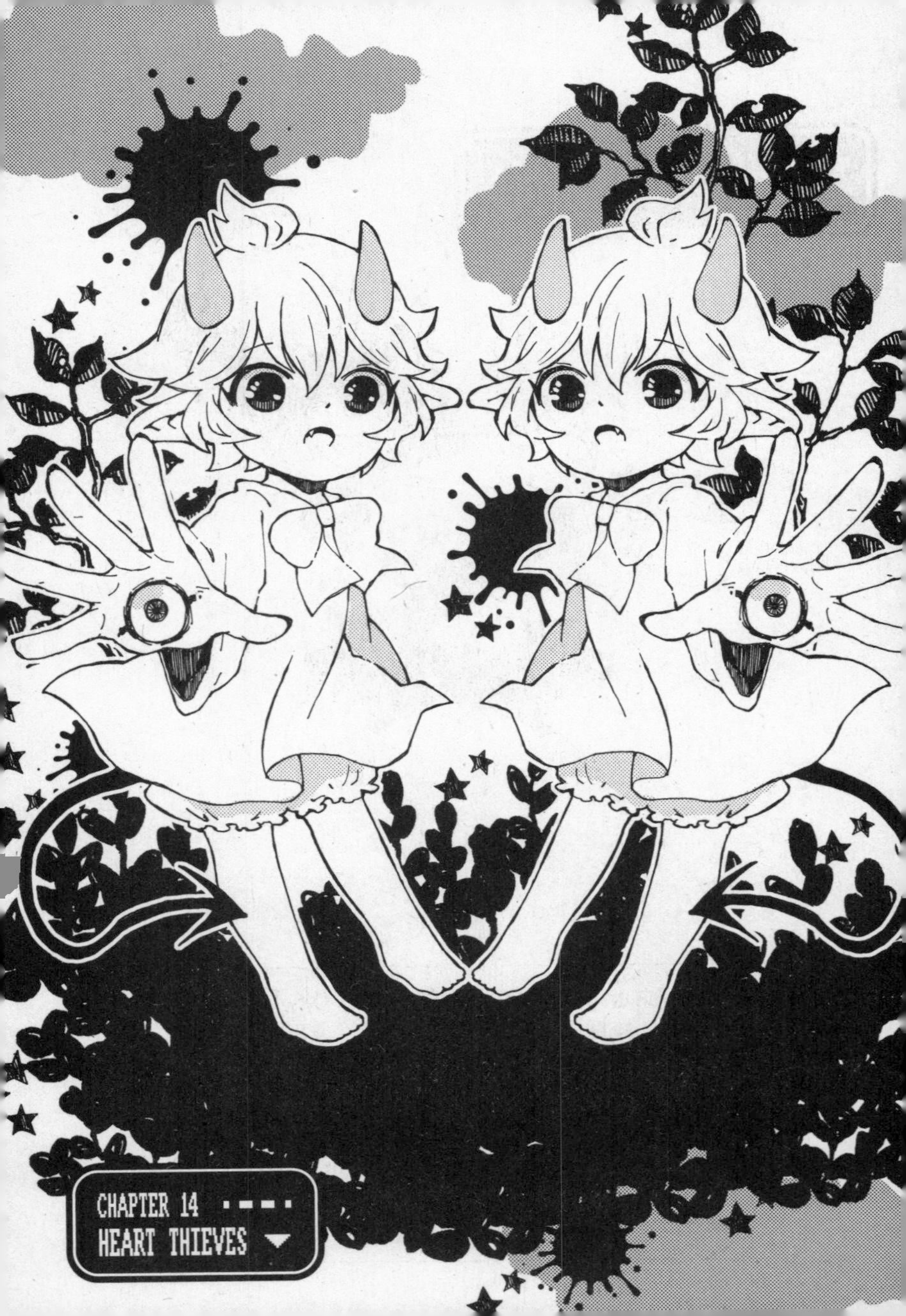
CHAPTER 14
HEART THIEVES

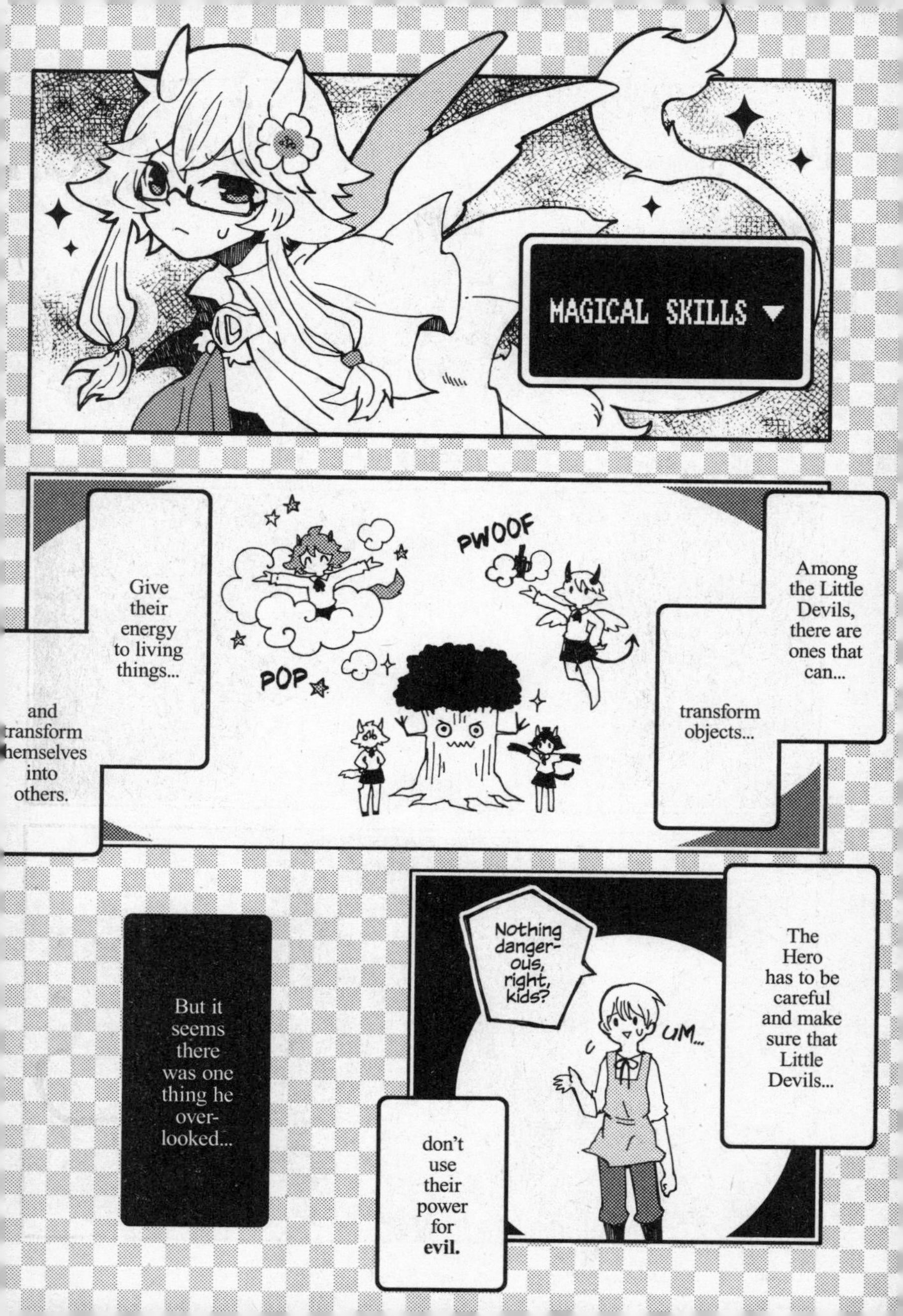
MAGICAL SKILLS ▼
Among the Little Devils, there are ones that can...
transform objects...
PWOOF
POP
Give their energy to living things...
and transform hemselves into others.
The Hero has to be careful and make sure that Little Devils...
Nothing danger-ous, right, kids?
UM...
don't use their power for **evil.**
But it seems there was one thing he over-looked...

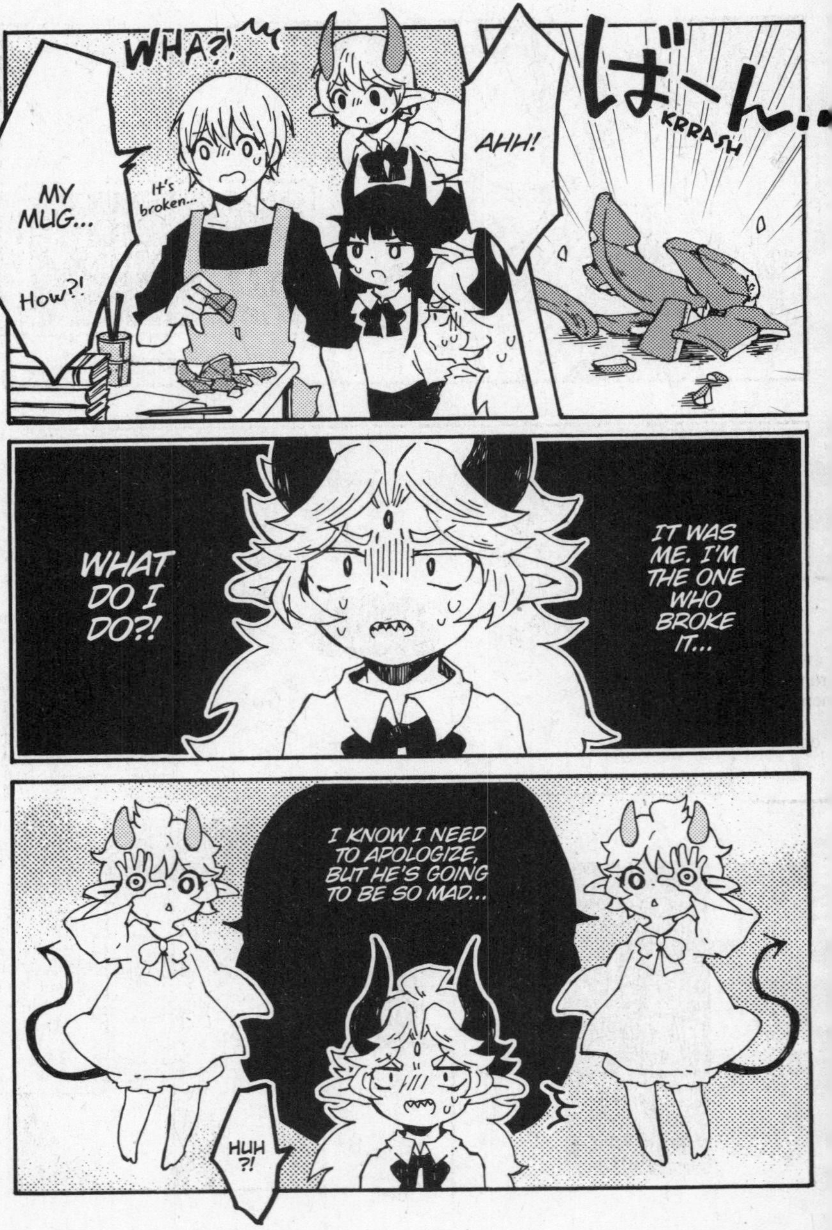
ばーん…
KRRASH
AHH!
WHA?!
It's broken...
MY MUG...
How?!
IT WAS ME. I'M THE ONE WHO BROKE IT...
WHAT DO I DO?!
I KNOW I NEED TO APOLOGIZE, BUT HE'S GOING TO BE SO MAD...
HUH ?!

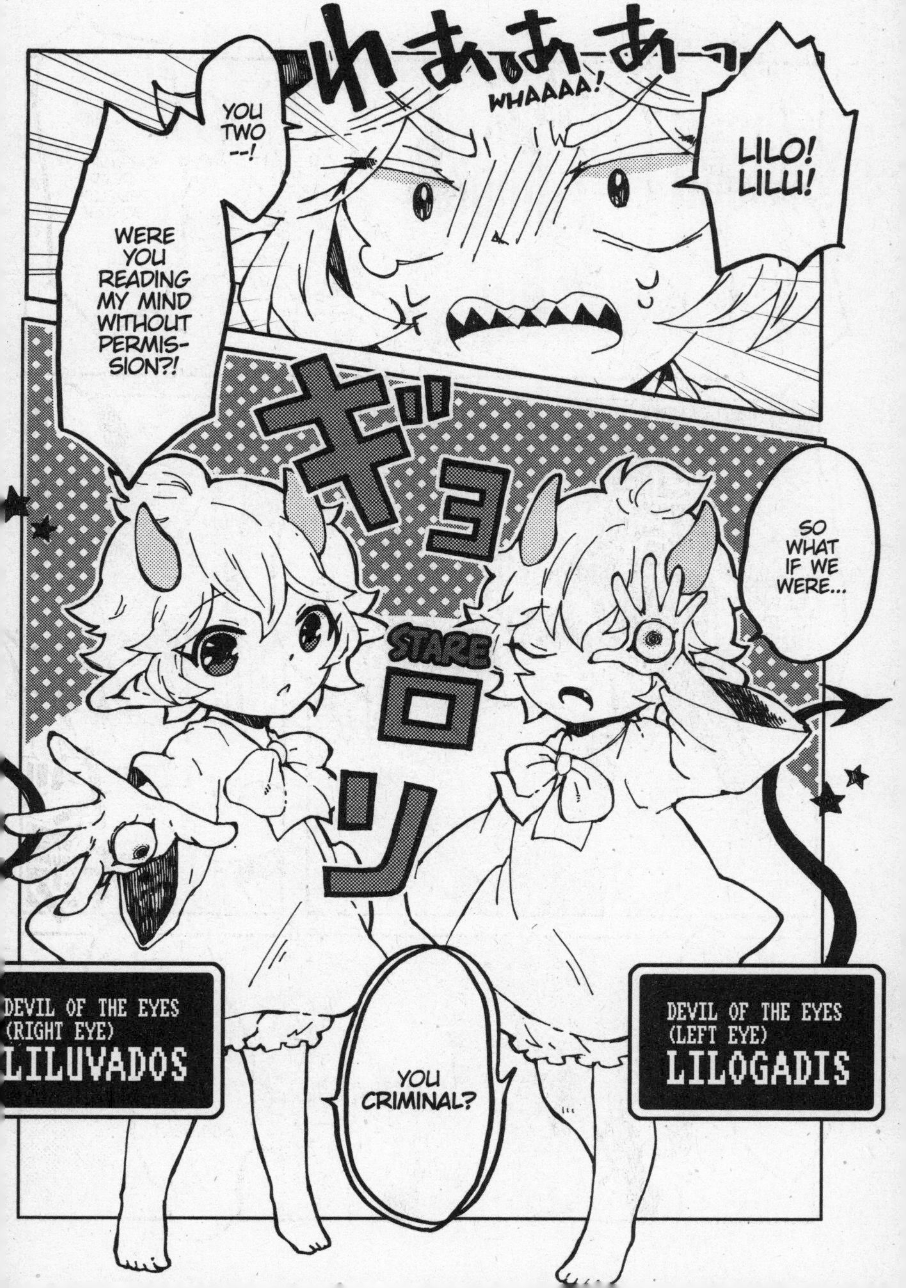
LILO! LILU!
WHAAAA!
YOU TWO--!
WERE YOU READING MY MIND WITHOUT PERMIS-SION?!
SO WHAT IF WE WERE...
ギョロリ
STARE
YOU CRIMINAL?
DEVIL OF THE EYES (LEFT EYE) LILOGADIS
DEVIL OF THE EYES (RIGHT EYE) LILUVADOS

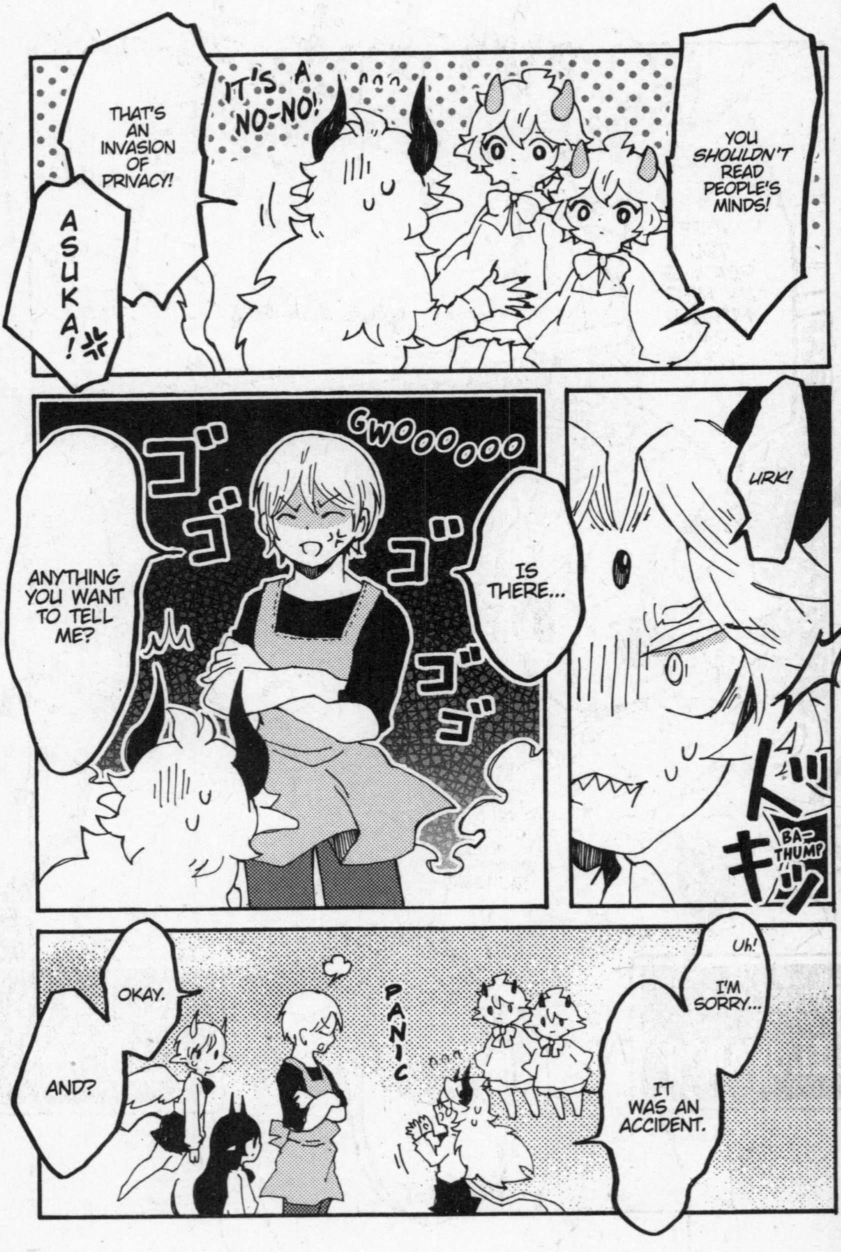
YOU SHOULDN'T READ PEOPLE'S MINDS!
IT'S A NO-NO!
THAT'S AN INVASION OF PRIVACY!
ASUKA!
URK!
BA-THUMP
GWOOOOOOO
IS THERE...
ANYTHING YOU WANT TO TELL ME?
Uh! I'M SORRY...
IT WAS AN ACCIDENT.
PANIC
OKAY.
AND?

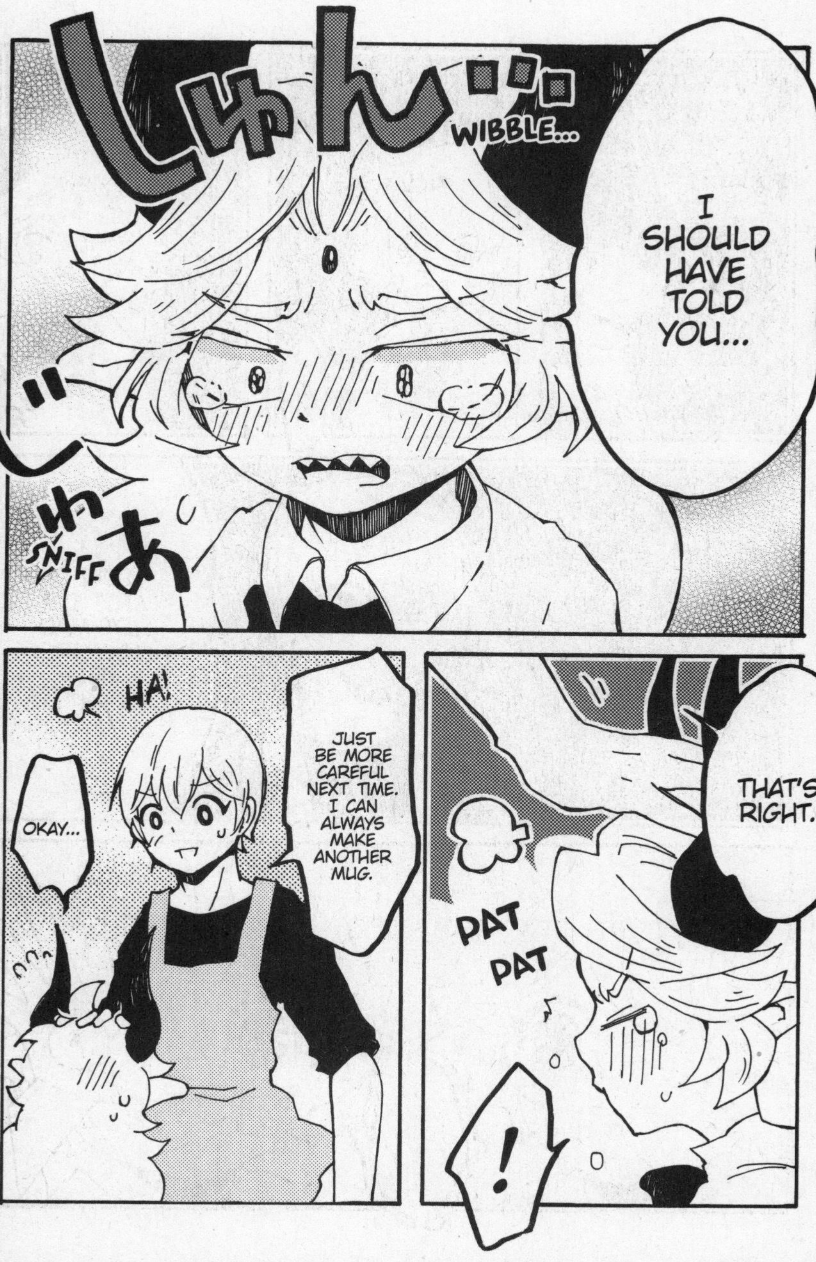
しゅん
WIBBLE...
I SHOULD HAVE TOLD YOU...
じわあ
SNIFF
THAT'S RIGHT.
PAT PAT
!
HA!
JUST BE MORE CAREFUL NEXT TIME. I CAN ALWAYS MAKE ANOTHER MUG.
OKAY...

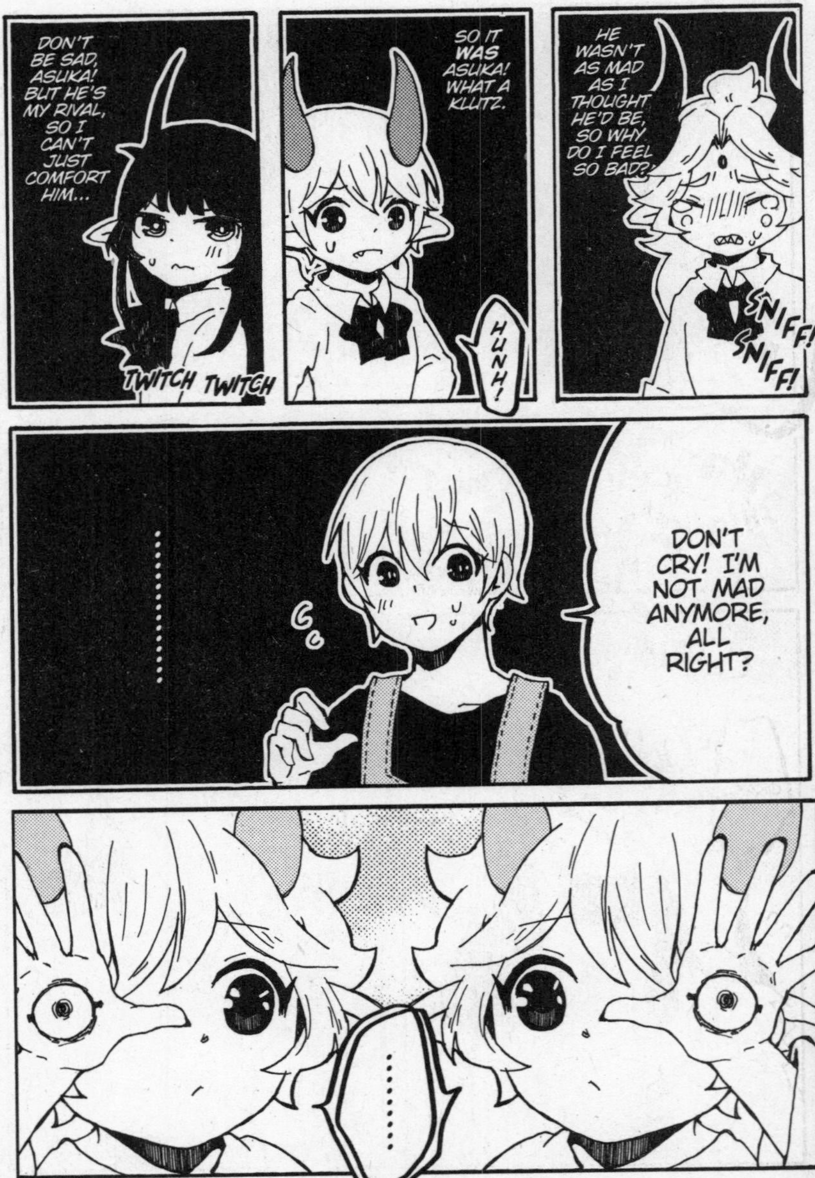
HE WASN'T AS MAD AS I THOUGHT HE'D BE, SO WHY DO I FEEL SO BAD?
SNIFF! SNIFF!
SO IT WAS ASUKA! WHAT A KLUTZ.
HUNH!
DON'T BE SAD, ASUKA! BUT HE'S MY RIVAL, SO I CAN'T JUST COMFORT HIM...
TWITCH TWITCH
DON'T CRY! I'M NOT MAD ANYMORE, ALL RIGHT?
......
...

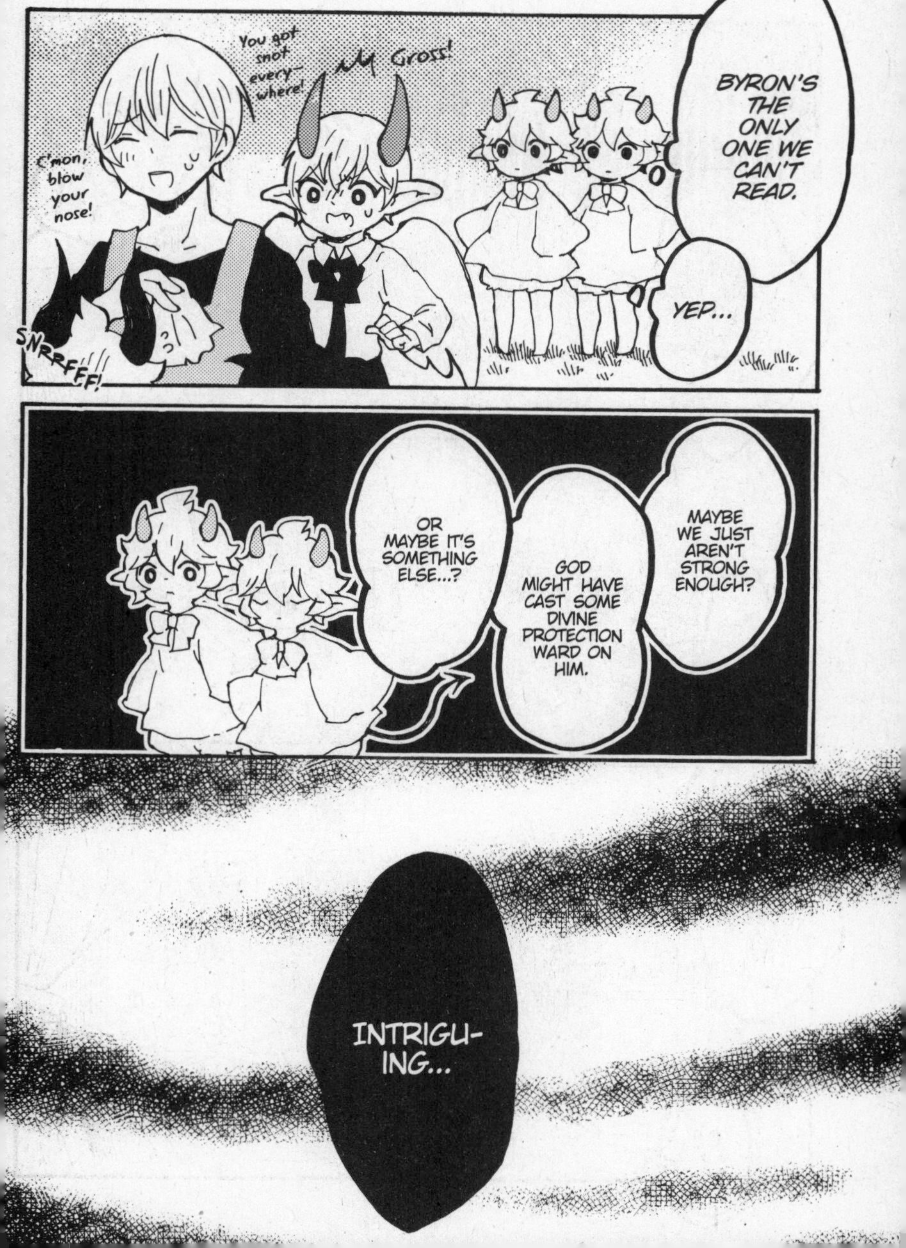
BYRON'S THE ONLY ONE WE CAN'T READ.
YEP...
Gross!
You got snot every-where!
C'mon, blow your nose!
SNRRFFF!
MAYBE WE JUST AREN'T STRONG ENOUGH?
GOD MIGHT HAVE CAST SOME DIVINE PROTECTION WARD ON HIM.
OR MAYBE IT'S SOMETHING ELSE...?
INTRIGU-ING...

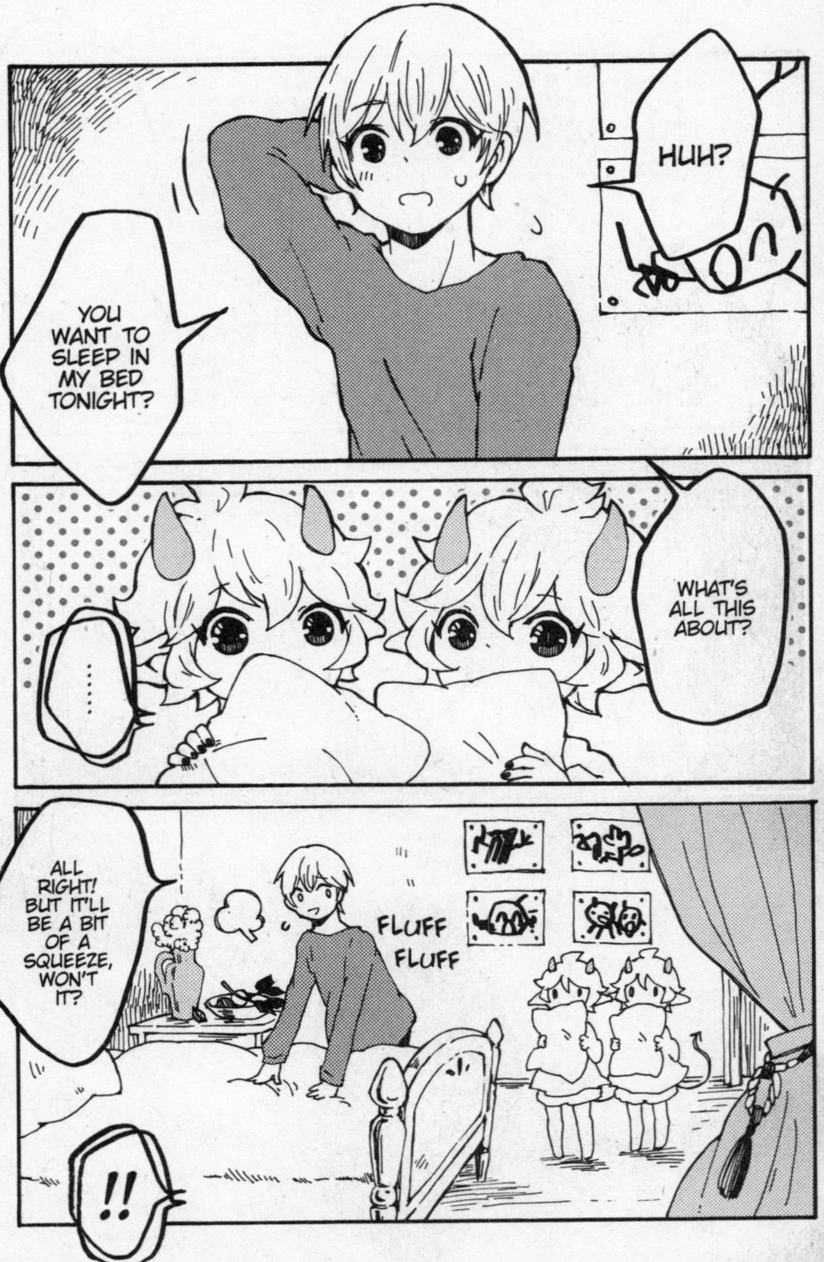
HUH?
YOU WANT TO SLEEP IN MY BED TONIGHT?
WHAT'S ALL THIS ABOUT?
......
FLUFF FLUFF
ALL RIGHT! BUT IT'LL BE A BIT OF A SQUEEZE, WON'T IT?
!!

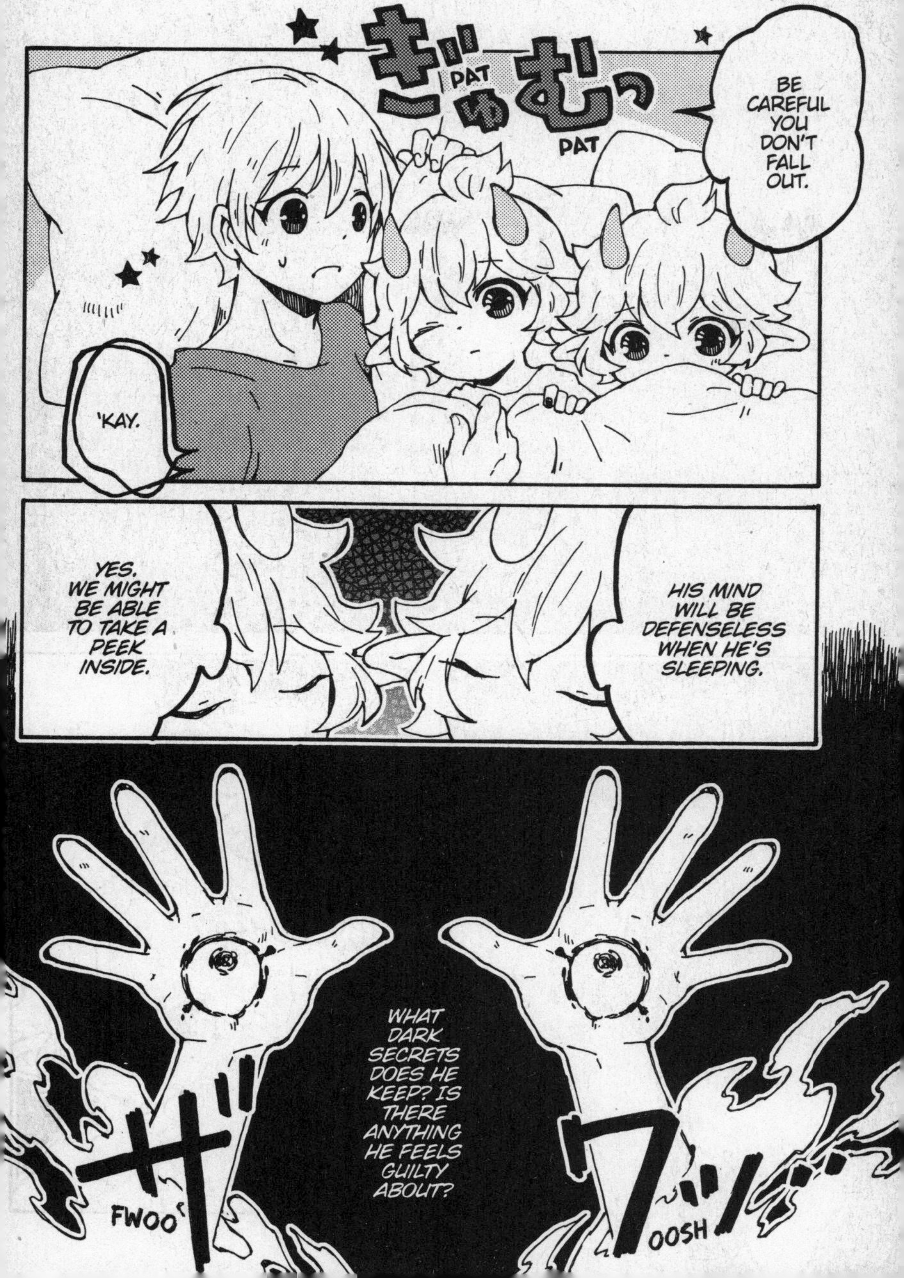
BE CAREFUL YOU DON'T FALL OUT.
ぎゅむっ
PAT PAT
'KAY.
HIS MIND WILL BE DEFENSELESS WHEN HE'S SLEEPING.
YES. WE MIGHT BE ABLE TO TAKE A PEEK INSIDE.
WHAT DARK SECRETS DOES HE KEEP? IS THERE ANYTHING HE FEELS GUILTY ABOUT?
FWOO
OOSH

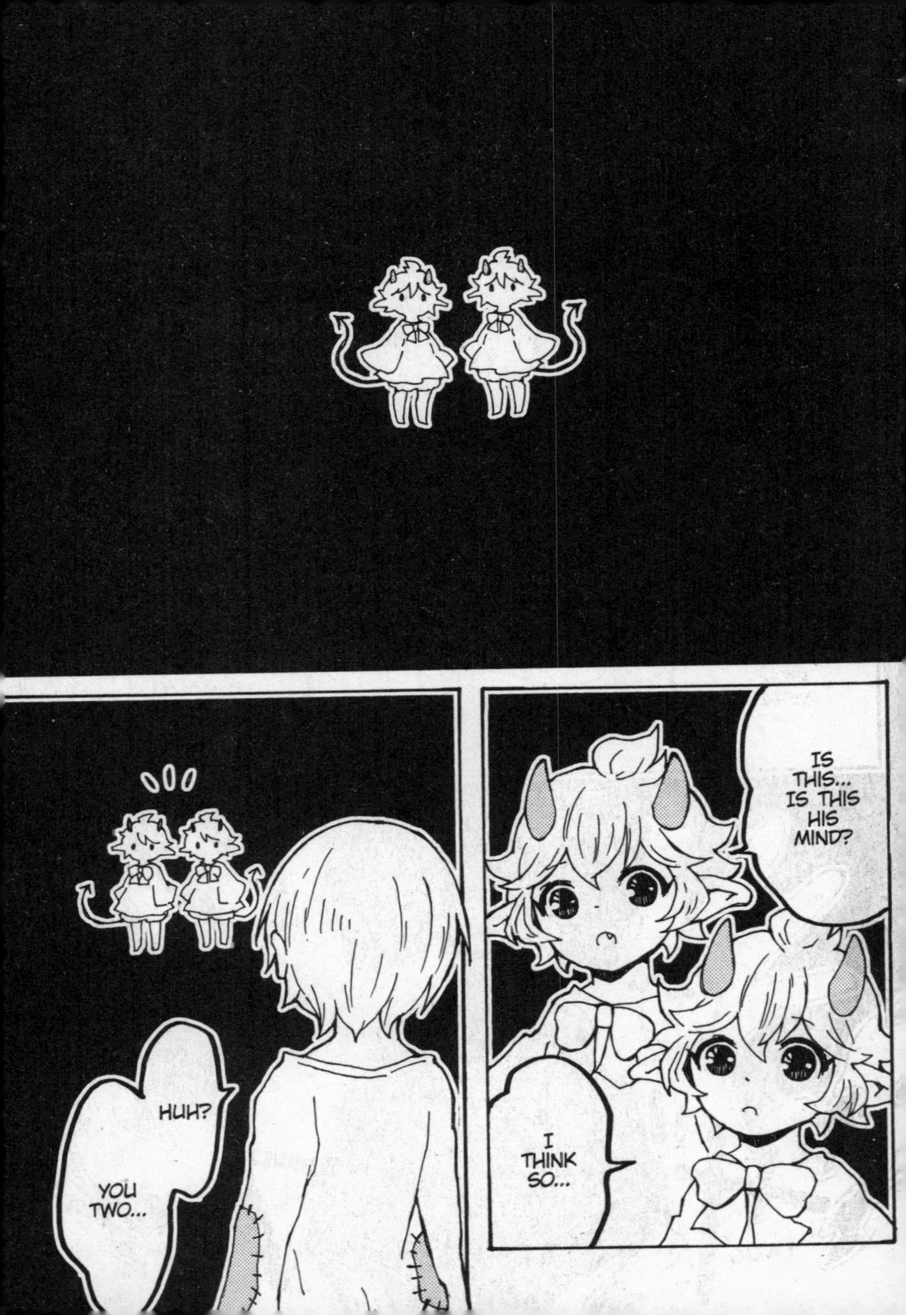
IS THIS... IS THIS HIS MIND?
I THINK SO...
HUH?
YOU TWO...

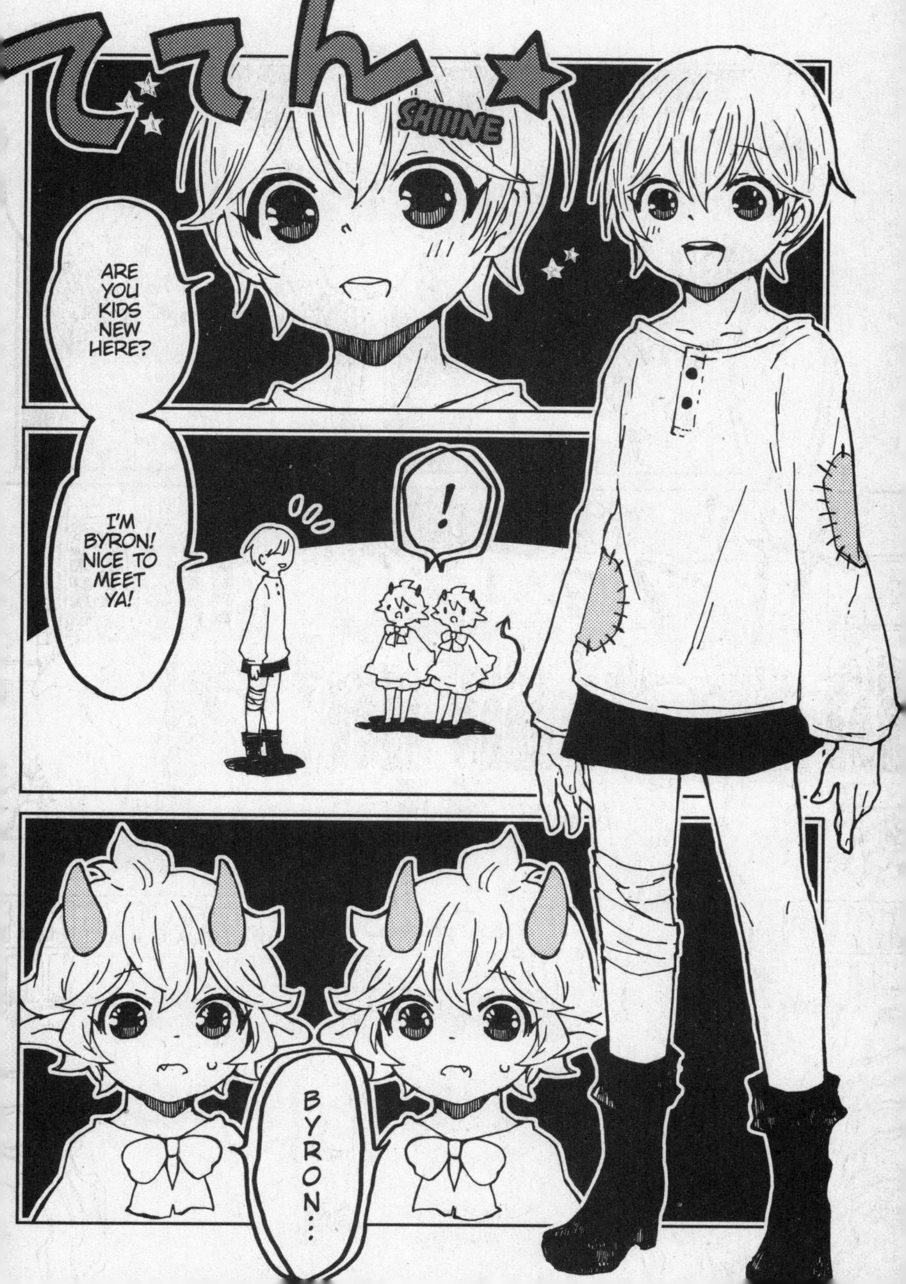
ててん
SHIIINE
ARE YOU KIDS NEW HERE?
I'M BYRON! NICE TO MEET YA!
!
BYRON...

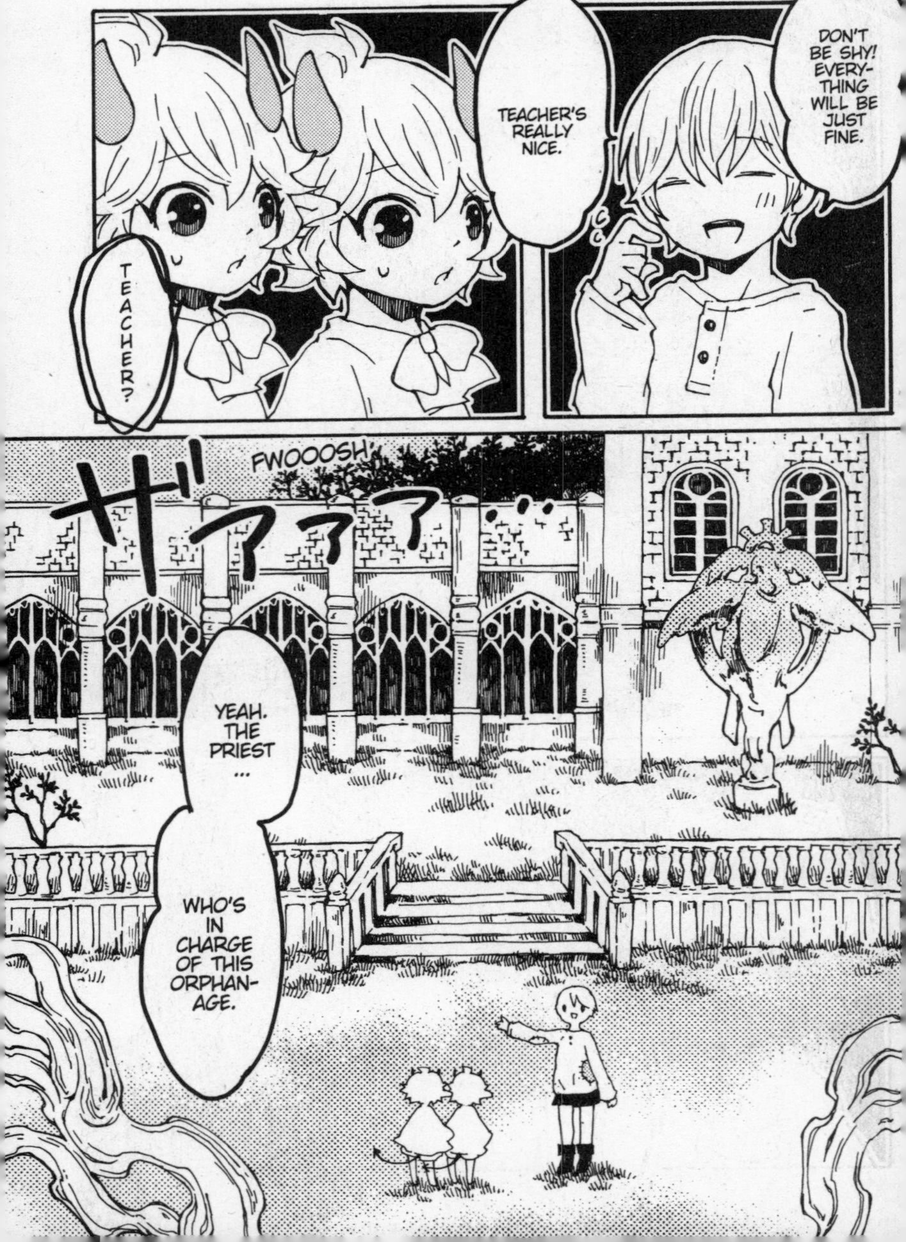
DON'T BE SHY! EVERYTHING WILL BE JUST FINE.
TEACHER'S REALLY NICE.
TEACHER?
ザアアア
FWOOOSH
YEAH. THE PRIEST...
WHO'S IN CHARGE OF THIS ORPHANAGE.

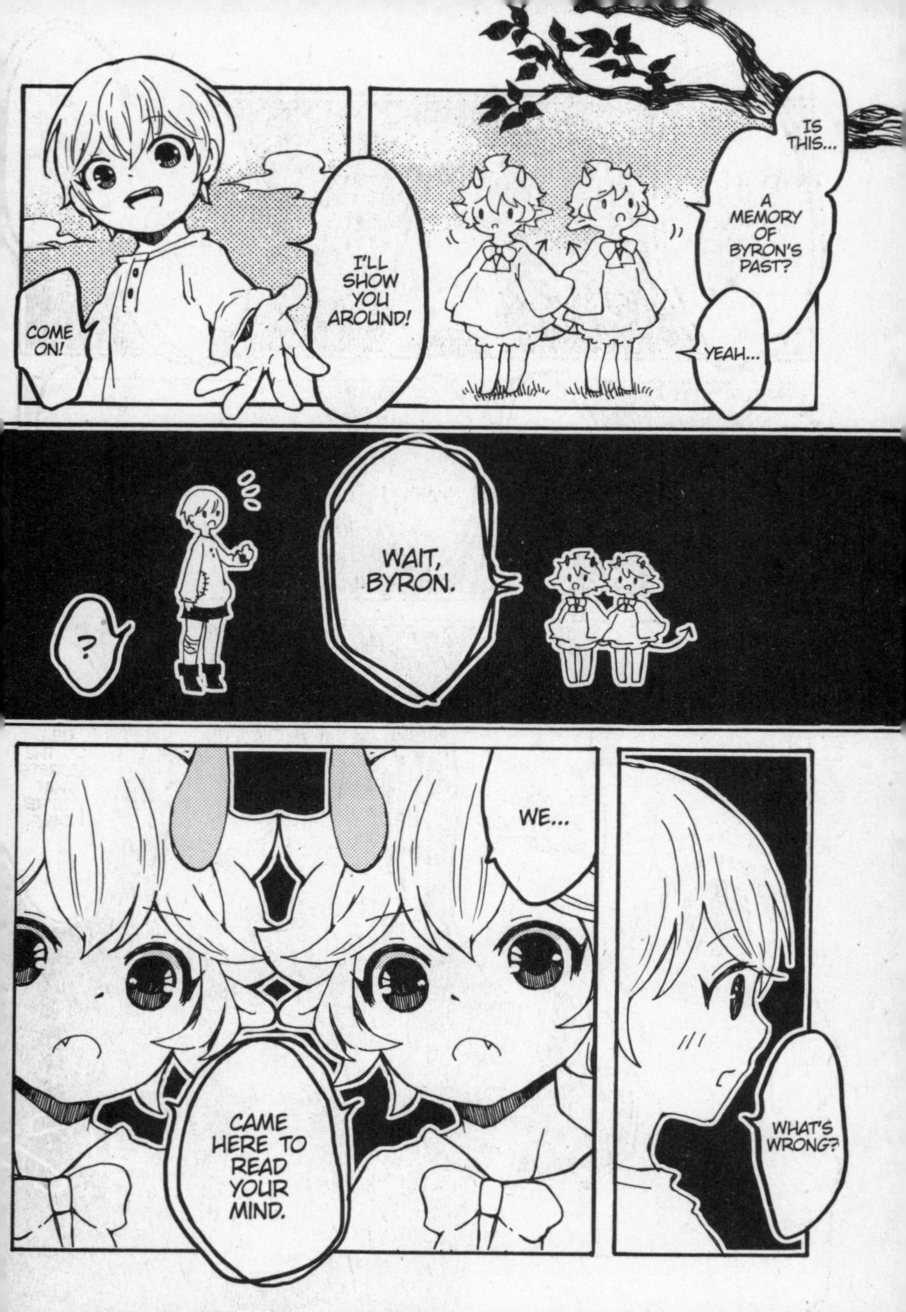
IS THIS... A MEMORY OF BYRON'S PAST?
YEAH...
I'LL SHOW YOU AROUND!
COME ON!
WAIT, BYRON.
?
WHAT'S WRONG?
WE...
CAME HERE TO READ YOUR MIND.

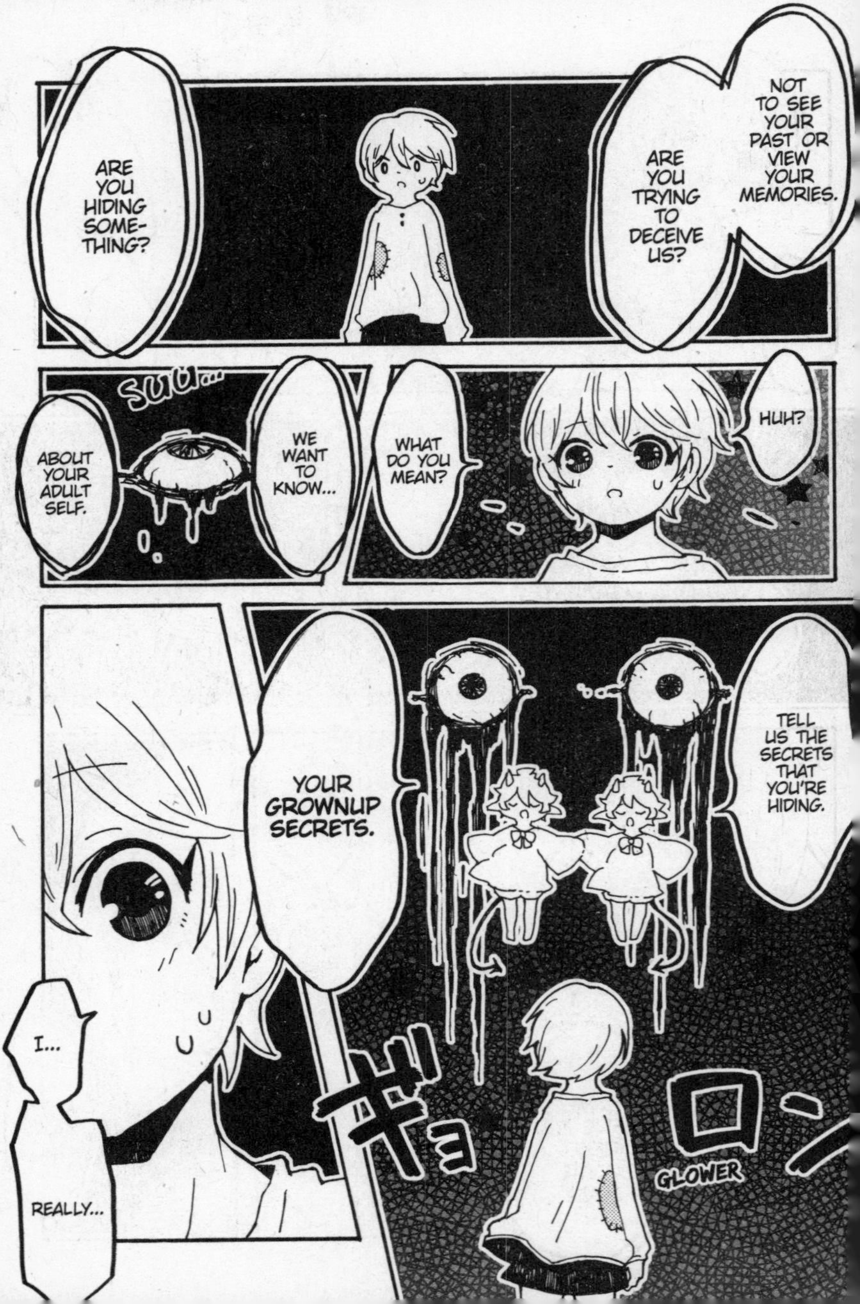
NOT TO SEE YOUR PAST OR VIEW YOUR MEMORIES.
ARE YOU TRYING TO DECEIVE US?
ARE YOU HIDING SOME-THING?
HUH?
WHAT DO YOU MEAN?
SUU...
WE WANT TO KNOW...
ABOUT YOUR ADULT SELF.
TELL US THE SECRETS THAT YOU'RE HIDING.
YOUR GROWNUP SECRETS.
ギョロン
GLOWER
I...
REALLY...

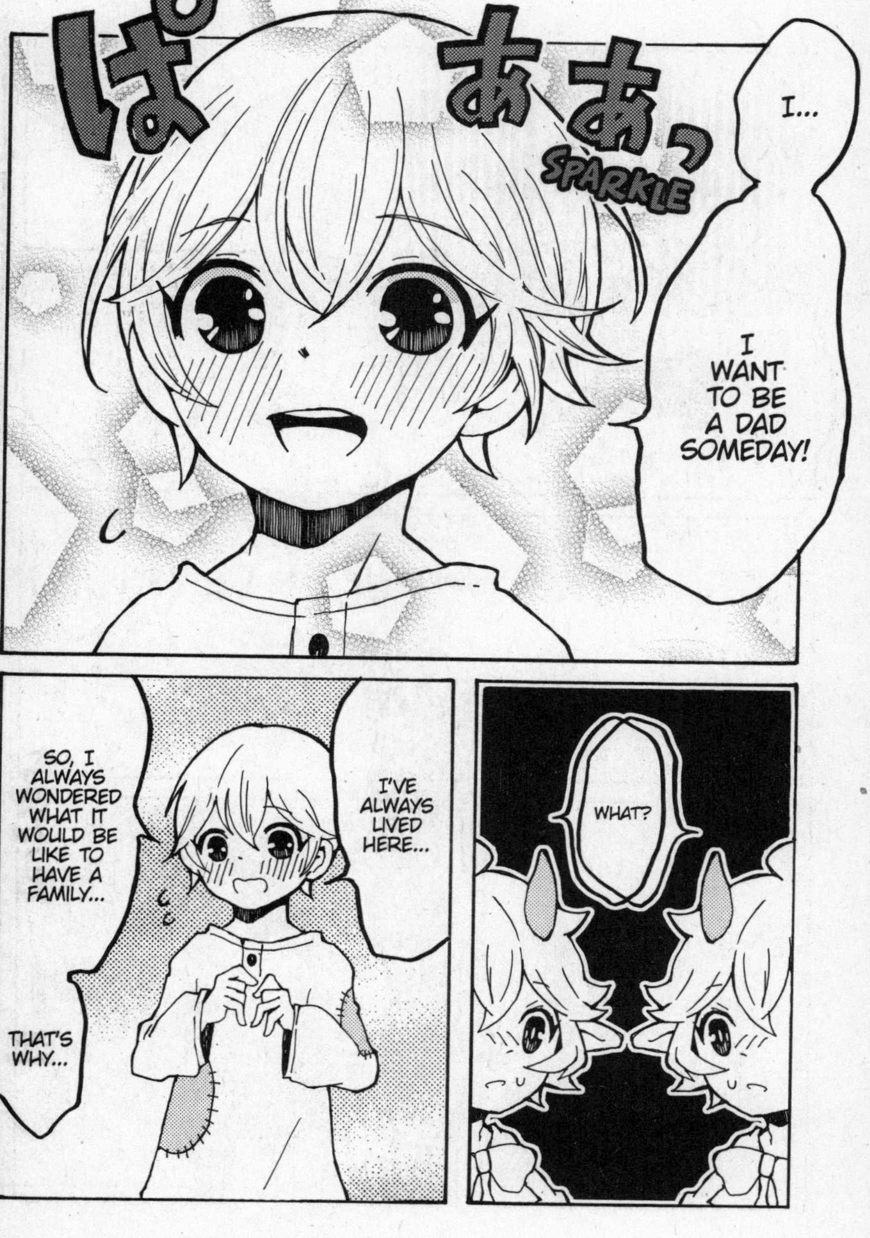
I... I WANT TO BE A DAD SOMEDAY!
ぱあぁっ
SPARKLE
WHAT?
I'VE ALWAYS LIVED HERE...
SO, I ALWAYS WONDERED WHAT IT WOULD BE LIKE TO HAVE A FAMILY...
THAT'S WHY...

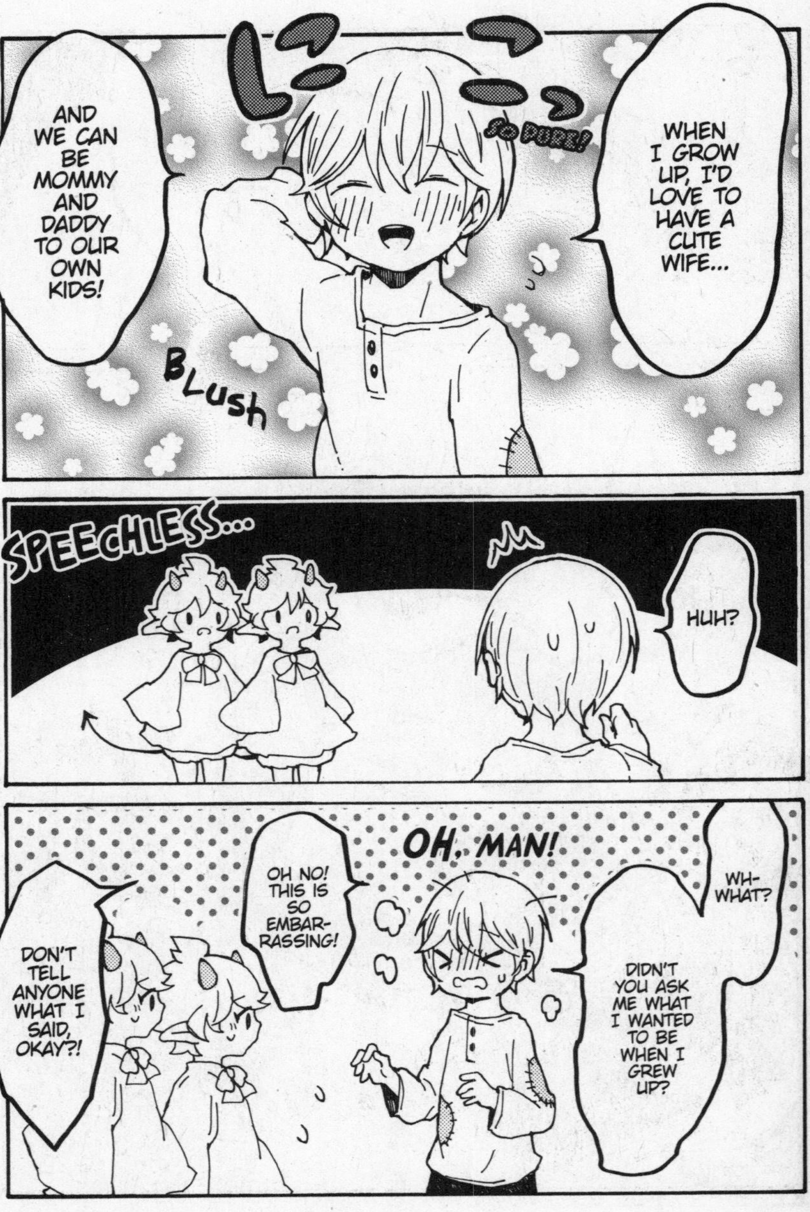
WHEN I GROW UP, I'D LOVE TO HAVE A CUTE WIFE...
SO PURE!
AND WE CAN BE MOMMY AND DADDY TO OUR OWN KIDS!
BLUSH
HUH?
SPEECHLESS...
WH- WHAT?
DIDN'T YOU ASK ME WHAT I WANTED TO BE WHEN I GREW UP?
OH, MAN!
OH NO! THIS IS SO EMBARRASSING!
DON'T TELL ANYONE WHAT I SAID, OKAY?!

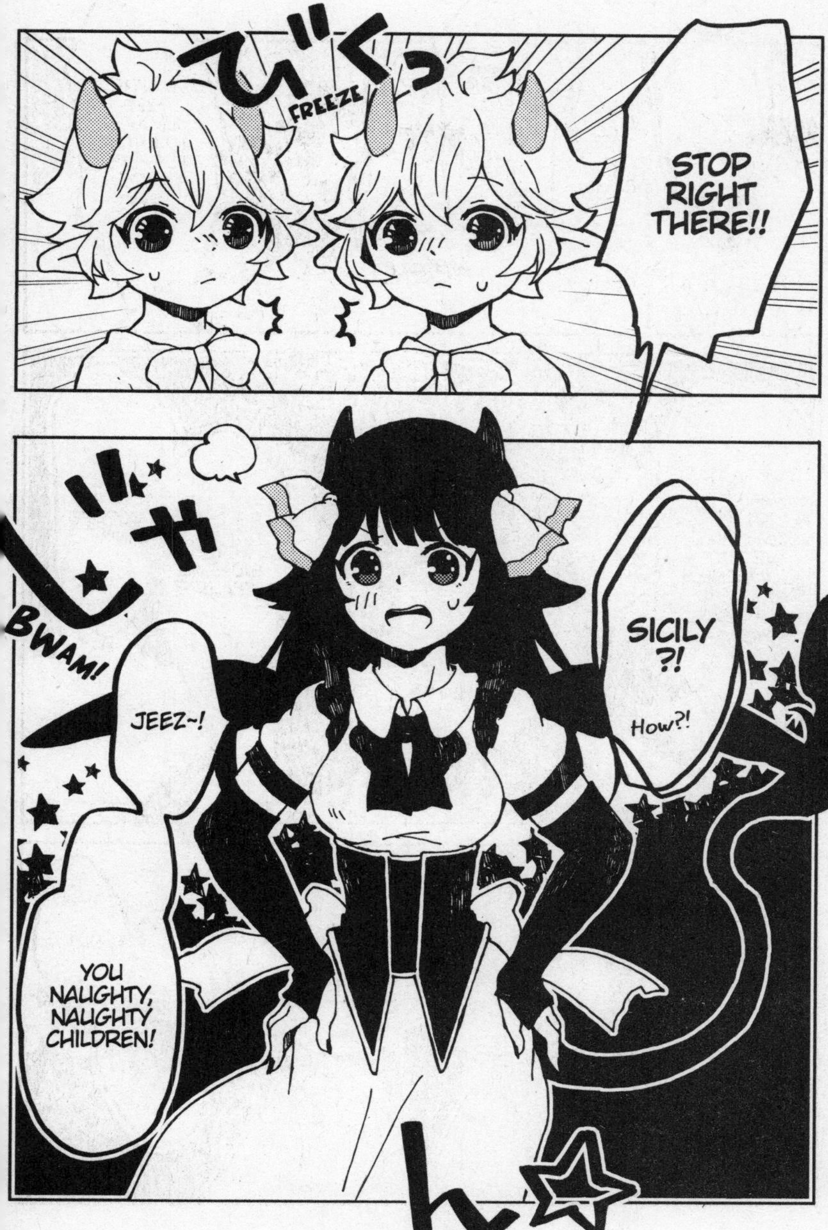
STOP RIGHT THERE!!
びくっ
FREEZE
SICILY ?!
How?!
JEEZ~!
BWAM!
YOU NAUGHTY, NAUGHTY CHILDREN!

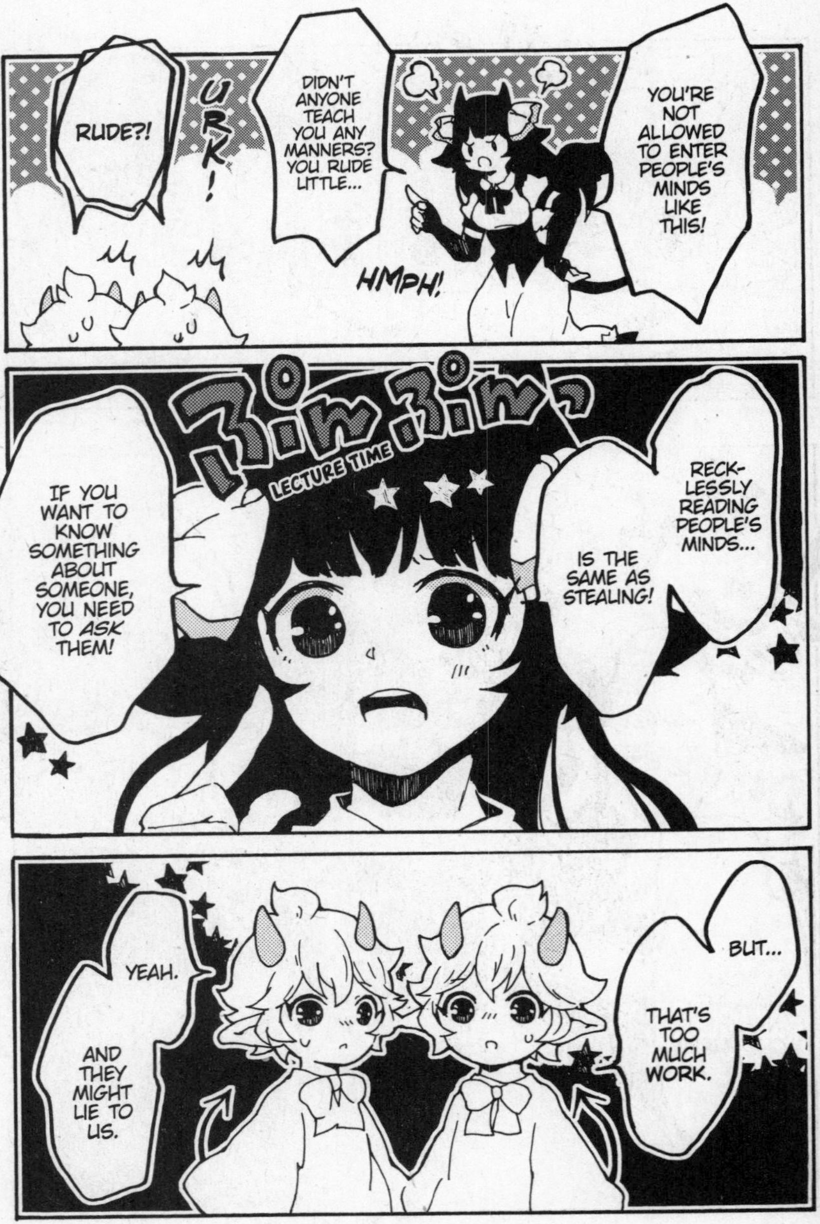
YOU'RE NOT ALLOWED TO ENTER PEOPLE'S MINDS LIKE THIS!
DIDN'T ANYONE TEACH YOU ANY MANNERS? YOU RUDE LITTLE...
HMPH!
URK!
RUDE?!
LECTURE TIME
RECK-LESSLY READING PEOPLE'S MINDS...
IS THE SAME AS STEALING!
IF YOU WANT TO KNOW SOMETHING ABOUT SOMEONE, YOU NEED TO *ASK* THEM!
BUT...
THAT'S TOO MUCH WORK.
YEAH.
AND THEY MIGHT LIE TO US.

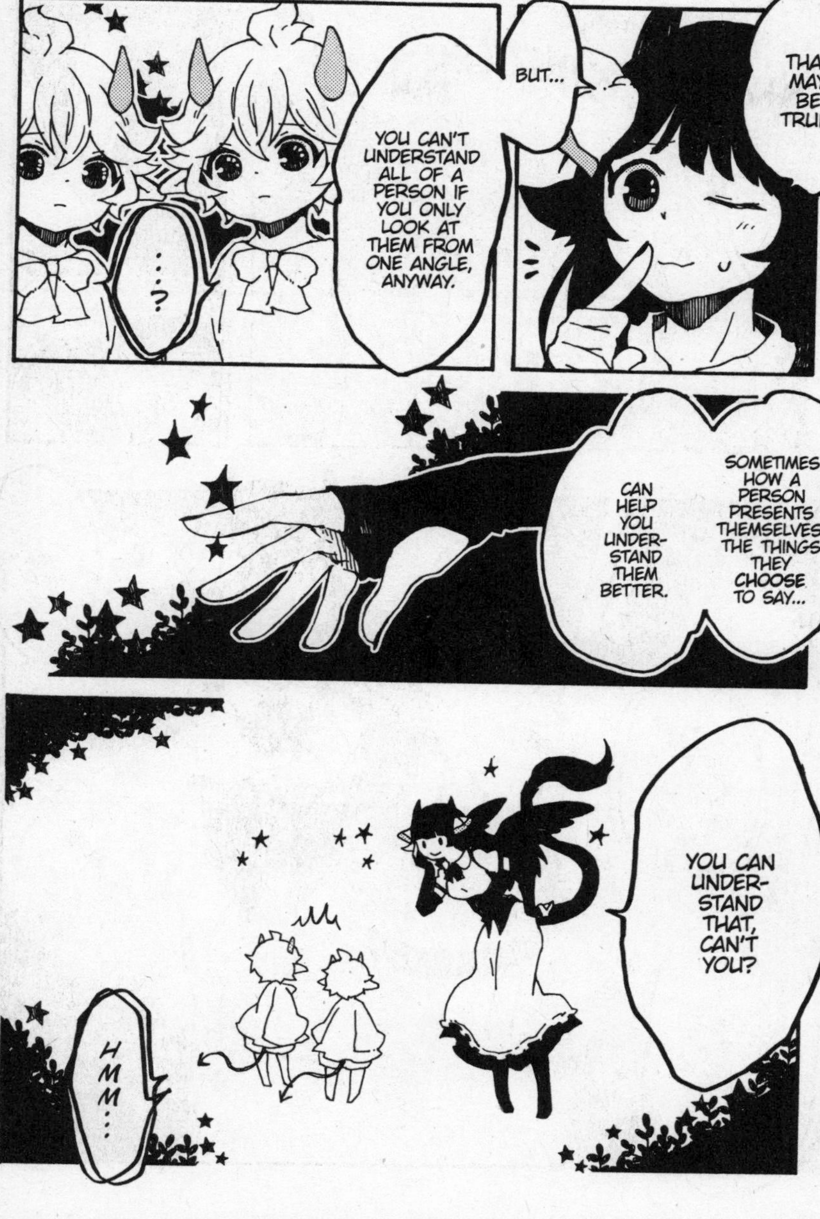
THAT MAY BE TRUE.
BUT...
YOU CAN'T UNDERSTAND ALL OF A PERSON IF YOU ONLY LOOK AT THEM FROM ONE ANGLE, ANYWAY.
...?
SOMETIMES HOW A PERSON PRESENTS THEMSELVES, THE THINGS THEY CHOOSE TO SAY...
CAN HELP YOU UNDER-STAND THEM BETTER.
YOU CAN UNDER-STAND THAT, CAN'T YOU?
HMM...

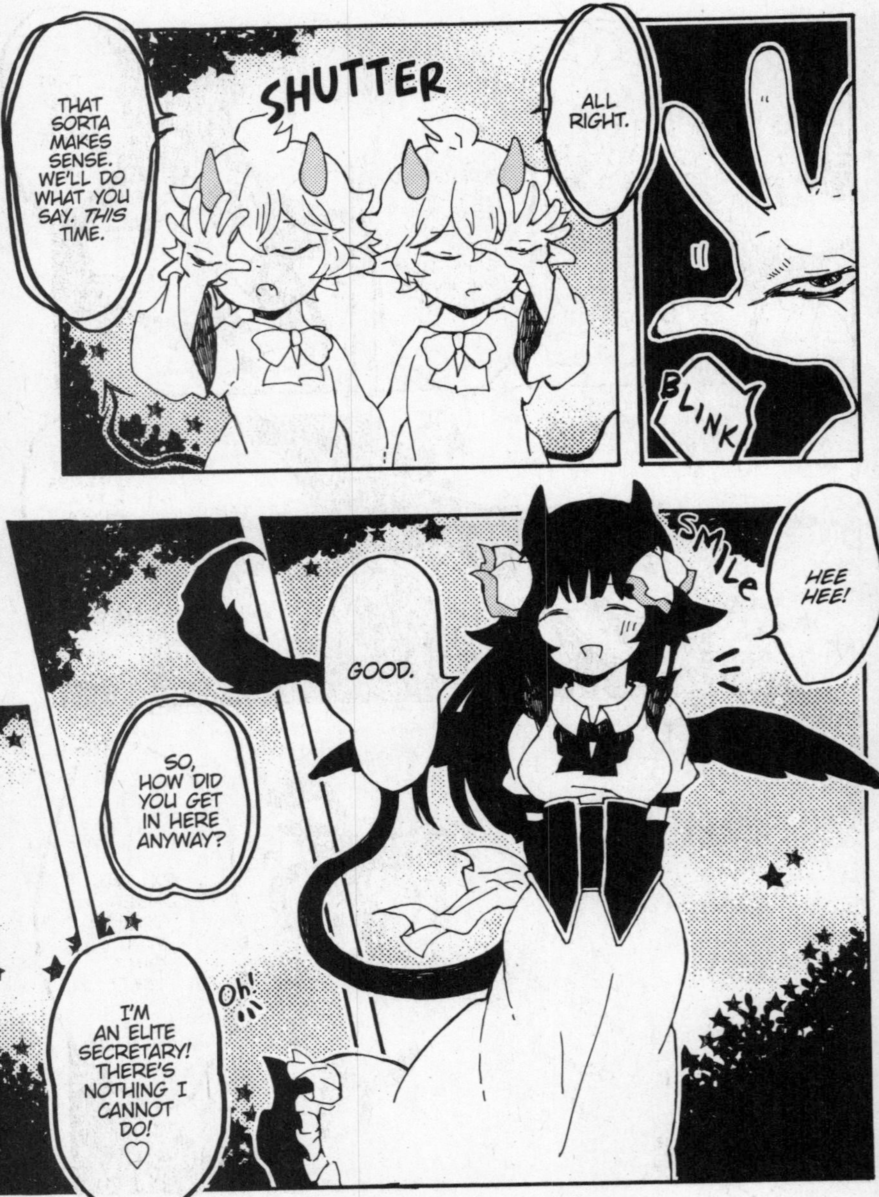
ALL RIGHT.
BLINK
SHUTTER
THAT SORTA MAKES SENSE. WE'LL DO WHAT YOU SAY. *THIS* TIME.
HEE HEE!
SMILE
GOOD.
SO, HOW DID YOU GET IN HERE ANYWAY?
Oh!
I'M AN ELITE SECRETARY! THERE'S NOTHING I CANNOT DO! ♡

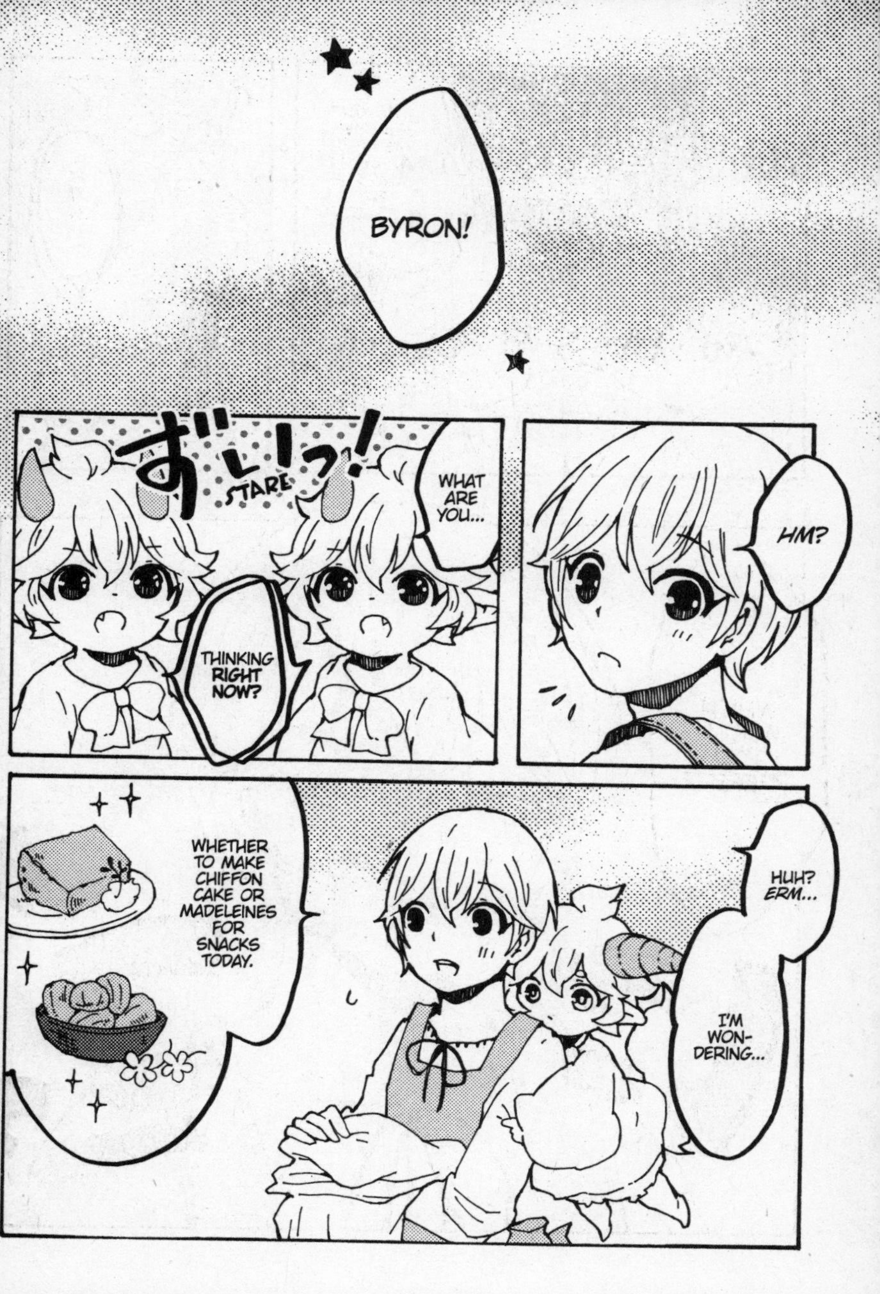
BYRON!
HM?
WHAT ARE YOU...
ずいっ!
STARE
THINKING RIGHT NOW?
HUH? ERM...
I'M WON-DERING...
WHETHER TO MAKE CHIFFON CAKE OR MADELEINES FOR SNACKS TODAY.

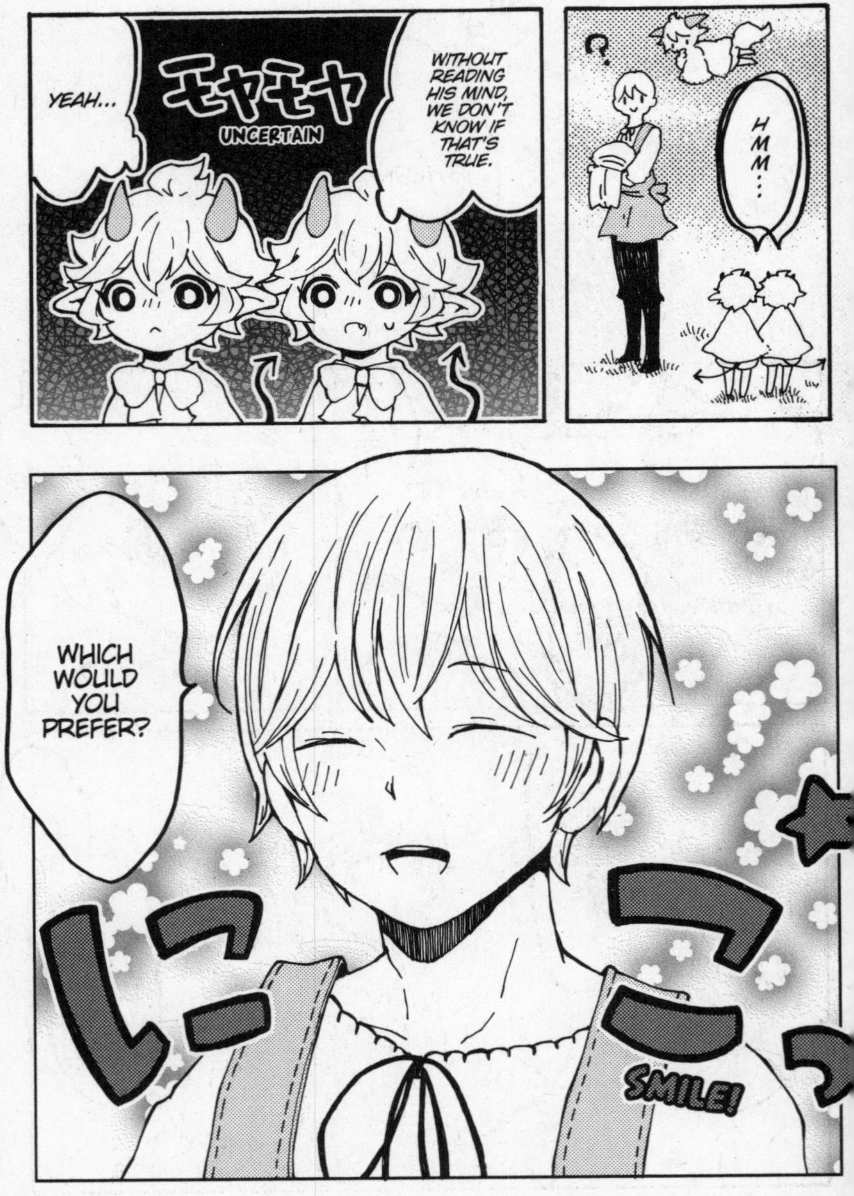
HMM...
WITHOUT READING HIS MIND, WE DON'T KNOW IF THAT'S TRUE.
モヤモヤ
UNCERTAIN
YEAH...
WHICH WOULD YOU PREFER?
SMILE!

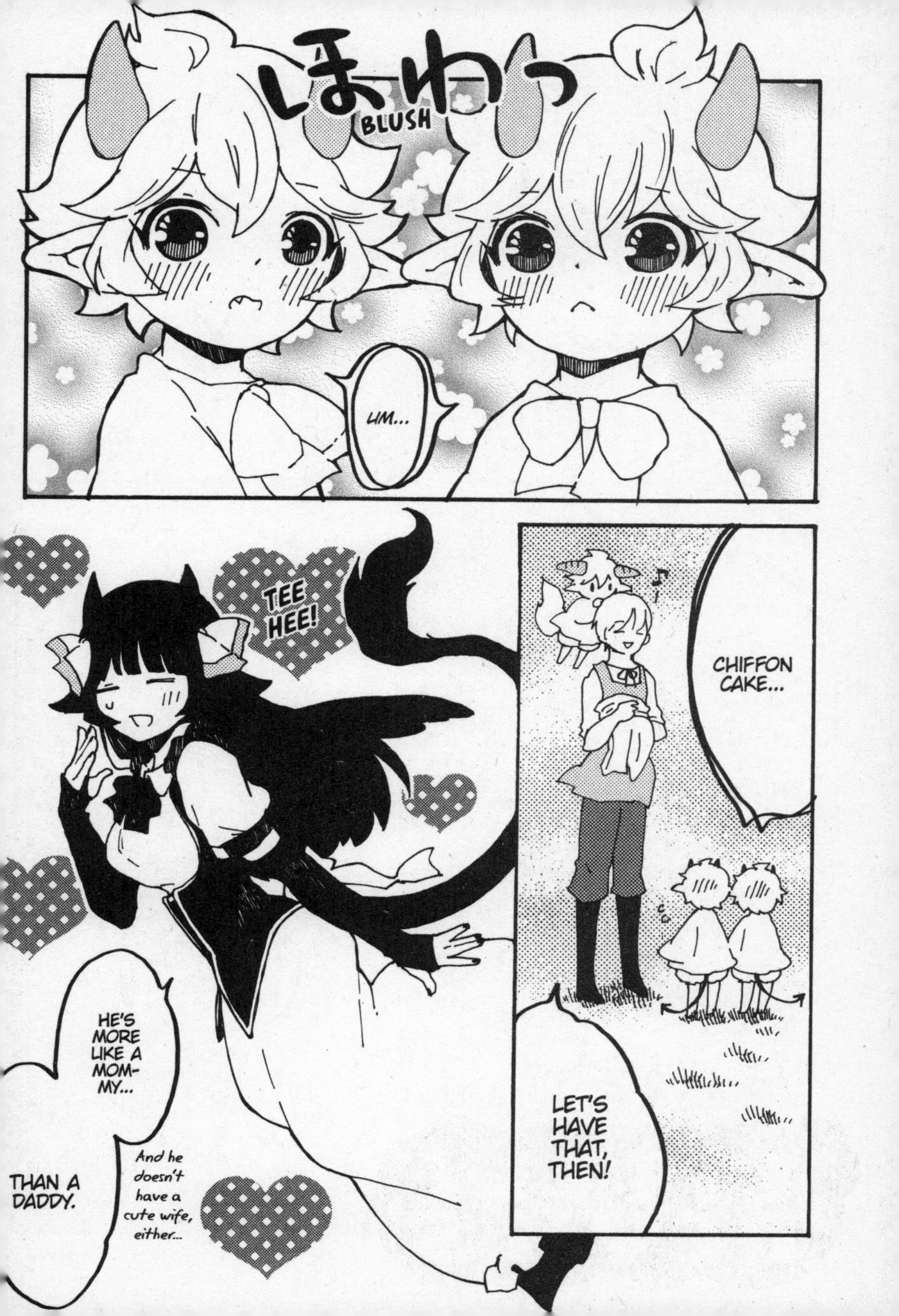
ほわっ
BLUSH
UM...
CHIFFON CAKE...
LET'S HAVE THAT, THEN!
TEE HEE!
HE'S MORE LIKE A MOMMY...
THAN A DADDY.
And he doesn't have a cute wife, either...

LITTLE DEVILS

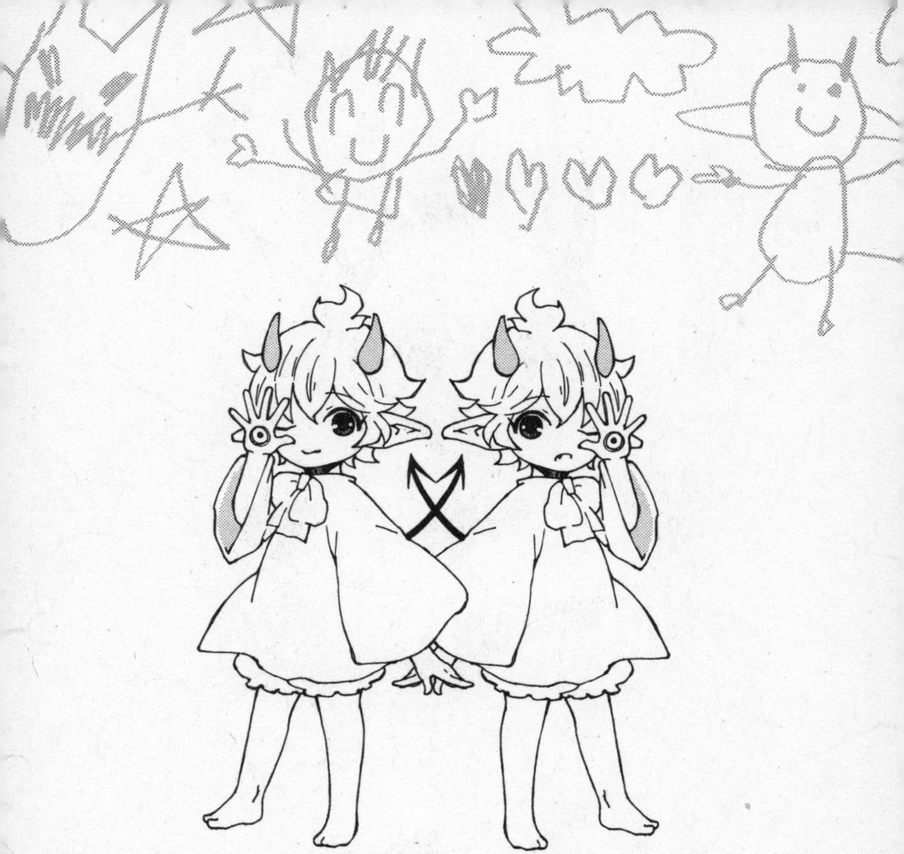

LILUVADOS AND LILOGADIS

These identical twins are a little strange. They can read people's minds, and because of that they never learned basic social skills.

They can't read the thoughts of anyone on a higher level than them, though.

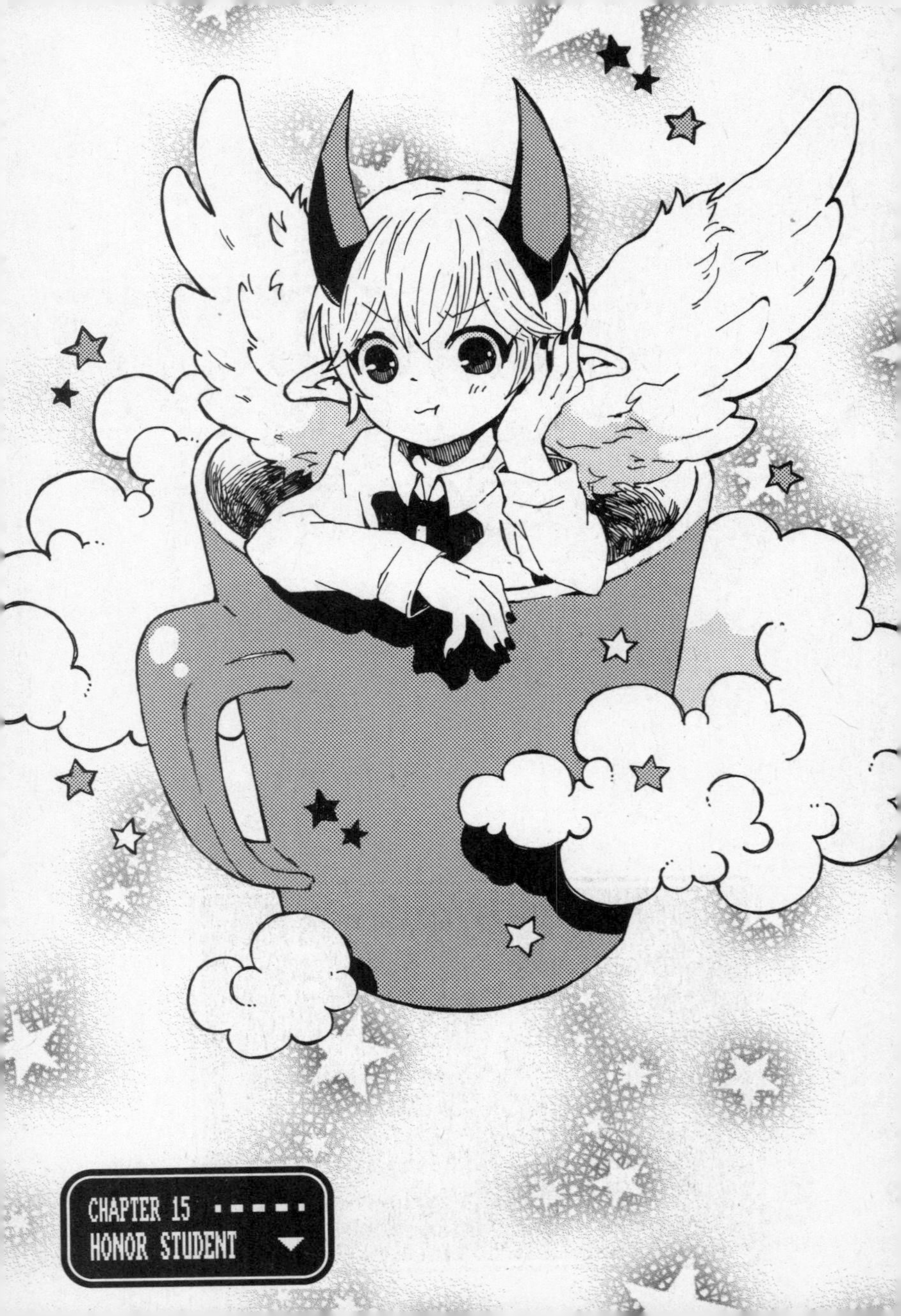

CHAPTER 15
HONOR STUDENT

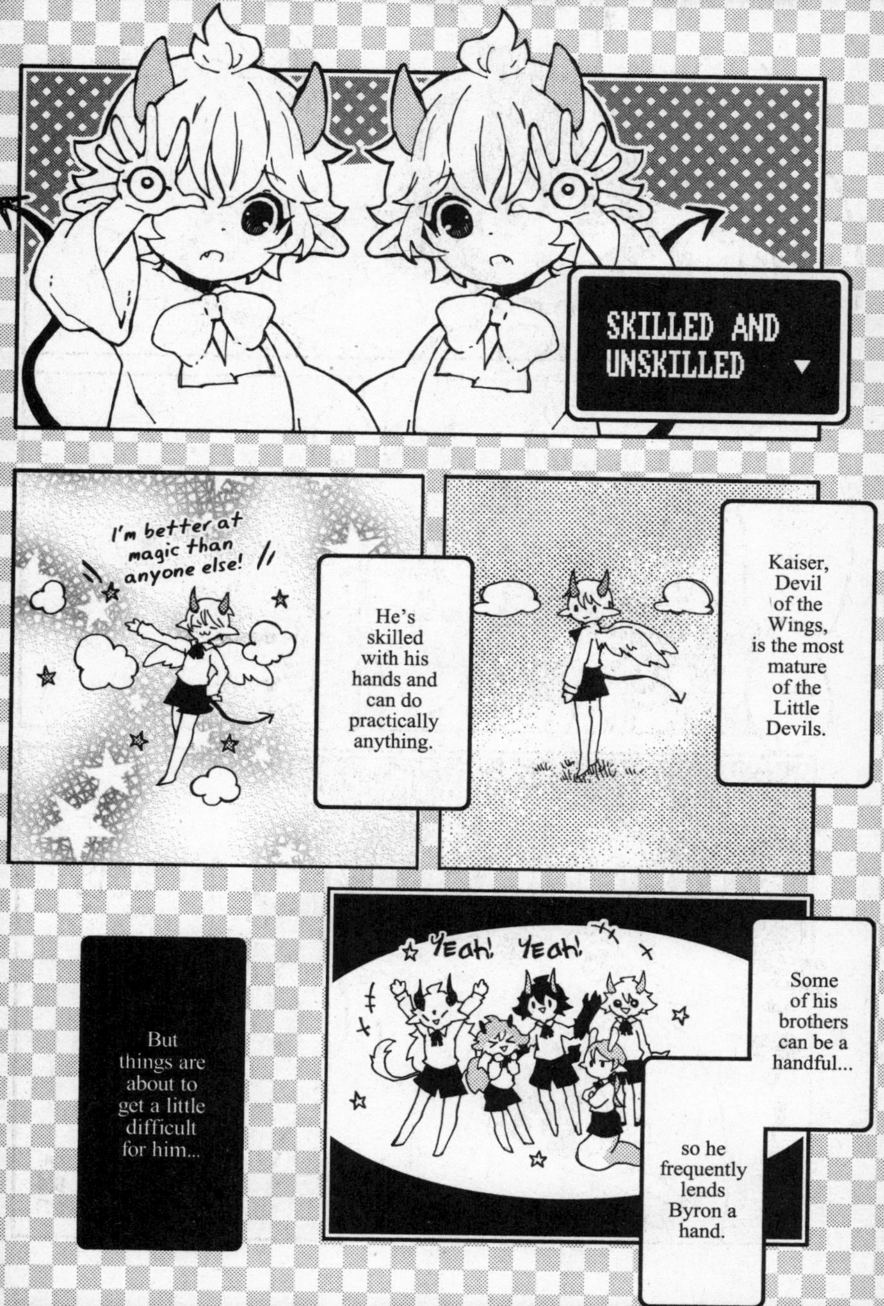
SKILLED AND UNSKILLED
Kaiser, Devil of the Wings, is the most mature of the Little Devils.
He's skilled with his hands and can do practically anything.
I'm better at magic than anyone else!
Some of his brothers can be a handful...
YEAH! YEAH!
so he frequently lends Byron a hand.
But things are about to get a little difficult for him...

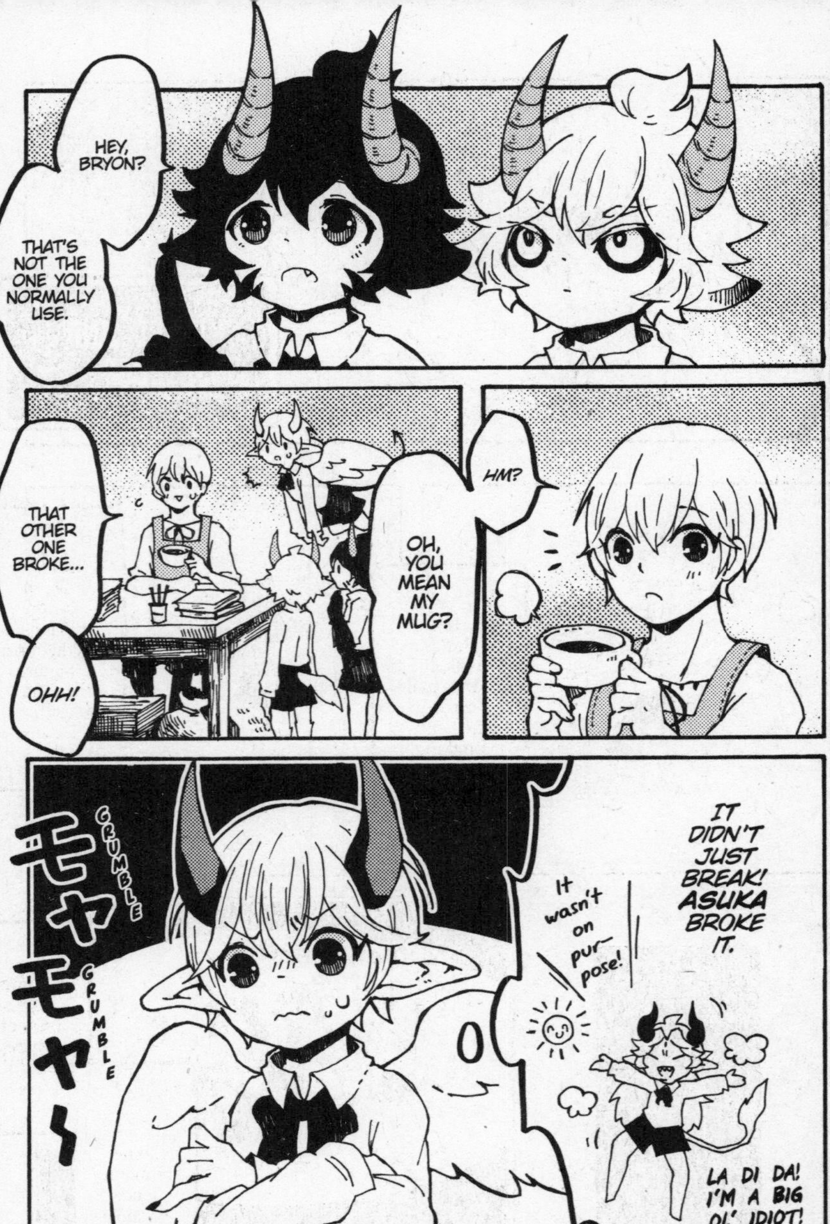
HEY, BRYON?
THAT'S NOT THE ONE YOU NORMALLY USE.
HM?
OH, YOU MEAN MY MUG?
THAT OTHER ONE BROKE...
OHH!
IT DIDN'T JUST BREAK! ASUKA BROKE IT.
It wasn't on pur-pose!
LA DI DA! I'M A BIG OL' IDIOT!
モヤモヤ~
GRUMBLE GRUMBLE

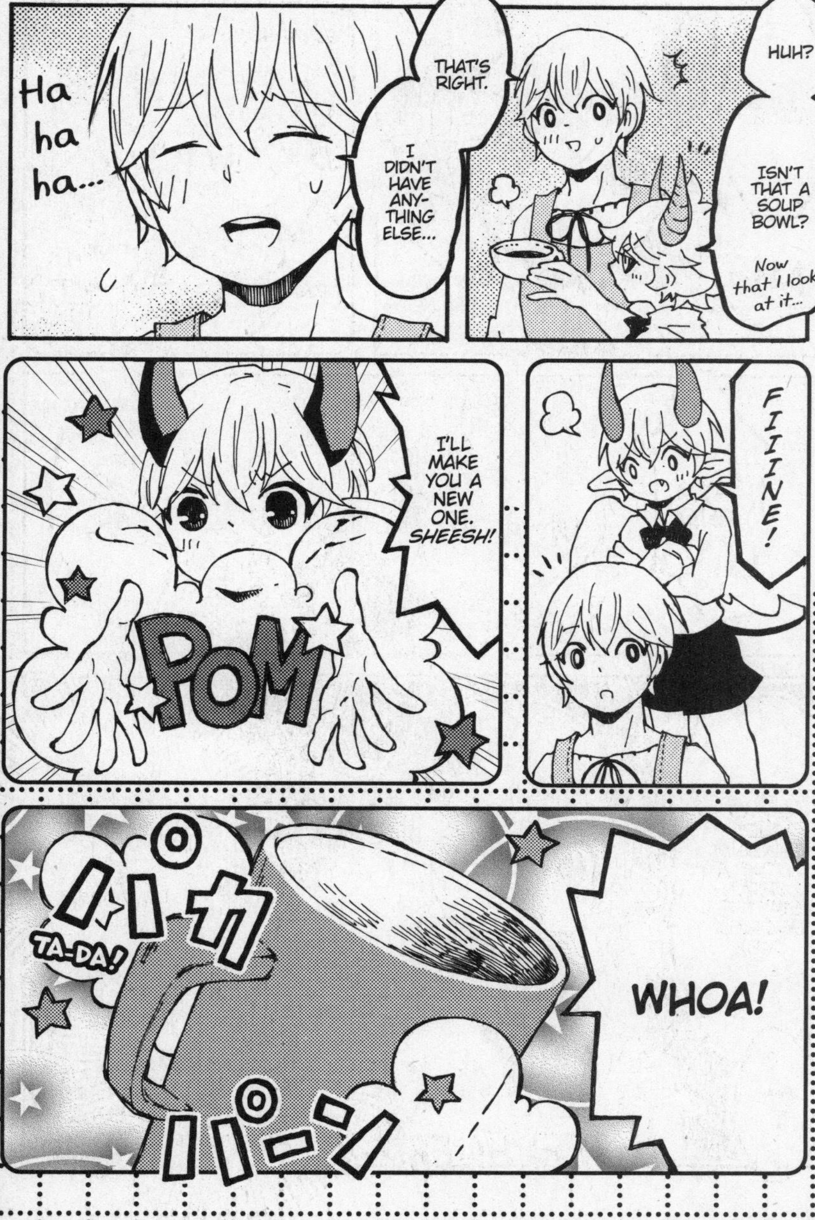
HUH?
ISN'T THAT A SOUP BOWL?
Now that I look at it...
THAT'S RIGHT.
I DIDN'T HAVE ANY-THING ELSE...
Ha ha ha...
FIIINE!
I'LL MAKE YOU A NEW ONE. SHEESH!
POM
WHOA!
パカ
TA-DA!
パーン!

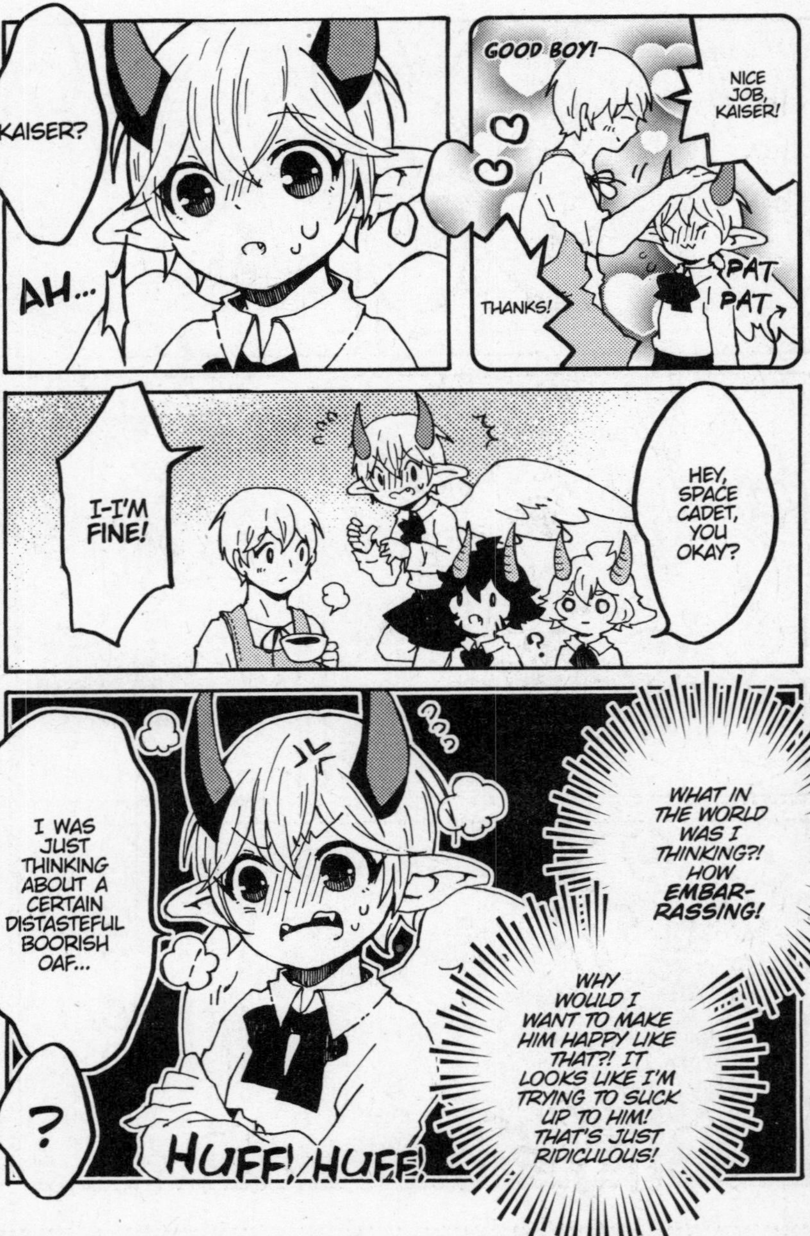
GOOD BOY!
NICE JOB, KAISER!
THANKS!
PAT PAT
KAISER?
AH...
HEY, SPACE CADET, YOU OKAY?
I-I'M FINE!
WHAT IN THE WORLD WAS I THINKING?! HOW EMBARRASSING!
WHY WOULD I WANT TO MAKE HIM HAPPY LIKE THAT?! IT LOOKS LIKE I'M TRYING TO SUCK UP TO HIM! THAT'S JUST RIDICULOUS!
I WAS JUST THINKING ABOUT A CERTAIN DISTASTEFUL BOORISH OAF...
?
HUFF! HUFF!

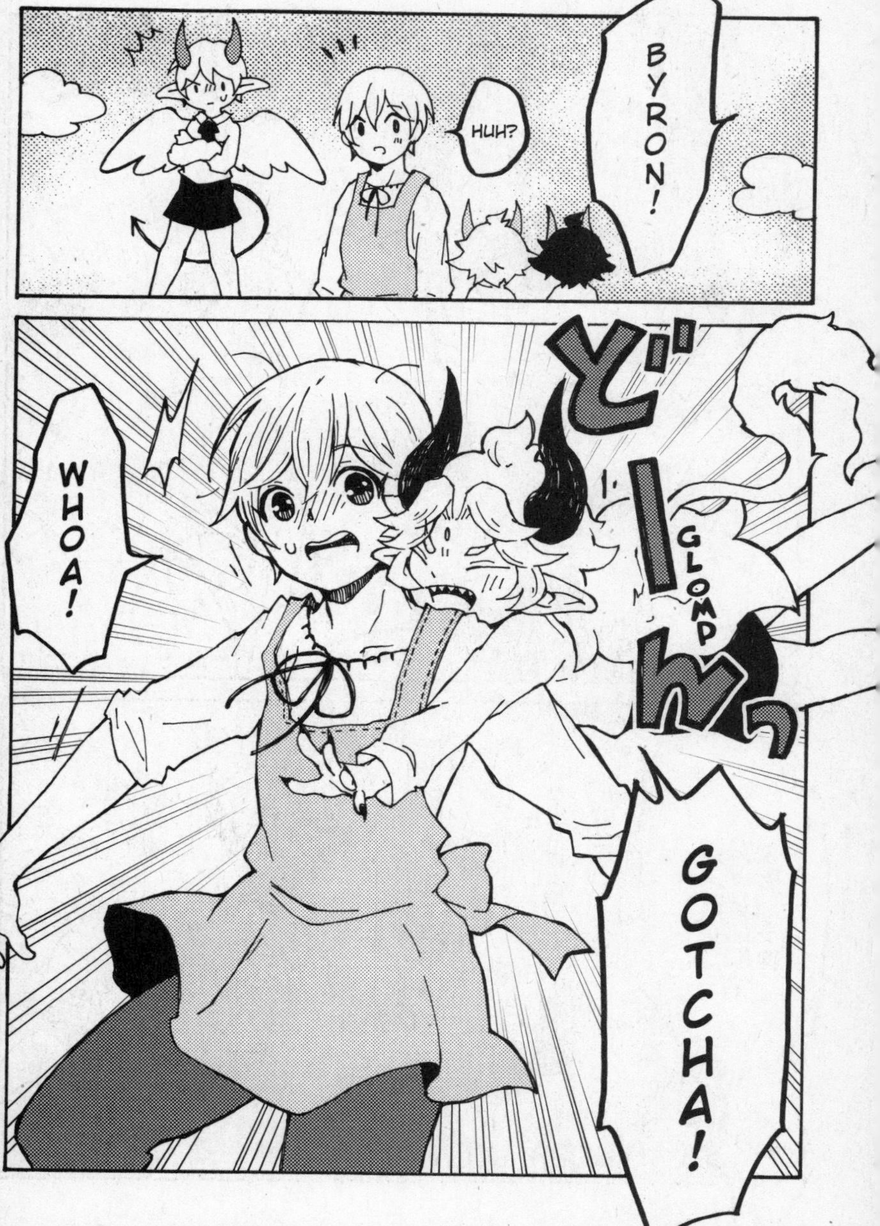
BYRON!
HUH?
どーんっ
GLOMP
GOTCHA!
WHOA!

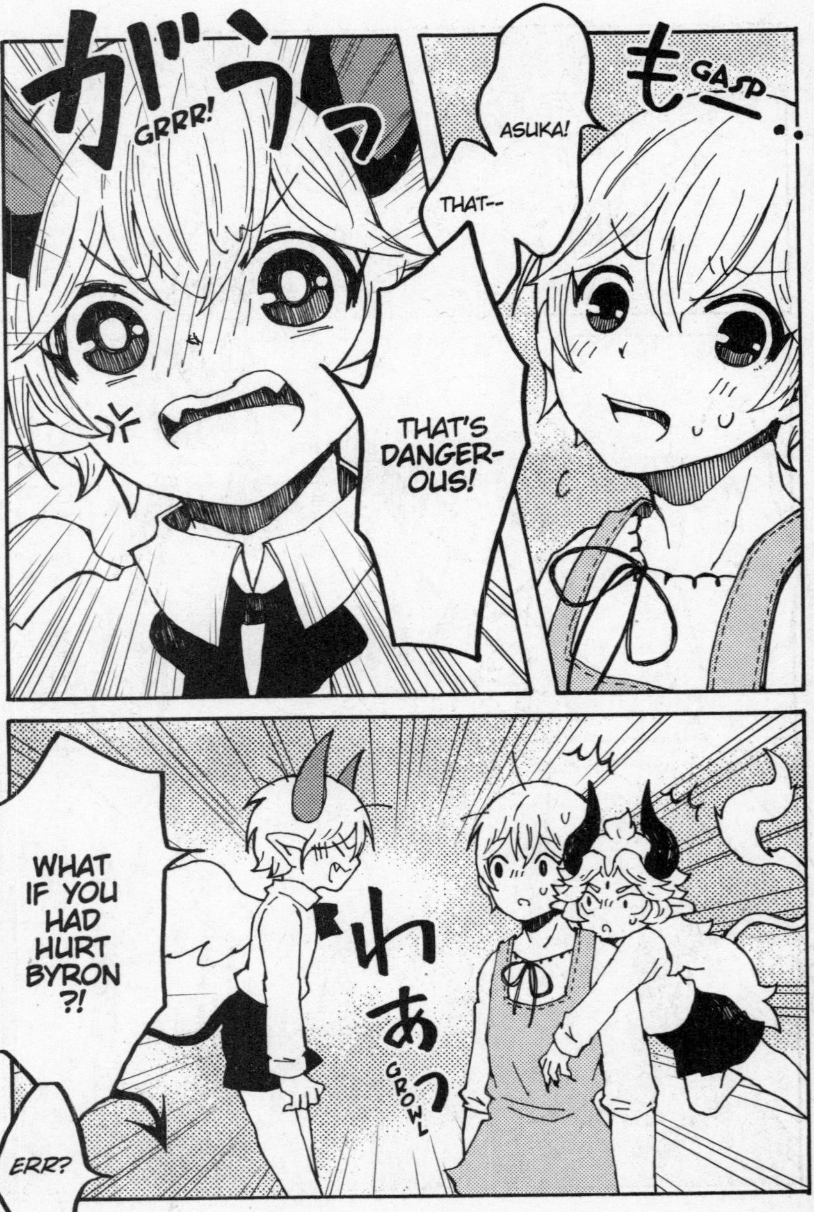
も
GASP
ASUKA!
THAT--
がうっ
GRRR!
THAT'S DANGER-OUS!
わあっ
GROWL
WHAT IF YOU HAD HURT BYRON?!
ERR?

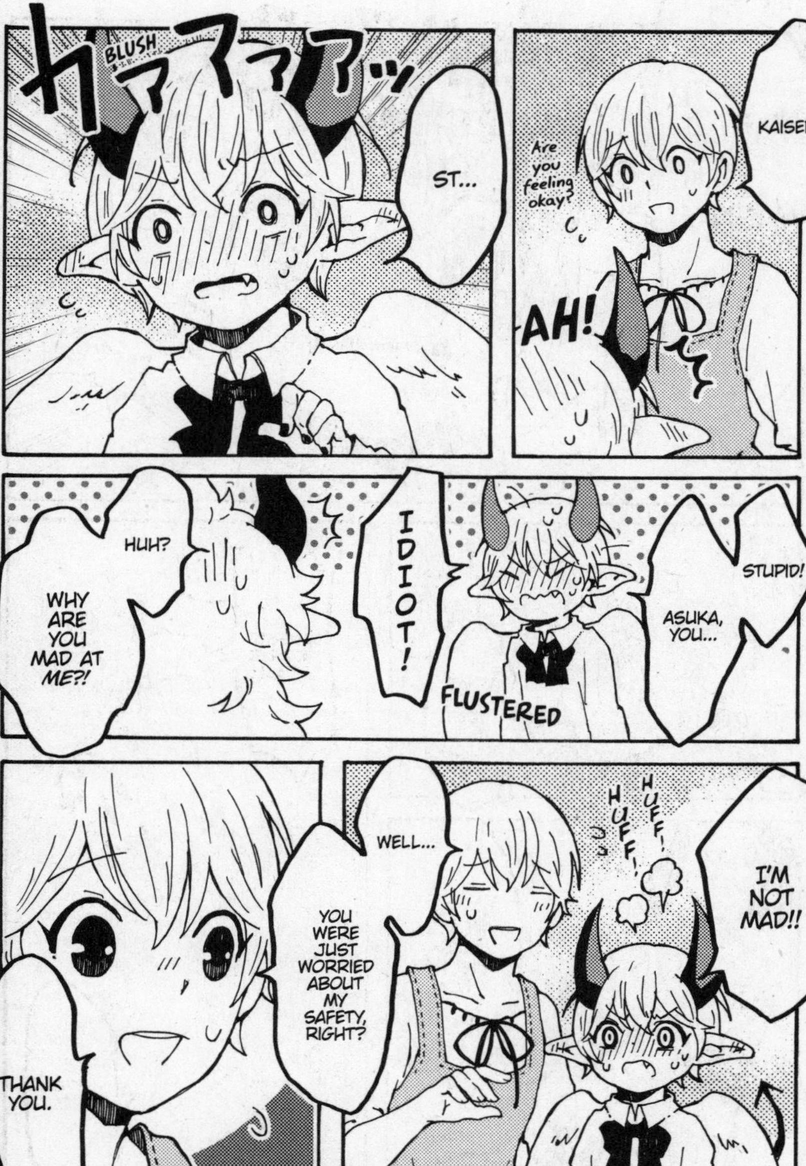
KAISER?
Are you feeling okay?
AH!
カァァァァッ
BLUSH
ST...
STUPID!
ASUKA, YOU...
IDIOT!
FLUSTERED
HUH?
WHY ARE YOU MAD AT ME?!
I'M NOT MAD!!
HUFF HUFF
HUFF HUFF
WELL...
YOU WERE JUST WORRIED ABOUT MY SAFETY, RIGHT?
THANK YOU.

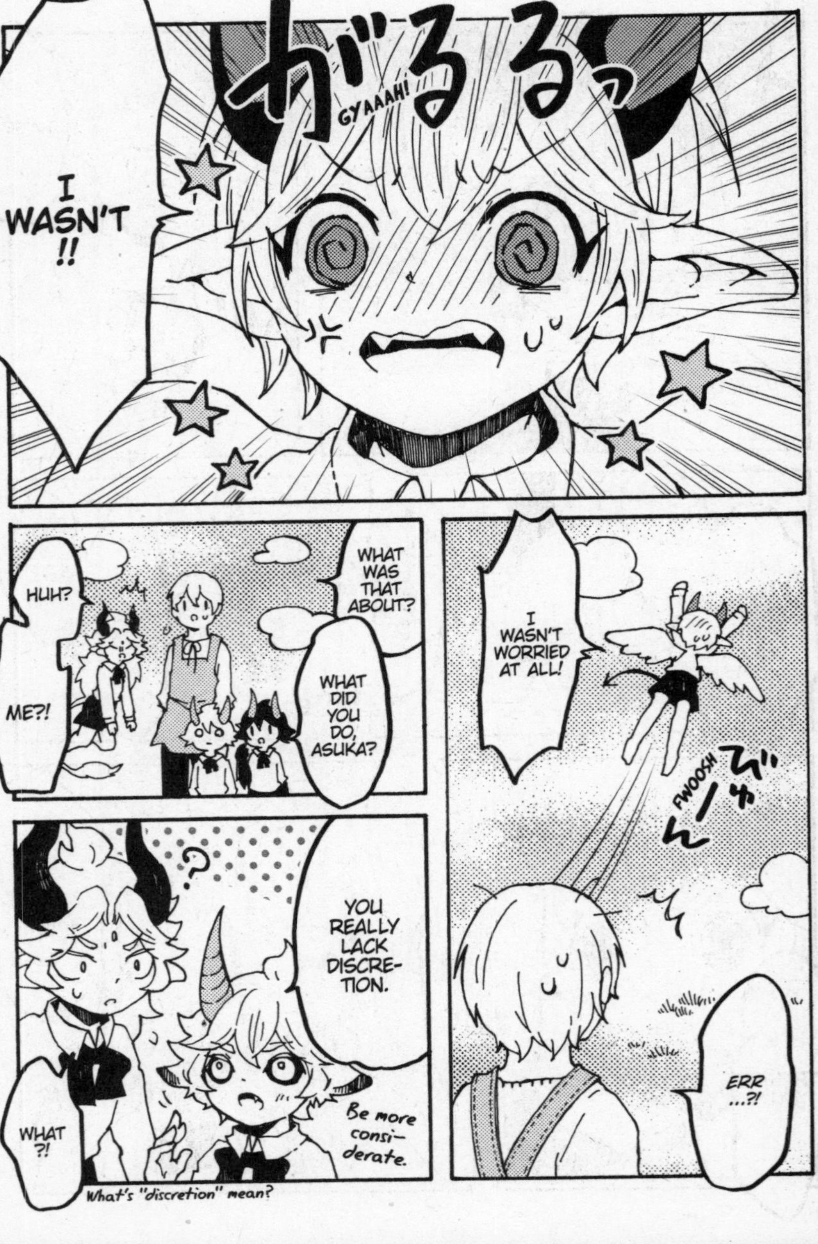
がるるっ
GYAAAH!
I WASN'T!!
I WASN'T WORRIED AT ALL!
びゅーん
FWOOSH
ERR...?!
WHAT WAS THAT ABOUT?
WHAT DID YOU DO, ASUKA?
HUH?
ME?!
YOU REALLY LACK DISCRETION.
Be more considerate.
WHAT?!
What's "discretion" mean?

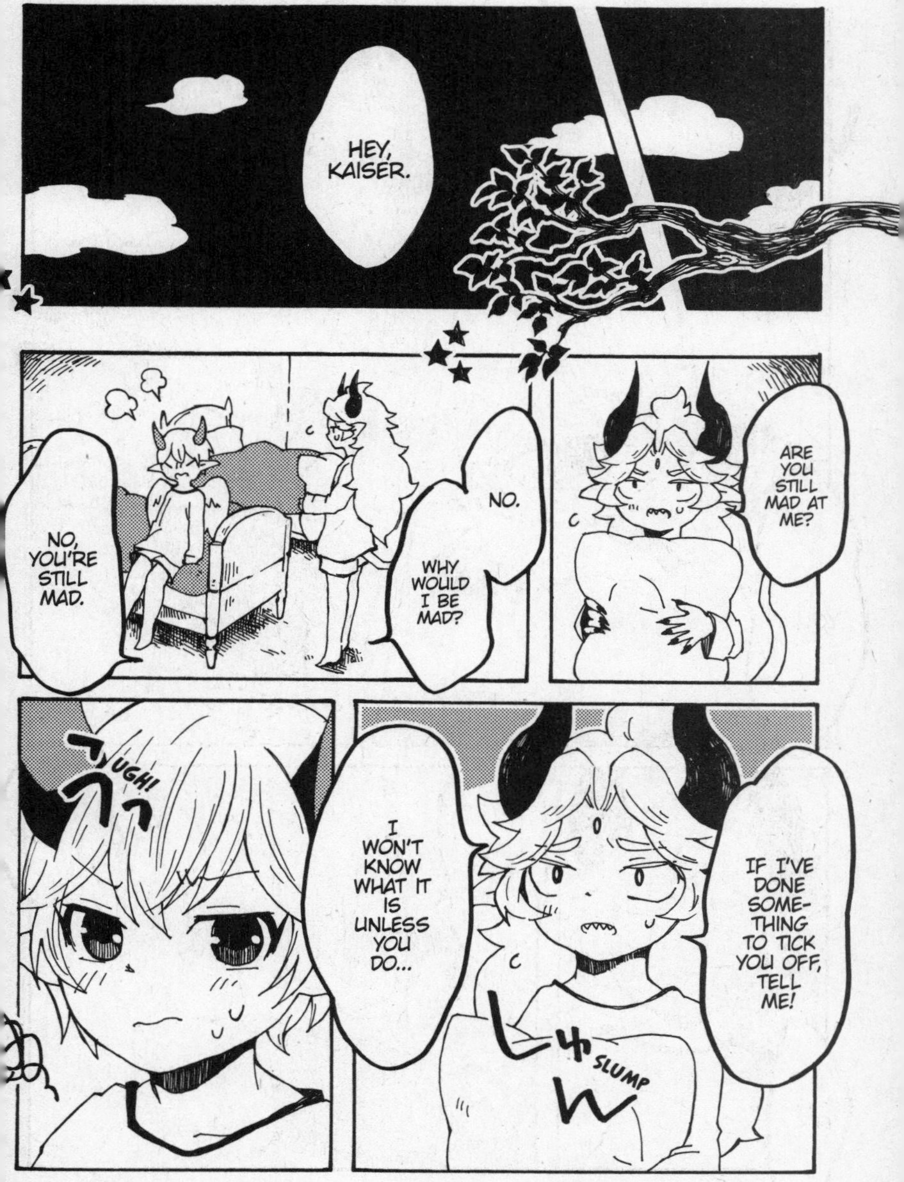
HEY, KAISER.
ARE YOU STILL MAD AT ME?
NO.
WHY WOULD I BE MAD?
NO, YOU'RE STILL MAD.
IF I'VE DONE SOME-THING TO TICK YOU OFF, TELL ME!
I WON'T KNOW WHAT IT IS UNLESS YOU DO...
SLUMP
UGH!

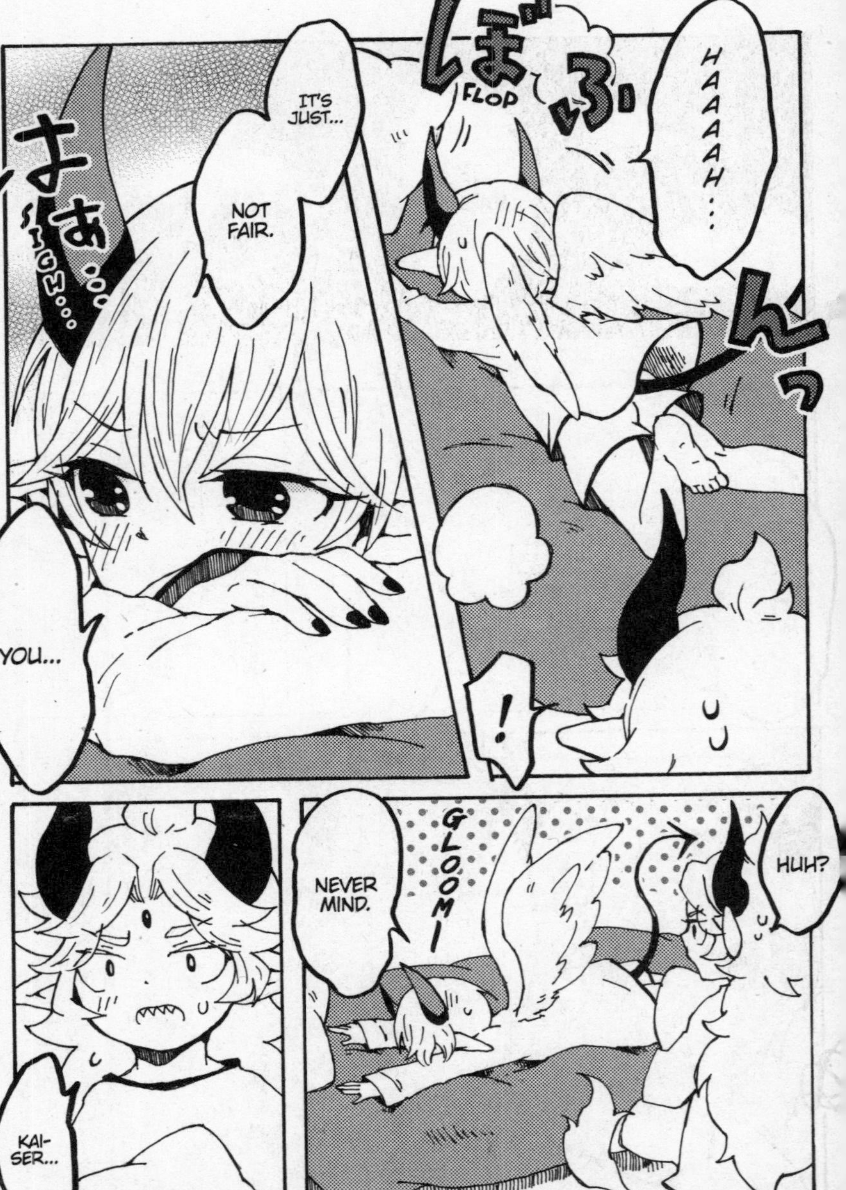
ぼふ
FLOP
HAAAAH...
んっ
!
IT'S JUST...
NOT FAIR.
はぁ
SIGH...
YOU...
HUH?
GLOOM
NEVER MIND.
KAI-SER...

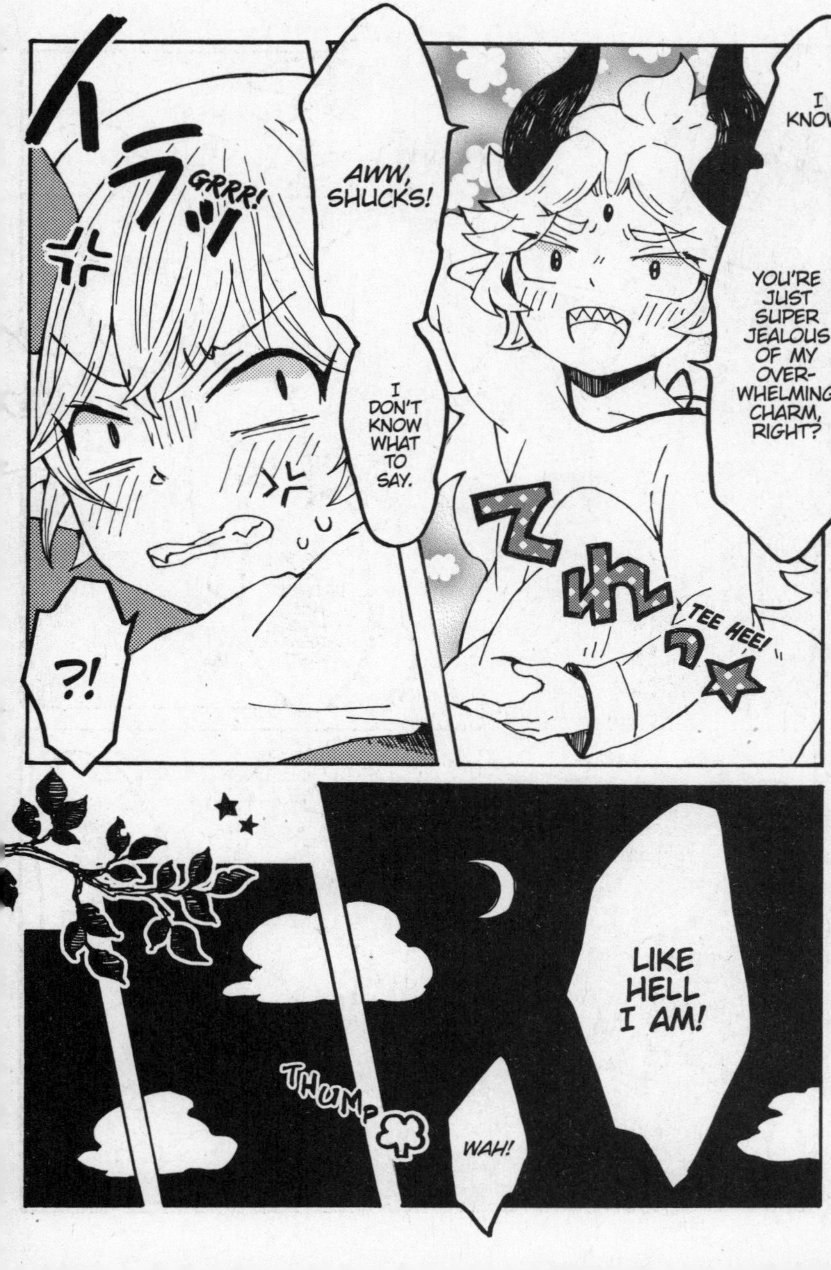
I KNOW!
YOU'RE JUST SUPER JEALOUS OF MY OVER-WHELMING CHARM, RIGHT?
TEE HEE!
AWW, SHUCKS!
I DON'T KNOW WHAT TO SAY.
GRRR!
?!
LIKE HELL I AM!
WAH!
THUMP

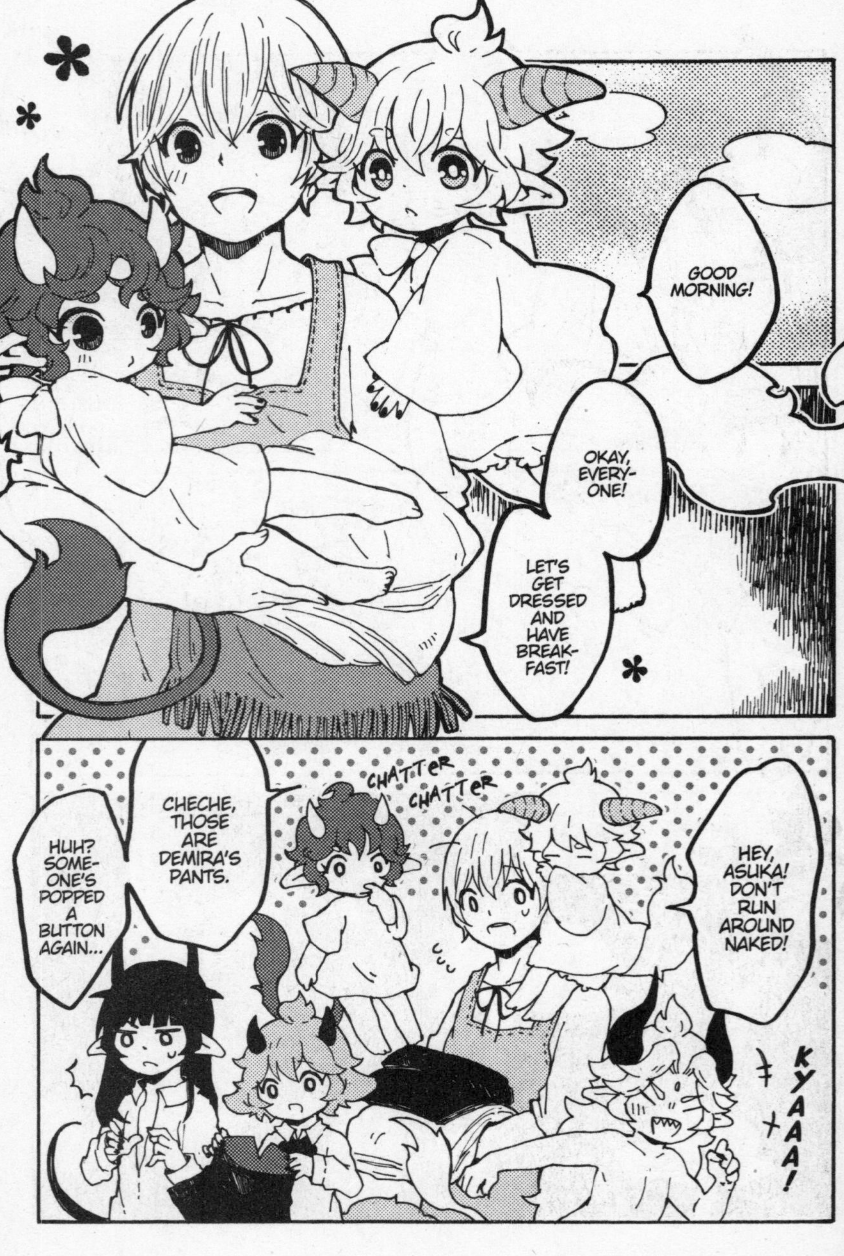
GOOD MORNING!
OKAY, EVERYONE!
LET'S GET DRESSED AND HAVE BREAKFAST!
HEY, ASUKA! DON'T RUN AROUND NAKED!
KYAAA!
CHATTER CHATTER
CHECHE, THOSE ARE DEMIRA'S PANTS.
HUH? SOMEONE'S POPPED A BUTTON AGAIN...

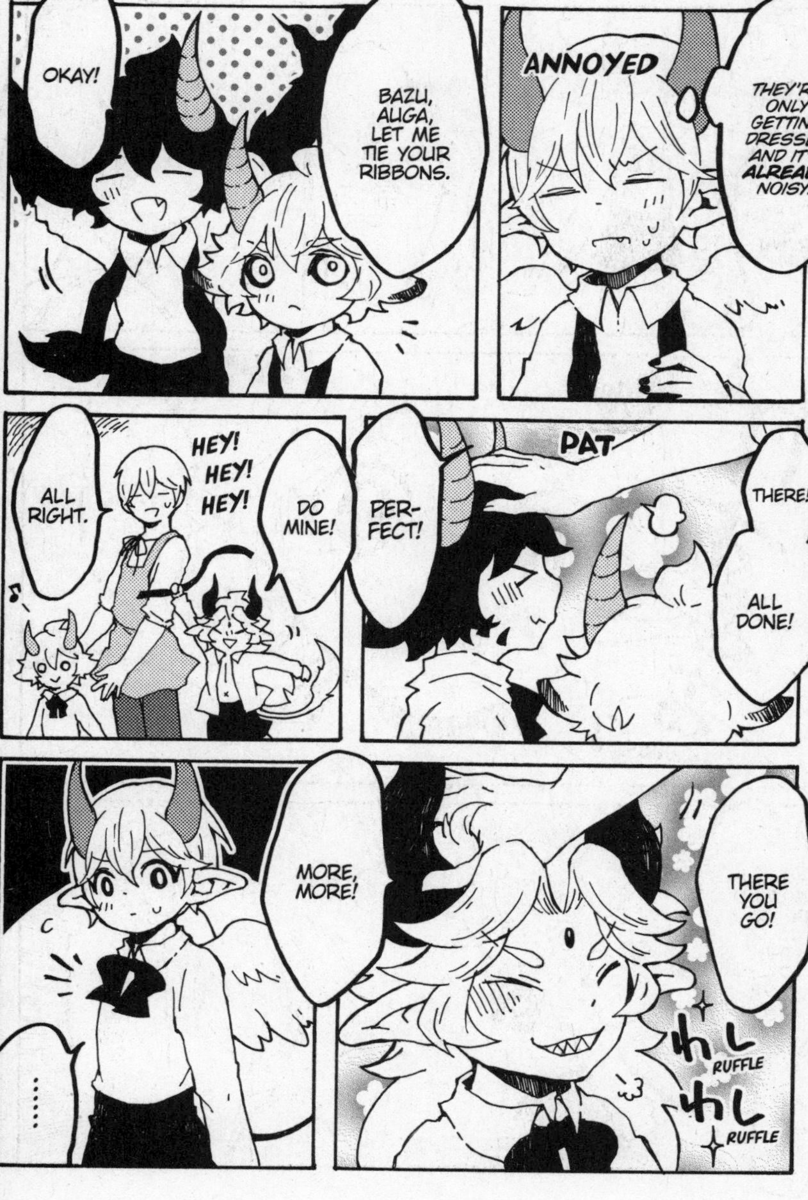
ANNOYED
THEY'RE ONLY GETTING DRESSED AND IT'S **ALREADY** NOISY!
BAZU, AUGA, LET ME TIE YOUR RIBBONS.
OKAY!
PAT
THERE!
ALL DONE!
PER-FECT!
DO MINE!
HEY! HEY! HEY!
ALL RIGHT.
THERE YOU GO!
わし RUFFLE
わし RUFFLE
MORE, MORE!
......

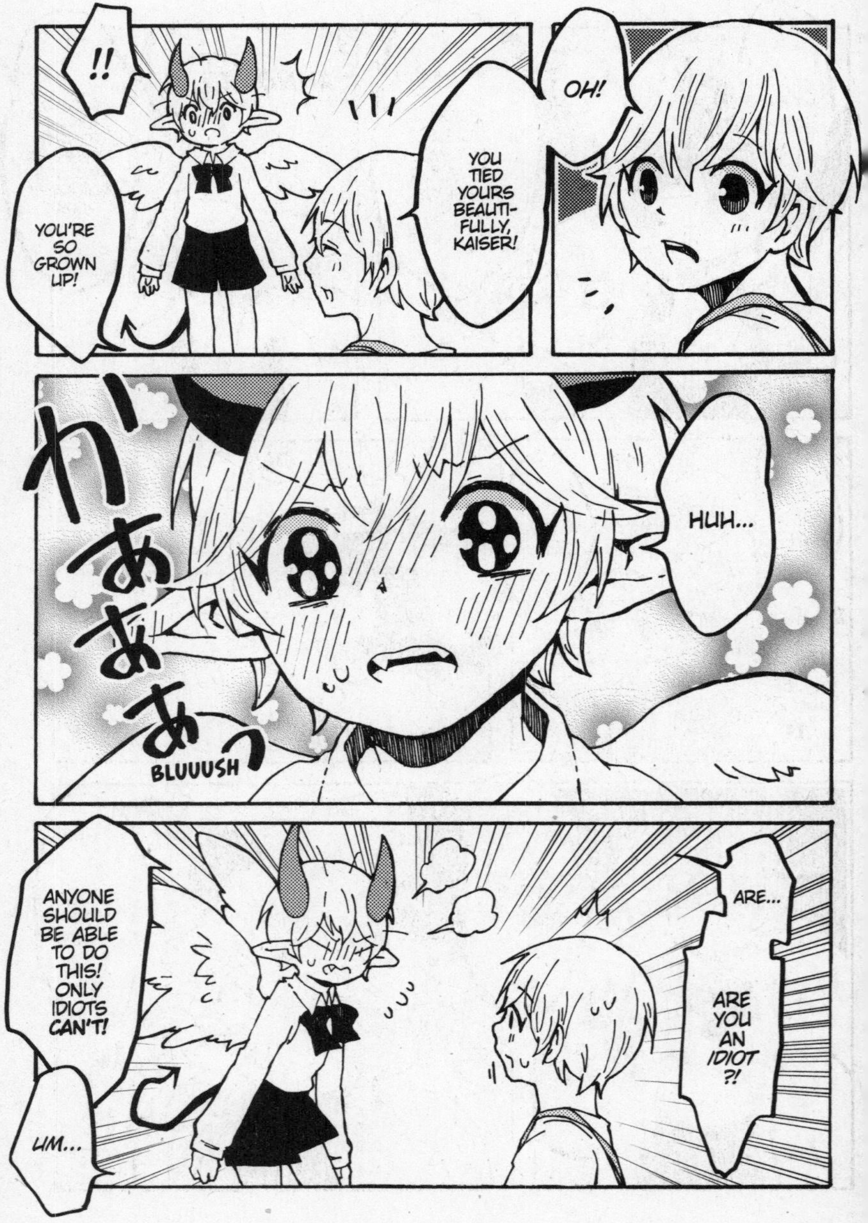
OH!
YOU TIED YOURS BEAUTIFULLY, KAISER!
!!
YOU'RE SO GROWN UP!
HUH...
かぁぁぁっ
BLUUUSH
ARE...
ARE YOU AN IDIOT?!
ANYONE SHOULD BE ABLE TO DO THIS! ONLY IDIOTS CAN'T!
UM...

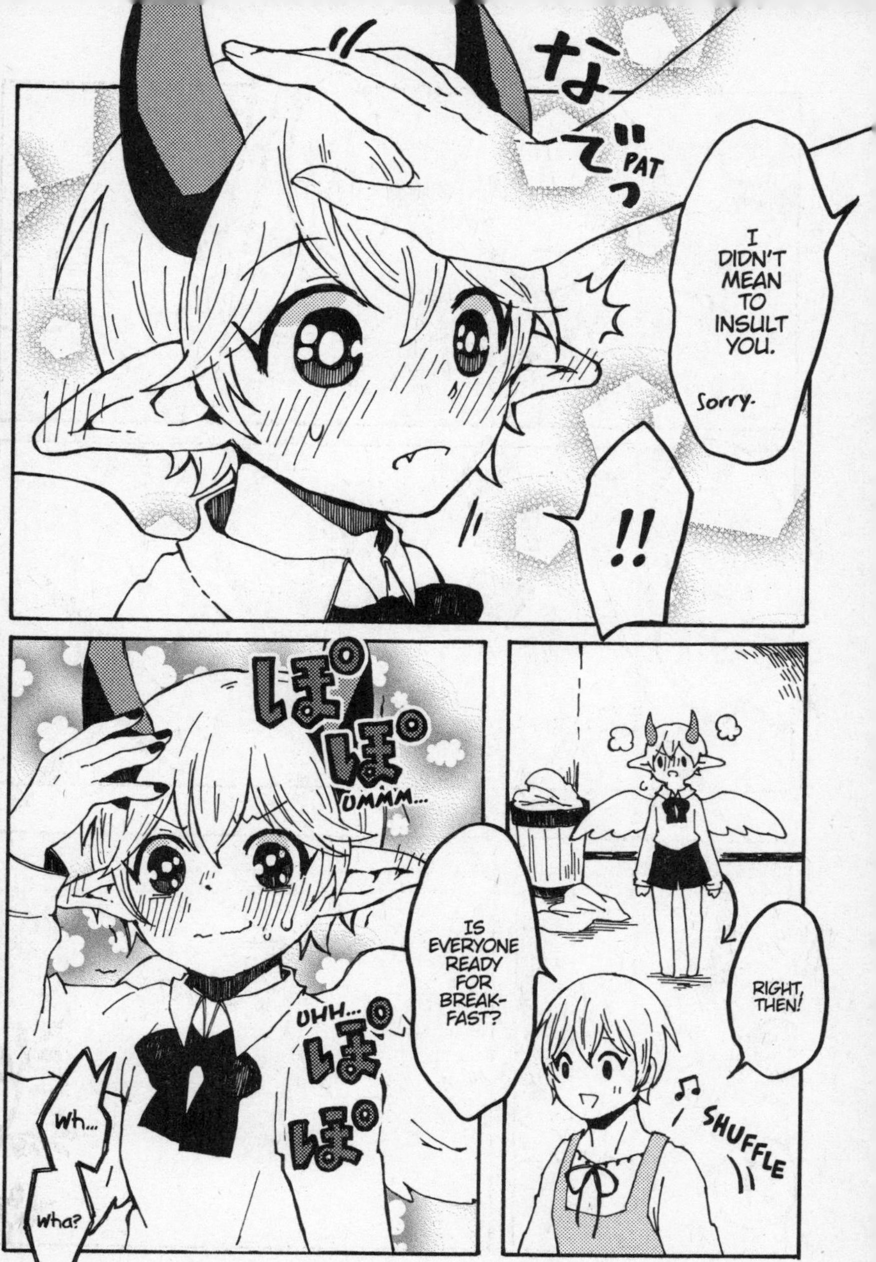
なでっ
PAT
I DIDN'T MEAN TO INSULT YOU.
Sorry.
!!
RIGHT, THEN!
IS EVERYONE READY FOR BREAK-FAST?
SHUFFLE
ぽぽ
UMMM...
UHH...
ぽぽ
Wh...
Wha?

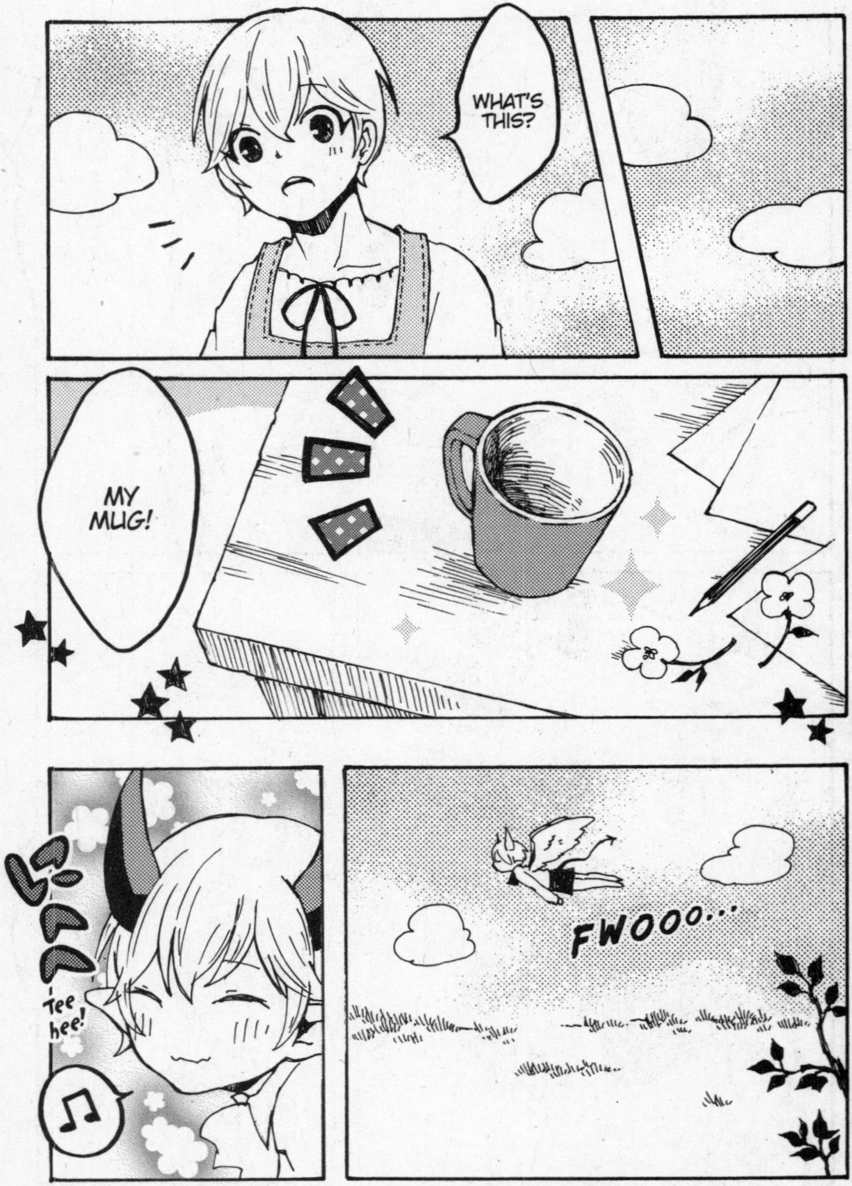
WHAT'S THIS?
MY MUG!
FWOOO...
Tee hee!

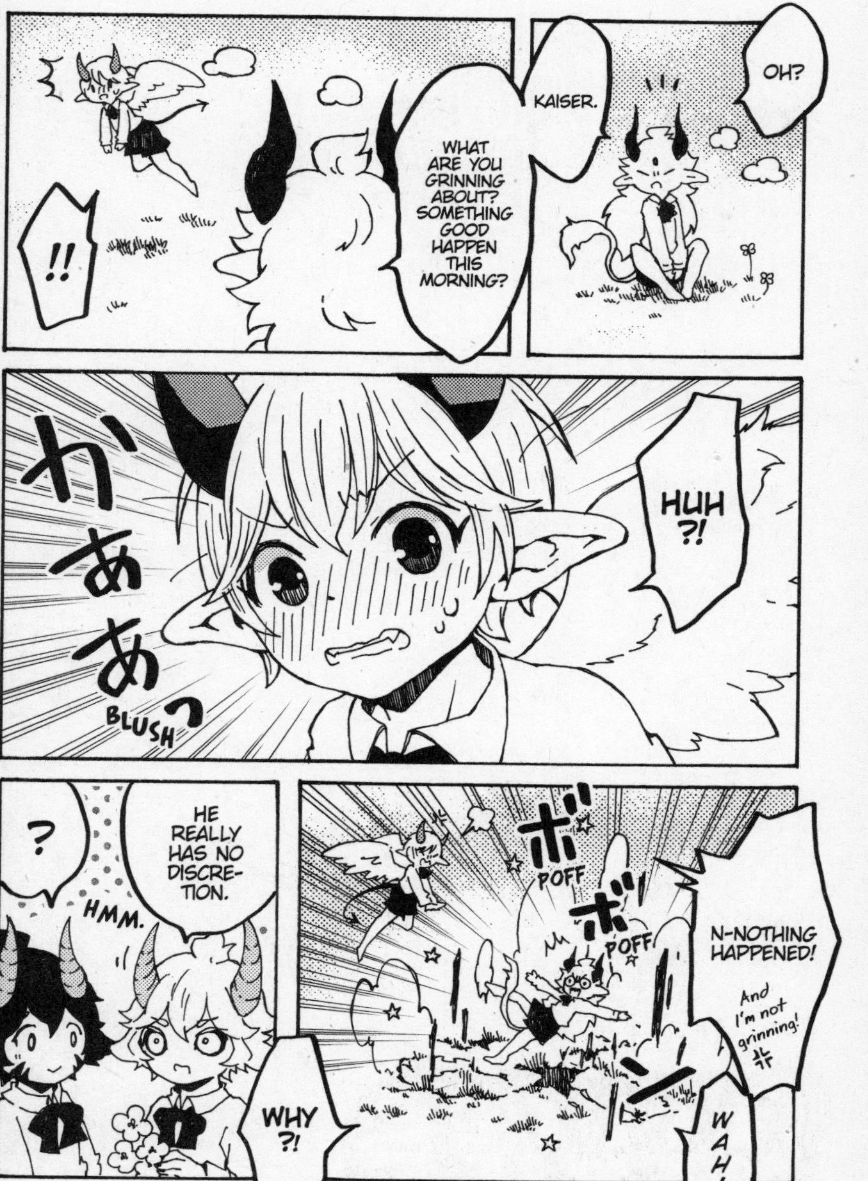
OH?
KAISER.
WHAT ARE YOU GRINNING ABOUT? SOMETHING GOOD HAPPEN THIS MORNING?
!!
HUH?!
かああっ
BLUSH
N-NOTHING HAPPENED!
And I'm not grinning!
ボ
POFF
ボ
POFF
WAH!
HE REALLY HAS NO DISCRE-TION.
?
HMM.
WHY?!

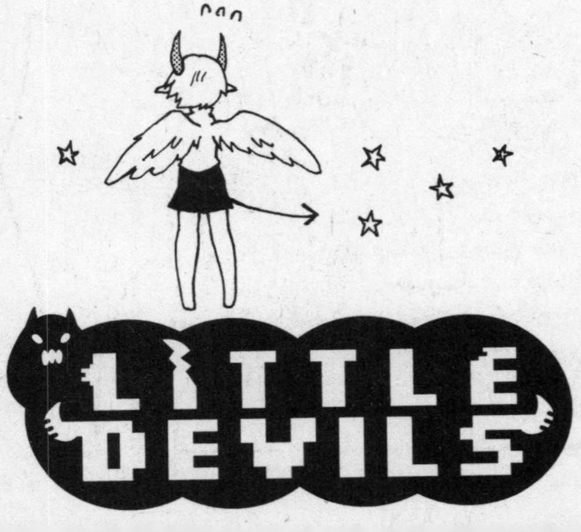

LITTLE DEVILS

THE LITTLE DEVILS' MAGIC: PART 2
CREATION MAGIC

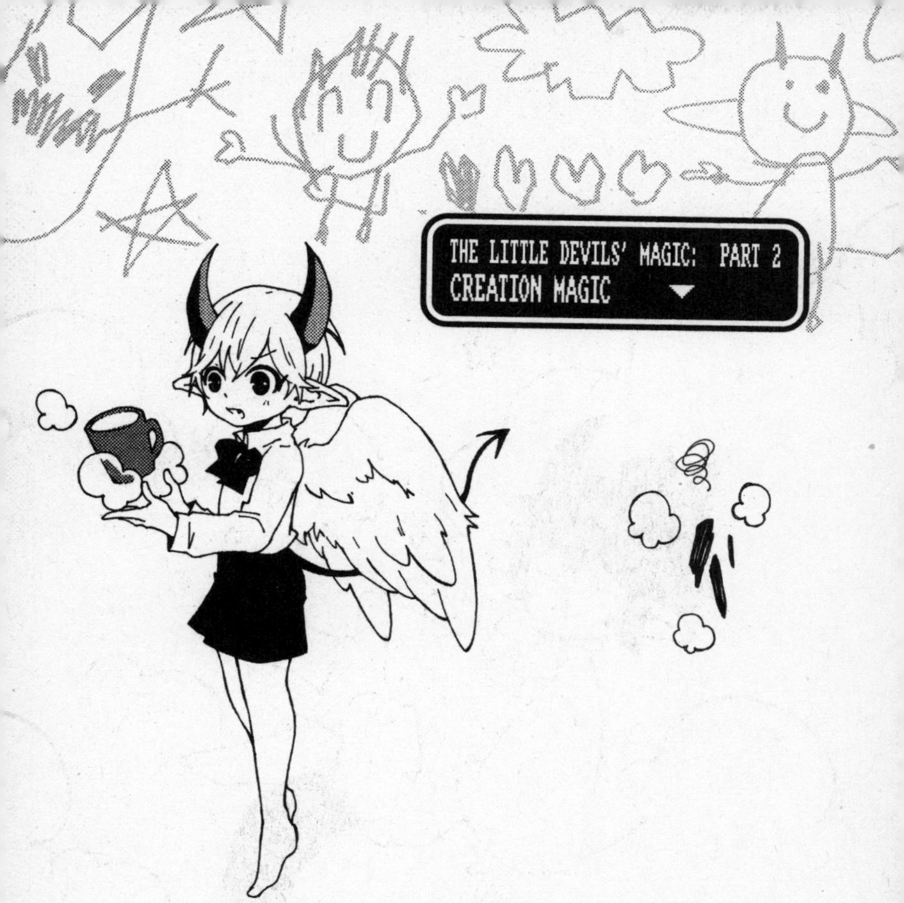

KAISER'S SPECIAL SKILL

He can duplicate any object after seeing it.
An incredibly useful ability, however...

- He needs materials which are similar to the original.
- Creation takes a lot of power and is very fatiguing.
- Kaiser's magic points (MP) are already low.

In other words, it has a lot of annoying downsides.

If he tries to make something without imagining it with enough detail, it turns into a lump of burnt charcoal.

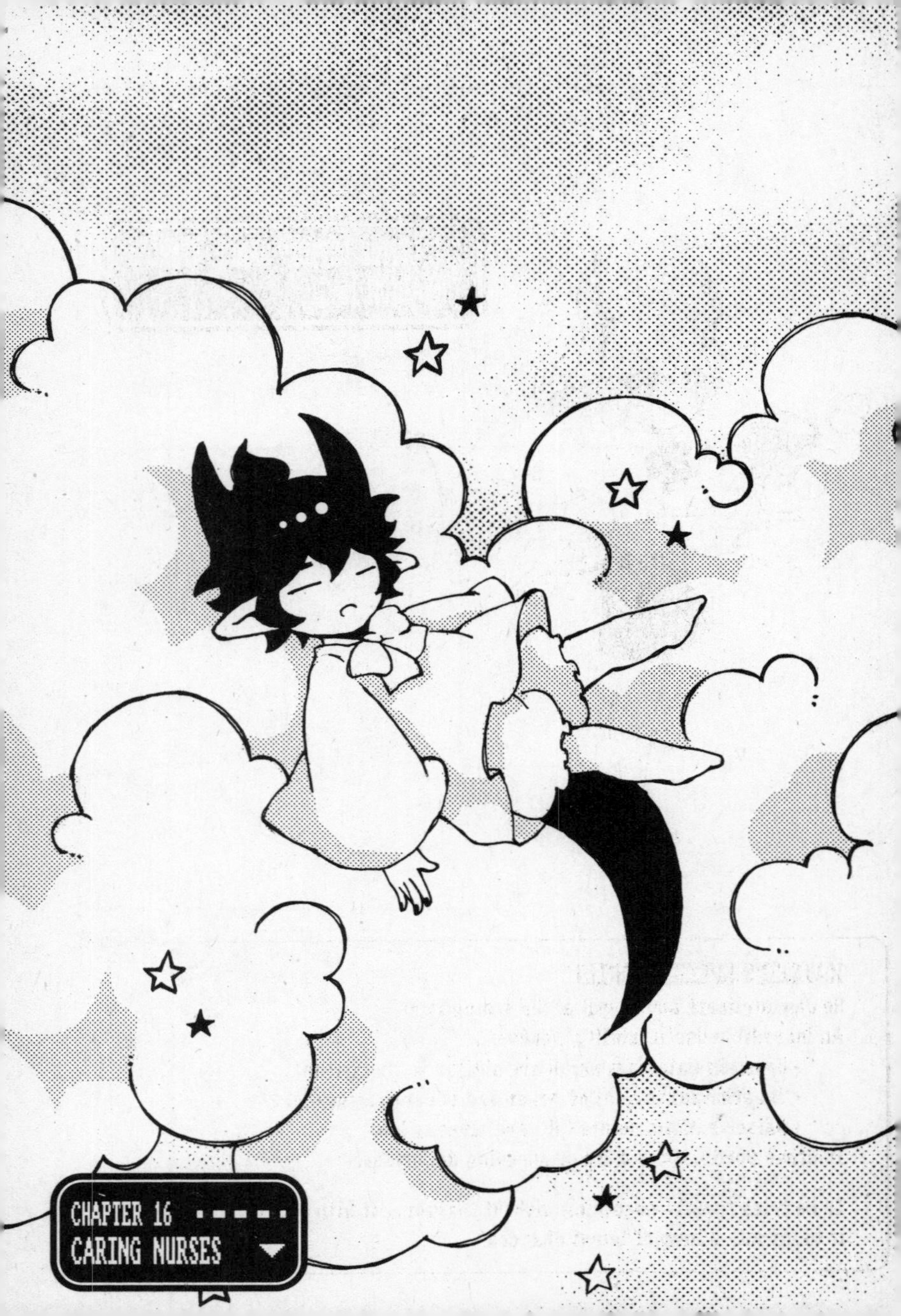
CHAPTER 16
CARING NURSES

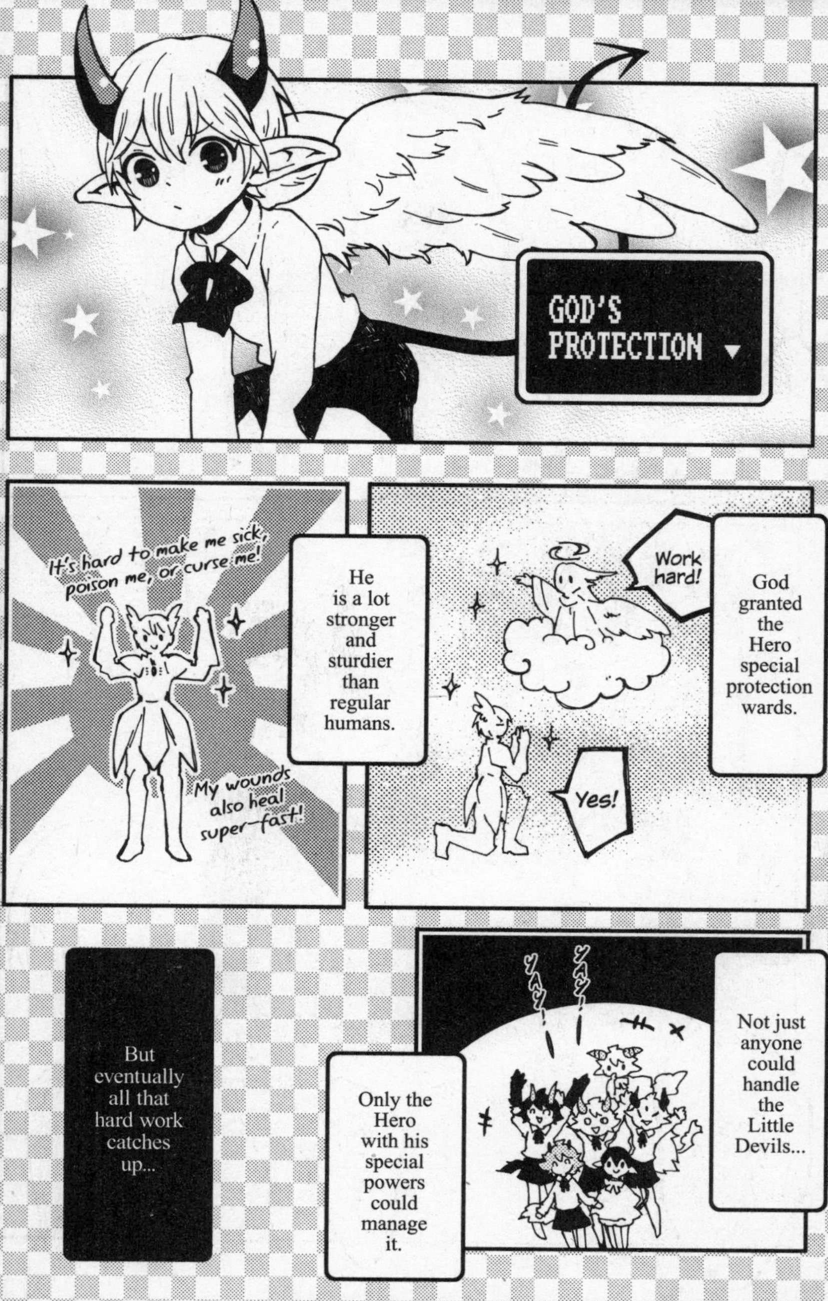
GOD'S PROTECTION ▼
God granted the Hero special protection wards.
Work hard!
Yes!
He is a lot stronger and sturdier than regular humans.
It's hard to make me sick, poison me, or curse me!
My wounds also heal super-fast!
Not just anyone could handle the Little Devils...
YAAY!
YAAY!
Only the Hero with his special powers could manage it.
But eventually all that hard work catches up...

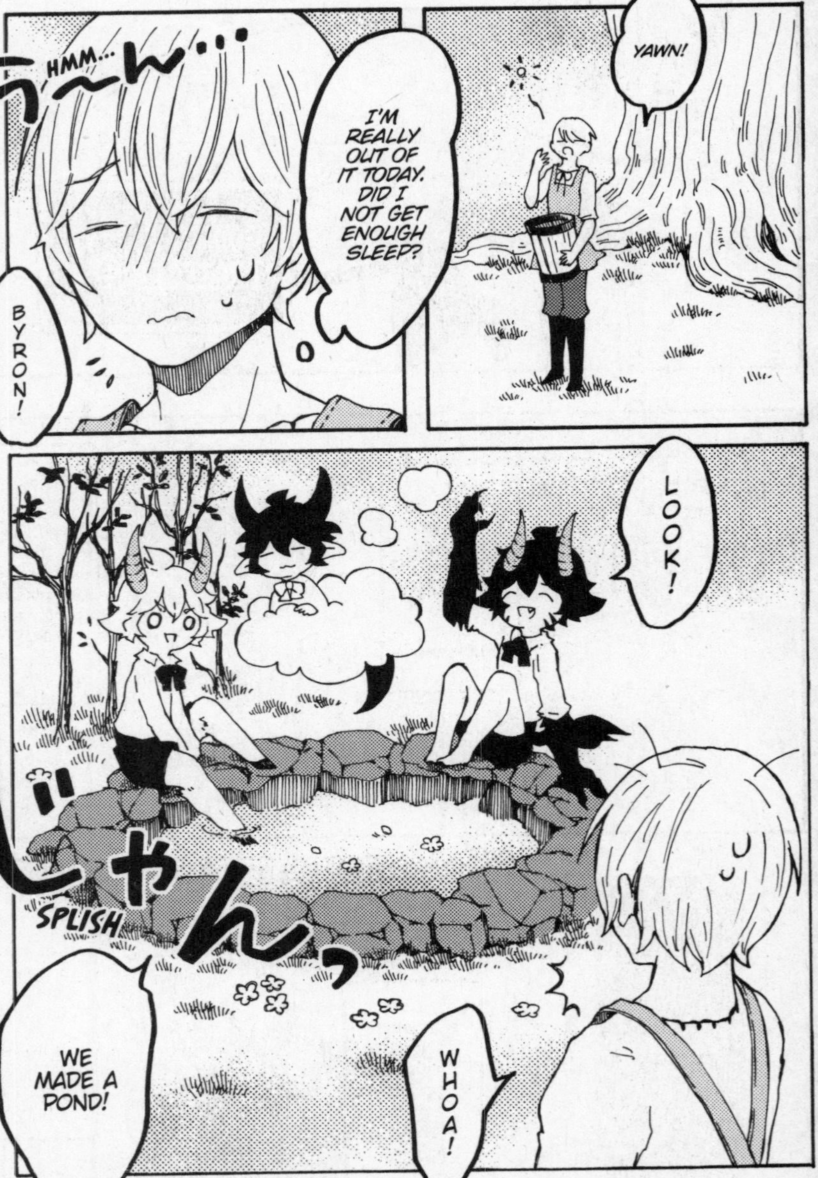
YAWN!
I'M REALLY OUT OF IT TODAY. DID I NOT GET ENOUGH SLEEP?
うーん…
HMM...
BYRON!
LOOK!
じゃん
SPLISH
WE MADE A POND!
WHOA!

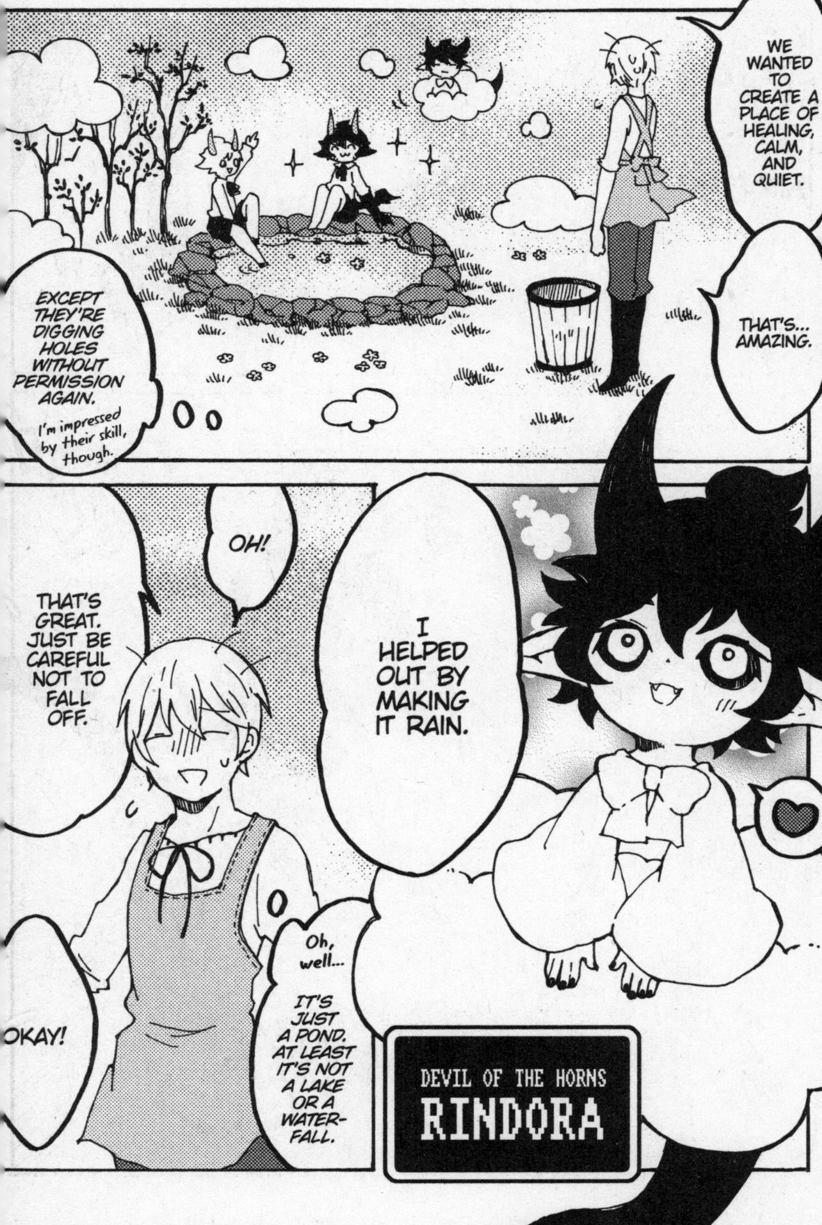
WE WANTED TO CREATE A PLACE OF HEALING, CALM, AND QUIET.
THAT'S... AMAZING.
EXCEPT THEY'RE DIGGING HOLES WITHOUT PERMISSION AGAIN.
I'm impressed by their skill, though.
I HELPED OUT BY MAKING IT RAIN.
DEVIL OF THE HORNS
RINDORA
OH!
THAT'S GREAT. JUST BE CAREFUL NOT TO FALL OFF.
OKAY!
Oh, well...
IT'S JUST A POND. AT LEAST IT'S NOT A LAKE OR A WATERFALL.

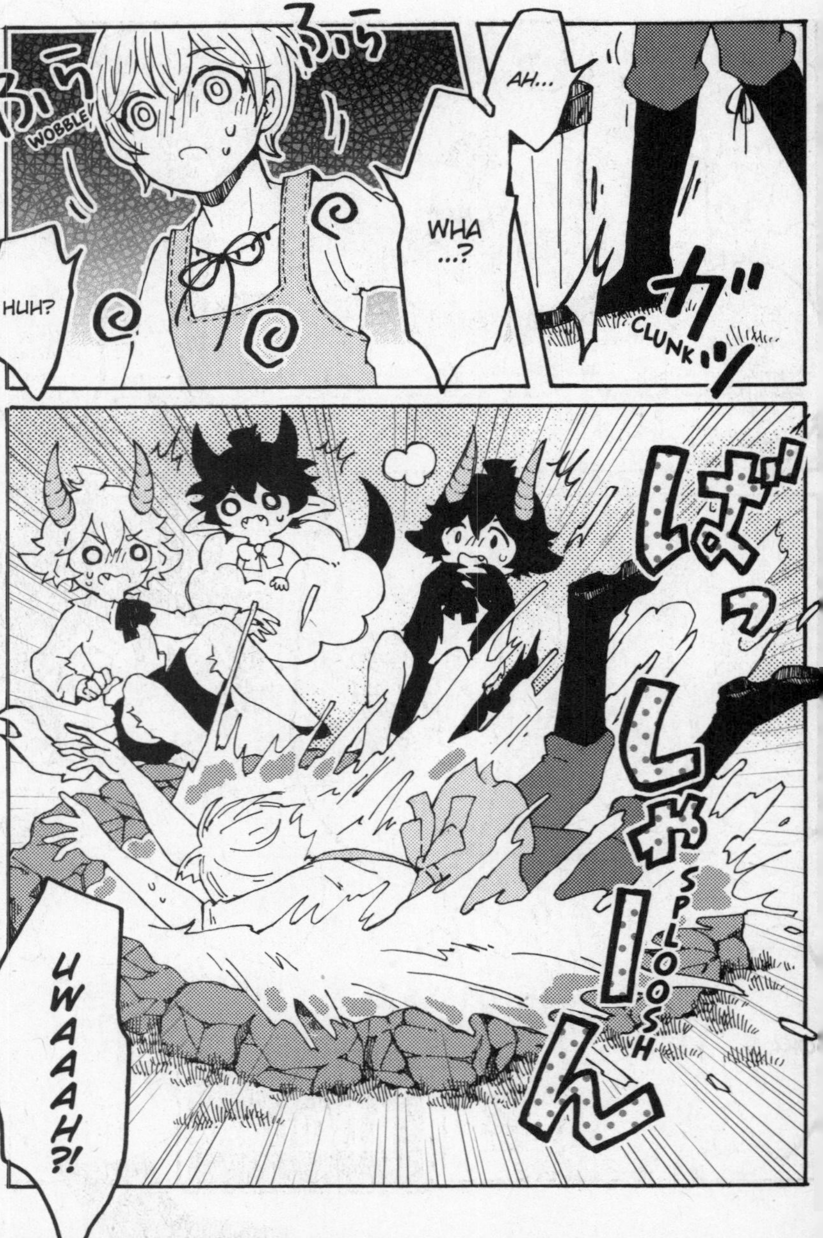
AH...
ガッ
CLUNK
ふら
WHA ...?
ふら
WOBBLE
HUH?
ばっしゃーん
SPLOOSH
UWAAAAH?!

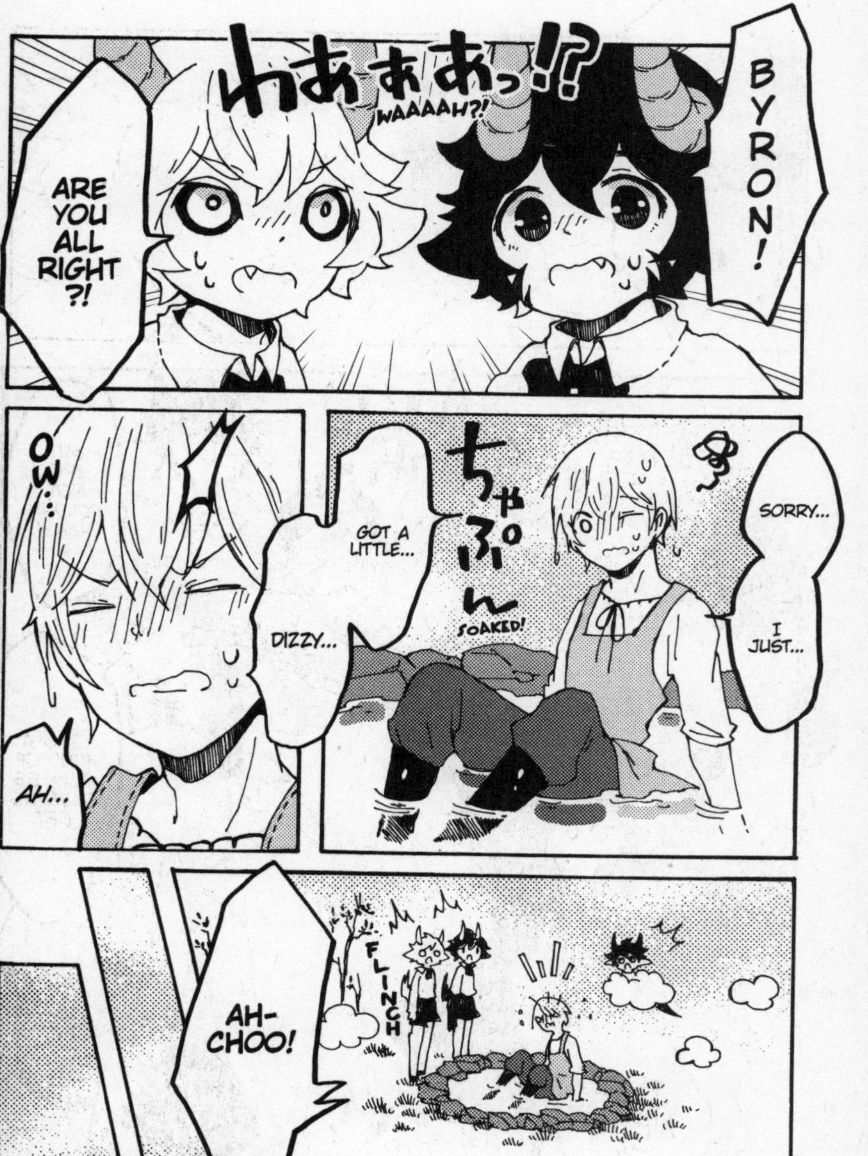
BYRON!
わあぁあっ!!?
WAAAAH?!
ARE YOU ALL RIGHT?!
SORRY...
I JUST...
ちゃぷーん
SOAKED!
GOT A LITTLE...
DIZZY...
OW...
AH...
FLINCH
AH-CHOO!

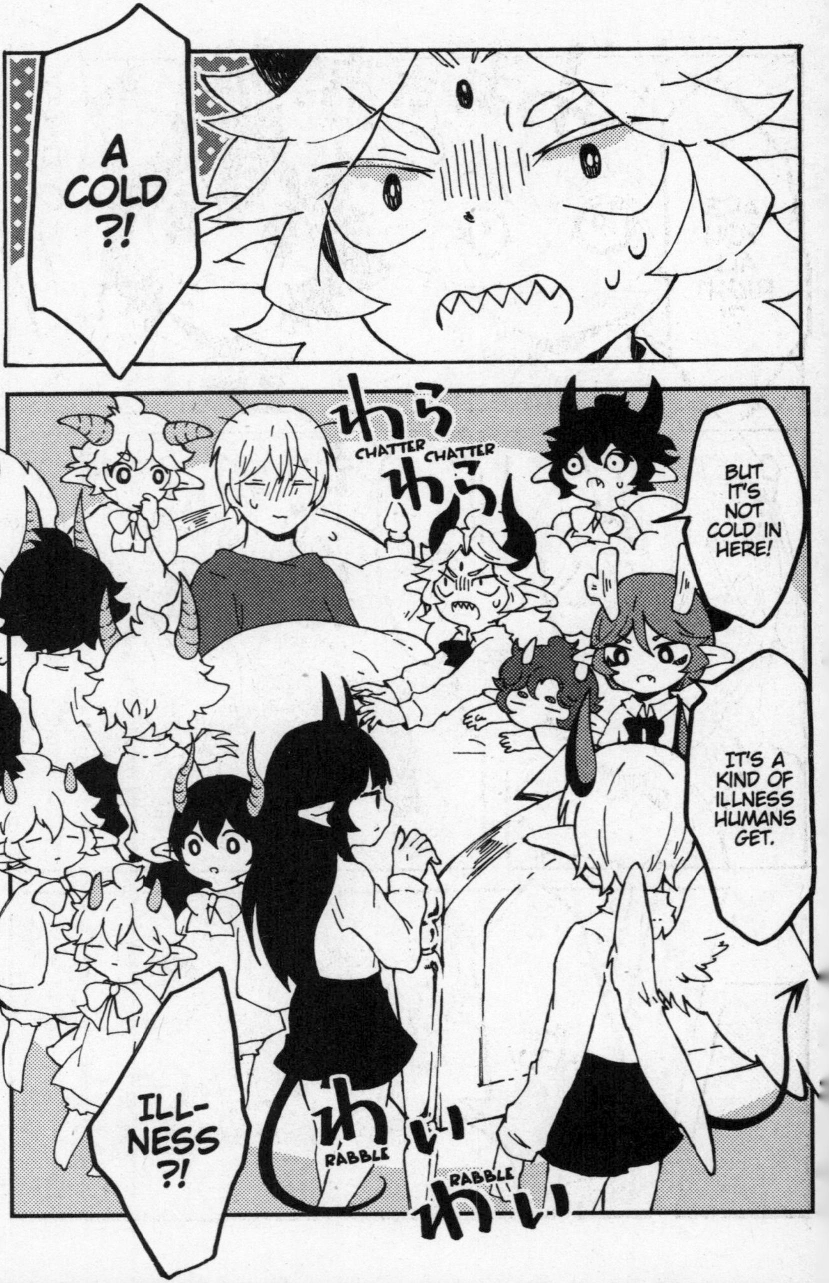
A COLD ?!
BUT IT'S NOT COLD IN HERE!
わら CHATTER
わら CHATTER
IT'S A KIND OF ILLNESS HUMANS GET.
わい RABBLE
わい RABBLE
ILL-NESS ?!

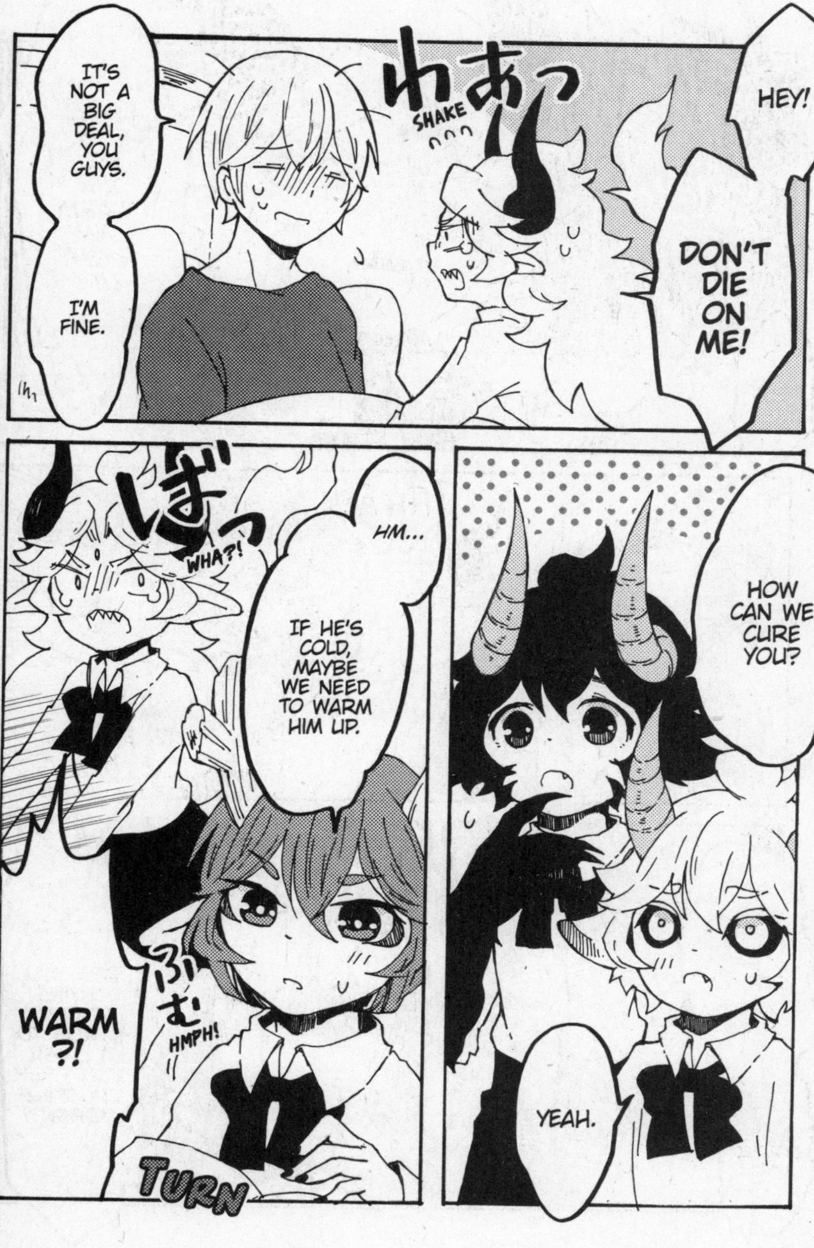
HEY!
DON'T DIE ON ME!
ゆあっ
SHAKE
IT'S NOT A BIG DEAL, YOU GUYS.
I'M FINE.
HOW CAN WE CURE YOU?
YEAH.
HM...
IF HE'S COLD, MAYBE WE NEED TO WARM HIM UP.
ぼっ
WHA?!
WARM ?!
ふむ
HMPH!
TURN

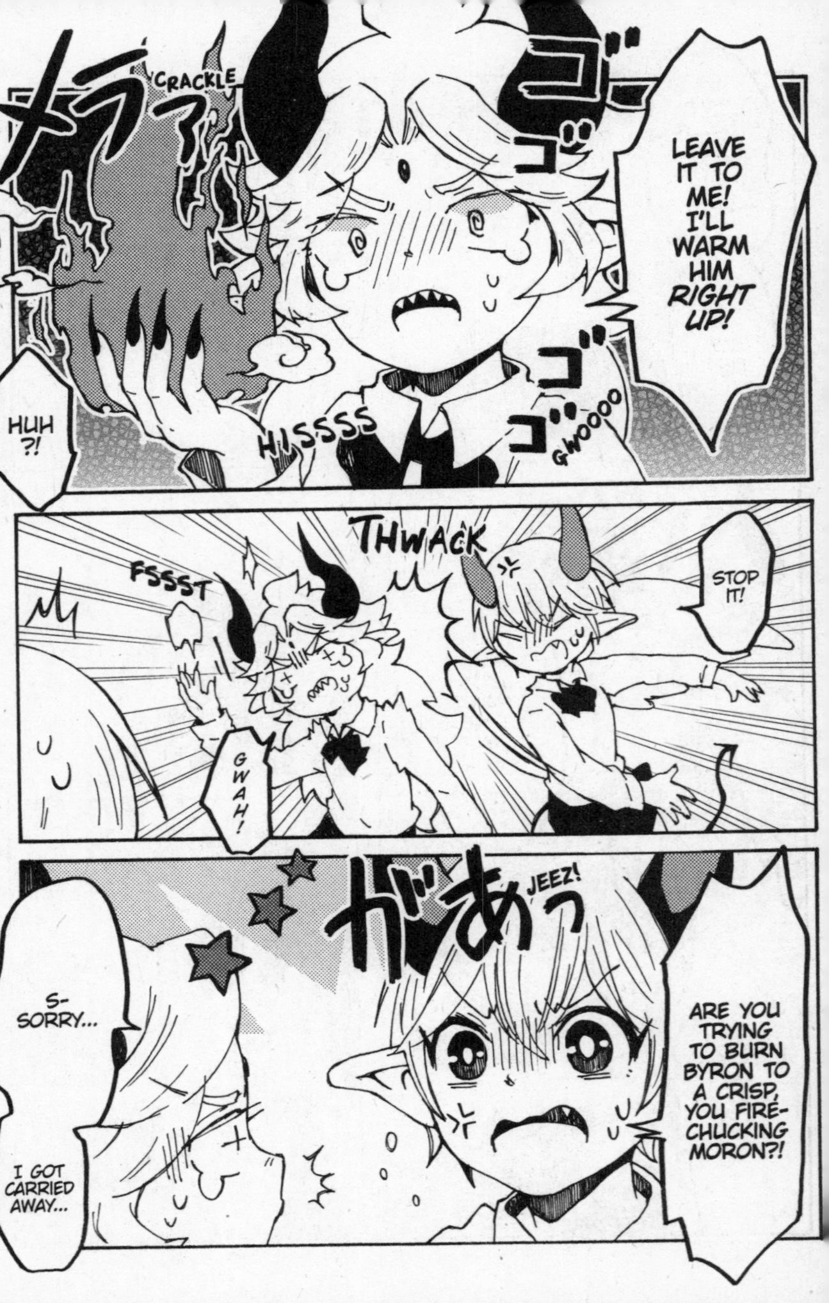
LEAVE IT TO ME! I'LL WARM HIM RIGHT UP!
ゴゴ
ゴゴ
GWOOOO
CRACKLE
メラァ
HISSSSS
HUH?!
STOP IT!
THWACK
FSSST
GWAH!
ARE YOU TRYING TO BURN BYRON TO A CRISP, YOU FIRE-CHUCKING MORON?!
JEEZ!
がぁっ
S-SORRY...
I GOT CARRIED AWAY...

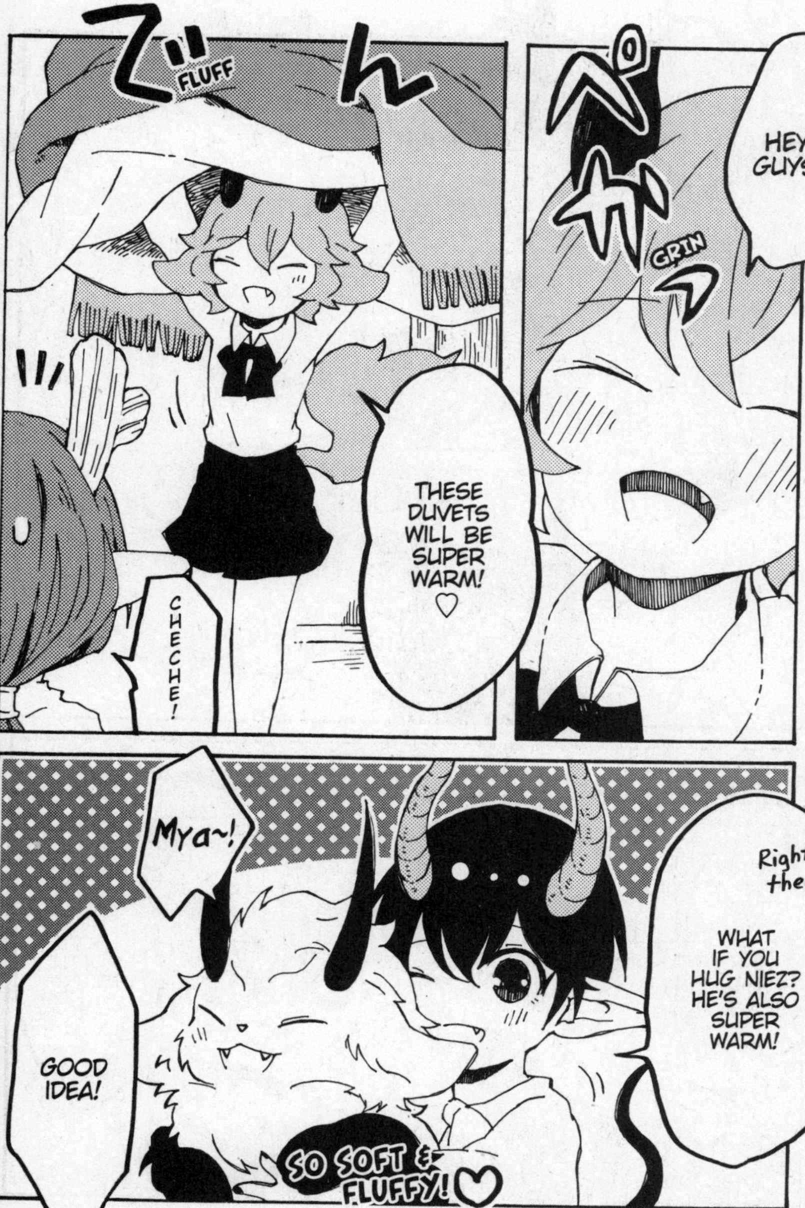
HEY, GUYS!
GRIN
FLUFF
THESE DUVETS WILL BE SUPER WARM! ♡
CHECHE!
Right, then!
WHAT IF YOU HUG NIEZ? HE'S ALSO SUPER WARM!
Mya~!
GOOD IDEA!
SO SOFT & FLUFFY! ♡

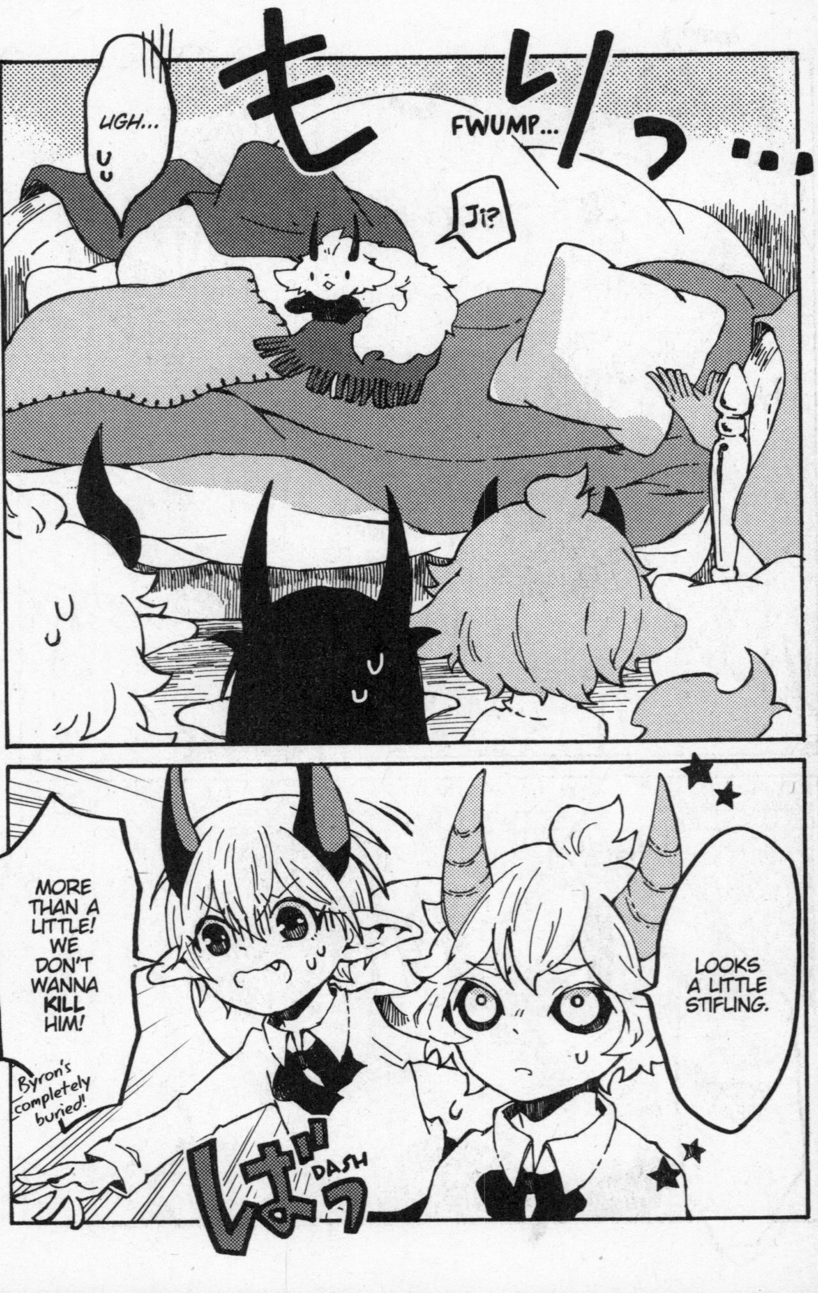

もりっ…
FWUMP...
UGH...
Ji?
LOOKS A LITTLE STIFLING.
MORE THAN A LITTLE! WE DON'T WANNA **KILL** HIM!
Byron's completely buried!
しばっ
DASH

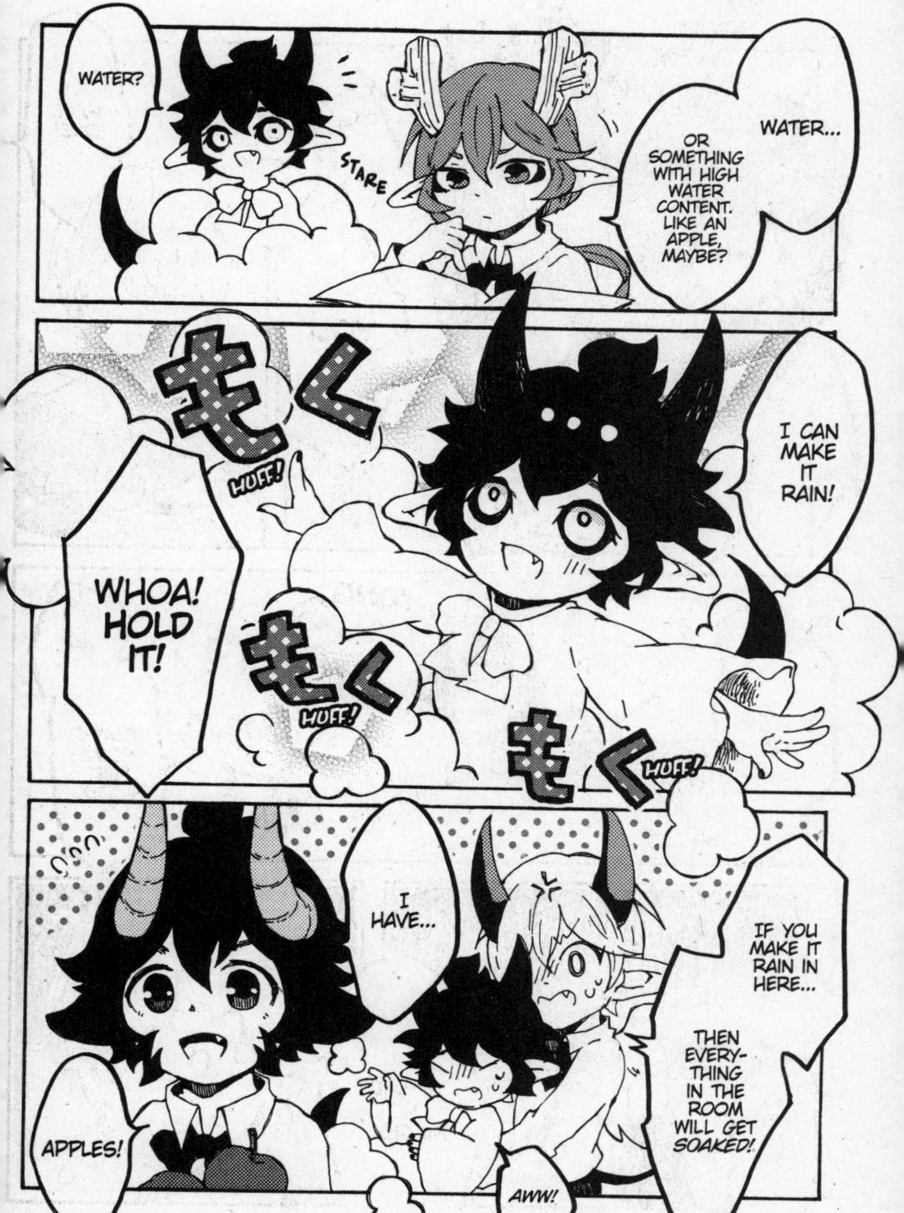
WATER...
OR SOMETHING WITH HIGH WATER CONTENT. LIKE AN APPLE, MAYBE?
STARE
WATER?
I CAN MAKE IT RAIN!
もく
HUFF!
もく
HUFF!
もく
HUFF!
WHOA! HOLD IT!
IF YOU MAKE IT RAIN IN HERE...
THEN EVERYTHING IN THE ROOM WILL GET SOAKED!
AWW!
I HAVE...
APPLES!

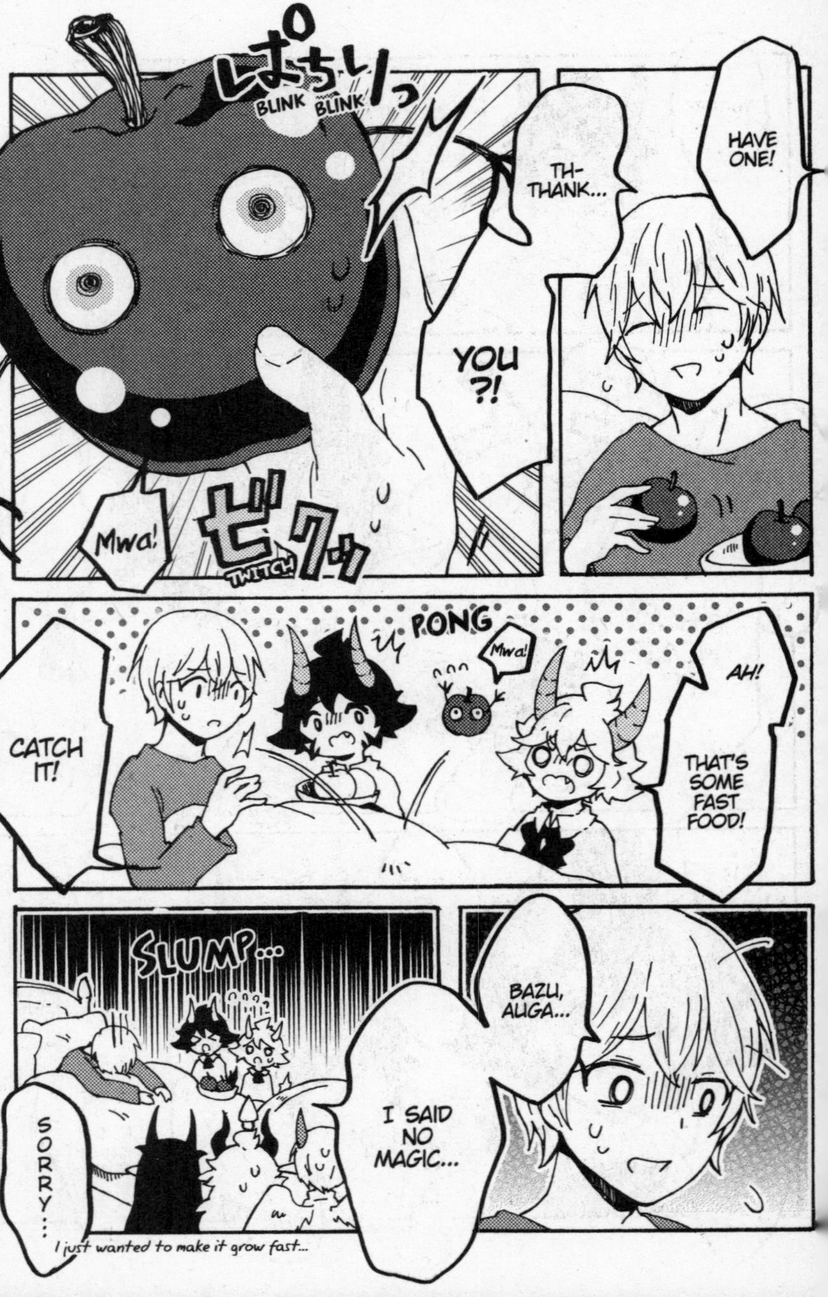
HAVE ONE!
TH-THANK...
YOU ?!
ぱちりっ
BLINK BLINK
Mwa!
ビクッ
TWITCH
AH!
THAT'S SOME FAST FOOD!
Mwa!
PONG
CATCH IT!
BAZU, AUGA...
I SAID NO MAGIC...
SLUMP...
SORRY...
I just wanted to make it grow fast...

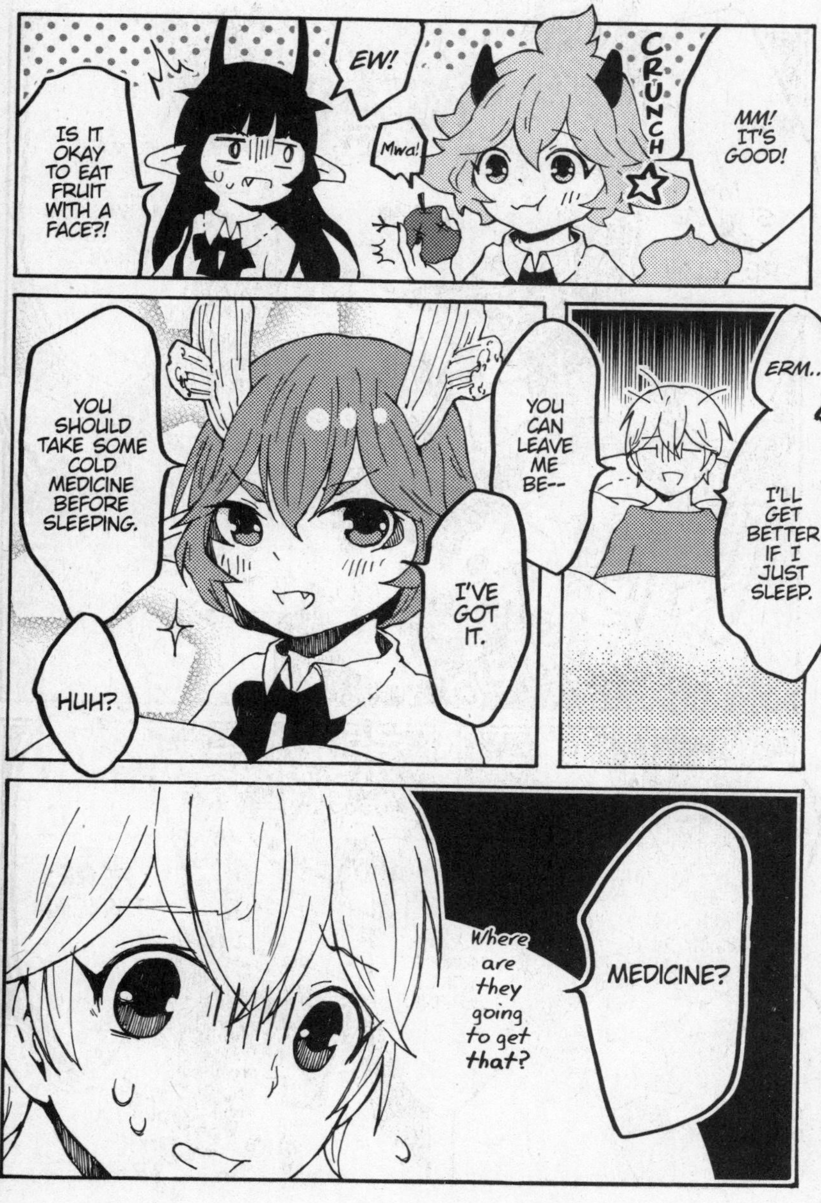
MM! IT'S GOOD!
CRUNCH
Mwa!
EW!
IS IT OKAY TO EAT FRUIT WITH A FACE?!
ERM...
YOU CAN LEAVE ME BE--
I'LL GET BETTER IF I JUST SLEEP.
I'VE GOT IT.
YOU SHOULD TAKE SOME COLD MEDICINE BEFORE SLEEPING.
HUH?
MEDICINE?
Where are they going to get that?

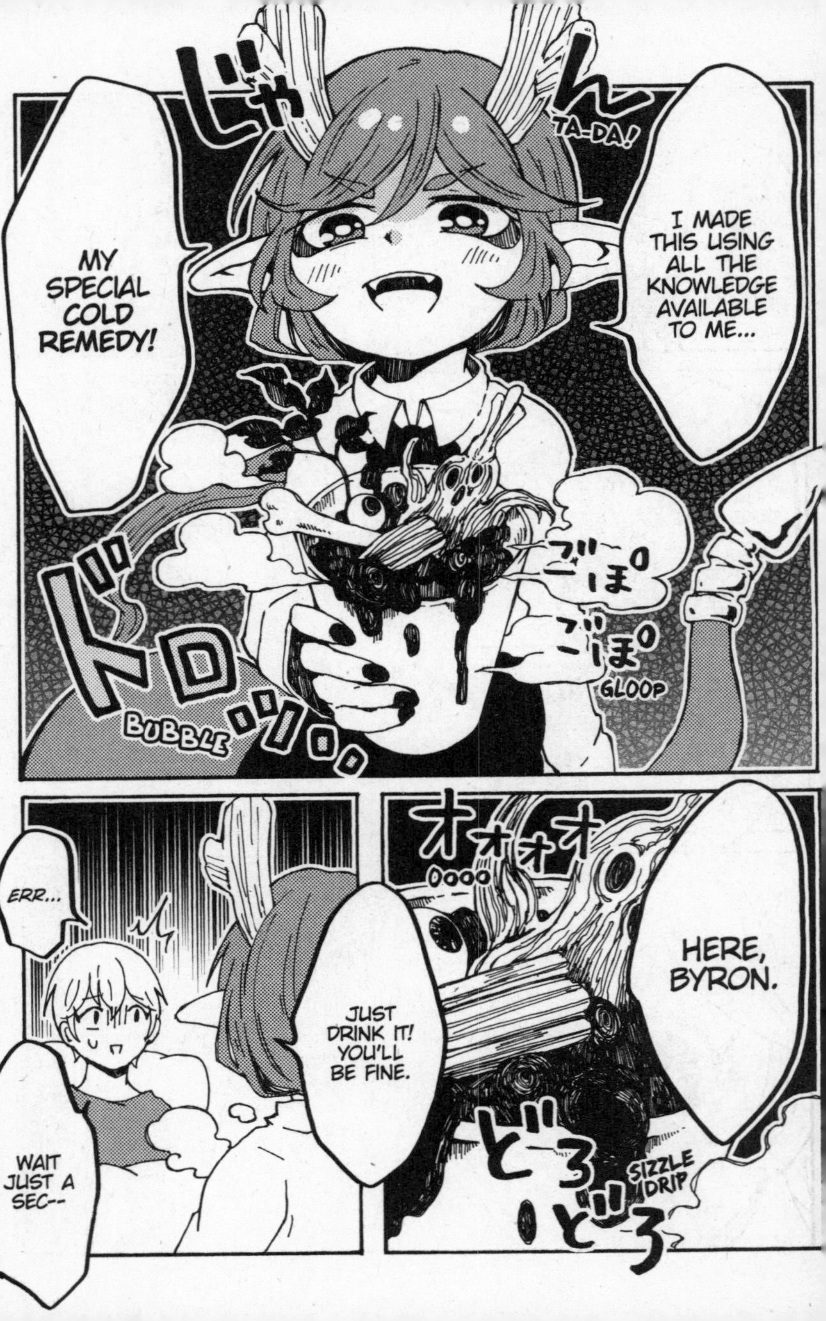

じゃん
TA-DA!
I MADE THIS USING ALL THE KNOWLEDGE AVAILABLE TO ME...
MY SPECIAL COLD REMEDY!
ごぽ ごぽ
GLOOP
ドロ
BUBBLE
オォォォ
oooo
HERE, BYRON.
JUST DRINK IT! YOU'LL BE FINE.
どろ どろ
SIZZLE DRIP
ERR...
WAIT JUST A SEC--

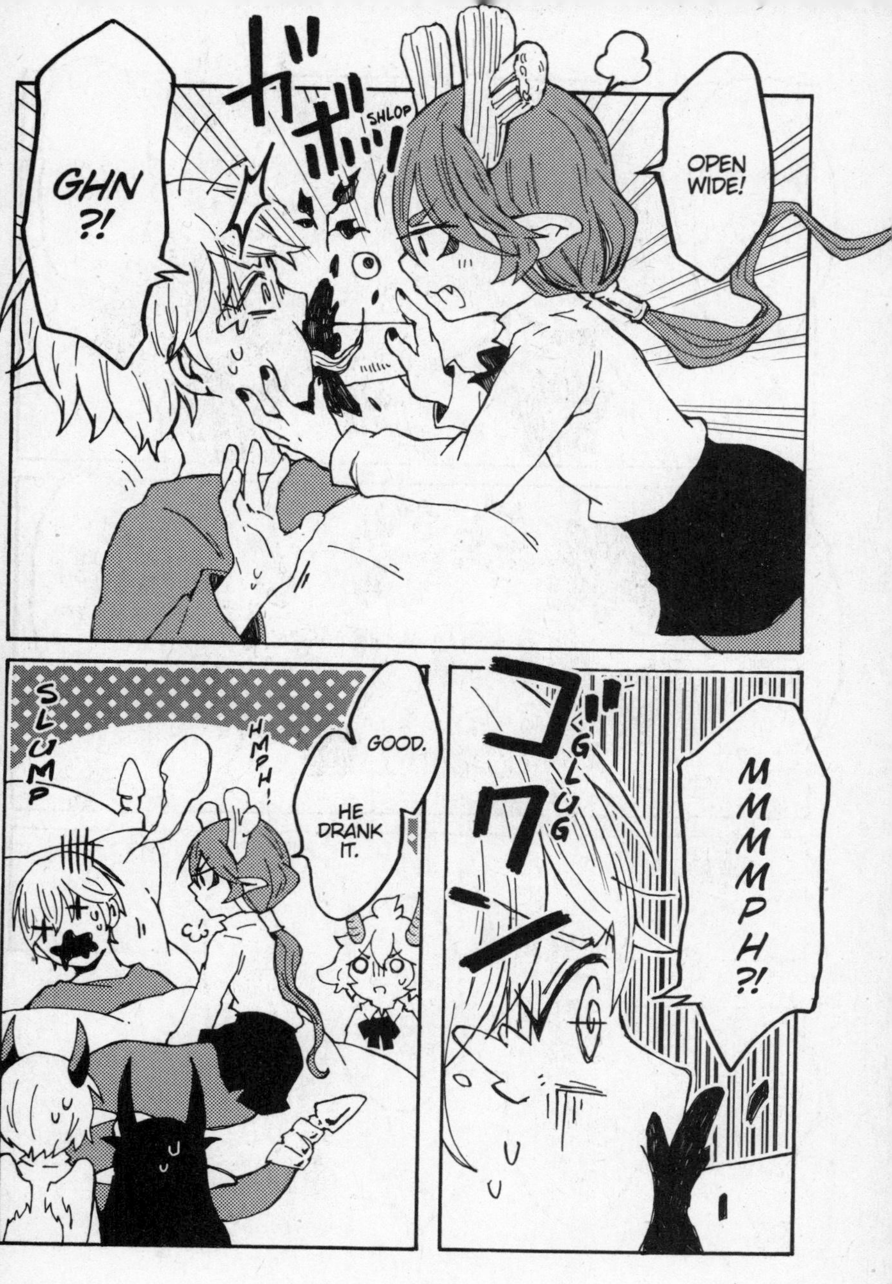
OPEN WIDE!
ガボッ
SHLOP
GHN ?!
MMMMMPH?!
ゴクーン
GLUG
GOOD.
HE DRANK IT.
HMPH!
SLUMP

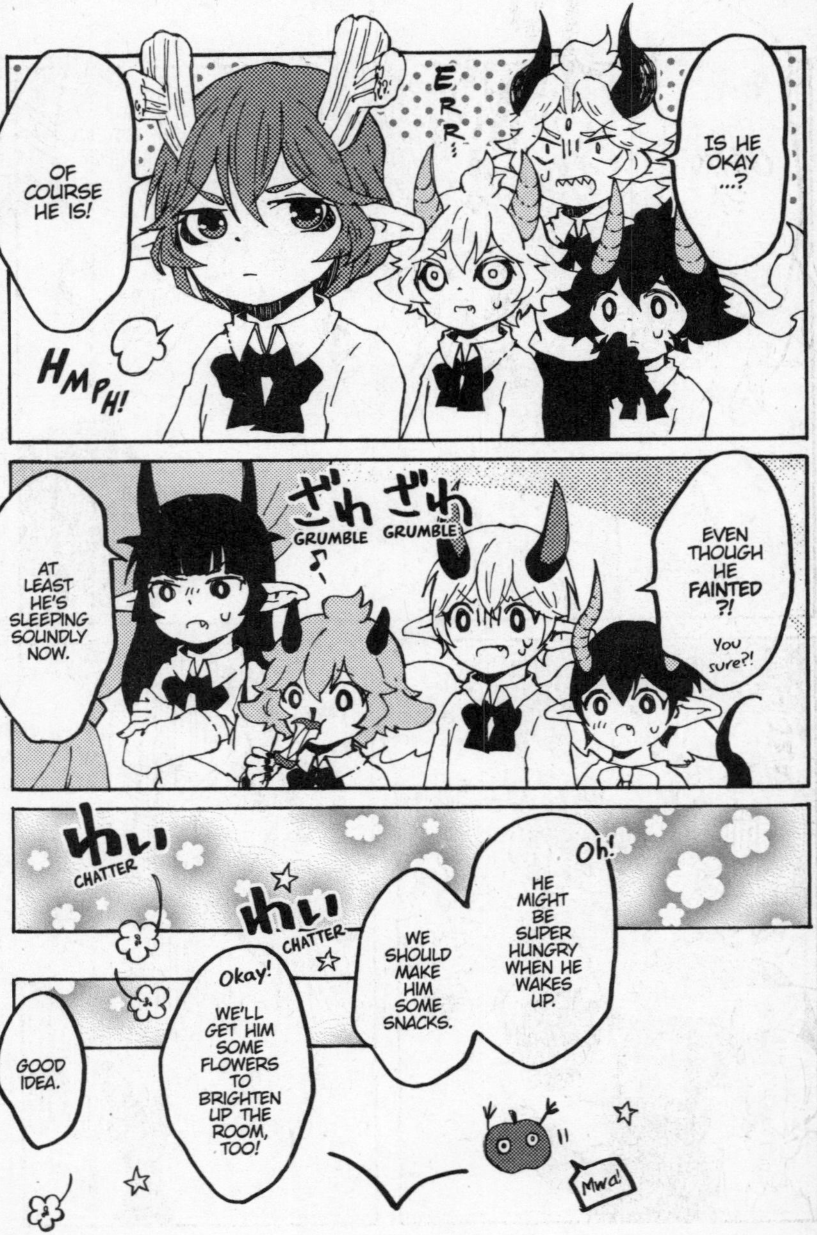
IS HE OKAY ...?
ERR...
OF COURSE HE IS!
HMPH!
EVEN THOUGH HE FAINTED ?!
You sure?!
ざわざわ
GRUMBLE GRUMBLE
AT LEAST HE'S SLEEPING SOUNDLY NOW.
Oh!
HE MIGHT BE SUPER HUNGRY WHEN HE WAKES UP.
わいわい
CHATTER
わいわい
CHATTER
WE SHOULD MAKE HIM SOME SNACKS.
Mwa!
Okay!
WE'LL GET HIM SOME FLOWERS TO BRIGHTEN UP THE ROOM, TOO!
GOOD IDEA.

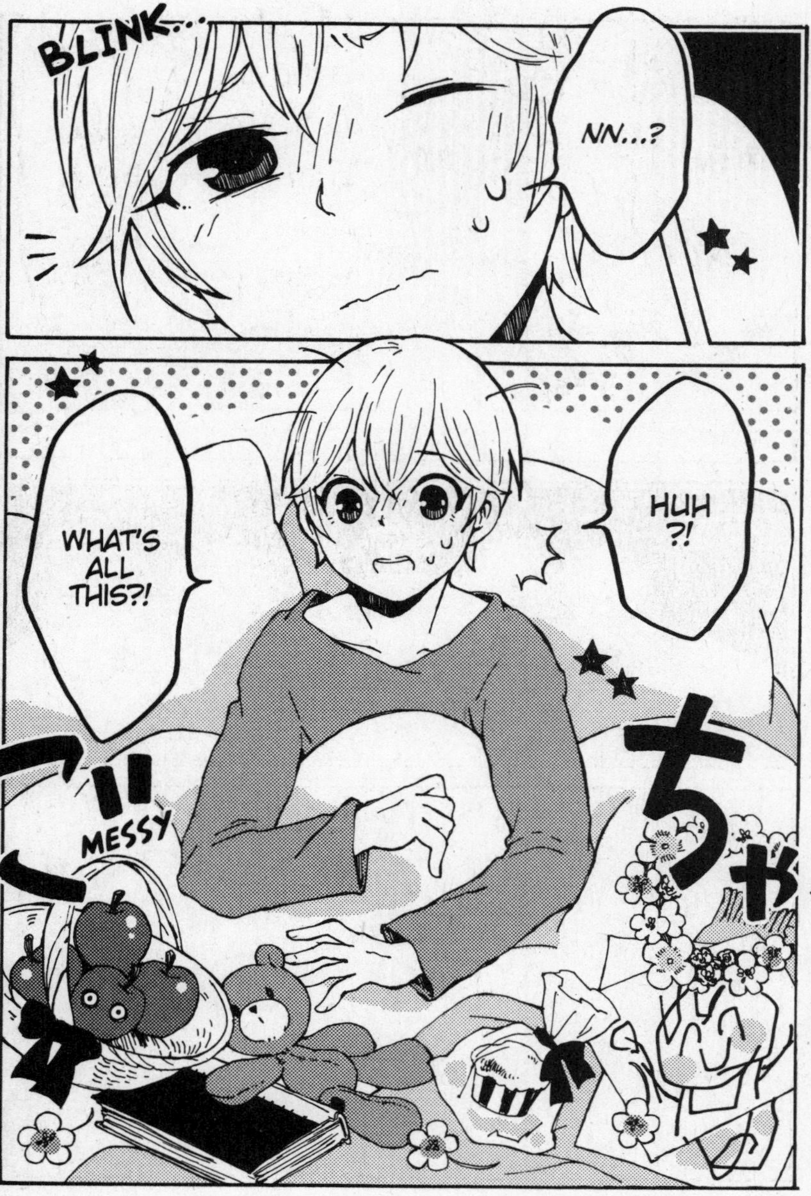
NN...?
BLINK...
HUH ?!
WHAT'S ALL THIS?!
ちゃ
MESSY

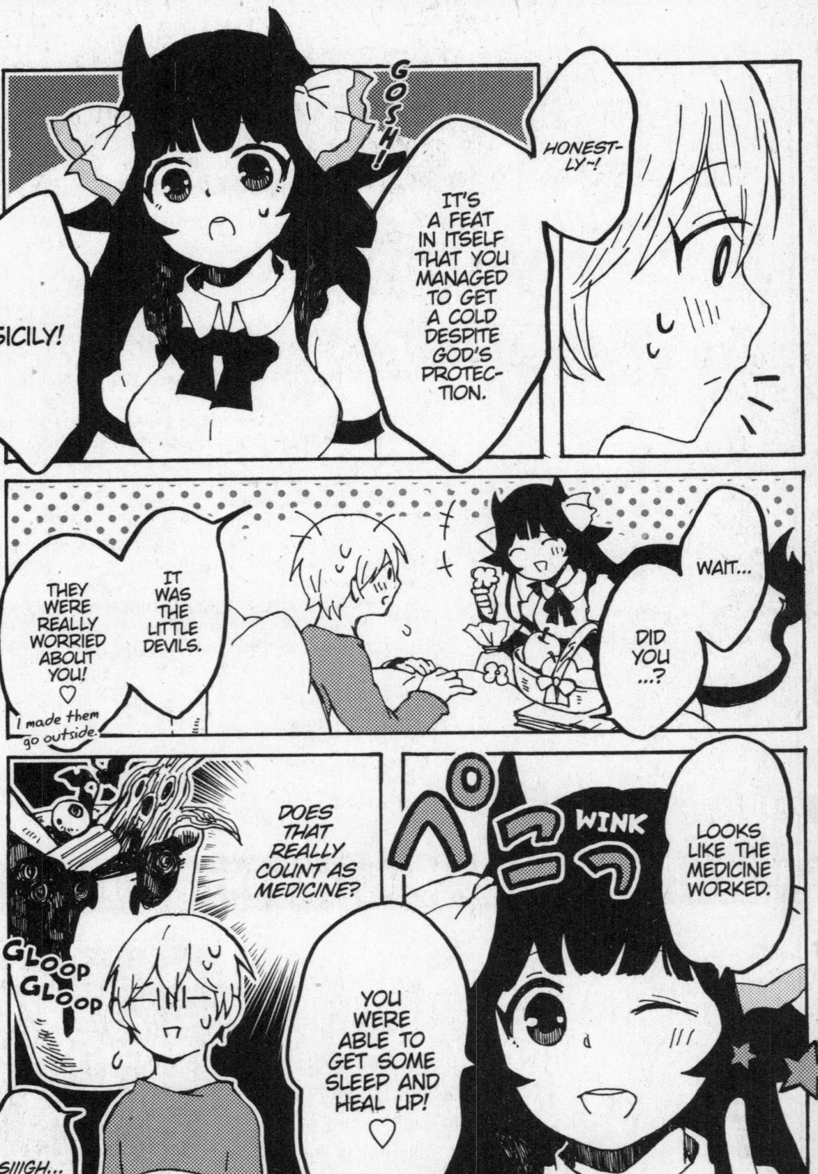
HONEST-LY~!
IT'S A FEAT IN ITSELF THAT YOU MANAGED TO GET A COLD DESPITE GOD'S PROTEC-TION.
GOSH!
SICILY!
WAIT...
DID YOU ...?
IT WAS THE LITTLE DEVILS.
THEY WERE REALLY WORRIED ABOUT YOU! ♡
I made them go outside.
WINK
LOOKS LIKE THE MEDICINE WORKED.
YOU WERE ABLE TO GET SOME SLEEP AND HEAL UP! ♡
DOES THAT REALLY COUNT AS MEDICINE?
GLOOP GLOOP
SIIIGH...

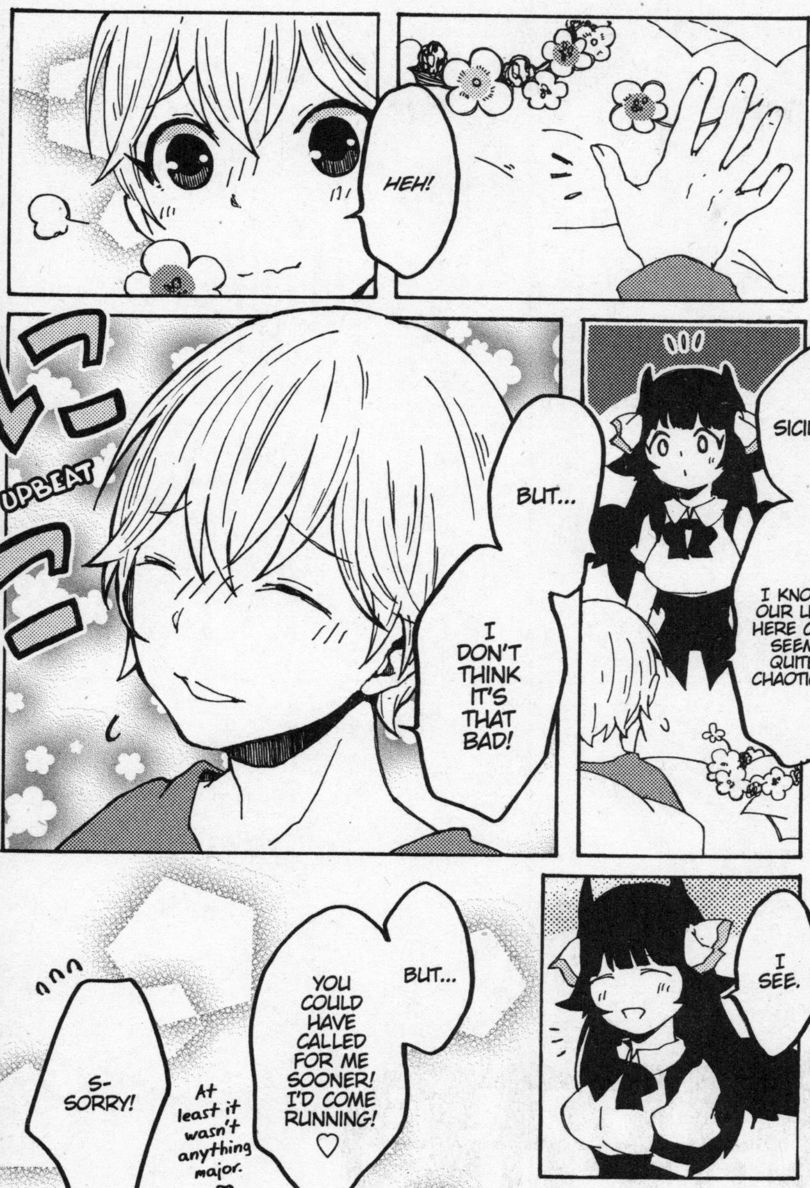
HEH!
SICILY...
I KNOW OUR LIFE HERE CAN SEEM QUITE CHAOTIC...
BUT...
I DON'T THINK IT'S THAT BAD!
UPBEAT
I SEE.
BUT...
YOU COULD HAVE CALLED FOR ME SOONER! I'D COME RUNNING! ♡
S-SORRY!
At least it wasn't anything major.

LITTLE
DEVILS

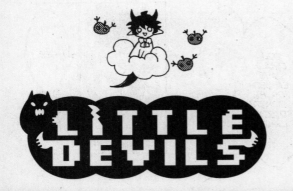

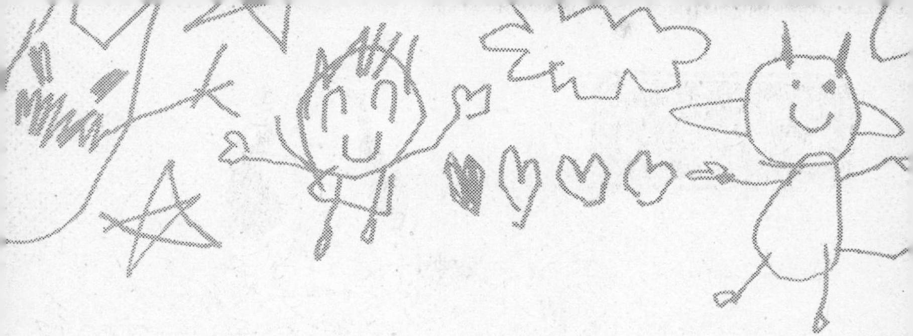

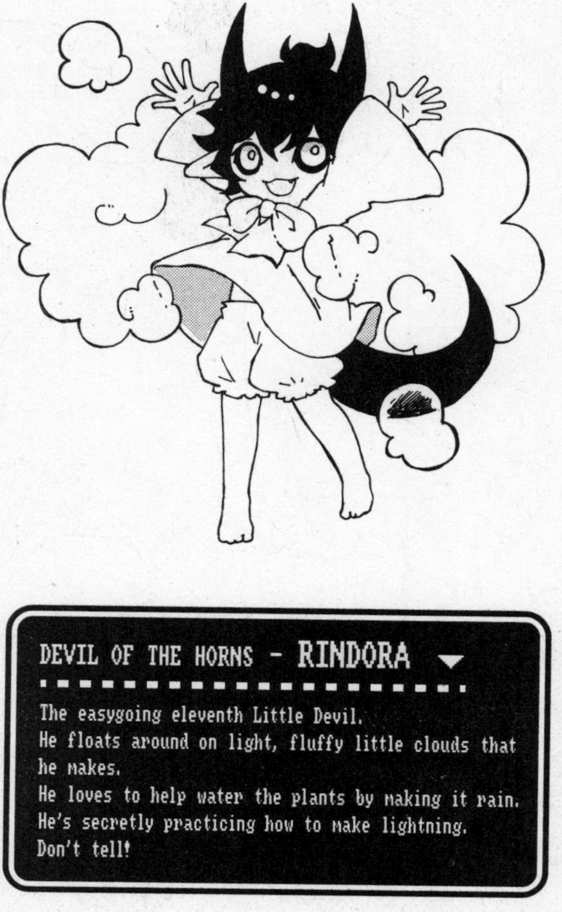

DEVIL OF THE HORNS - RINDORA

The easygoing eleventh Little Devil.
He floats around on light, fluffy little clouds that he makes.
He loves to help water the plants by making it rain.
He's secretly practicing how to make lightning.
Don't tell!

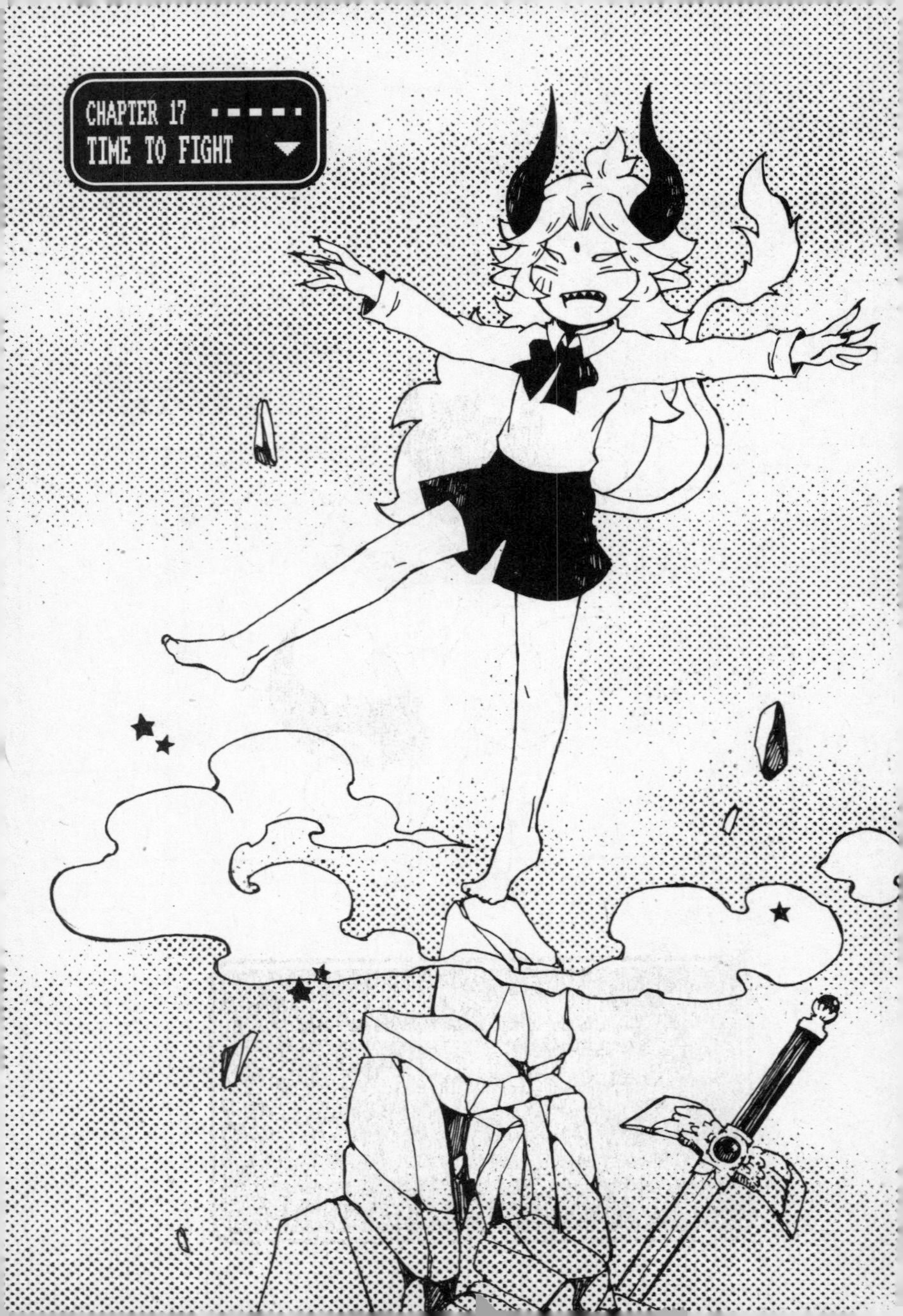
CHAPTER 17
TIME TO FIGHT

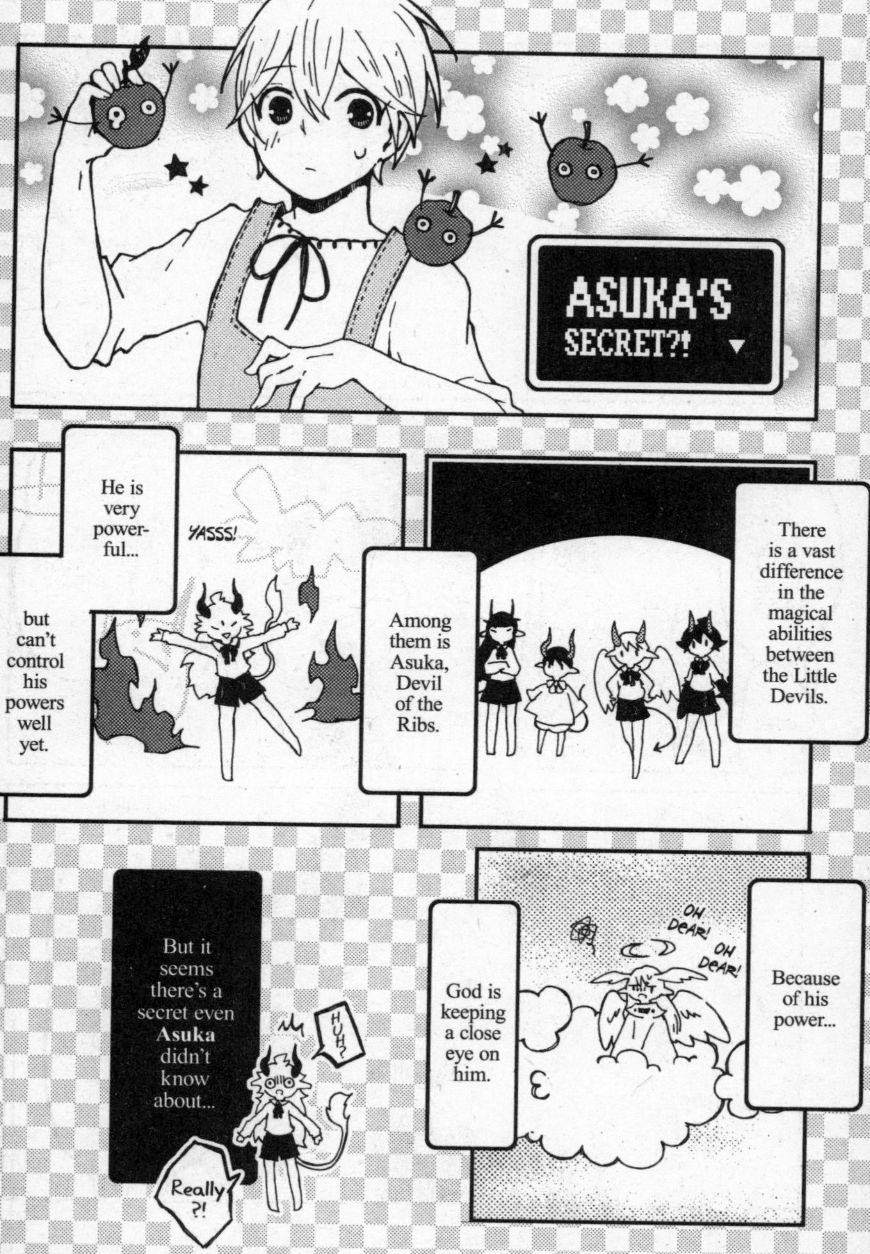
ASUKA'S SECRET?!
There is a vast difference in the magical abilities between the Little Devils.
Among them is Asuka, Devil of the Ribs.
He is very powerful...
YASSS!
but can't control his powers well yet.
Because of his power...
OH DEAR! OH DEAR!
God is keeping a close eye on him.
But it seems there's a secret even Asuka didn't know about...
HUH?
Really?!

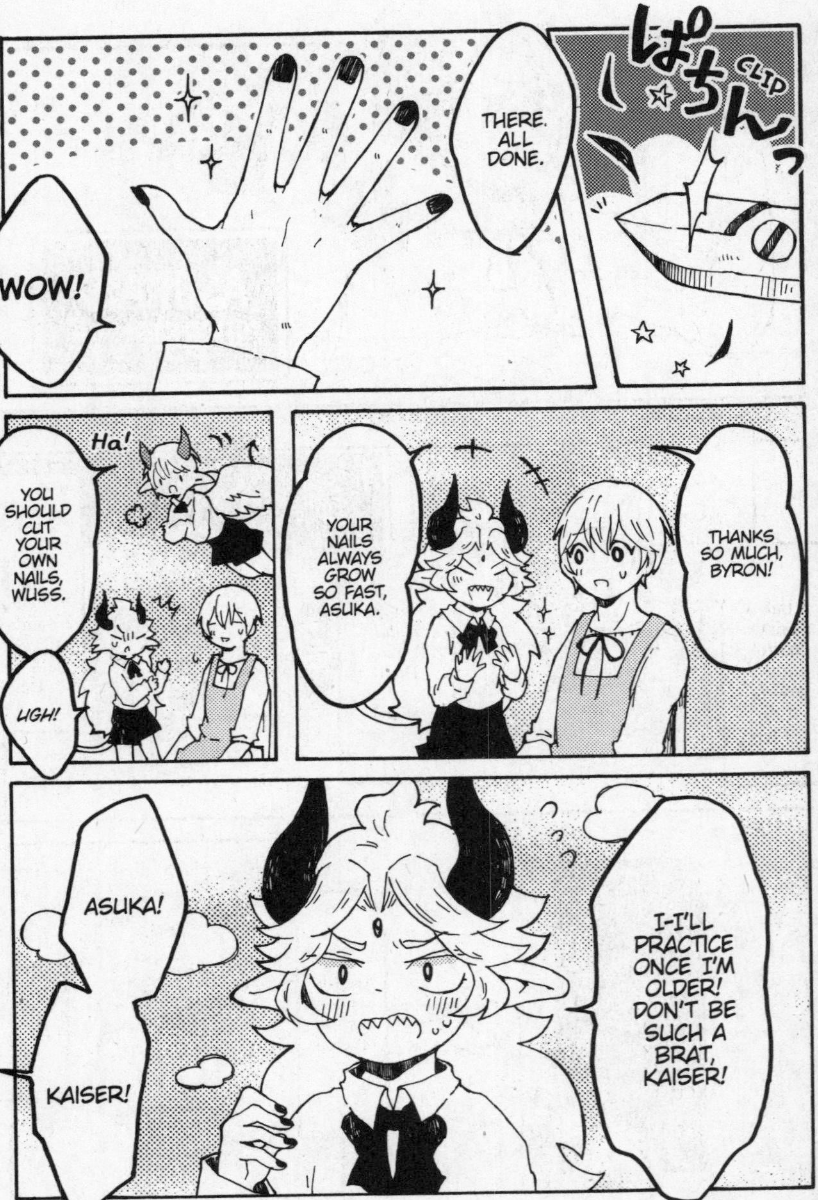
ぱちんっ
CLIP
THERE. ALL DONE.
WOW!
THANKS SO MUCH, BYRON!
YOUR NAILS ALWAYS GROW SO FAST, ASUKA.
Ha!
YOU SHOULD CUT YOUR OWN NAILS, WUSS.
UGH!
I-I'LL PRACTICE ONCE I'M OLDER! DON'T BE SUCH A BRAT, KAISER!
ASUKA!
KAISER!

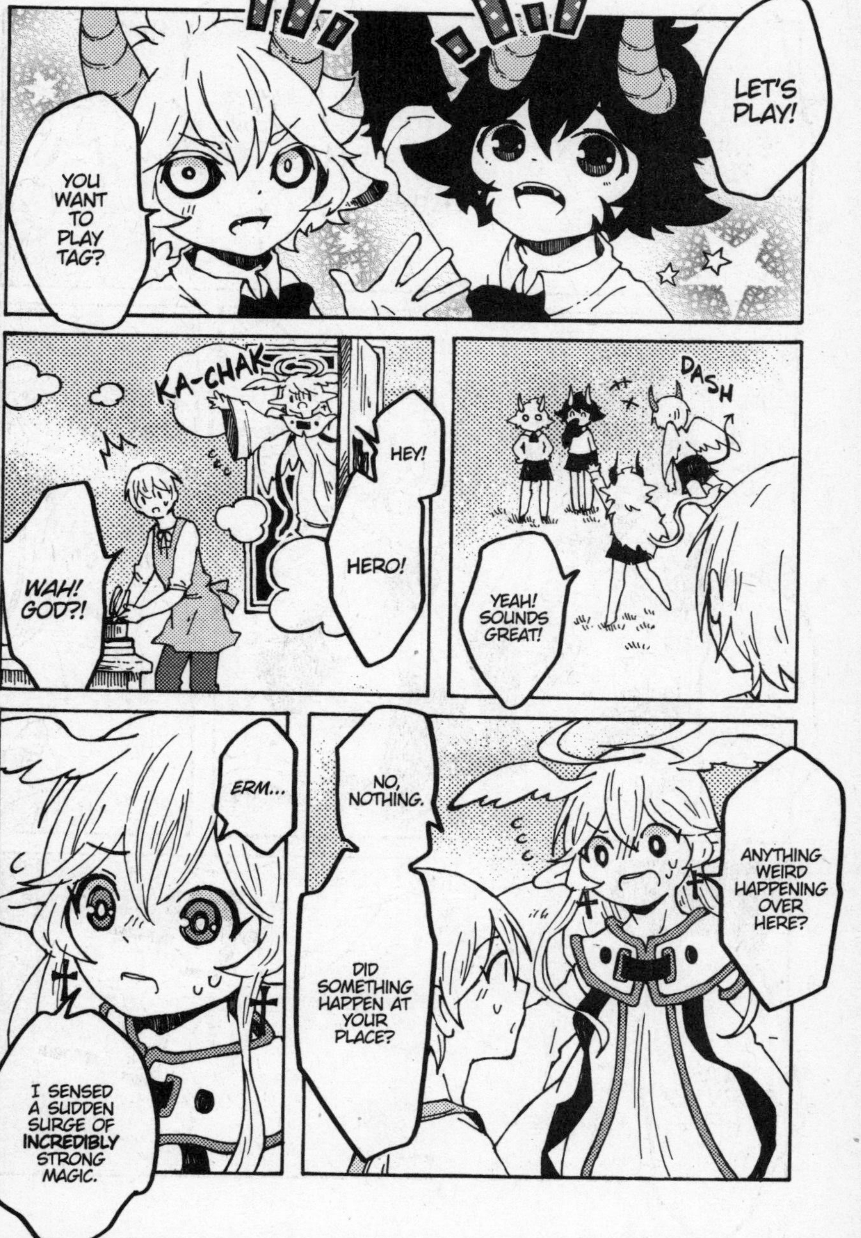
LET'S PLAY!
YOU WANT TO PLAY TAG?
DASH
YEAH! SOUNDS GREAT!
HEY!
HERO!
KA-CHAK
WAH! GOD?!
ANYTHING WEIRD HAPPENING OVER HERE?
NO, NOTHING.
DID SOMETHING HAPPEN AT YOUR PLACE?
ERM...
I SENSED A SUDDEN SURGE OF INCREDIBLY STRONG MAGIC.

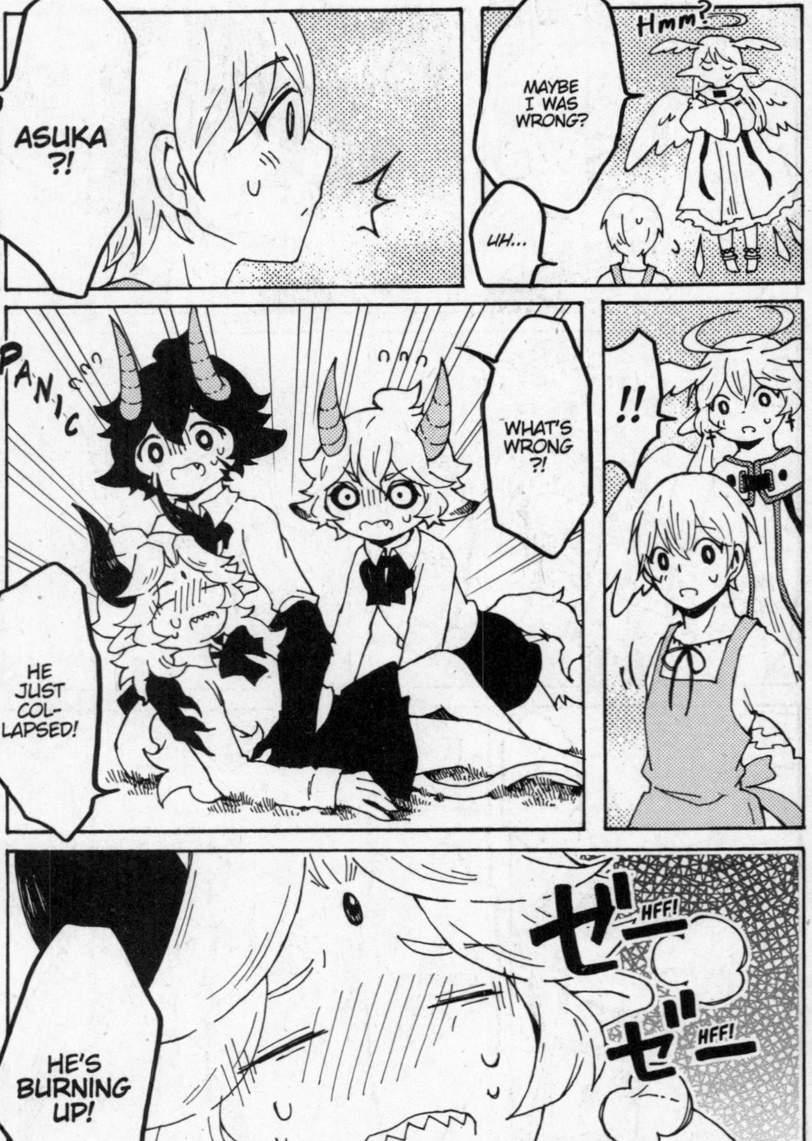
Hmm?
MAYBE I WAS WRONG?
UH...
ASUKA ?!
!!
WHAT'S WRONG ?!
PANIC
HE JUST COL-LAPSED!
ゼー HFF!
ゼー HFF!
HE'S BURNING UP!

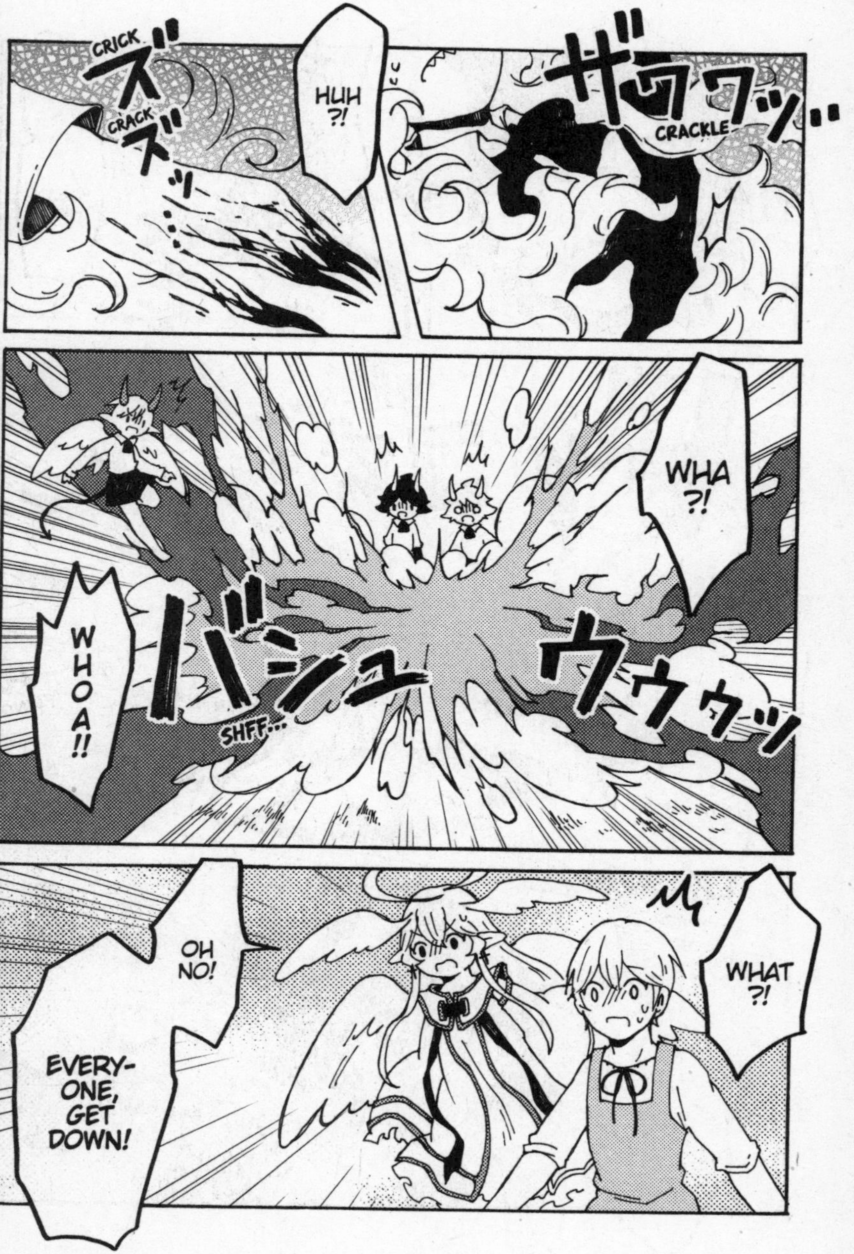

ザワワッ
CRACKLE
HUH ?!
ズズッ
CRICK
CRACK
WHA ?!
バシュウウウッ
SHFF...
WHOA!!
WHAT ?!
OH NO!
EVERY-ONE, GET DOWN!

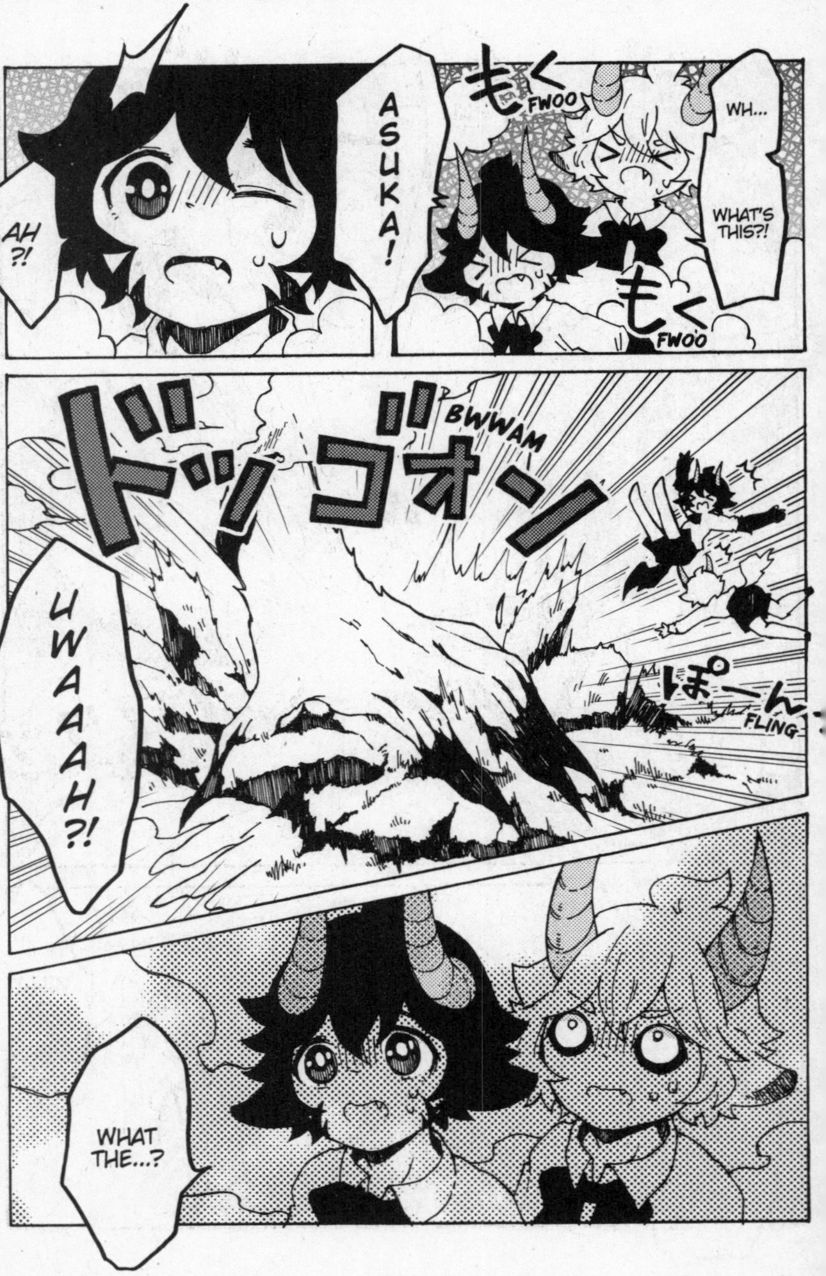
WH... WHAT'S THIS?!
もく
FWOO
ASUKA!
もく
FWOO
AH ?!
ドッゴオーン
BWWAM
ぽーん
FLING
UWAAAAH?!
WHAT THE...?

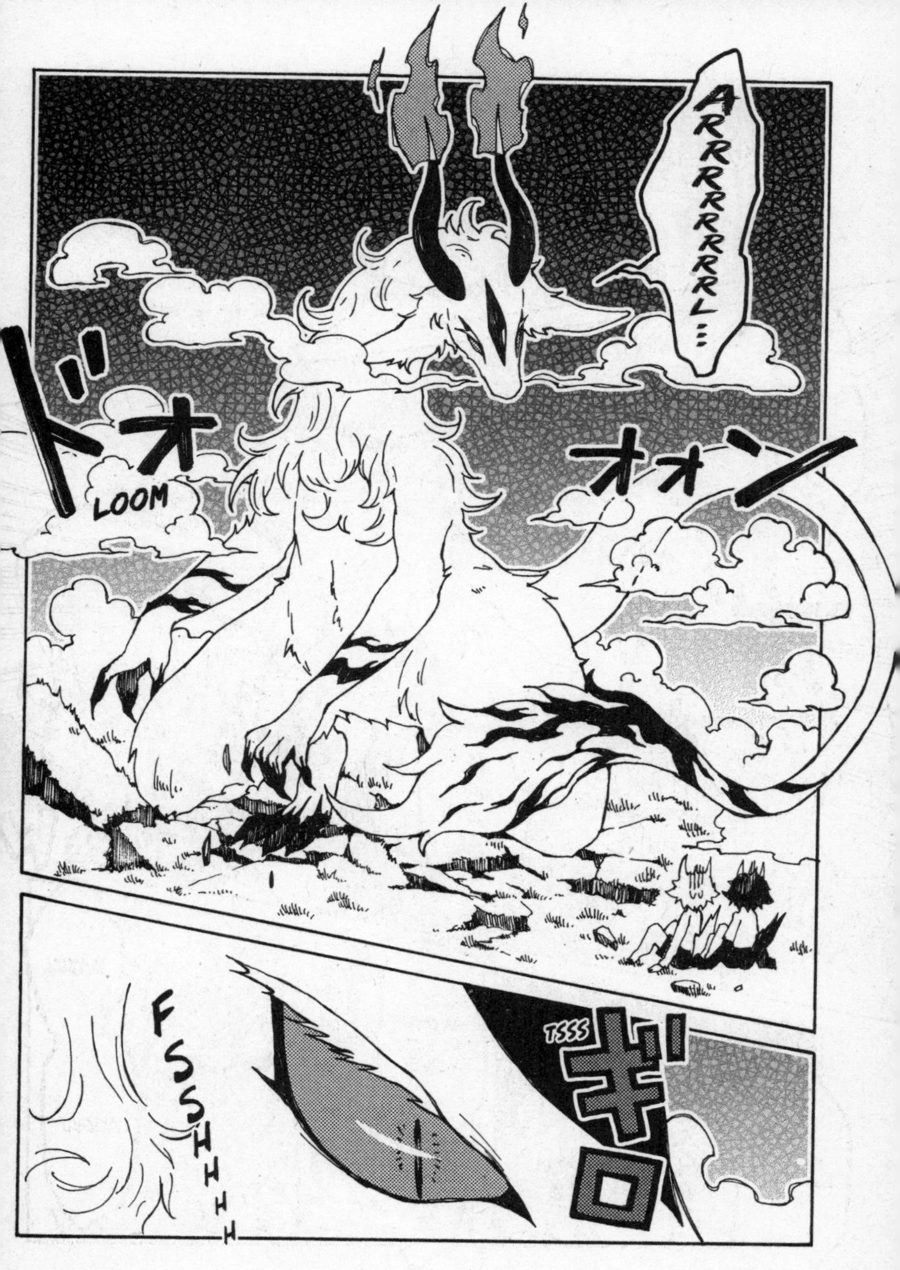
ARRRRRRRRL...
ドオ
LOOM
オオン
TSSS
ギロ
FSSHHHH

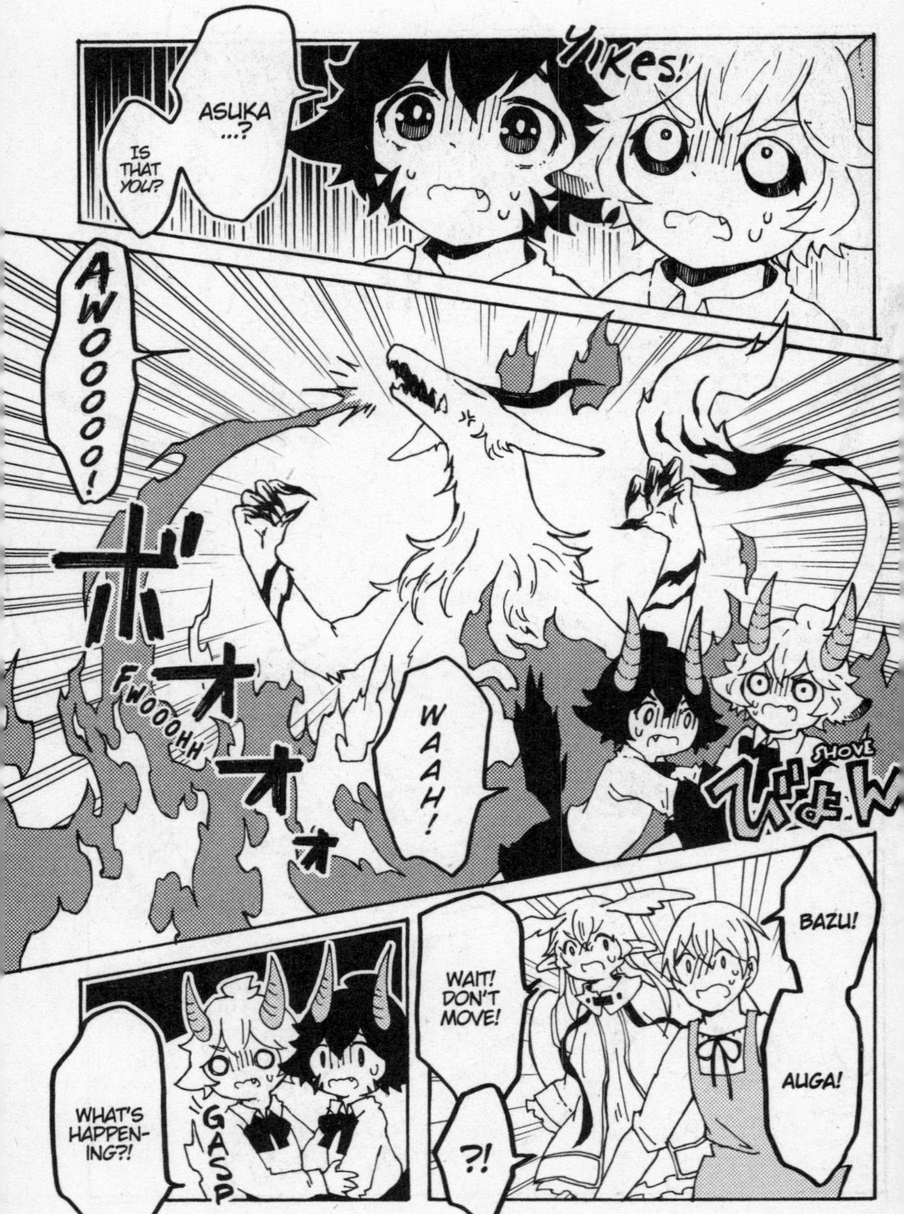
YIKES!
ASUKA ...?
IS THAT YOU?
AWOOOOOOO!
ボーオオオ
FWOOOHH
WAAH!
SHOVE
ぴょん
BAZU!
AUGA!
WAIT! DON'T MOVE!
?!
GASP
WHAT'S HAPPEN-ING?!

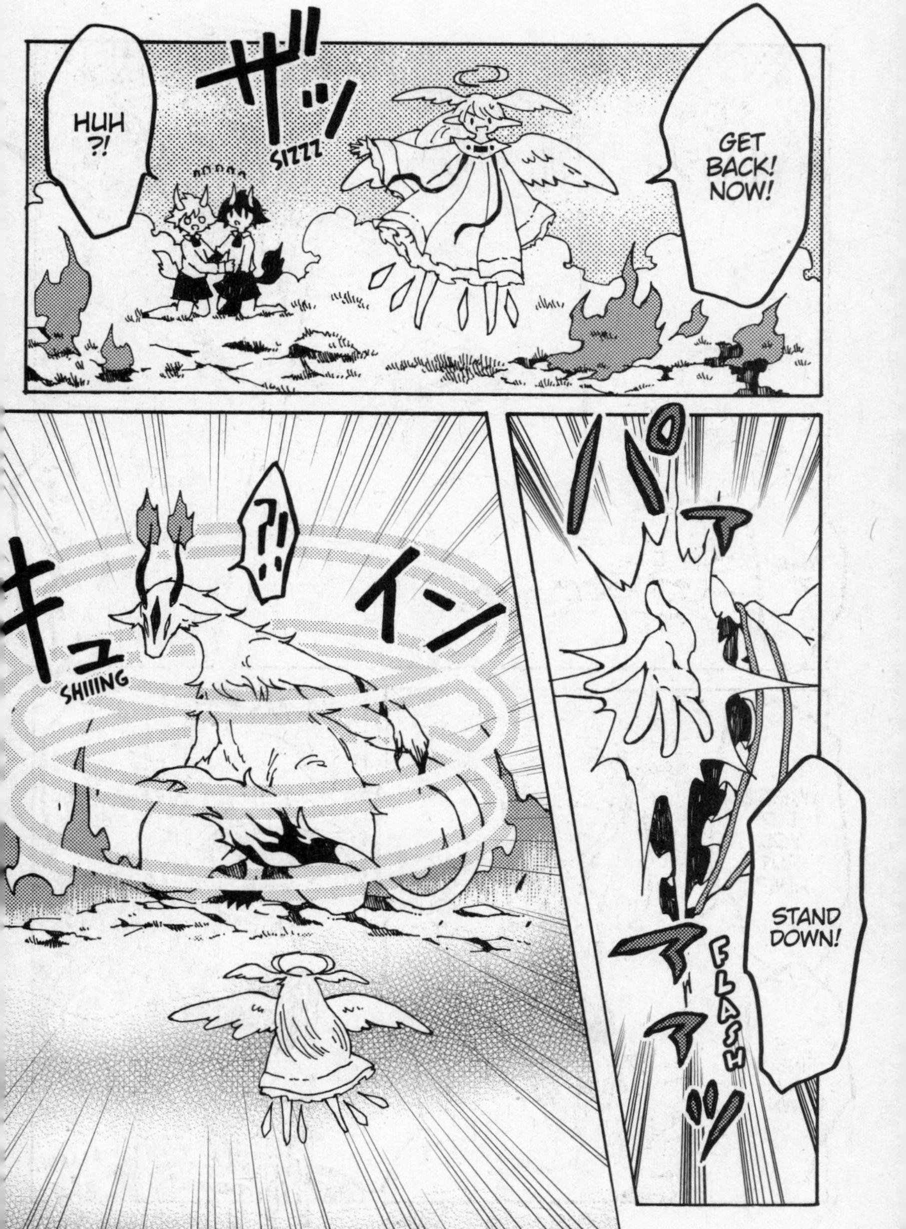
GET BACK! NOW!
ザッ
SIZZZ
HUH ?!
パァァァッ
FLASH
STAND DOWN!
キュイン
SHIIING
?!

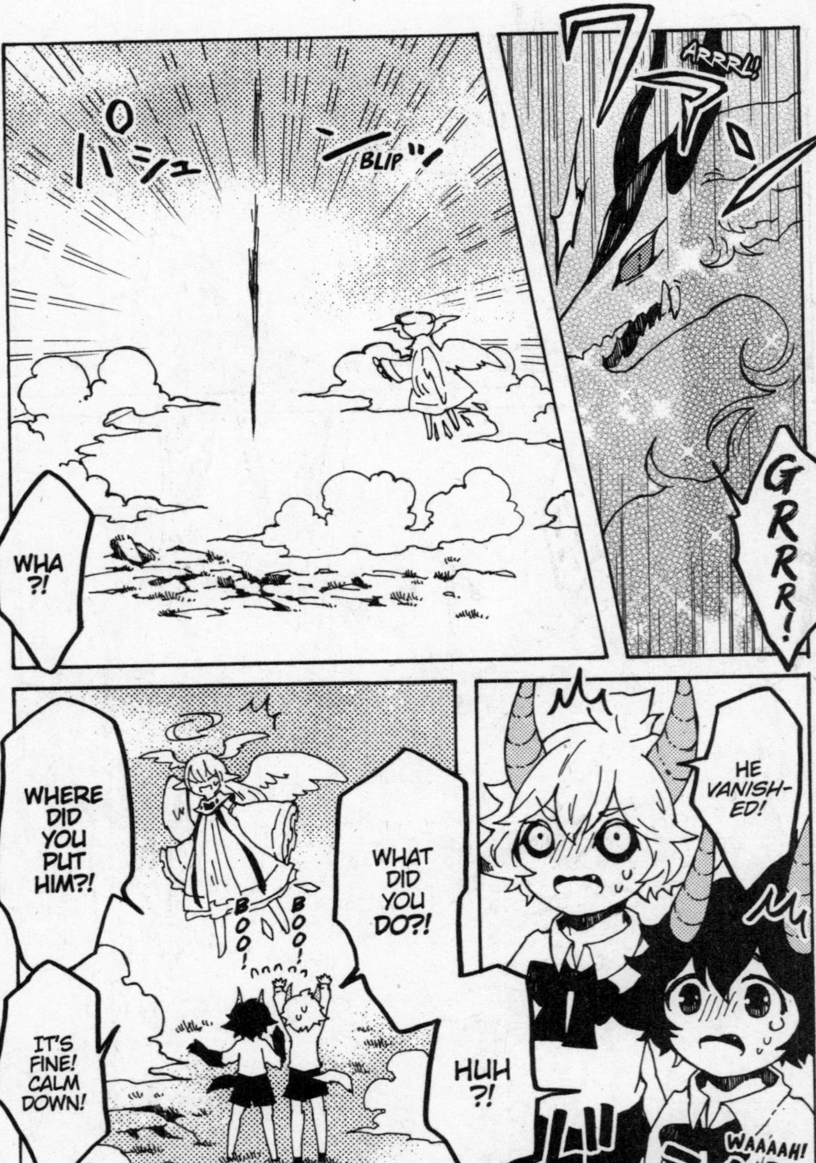
ARRRL!!
GRRRR!
BLIP
WHA?!
HE VANISH-ED!
HUH?!
WAAAAH!
WHERE DID YOU PUT HIM?!
WHAT DID YOU DO?!
BOO! BOO!
IT'S FINE! CALM DOWN!

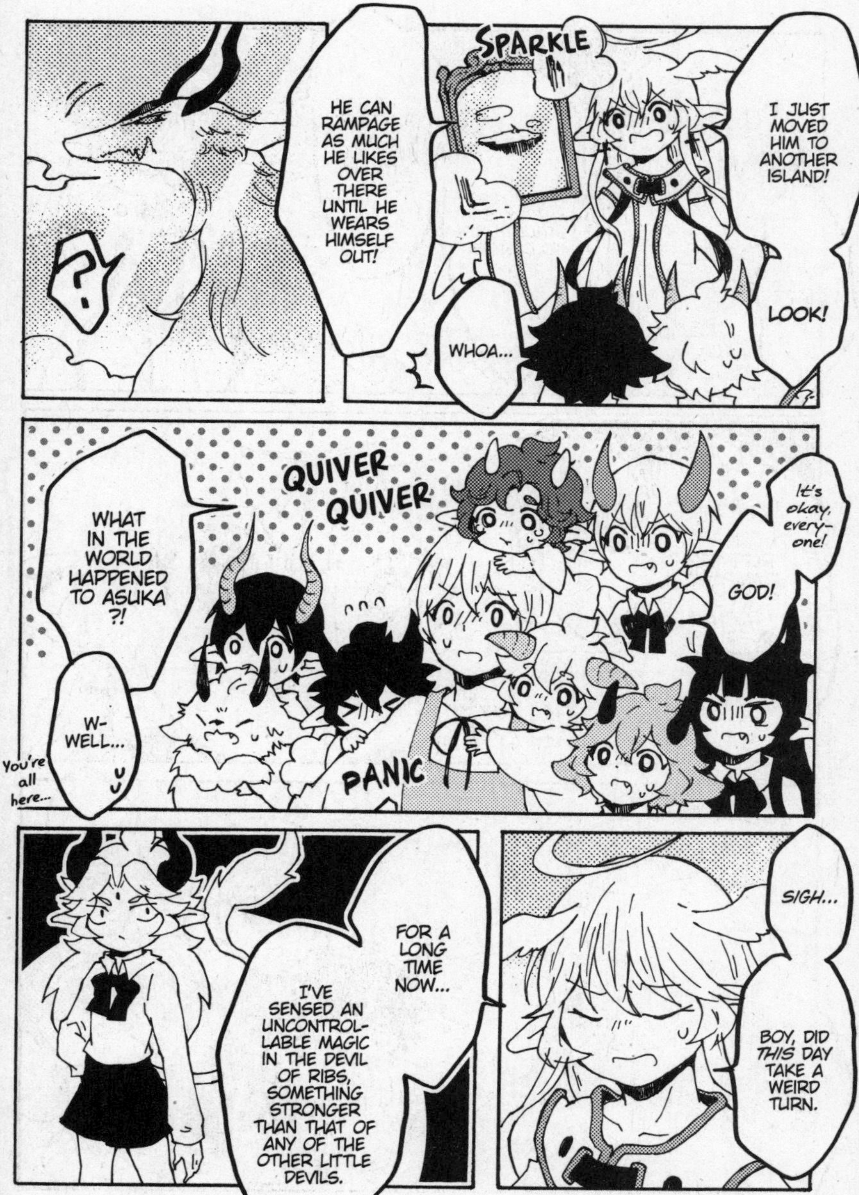
SPARKLE
I JUST MOVED HIM TO ANOTHER ISLAND!
LOOK!
HE CAN RAMPAGE AS MUCH HE LIKES OVER THERE UNTIL HE WEARS HIMSELF OUT!
WHOA...
?
QUIVER QUIVER
It's okay, every-one!
GOD!
WHAT IN THE WORLD HAPPENED TO ASUKA?!
PANIC
W-WELL...
You're all here...
SIGH...
BOY, DID THIS DAY TAKE A WEIRD TURN.
FOR A LONG TIME NOW...
I'VE SENSED AN UNCONTROL-LABLE MAGIC IN THE DEVIL OF RIBS, SOMETHING STRONGER THAN THAT OF ANY OF THE OTHER LITTLE DEVILS.

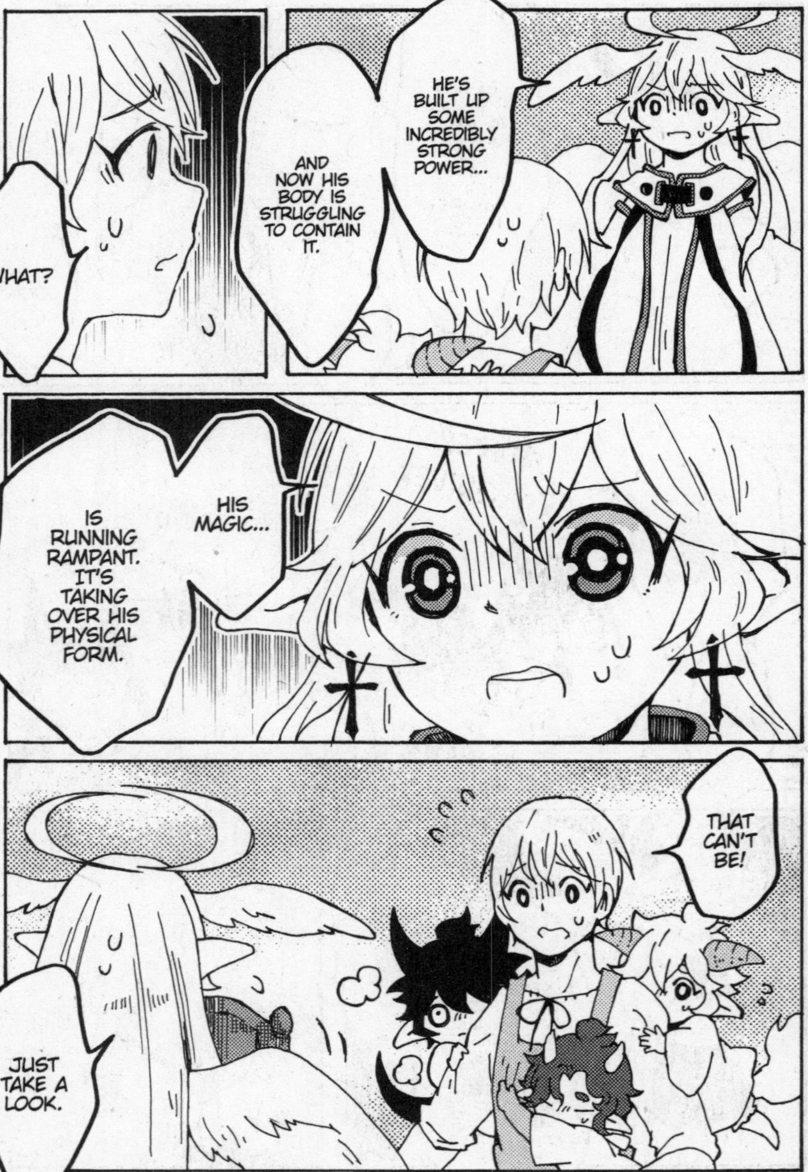
HE'S BUILT UP SOME INCREDIBLY STRONG POWER...
AND NOW HIS BODY IS STRUGGLING TO CONTAIN IT.
WHAT?
HIS MAGIC...
IS RUNNING RAMPANT. IT'S TAKING OVER HIS PHYSICAL FORM.
THAT CAN'T BE!
JUST TAKE A LOOK.

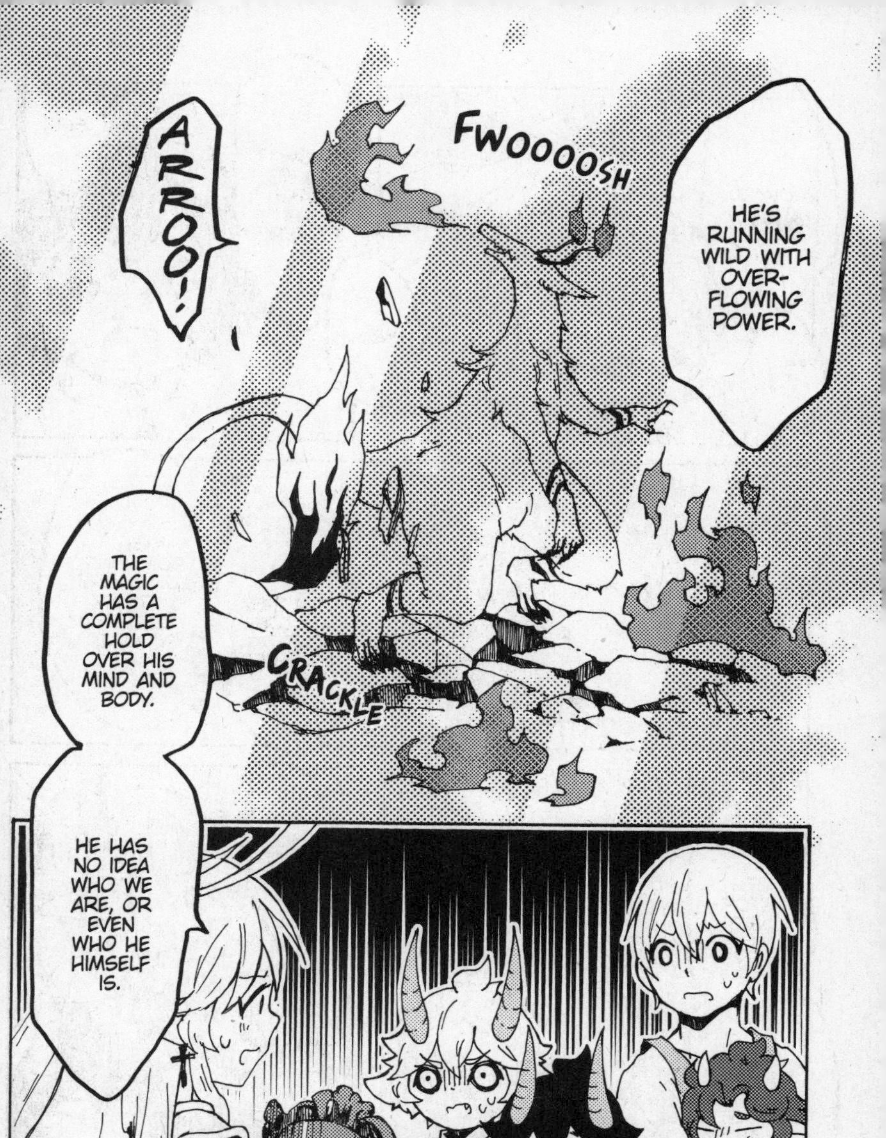
HE'S RUNNING WILD WITH OVER-FLOWING POWER.
FWOOOOSH
ARROO!
THE MAGIC HAS A COMPLETE HOLD OVER HIS MIND AND BODY.
CRACKLE
HE HAS NO IDEA WHO WE ARE, OR EVEN WHO HE HIMSELF IS.

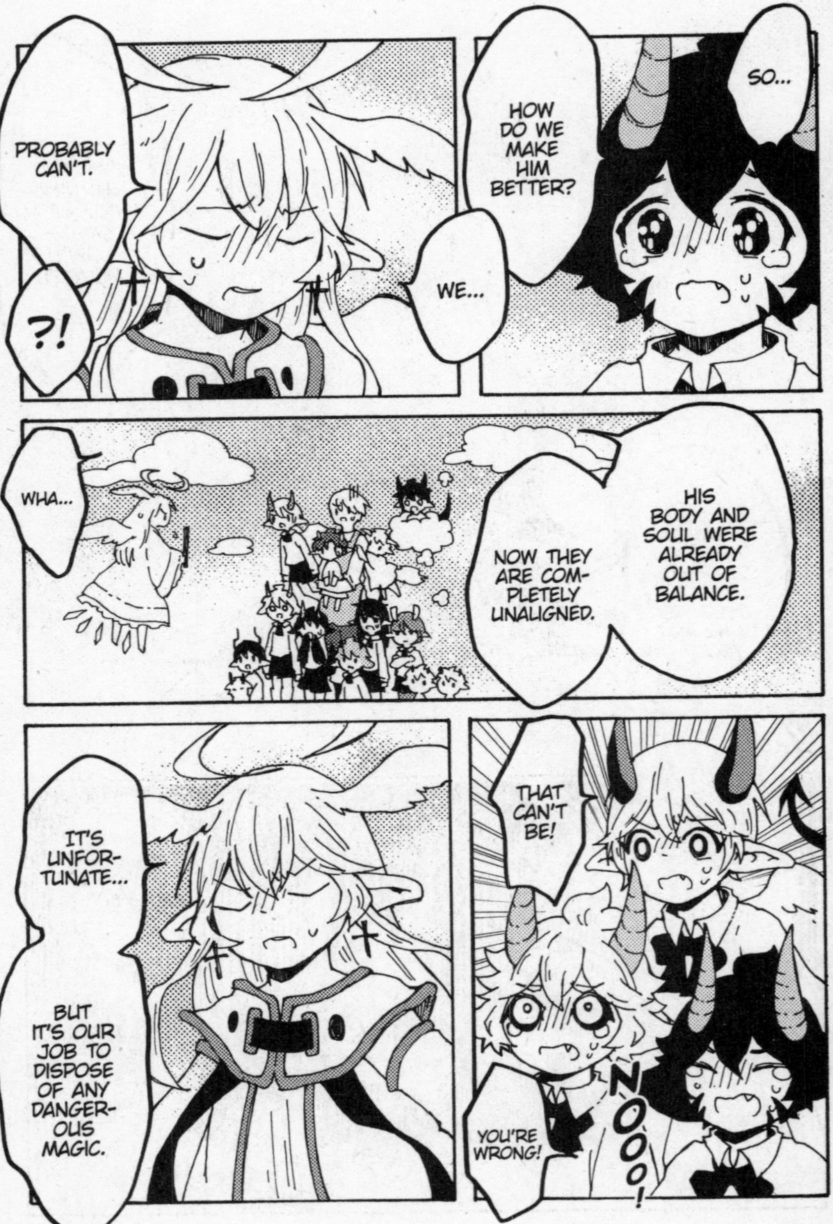
SO...
HOW DO WE MAKE HIM BETTER?
WE...
PROBABLY CAN'T.
?!
HIS BODY AND SOUL WERE ALREADY OUT OF BALANCE.
NOW THEY ARE COM-PLETELY UNALIGNED.
WHA...
THAT CAN'T BE!
NOOOO!
YOU'RE WRONG!
IT'S UNFOR-TUNATE...
BUT IT'S OUR JOB TO DISPOSE OF ANY DANGER-OUS MAGIC.

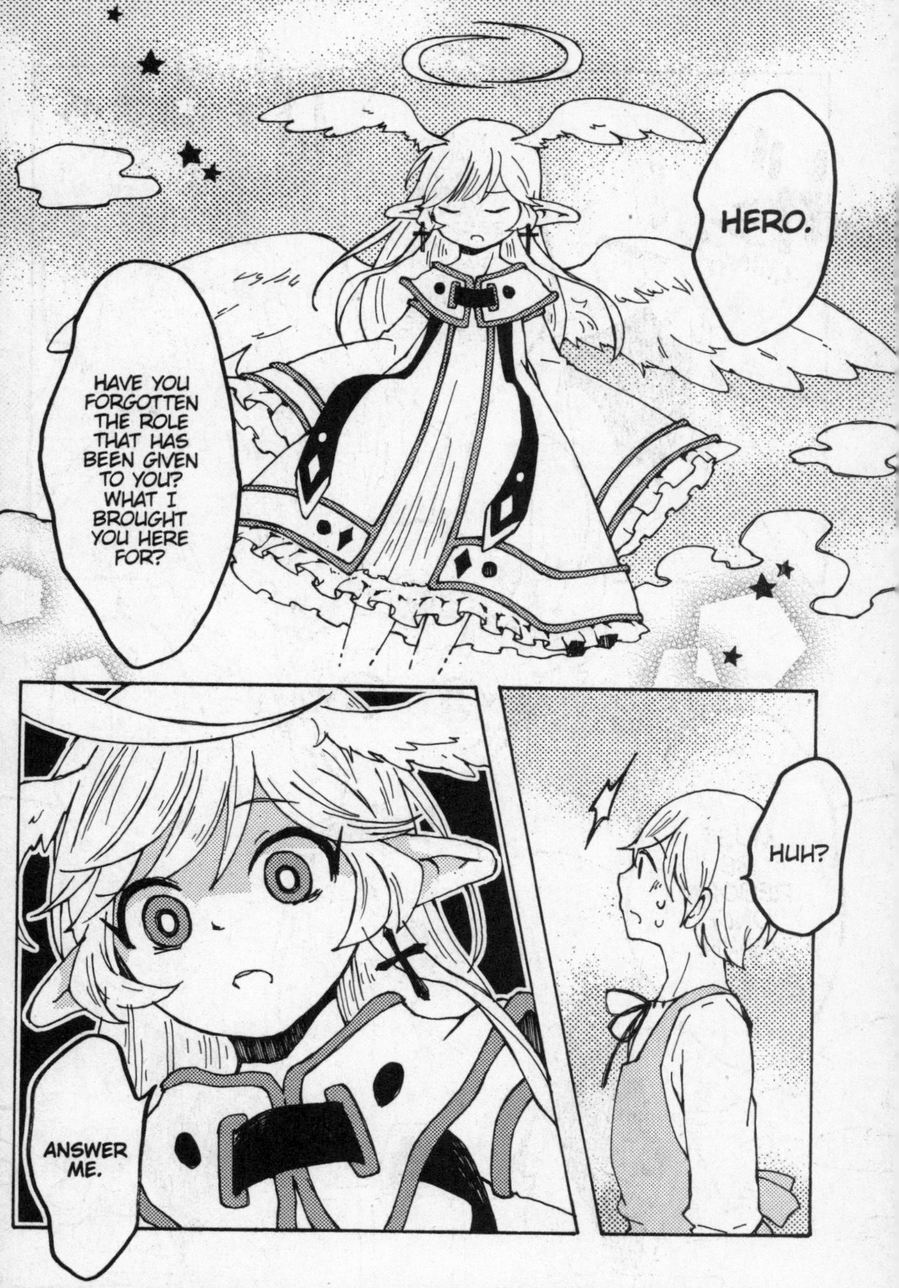
HERO.
HAVE YOU FORGOTTEN THE ROLE THAT HAS BEEN GIVEN TO YOU? WHAT I BROUGHT YOU HERE FOR?
HUH?
ANSWER ME.

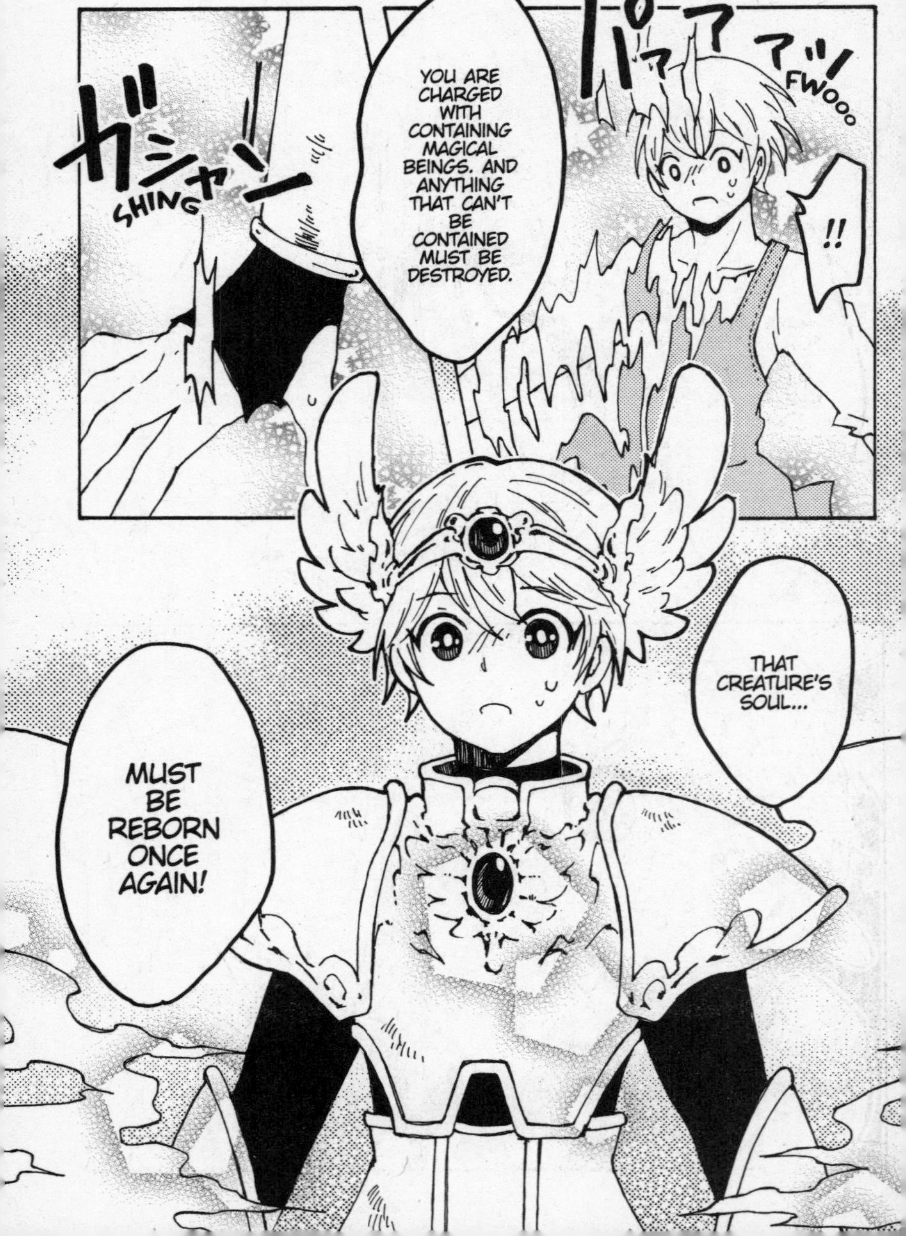
FWOOO
!!
YOU ARE CHARGED WITH CONTAINING MAGICAL BEINGS. AND ANYTHING THAT CAN'T BE CONTAINED MUST BE DESTROYED.
SHING
THAT CREATURE'S SOUL...
MUST BE REBORN ONCE AGAIN!

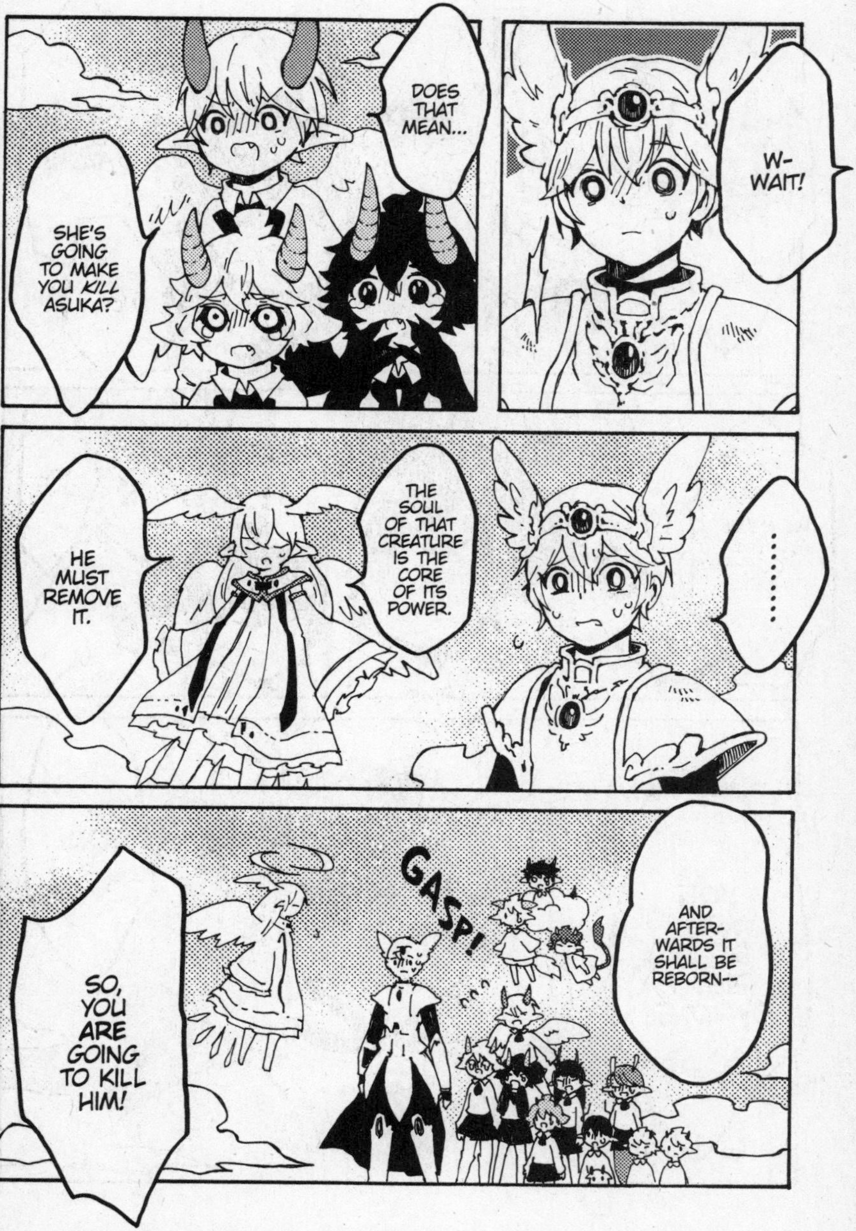
W-WAIT!
DOES THAT MEAN...
SHE'S GOING TO MAKE YOU *KILL* ASUKA?
......
THE SOUL OF THAT CREATURE IS THE CORE OF ITS POWER.
HE MUST REMOVE IT.
AND AFTER-WARDS IT SHALL BE REBORN--
GASP!
SO, YOU ARE GOING TO KILL HIM!

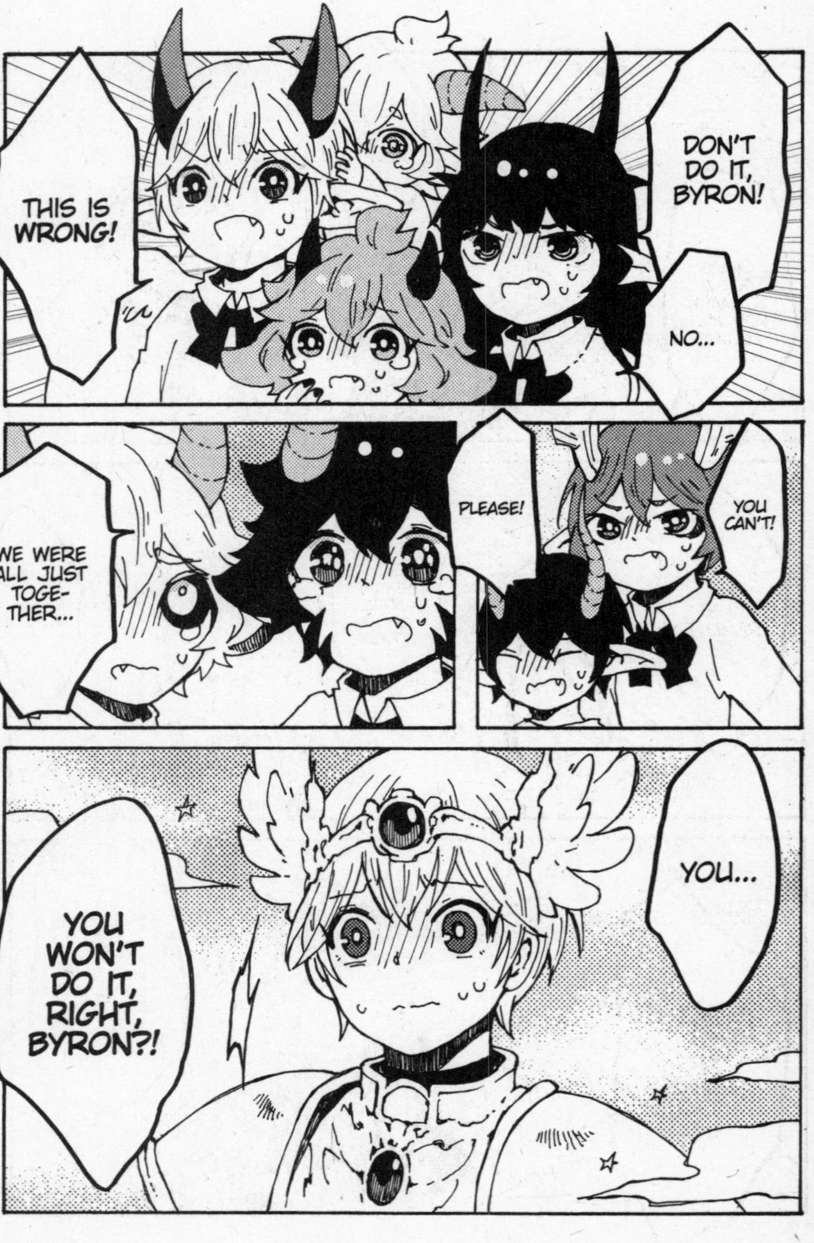
DON'T DO IT, BYRON!
NO...
THIS IS WRONG!
YOU CAN'T!
PLEASE!
WE WERE ALL JUST TOGE-THER...
YOU...
YOU WON'T DO IT, RIGHT, BYRON?!

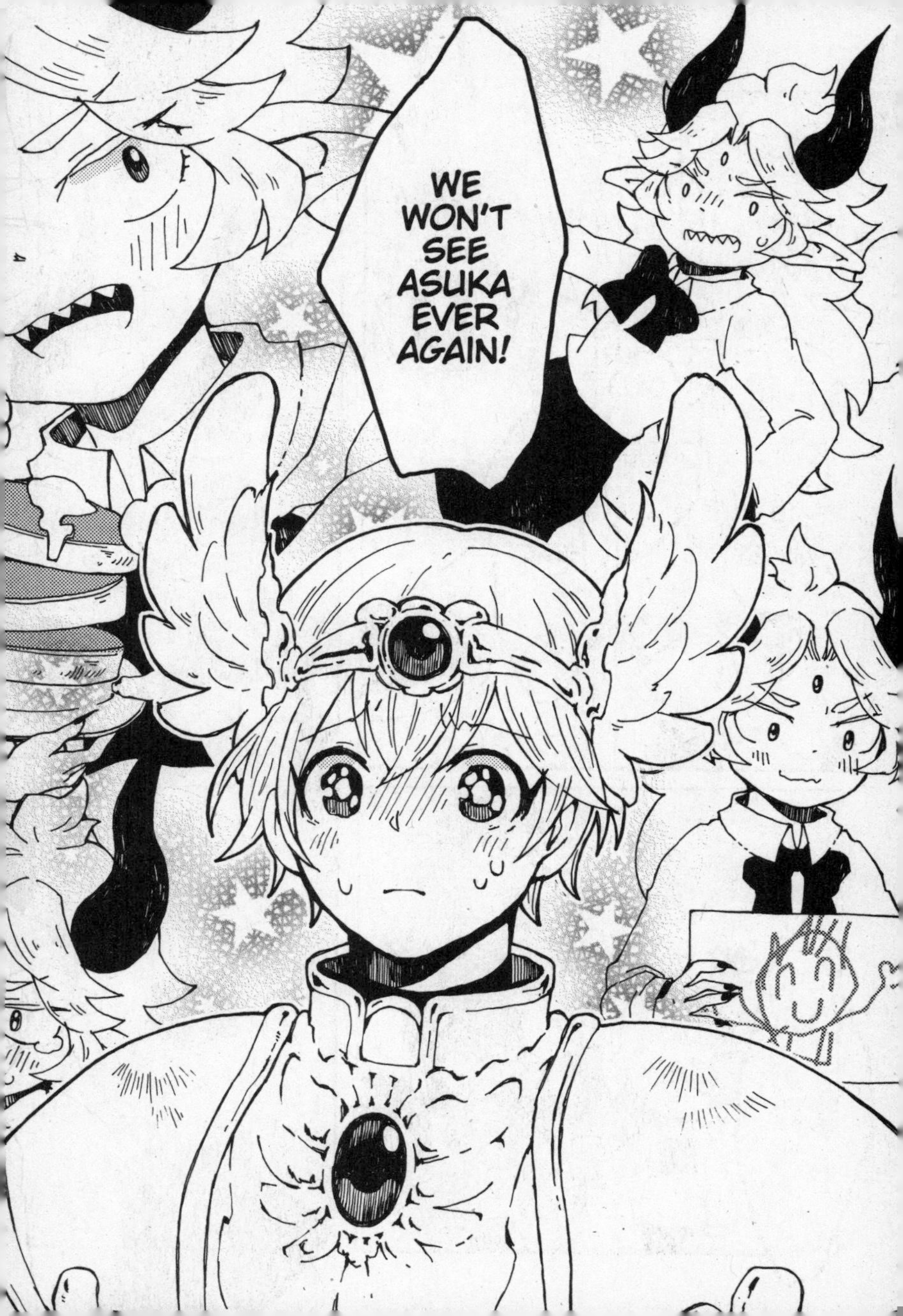
WE WON'T SEE ASUKA EVER AGAIN!

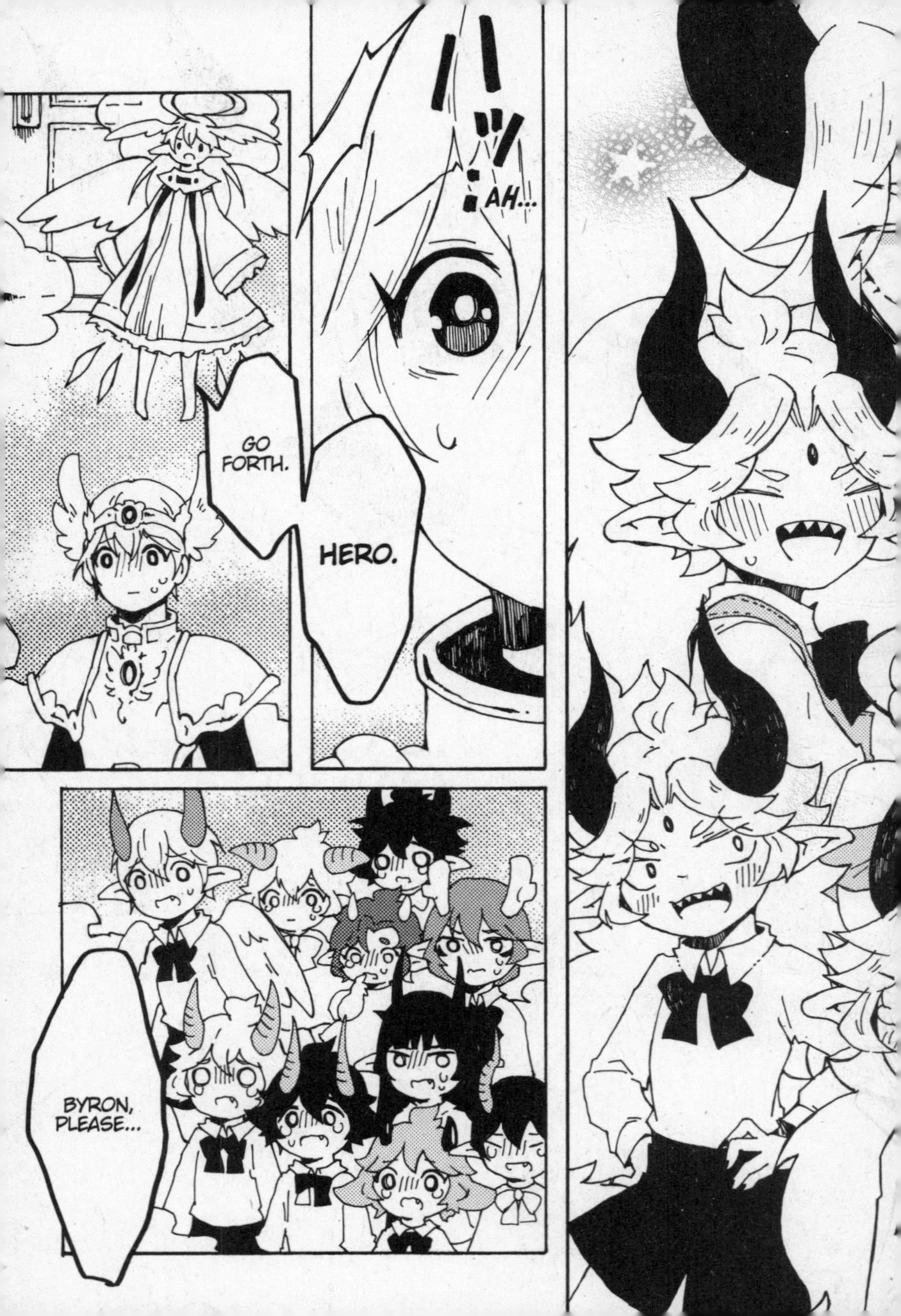
ハッ
AH...
GO FORTH.
HERO.
BYRON, PLEASE...

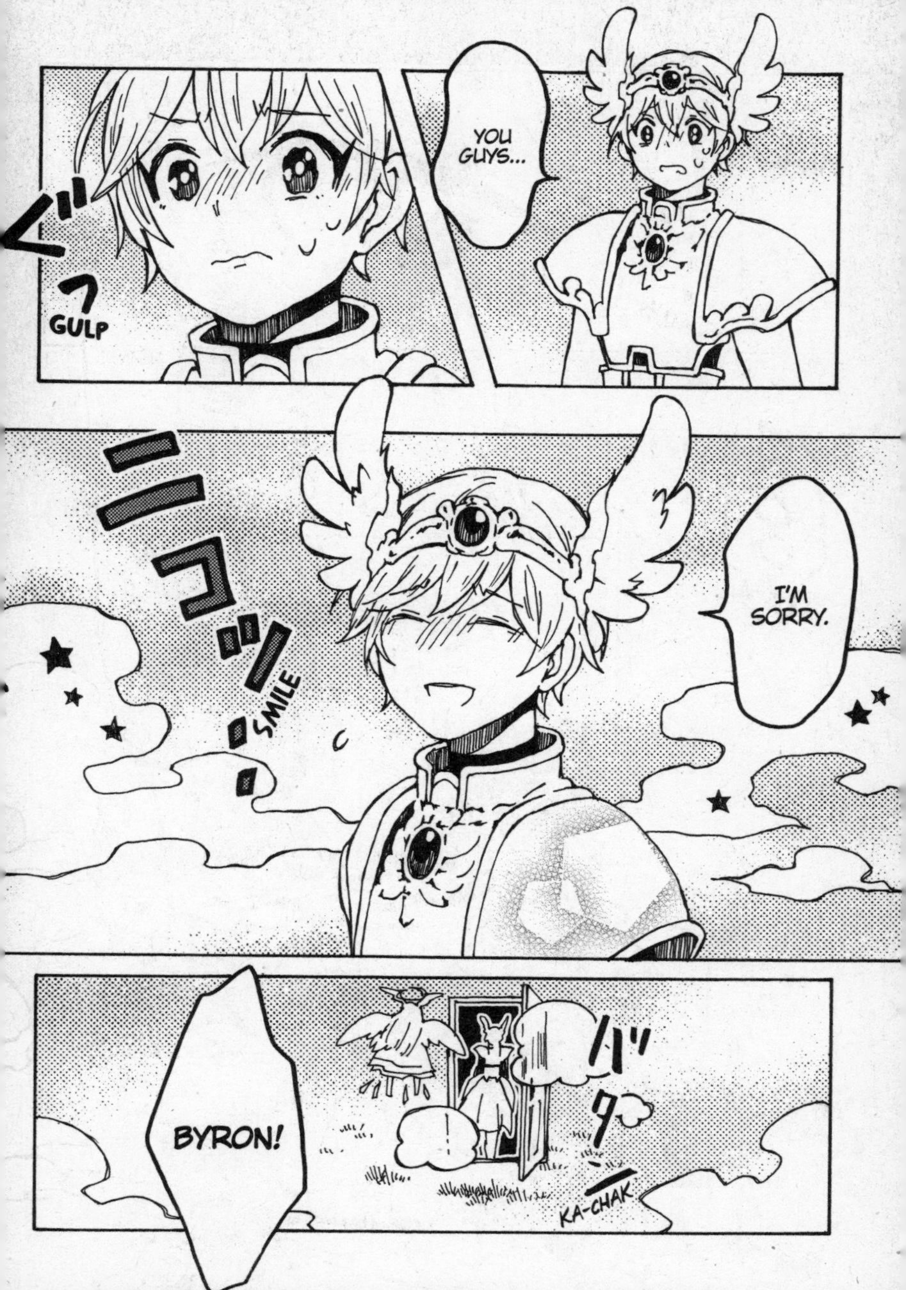
YOU GUYS...
GULP
I'M SORRY.
SMILE
BYRON!
KA-CHAK

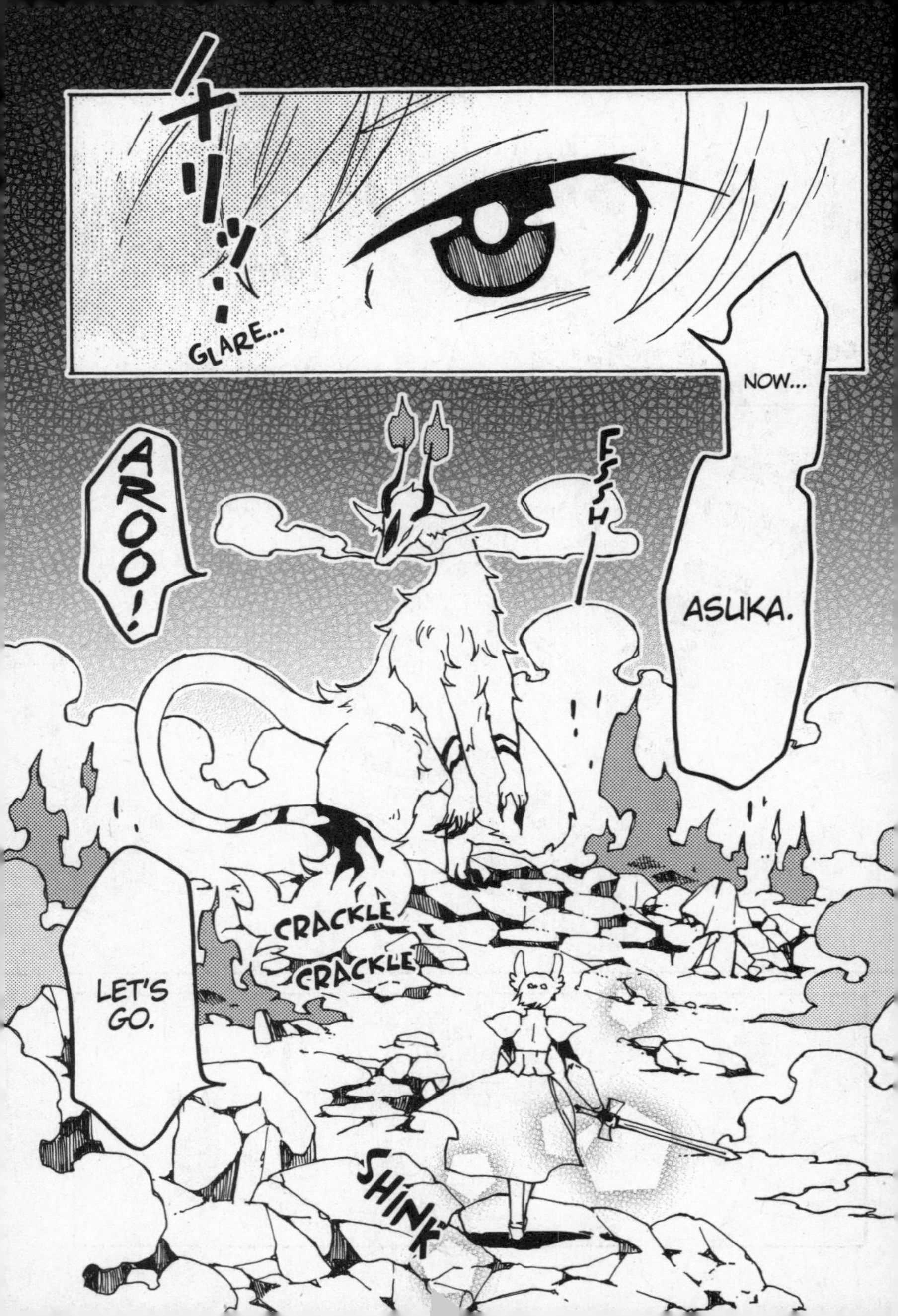
GLARE...
NOW...
ASUKA.
FSSH
AROO!
CRACKLE
CRACKLE
LET'S GO.
SHINK

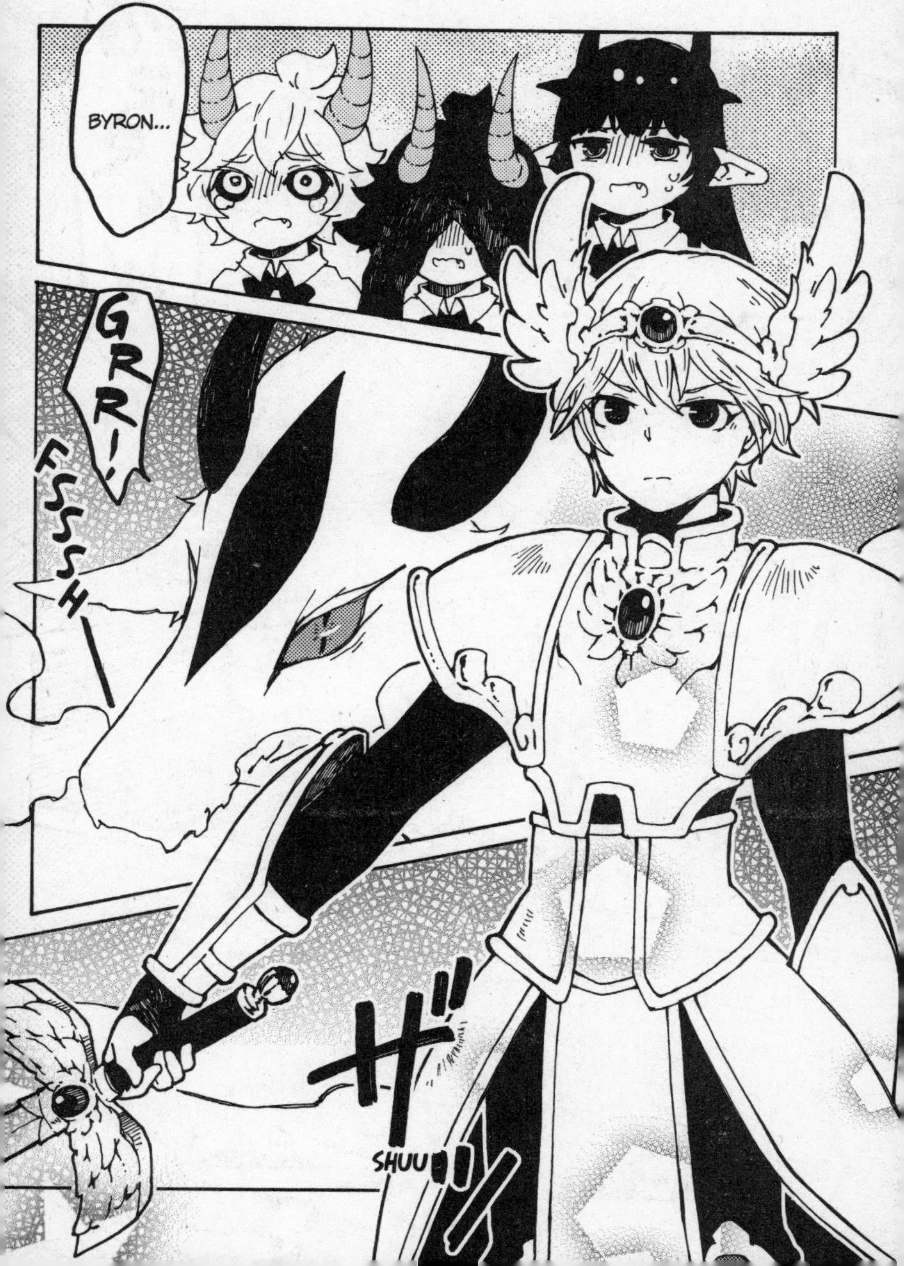
BYRON...
GRR!
FSSSH
SHUU

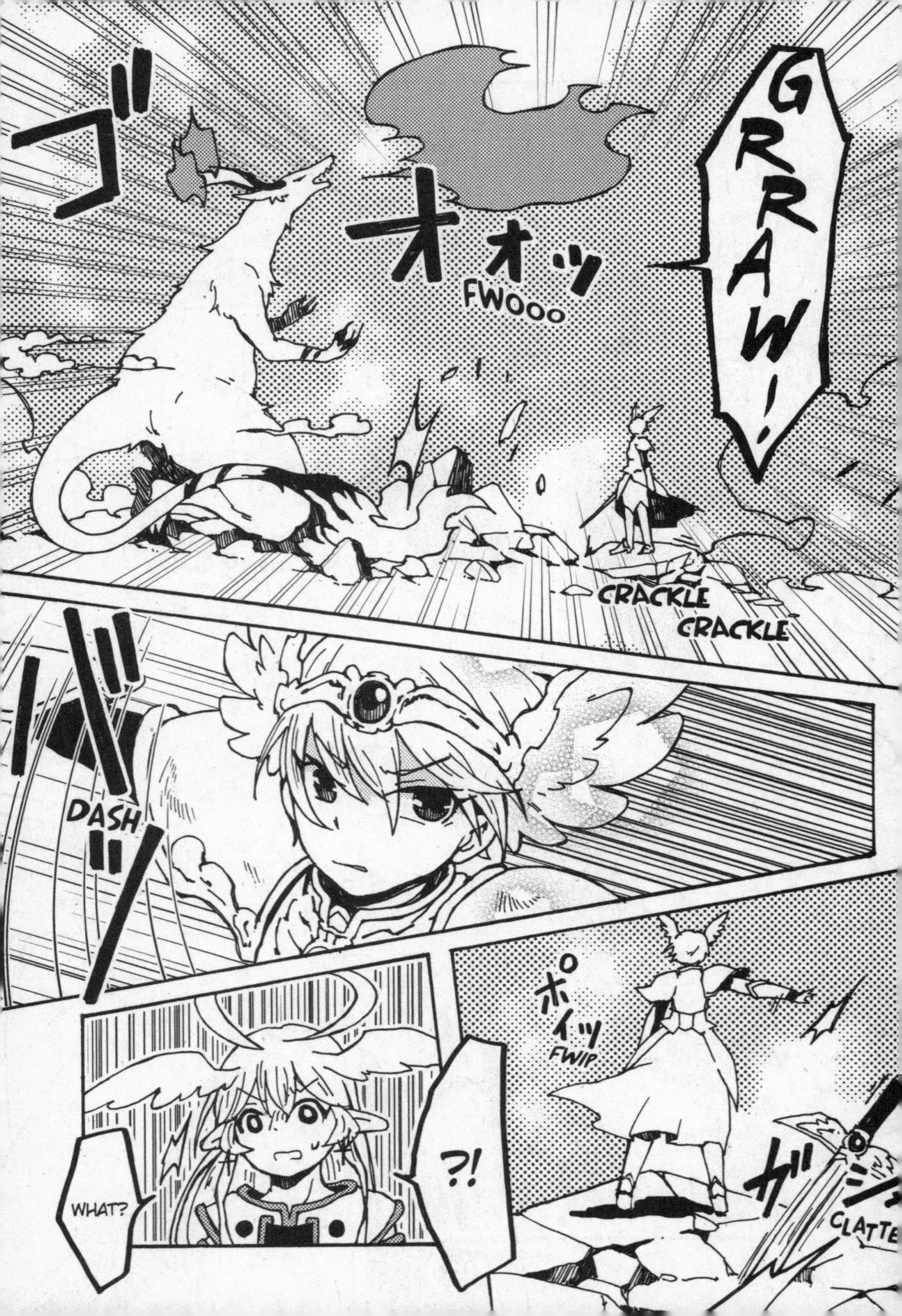
GRRAW!
ゴオオッ
FWOOO
CRACKLE
CRACKLE
DASH
ポイッ
FWIP
CLATTE
?!
WHAT?

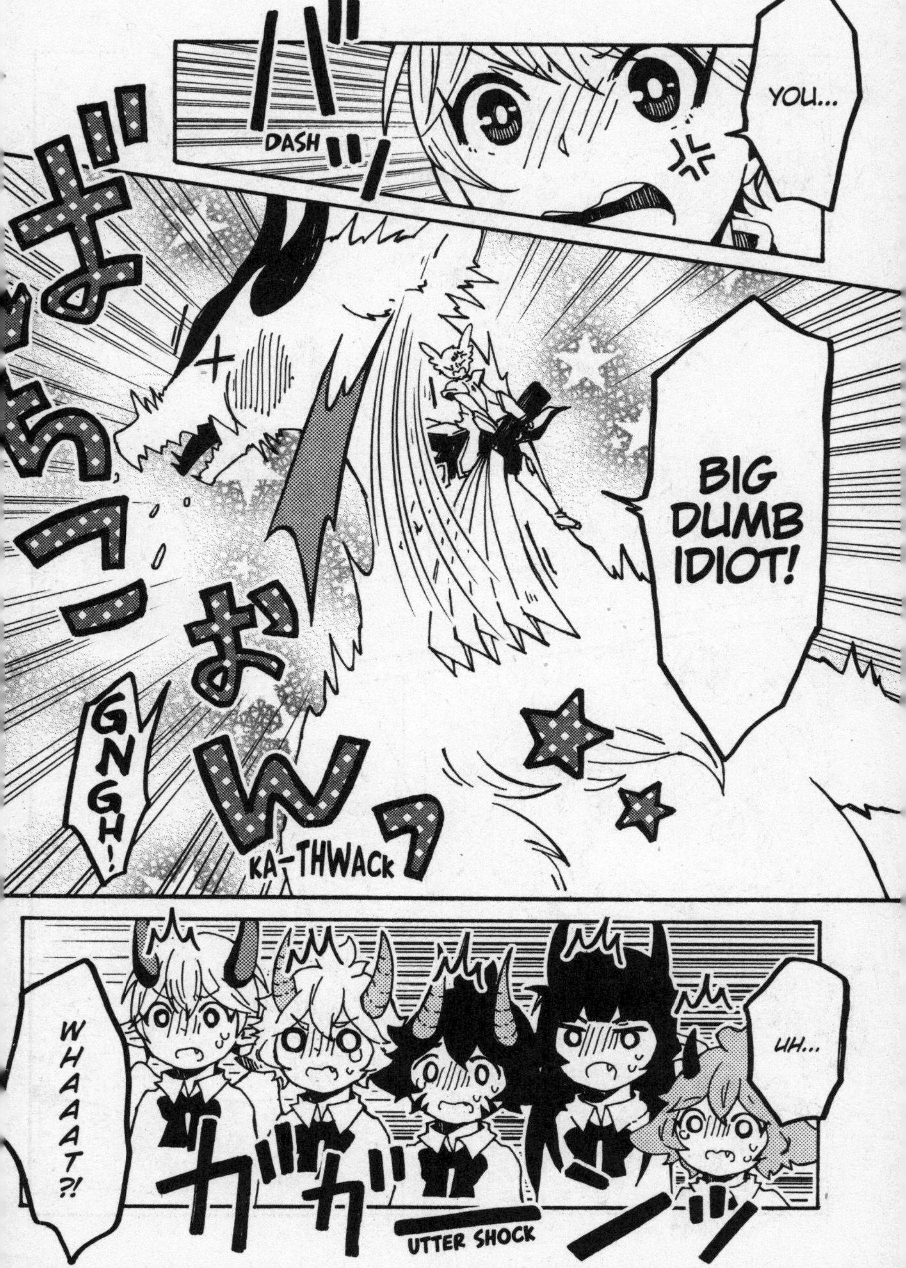
YOU...
DASH
BIG DUMB IDIOT!
GNGH!
KA-THWACK
UH...
WHAAAAT?!
UTTER SHOCK

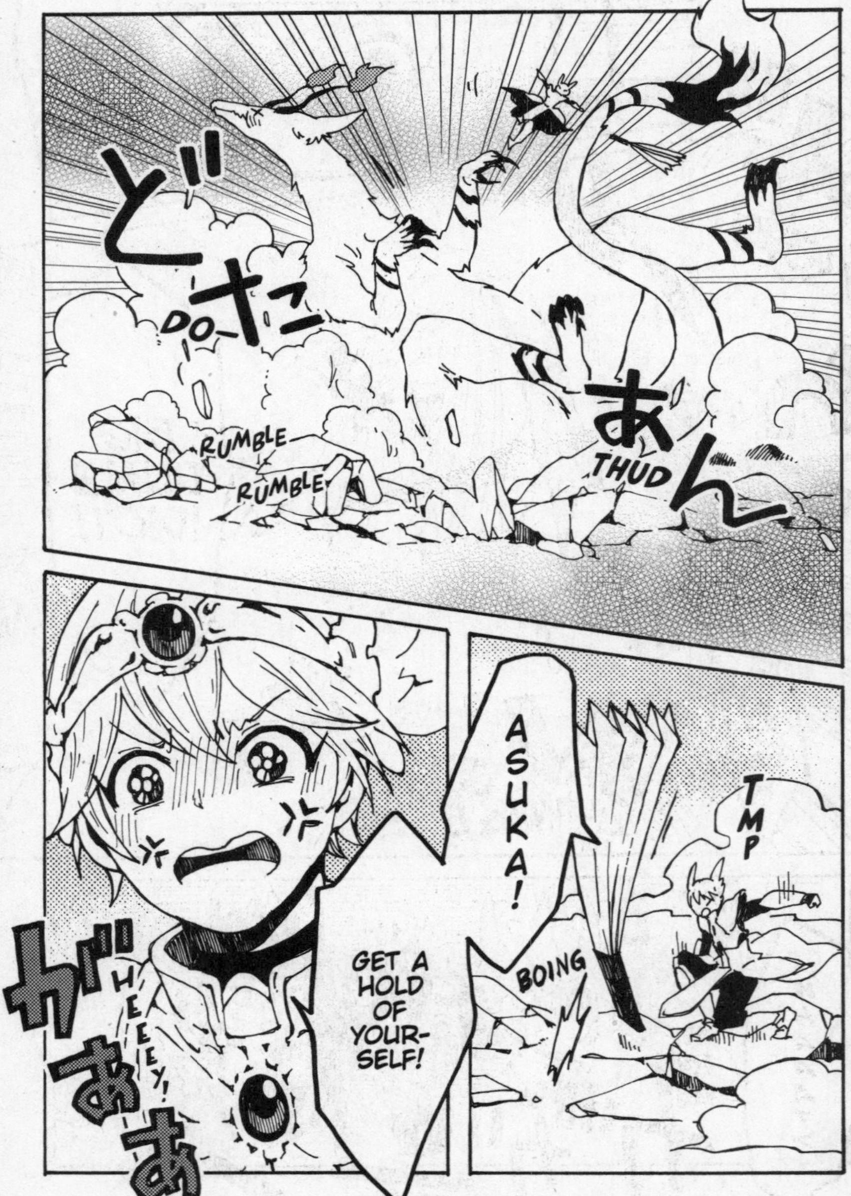
どかーん
DO-
RUMBLE
RUMBLE
THUD
ASUKA!
GET A HOLD OF YOURSELF!
TMP
BOING
がぁぁ
HEEEEY!

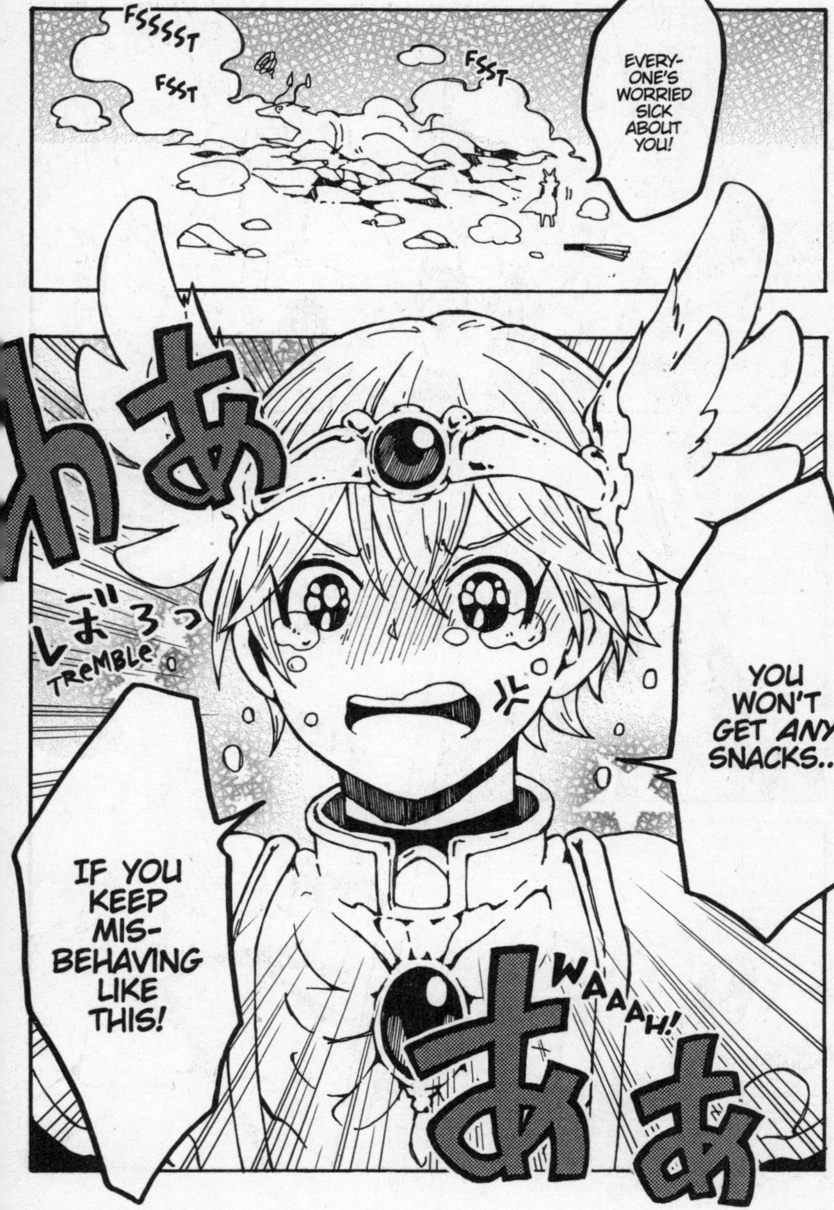
EVERY-ONE'S WORRIED SICK ABOUT YOU!
FSSST
FSSSSST
FSST
YOU WON'T GET ANY SNACKS...
わあ
TREMBLE
IF YOU KEEP MIS-BEHAVING LIKE THIS!
WAAAAH!
ああ

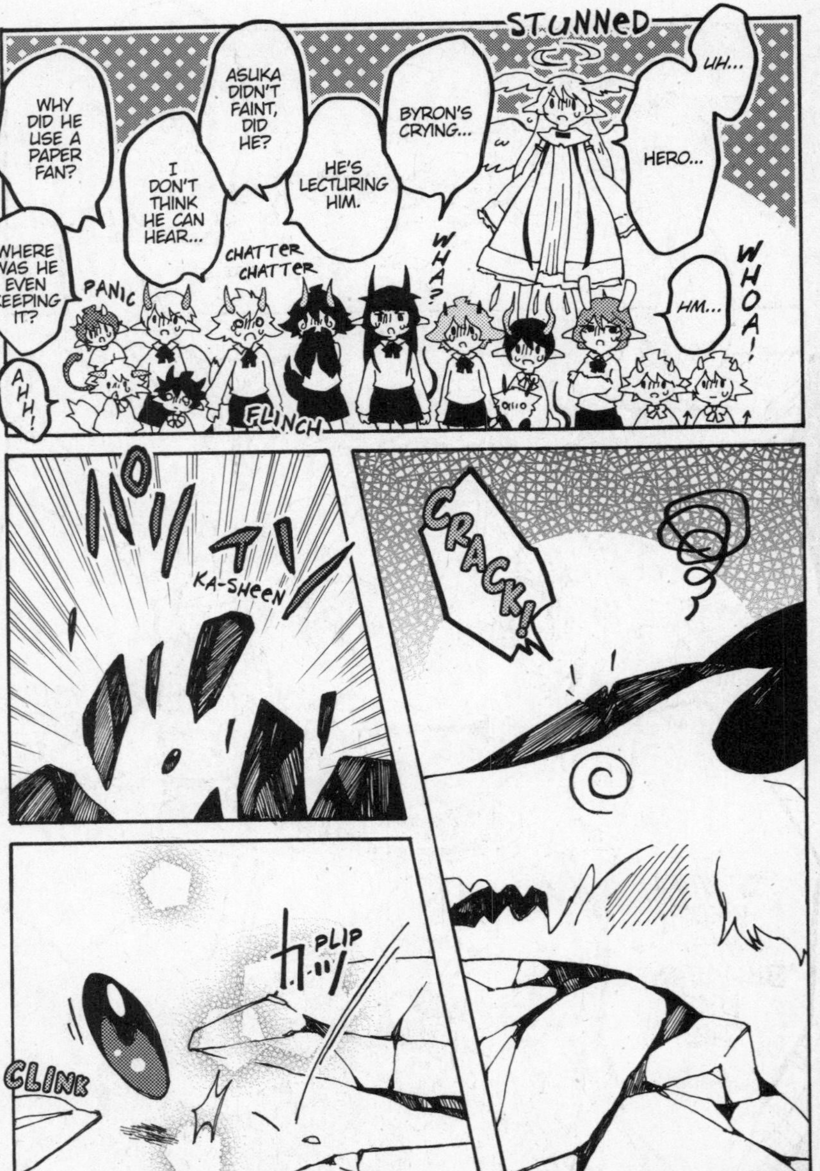
STUNNED
UH...
HERO...
HM...
WHOA!
WHA?
BYRON'S CRYING...
HE'S LECTURING HIM.
ASUKA DIDN'T FAINT, DID HE?
CHATTER CHATTER
I DON'T THINK HE CAN HEAR...
FLINCH
WHY DID HE USE A PAPER FAN?
WHERE WAS HE EVEN KEEPING IT?
PANIC
AHH!
CRACK!
KA-SHEEN
PLIP
CLINK

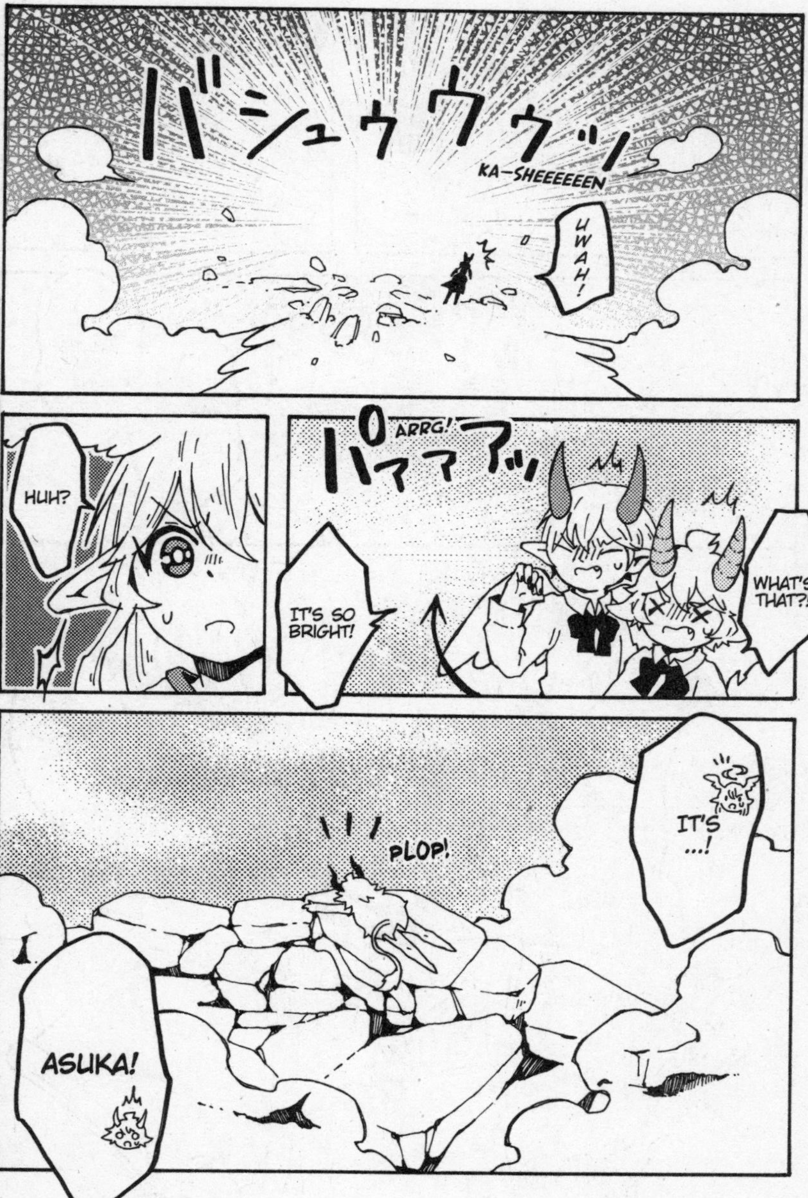
バシュウウウッ
KA-SHEEEEEEN
UWAH!
パァァアッ
ARRG!
WHAT'S THAT?!
IT'S SO BRIGHT!
HUH?
IT'S ...!
PLOP!
ASUKA!

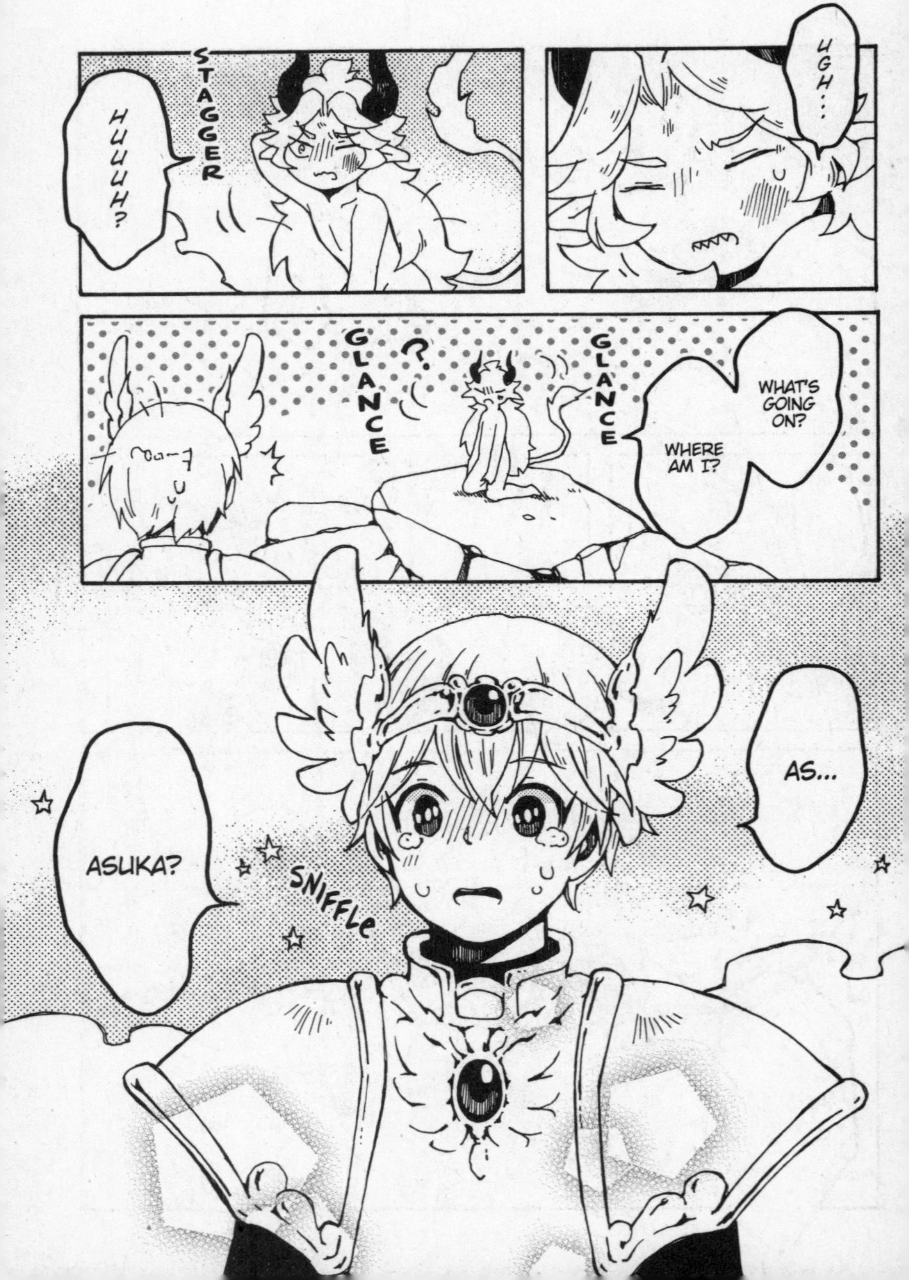
UGH...
STAGGER
HUUUH?
WHAT'S GOING ON?
WHERE AM I?
GLANCE
?
GLANCE
AS...
SNIFFLE
ASUKA?

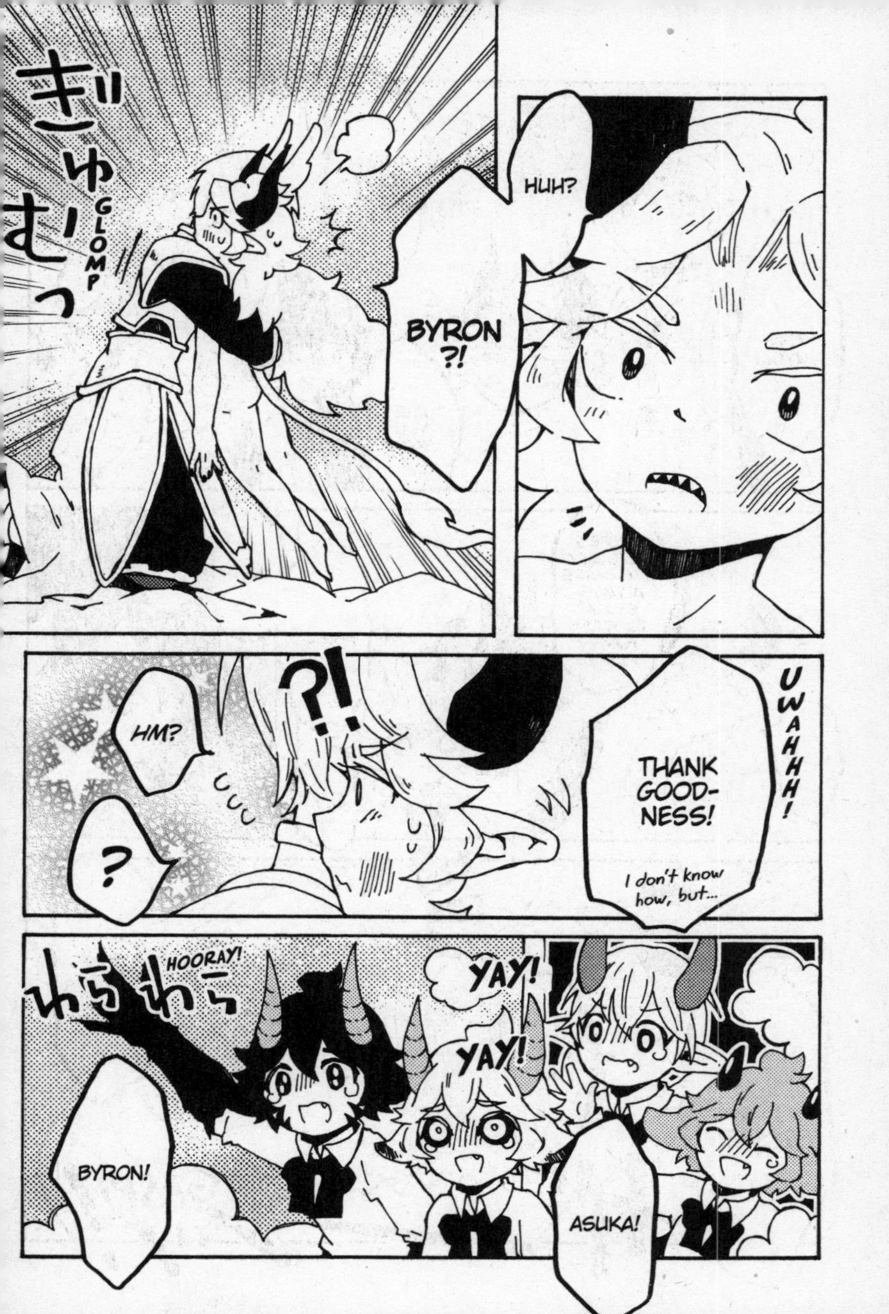
HUH?
BYRON ?!
ぎゅーむっ
GLOMP
UWAHHHH!
THANK GOODNESS!
I don't know how, but...
?!
HM?
?
ASUKA!
YAY!
YAY!
HOORAY!
わらわら
BYRON!

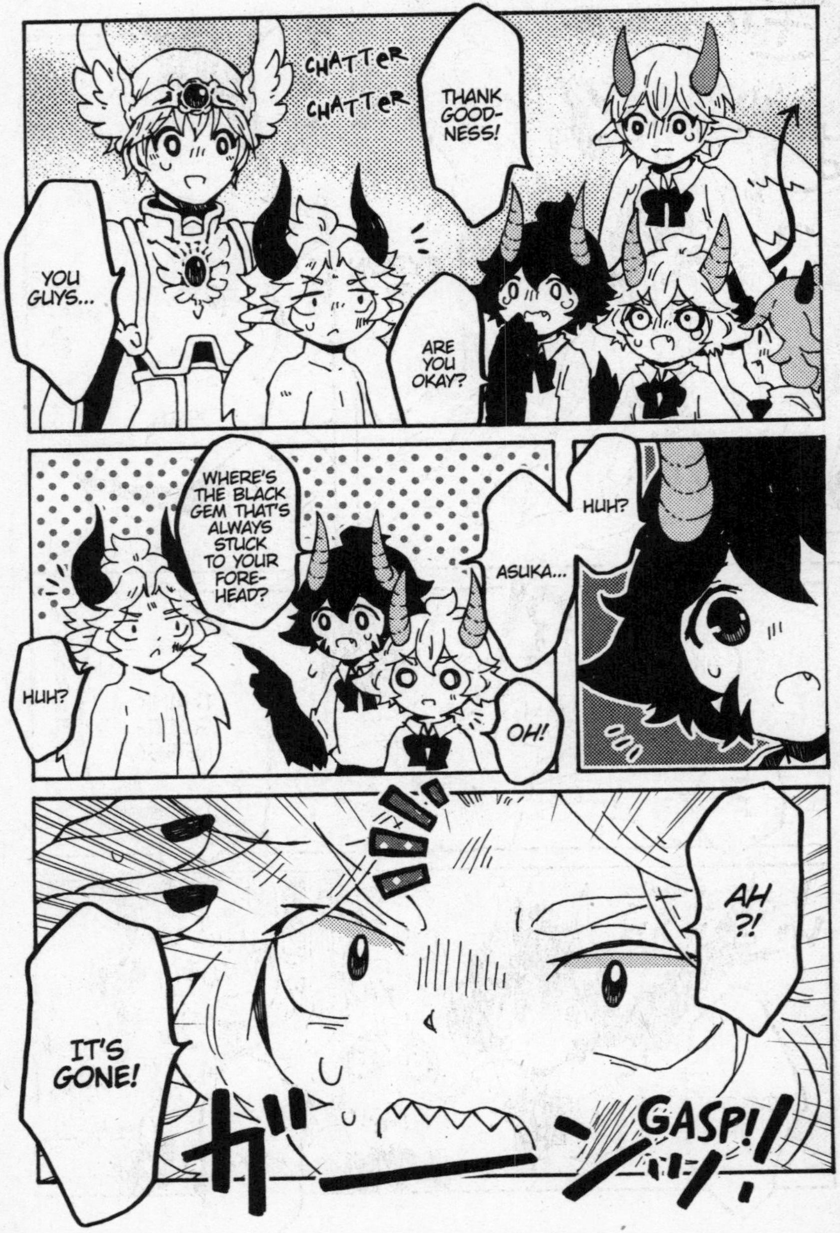
THANK GOODNESS!
CHATTER CHATTER
ARE YOU OKAY?
YOU GUYS...
HUH?
ASUKA...
WHERE'S THE BLACK GEM THAT'S ALWAYS STUCK TO YOUR FOREHEAD?
OH!
HUH?
AH ?!
GASP!
IT'S GONE!
ガー

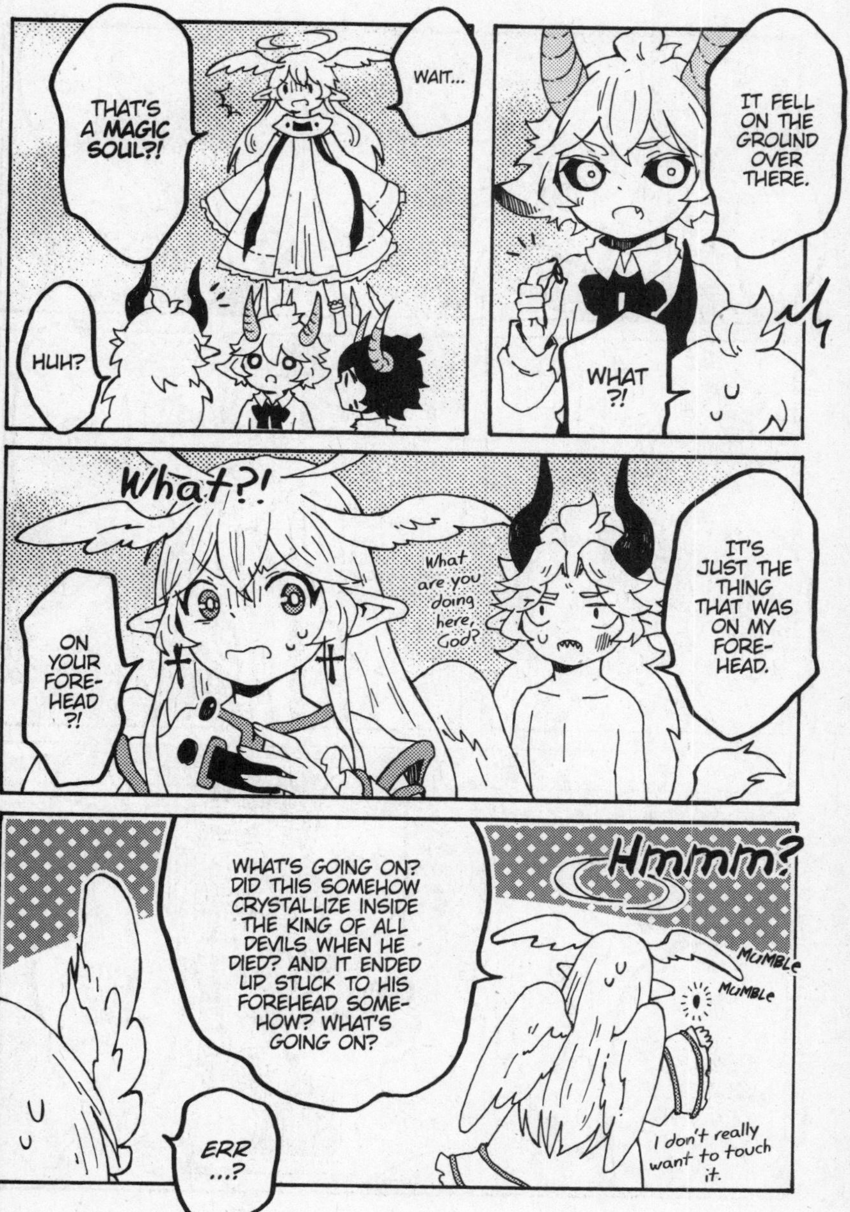
IT FELL ON THE GROUND OVER THERE.
WHAT ?!
WAIT...
THAT'S A MAGIC SOUL?!
HUH?
IT'S JUST THE THING THAT WAS ON MY FORE-HEAD.
What are you doing here, God?
What?!
ON YOUR FORE-HEAD ?!
Hmmm?
MUMBLE
MUMBLE
WHAT'S GOING ON? DID THIS SOMEHOW CRYSTALLIZE INSIDE THE KING OF ALL DEVILS WHEN HE DIED? AND IT ENDED UP STUCK TO HIS FOREHEAD SOME-HOW? WHAT'S GOING ON?
I don't really want to touch it.
ERR ...?

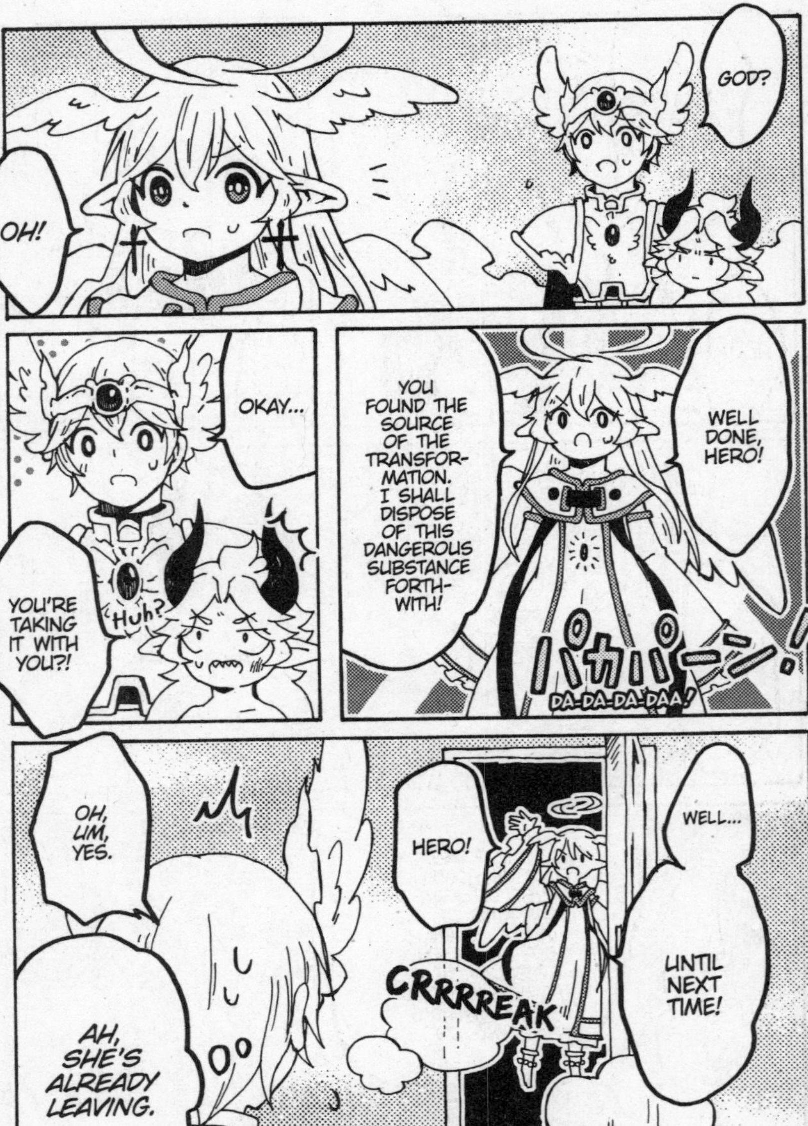
GOD?
OH!
WELL DONE, HERO!
YOU FOUND THE SOURCE OF THE TRANSFORMATION. I SHALL DISPOSE OF THIS DANGEROUS SUBSTANCE FORTHWITH!
パカパーン!
DA-DA-DA-DAA!
OKAY...
Huh?
YOU'RE TAKING IT WITH YOU?!
WELL...
UNTIL NEXT TIME!
HERO!
CRRRRREAK
OH, UM, YES.
AH, SHE'S ALREADY LEAVING.

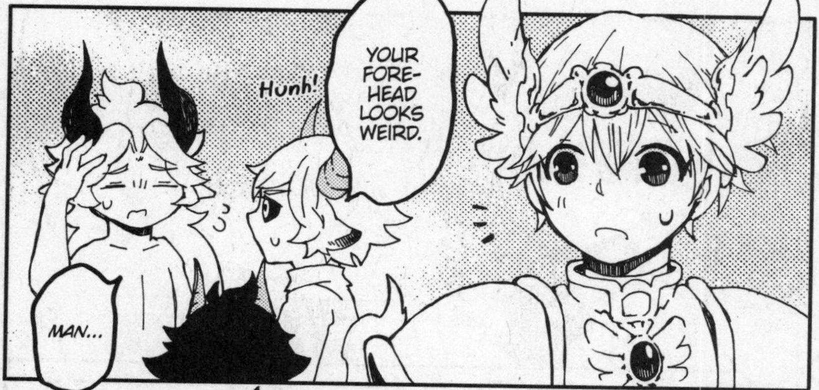
YOUR FORE-HEAD LOOKS WEIRD.
Hunh!
MAN...

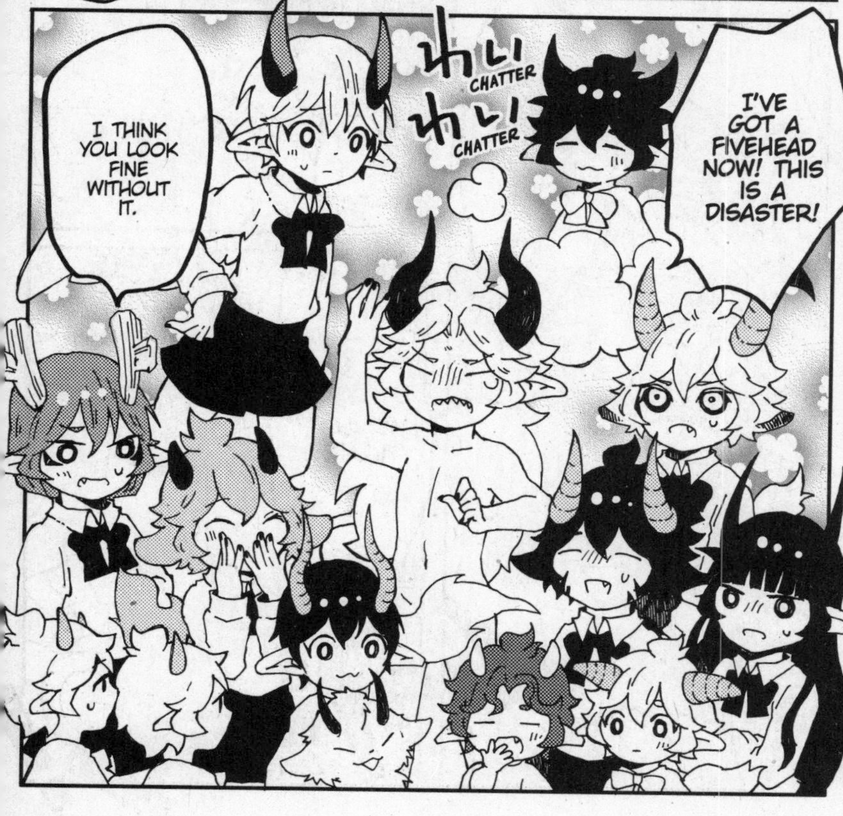
I'VE GOT A FIVEHEAD NOW! THIS IS A DISASTER!
わい CHATTER
わい CHATTER
I THINK YOU LOOK FINE WITHOUT IT.

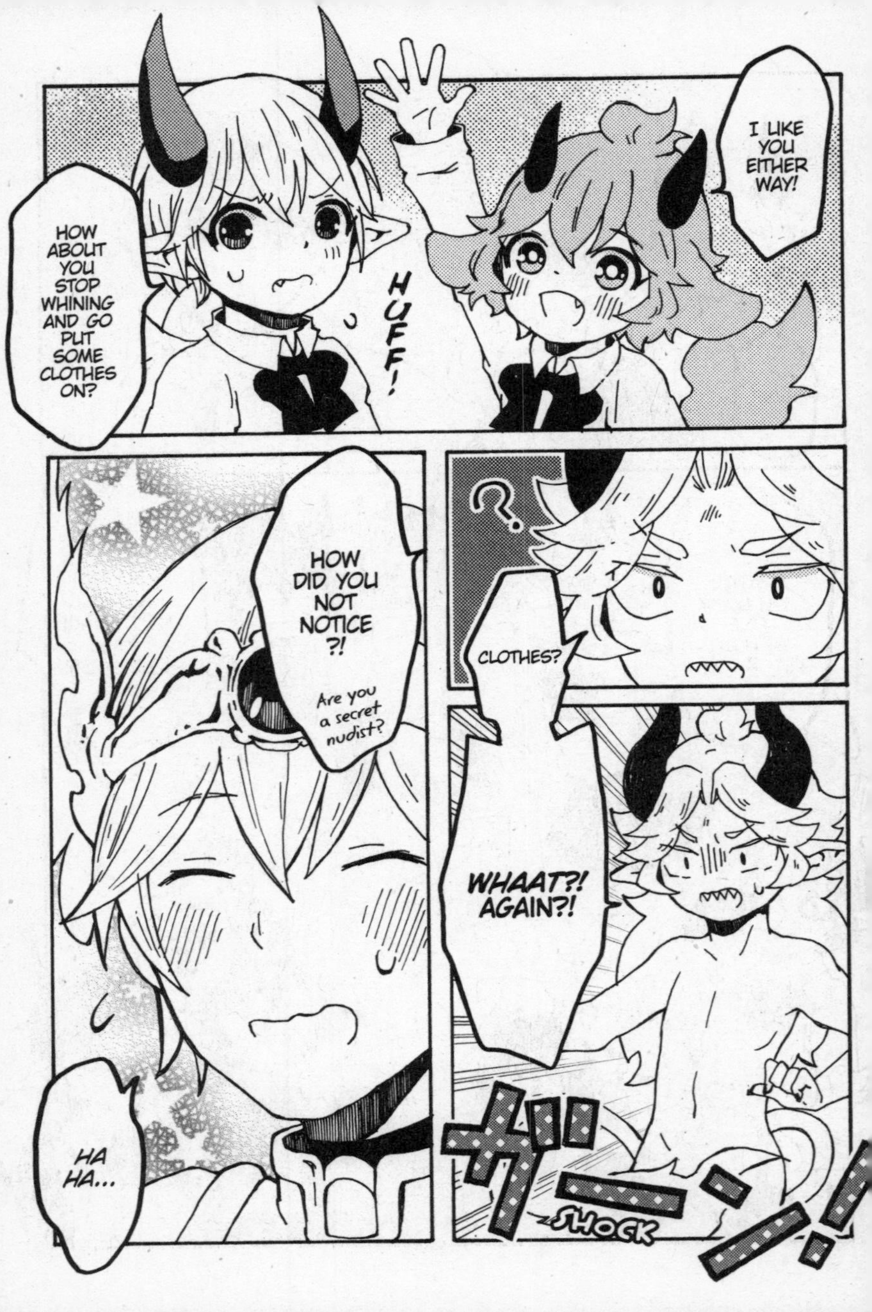
I LIKE YOU EITHER WAY!
HUFF!
HOW ABOUT YOU STOP WHINING AND GO PUT SOME CLOTHES ON?
?
CLOTHES?
WHAAT?! AGAIN?!
SHOCK
HOW DID YOU NOT NOTICE ?!
Are you a secret nudist?
HA HA...

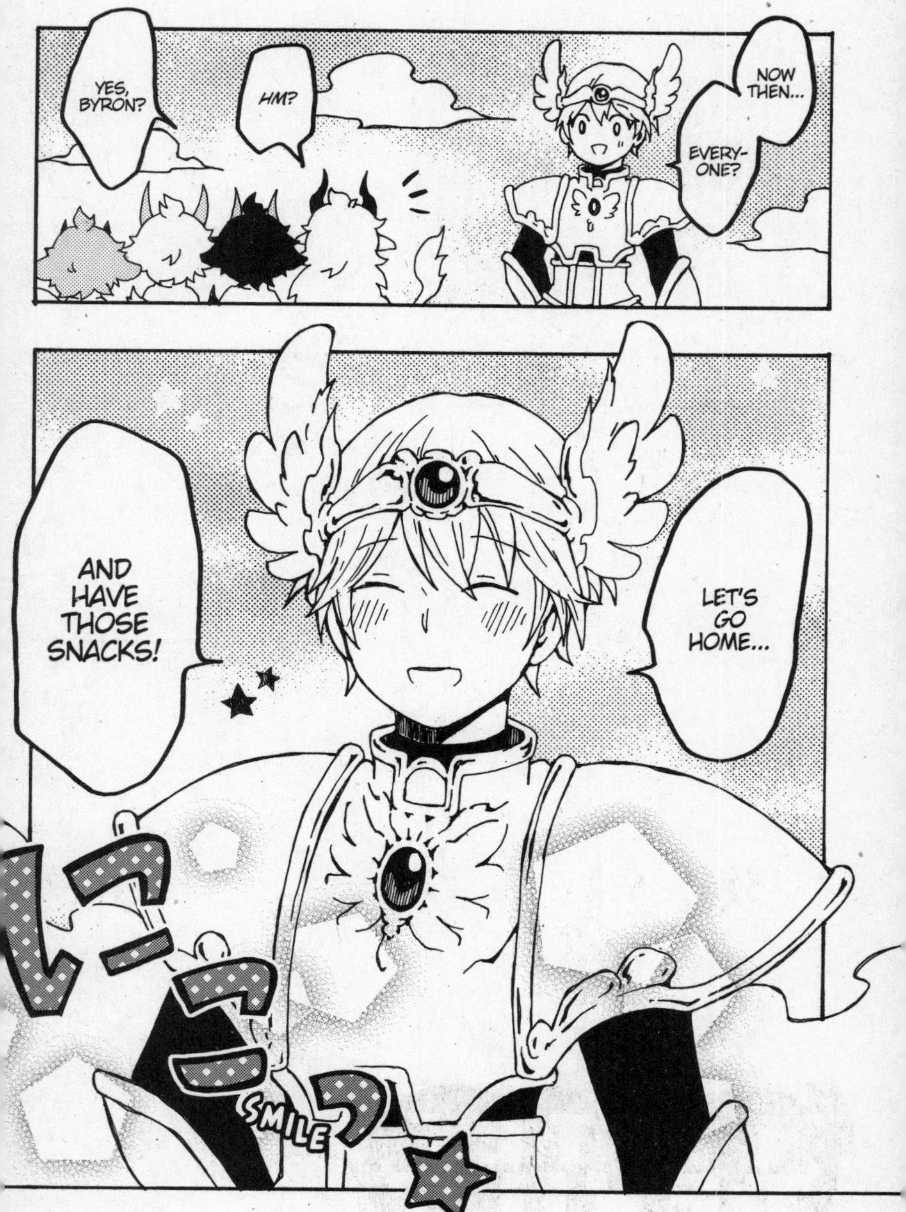
NOW THEN...
EVERY-ONE?
HM?
YES, BYRON?
LET'S GO HOME...
AND HAVE THOSE SNACKS!
SMILE

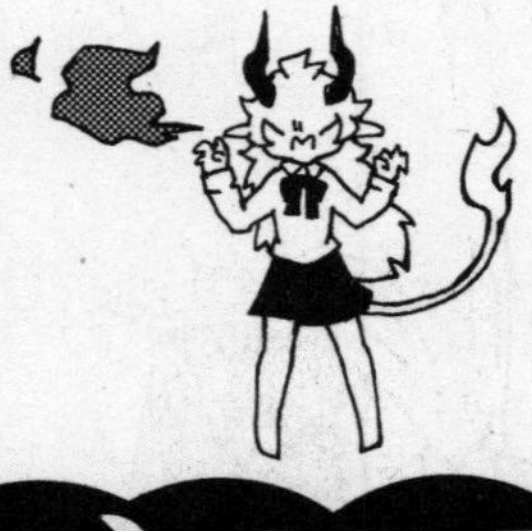

LITTLE DEVILS

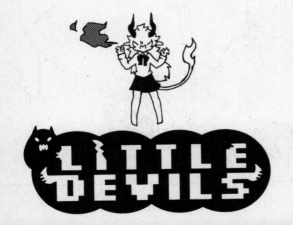

AFTERWORD

Uuumi

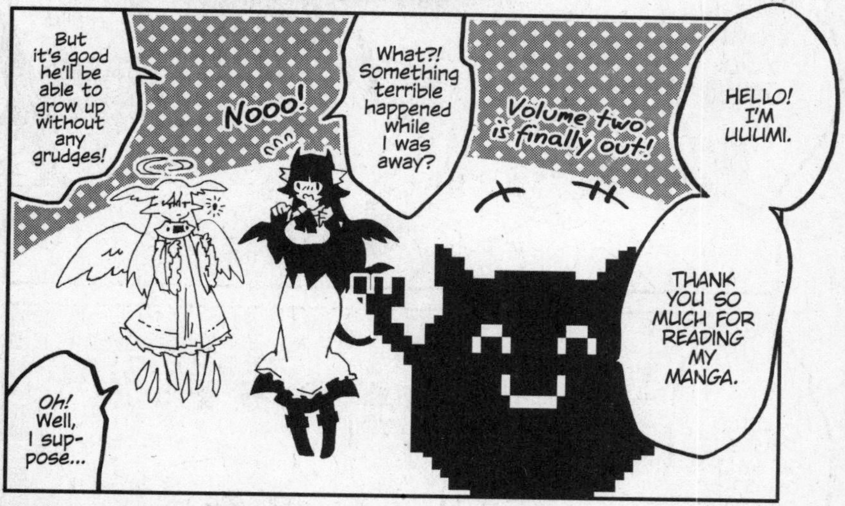
HELLO! I'M UUUMI.
THANK YOU SO MUCH FOR READING MY MANGA.
Volume two is finally out!
What?! Something terrible happened while I was away?
Nooo!
But it's good he'll be able to grow up without any grudges!
Oh! Well, I sup-pose...

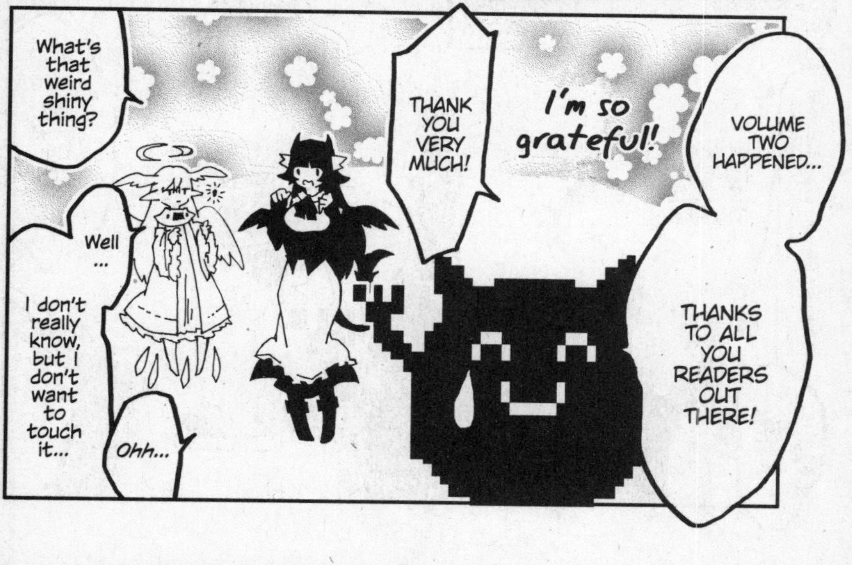
VOLUME TWO HAPPENED...
THANKS TO ALL YOU READERS OUT THERE!
I'm so grateful!
THANK YOU VERY MUCH!
What's that weird shiny thing?
Well...
I don't really know, but I don't want to touch it...
Ohh...

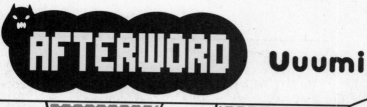

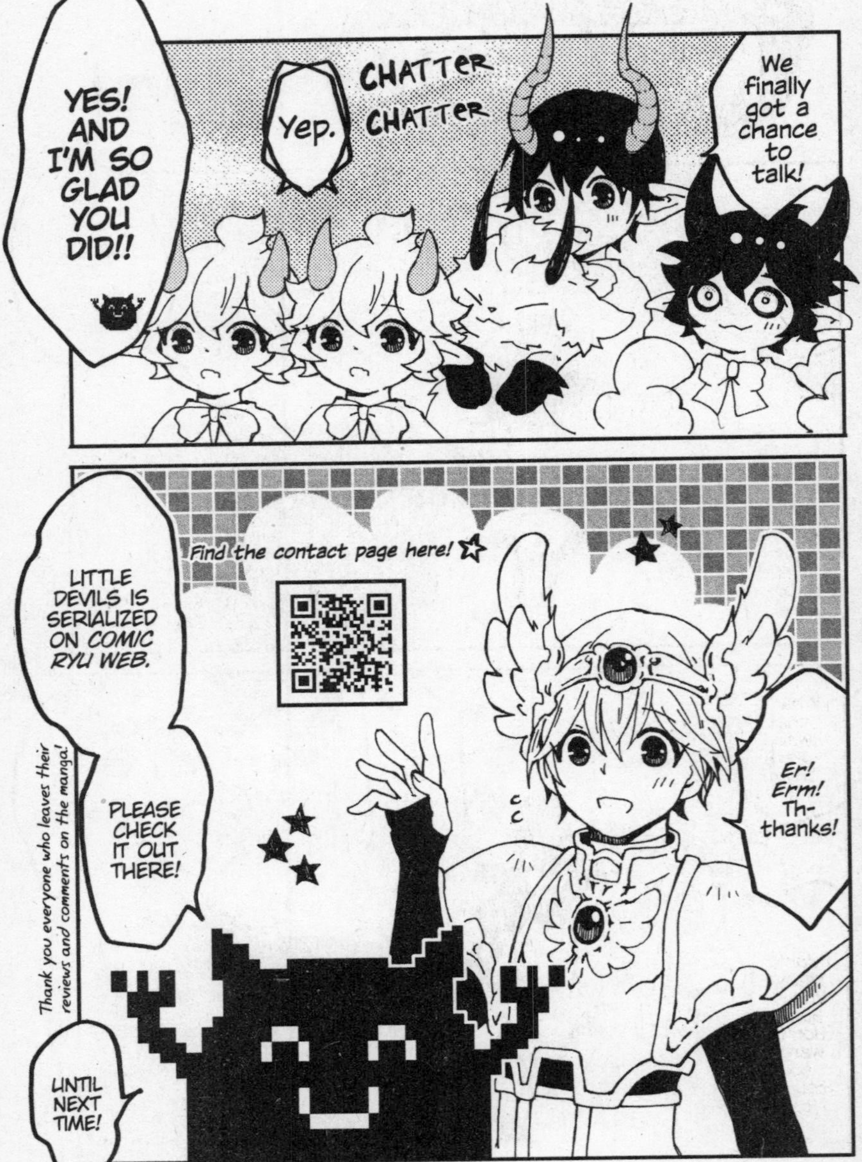
We finally got a chance to talk!
CHATTER CHATTER
Yep.
YES! AND I'M SO GLAD YOU DID!!
Er! Erm! Th-thanks!
Find the contact page here!
LITTLE DEVILS IS SERIALIZED ON *COMIC RYU WEB*.
PLEASE CHECK IT OUT THERE!
Thank you everyone who leaves their reviews and comments on the manga!
UNTIL NEXT TIME!

♡ Special Thanks ♡

I am so grateful to my editor
Ikai-san for being there from the
start of Little Devils ♡

Thank you so much!

SEVEN SEAS ENTERTAINMENT PRESENTS

LITTLE DEVILS

story and art by UUUMI

VOLUME 2

TRANSLATION
Jennifer O'Donnell

ADAPTATION
Casey Lucas

LETTERING AND RETOUCH
Ochie Caraan

COVER DESIGN
KC Fabellon

PROOFREADER
Janet Houck
B. Lana Guggenheim

EDITOR
Shannon Fay

PRODUCTION ASSISTANT
CK Russell

PRODUCTION MANAGER
Lissa Pattillo

EDITOR-IN-CHIEF
Adam Arnold

PUBLISHER
Jason DeAngelis

Seven Seas books may be purchased in bulk for promotional, educational, or business use. Please contact your local bookseller or the Macmillan Corporate and Premium Sales Department at 1-800-221-7945, extension 5442, or by e-mail at MacmillanSpecialMarkets@macmillan.com.

ISBN: 978-1-626929-31-9

Printed in Canada

First Printing: March 2019

10 9 8 7 6 5 4 3 2 1

FOLLOW US ONLINE: ***www.sevenseasentertainment.com***

READING DIRECTIONS

This book reads from ***right to left***, Japanese style. If this is your first time reading manga, you start reading from the top right panel on each page and take it from there. If you get lost, just follow the numbered diagram here. It may seem backwards at first, but you'll get the hang of it! Have fun!!

1
2
3
4
5
6
7
8
9

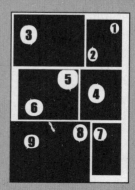